Ripley's Believe It or Not! 2008

The Remarkable... Revealed

BOOKS

Developed and produced by Miles Kelly Publishing Ltd
in association with Ripley Publishing

PUBLISHING

Executive Vice President Norm Deska
Vice President, Archives and Exhibits Edward Meyer
Archives Executive Assistant Viviana Ray
Researcher Lucas Stram

PUBLISHING

Publishing Director Anne Marshall

Managing Editor Rebecca Miles
Text Geoff Tibballs
Interviews Jo Wiltshire
Editors Sally McFall, Judy Barratt
Editorial Assistant Gemma Simmons
Indexer Hilary Bird

Art Director Jo Brewer
Project Designer/Cover Design Warris Kidwai
Reprographics Stephan Davis
Picture Researchers Gemma Simmons, Laura Faulder
Production Manager Sally Knowles

Sales and Marketing Morty Mint

Copyright © 2007 by Ripley Entertainment Inc.

First published in Great Britain in 2007 by
Random House Books

Random House Books
Random House, 20 Vauxhall Bridge Road,
London SW1V 2SA

Addresses for companies within The Random House Group
Limited can be found at:
www.randomhouse.co.uk/offices.htm

The Random House Group Limited Reg. No. 954009

www.randomhouse.co.uk

All rights reserved. Ripley's, Believe It or Not!,
and Ripley's Believe It or Not! are registered
trademarks of Ripley Entertainment Inc.

ISBN: 9781905211135
10 9 8 7 6 5 4 3 2 1

No part of this publication may be reproduced in whole or in
part, or stored in a retrieval system, or transmitted in any form
or by any means, electronic, mechanical, photocopying,
recording, or otherwise, without written permission from the
publisher. For information regarding permission, write to VP
Intellectual Property, Ripley Entertainment Inc., Suite 188,
7576 Kingspointe Parkway, Orlando, Florida 32819
email: publishing@ripleys.com

A CIP catalogue record for this book
is available from the British Library

Printed in China

PUBLISHER'S NOTE
Whle every effort has been made to verify the accuracy of the
entries in this book, the Publishers cannot be held responsible
for any errors contained in the work. They would be glad to
receive any information from readers.

WARNING
Some of the stunts and activities in this book are undertaken
by experts and should not be attempted by anyone without
adequate training and supervision.

CONTENTS

Robert Ripley, creator of the world famous daily cartoon strip "Ripley's Believe It or Not!" combed the globe in a relentless quest for odd people, places, and things.

In December 1918, while working as a sports columnist for the *New York Globe*, Robert Ripley created his first collection of odd facts and feats. The cartoons, based on unusual athletic achievements, were submitted under the heading "Champs and Chumps," but his editor wanted a title that would describe the incredible nature of the content, so after much deliberation it was changed to "Believe It or Not!" The cartoon was an instant success and the phrase "believe it or not" soon entered everyday speech.

Ripley's passion was travel and by 1940 he had visited no fewer than 201 countries. Wherever he went, he searched out the bizarre for inclusion in his syndicated newspaper cartoons, which had blossomed to reach worldwide distribution, being translated into 17 different languages and boasting a readership of 80 million people. During one trip he crossed two continents and covered more than 24,000 mi (39,000 km) from New York to Cairo and back to satisfy his appetite for the weird.

MUSEUMS

Ripley's remarkable collection is now showcased in no fewer than 29 museums across nine countries. Ripley called his museums "Odditoriums," and built the first one in Chicago in 1933. Exhibits here ranged from genuine shrunken heads from the Upper Amazon to *The Last Supper* painted on a dime, and the effect the new museum had on the visiting public was startling. According to Ripley himself: "At Chicago one hundred people fainted every day and we had to have six beds." By the time the New York City Odditorium was opened in 1940, visitors were getting used to Ripley's—there were only three beds available and "hardly anyone fainted."

THE LEGACY LIVES ON

Although Robert Ripley died in 1949 (after collapsing on the set of his weekly television show), his "Believe It or Not!" cartoons are still produced on a daily basis—just as they have been every day since 1918—making it the longest running syndicated cartoon in the world. Intrepid researchers follow in his footsteps, continually scouring the world and enabling Ripley's to remain the undisputed king of the strange and unbelievable.

With a huge database of incredible facts, people, and events, a massive photographic archive, a TV show syndicated around the world, and a warehouse stuffed with unique and fascinating exhibits, Ripley's is able to present a celebration of the amazing diversity of our world, without ever passing judgment.

From the outset, Robert Ripley encouraged his readers to submit material and photographs—his weekly mailbag sometimes exceeded 170,000 letters! The one man who started it all was once commemorated by a memorial in his hometown church of Santa Rosa, California. The entire church was made from a single giant redwood tree... Today, there is a still a team of people waiting to hear from you, collecting new amazing facts.

Anyone with a strange fact should contact...

www.ripleys.com

For information regarding submission, email bionresearch@ripleys.com, or write to BION Research, Ripley Entertainment Inc., 7576 Kingspointe Parkway, #188, Orlando, Florida, 32819, U.S.A.

Truckloads of ripe tomatoes arrive for the annual tomato fight in Buñol, Spain—page 10

Flaming tar barrels carried through the streets light up an English town—page 15

Franz-Wolfgang Coersten, cherry-pit spitter, practices for the world championships—page 37

WEIRD WORLD

BATTLE OF THE TOMATOES

At Buñol in Spain every August, 30,000 people take part in a huge tomato fight—a two-hour battle during which more than 150,000 lb (68,000 kg) of over-ripe tomatoes are thrown.

The La Tomatina festival, which draws visitors from all over the world, dates back to 1944 when the local carnival in Buñol was marred by hooligans hurling tomatoes at the procession. But the fruity frolics proved so popular that they were re-created the following year and now the carnival is little more than a sideshow to the huge tomato fight.

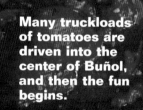

Many truckloads of tomatoes are driven into the center of Buñol, and then the fun begins.

The tons of tomatoes are brought in each year on large trucks from the Extremadura region of Spain, where the fruit is cheaper. Participants are encouraged to wear protective goggles and gloves and must squash the tomatoes before throwing them to reduce the risk of injury.

Although it is a free-for-all, there are vague rules, and anyone caught tearing another person's clothing is likely to be ejected. Meanwhile, storekeepers take steps to cover their storefronts to guard against the widespread carnage.

The action starts around 11 a.m. A ham is placed on the top of a greased pole and as soon as someone is able to climb the pole and bring down the ham, the tomato fight begins.

A cannon is fired to signal the end of the battle, after which fire truck hoses spray the town's streets and the combatants with welcome water, and Buñol returns to normality for another year—until the next battle.

The small town of Buñol turns red with squashed tomatoes before being hosed down for another year.

PLANE VANE
In Whitehorse, Yukon, Canada, there is a giant weather vane—an actual DC-3 airplane mounted on a swivel—that always points its nose to the wind.

BICYCLE FENCE
In Egmont Village, New Zealand, there is a fence made out of old bicycles.

⚠ HEDGECUTTERS
On Lord Lansdowne's estate in Perthshire, Scotland, in 1933, a 100-ft (30-m) high hedge ran for ⅓ mi (0.5 km). Hedgecutting required six men, a long rope, and elaborate scaffolding!

VAST BUILDING
The Boeing Commercial Airplane factory in Everett, Washington, is such a huge building that the entire Disneyland amusement park, including its parking lots, could fit inside.

BRIDGE LAYOUT
Because of the layout of the Boston University Bridge in Boston, Massachusetts, it is possible for a boat going under it to float beneath a train, passing under a car, driving under an airplane!

NO MENUS
In Salt Lake City, Utah, there is a restaurant called the One World Café in which there are no menus and patrons pay what they feel their meal is worth.

GRIT ROLL
In St. George, South Carolina, there is an annual Roll in the Grits contest, where contestants wallow in a swimming pool filled with grits in order to see how much they can collect on their body.

DESIGNER KENNELS
Dog owners in Olmsted Falls, Ohio, are required by law to have waterproof doghouses that are equipped with self-closing doors!

FAST FOOD
The Karne Garibaldi restaurant in Guadalajara, Mexico, claims to serve a customer's food within just 13 seconds of the order being made.

VARIABLE RAINFALL
At its peak, enough water flows along the Iguaçu River and over the Iguaçu Falls, located on the border between Brazil and Argentina, to fill six Olympic swimming pools every second. Yet in some years rainfall in the region is so low that the river dries up completely.

ANGEL MUSEUM
A museum in Beloit, Wisconsin, boasts a display of more than 7,500 angels, including ones made from pasta, porcelain, coal, tin, pine cones, drinking straws, and seal skin.

PYRAMID SHIFT
Owing to the movement of the Earth's crust, the Pyramids of Egypt have shifted 2½ mi (4 km) to the south of where they were originally built some 5,000 years ago.

LEGAL TARGETS
Under an ancient bylaw that has never been repealed, it is still legal for citizens of York, England, to shoot Scotsmen with a bow and arrow within the city walls.

A PAIN IN THE NECK

"Antzar Eguna" (Day of the Goose) is the highlight of a centuries-old fiesta that takes place each year in the Basque village of Lekeitio in northern Spain. It features an unusual competition whereby contestants hang on to a dead goose's neck while the bird is raised and lowered into a river. The aim of the contest is to decapitate the bird while withstanding the vigorous dunking.

BEER 'N' BACON

The Pub in the Paddock at Pyengana, Tasmania, is home to a pair of pigs that drink along with the patrons.

TALL DUTCH

The Netherlands may be one of the Low Countries, but its people are officially the tallest in the world. A 2006 survey revealed that the average Dutchman stands just over 6 ft (1.83 m) while Dutch women average nearly 5 ft 7 in (1.69 m).

ROBOT KITCHEN ▷

A new restaurant in a Hong Kong shopping mall is causing something of a stir with diners because of its unusual waiting staff. The owners of Robot Kitchen claim that it's the first restaurant in the world to have robots as waiters. Seen here is Robot No. 2, who can recognize voice patterns and take meal orders, which are sent by infrared technology to the kitchen. It also helps to serve the meals to customers.

GOAT COUTURE

It's not only the people who wear fancy dress at the famous Lake County Fair in the city of Crown Point, Indiana—they dress their goats up, too! The dairy goat costume contest is for the best-dressed owner and animal combination, and in 2006 it featured one goat that was dressed as a chicken and another who was sporting a clown costume.

SKY HIGH

A new cocktail from Croatia can be mixed only by a bartender free-falling from 10,000 ft (3,000 m). The Wings of Zadar cocktail is poured upside down so that the drink flies upwards into the mixer and is then shaken as the skydiving barman performs a series of somersaults. Chilled by the freezing air rushing over the shaker, it is served on landing. Naturally the price of the cocktail is sky high.

CONCRETE COMMANDMENTS

In Murphy, North Carolina, there is a huge set of the Ten Commandments written in concrete letters 4 x 5 ft (1.2 x 1.5 m) in size.

HUGE HYDRANT

An operational fire hydrant that is 30 ft (9 m) high has been built in Elm Creek, Manitoba, Canada, complete with a 12 ft (3.6 m) chain. It took volunteer firefighters seven months to build.

HARK AT BARKERS

Every year, West Salem, Wisconsin, stages a Bark in the Park, where local dogs compete to produce the loudest bark. Levels have been known to exceed 110 decibels.

BUSH TUCKER
ZEBRA
CAMEL
RATTLESNAKE
IMPALER
OSTRICH
KANGAROO

◁ WHAT'S FOR DINNER?

Steve Ritchie is a butcher from London, England, with a difference. Proprietor of Theobald's Specialist Butcher shop in the Clerkenwell district of the city, he sells a range of highly exotic meats, including zebra, camel, rattlesnake, ostrich, and kangaroo.

Roll out the Barrel

The streets of Ottery St. Mary in Devon, England, are lit up each November 5 by flaming tar barrels, which are carried by the town's strongest men as part of a custom dating back over 300 years.

Seventeen heavy barrels are pre-coated with tar and primed with paraffin. They are lit in turn and carried through the streets on the shoulders of muscular men whose arms are swathed in protective sacking, soaked in water. When each man can stand the heat no longer, the barrel is passed to another. The last barrel is rolled into the main square around midnight, after which the tar-barrelers triumphantly tear off their protective cladding and toss it into the flames. The tradition of tar-barrel rolling is believed to cleanse the streets of evil spirits.

Women and boys also compete in the festival, earlier in the evening, carrying barrels that are lighter than the men's.

THE HIGH LIFE

For the past 19 years, 46-year-old Andrew Thurnheer of Danby, New York, has lived 40 ft (12 m) off the ground in a two-story tree house that he built himself. Located on his parents' cattle farm, the tree house features an electric motor-powered hoist for an elevator, a shower, and a propane heater. A ground-level outhouse stands nearby.

PLATYPUS TOSS

At the Nymboida Heritage Festival, held each year in New South Wales, Australia, competitors take turns to hurl a giant plastic platypus as far as they can.

SHORT RIVERS

The D River, which flows from Devil's Lake into the Pacific Ocean near Lincoln City, Oregon, flows for just 120 ft (37 m). The Roe River, which originates near Great Falls, Montana, and flows into the Missouri River, is not much longer at 201 ft (61 m).

A GOOD TERN

New Hampshire has an official State Seagull Harasser—a paid position that provides for a "continuous human presence" to frighten off seagulls on Seavey Island in order to provide a better habitat for nesting terns.

PIZZA CITY △

To celebrate the 859th anniversary of the founding of their city, pizza lovers in the Russian capital, Moscow, created a map of the city made from pizza. Almost 20 ft (6 m) in diameter, the prodigious pizza featured sculptures of the Kremlin and other Moscow landmarks made from gooey cheese on the top.

WELSH COLONY

There is a Welsh-speaking colony in the province of Chubut in Argentine Patagonia! It began in 1865 when 153 Welsh settlers arrived in South America.

WOOD MEASURER

The town of Brookline, Massachusetts, has had an official measurer of wood and bark for over two centuries.

SHORT STREET

In Wick, Scotland, there is a street that is just 81 in (205 cm) long. Unsurprisingly, there is only one address on Ebenezer Place.

LIMITED VOCABULARY

Despite more than 200 years of contact with the rest of the world, Brazil's Piraha tribe has almost no words for counting, colors, time, or relationships.

◁ CATWALK CRUSTACEAN

Hermit crabs disguised as the Green Goblin and Spider-man walk through a display during the annual Miss Crustacean Beauty Pageant held in Ocean City, New Jersey. Each entry features a theme and a set for its crab or crabs, and children from across the U.S.A. come to compete in the contest, which is billed as the world's only beauty pageant for hermit crabs.

FUN BURIAL

Dutch entertainer Eddy Daams has launched a new extreme sport—fun burials—in which competitors are buried 5 ft (1.5 m) down in a coffin for an hour under a concrete block weighing 3½ tons. The coffin has an oxygen supply and a panic button and is linked by webcam to a computer so that friends and family can watch.

DEER DROP

The deer pellet drop is the highlight of the Friends of Black Moshannon Summer Festival near Philipsburg, Pennsylvania. Competitors must hold a piece of deer excrement near the tip of their nose and drop it into a milk bottle at their feet. Winners of the women's section earn a pair of deer-pellet earrings.

RUBBER RESIDENCE

Pat and Chuck Potter of Bancroft, Ontario, Canada, built a home that is 100 ft (30 m) long on the side of a hill using 1,200 old car tires, and solar panels for heat.

IN THE DARK

A new restaurant opened in London, England, in 2006 where diners eat in total darkness. Customers do not know what they are eating, the idea being that not being able to see what is on your plate heightens the senses and liberates the taste buds. The food is served by partly sighted or blind waiters and anything that might shatter the blackness, such as a cell phone display or a burning cigarette, is banned.

RAINMAKERS

A Chinese government agency aims to control the country's weather! The Beijing Weather Modification Office mobilizes cloud-seeding aircraft, artillery, and rockets to induce rainfall and so prevent drought in agricultural areas. It is also trying to guarantee blue skies for the 2008 Beijing Olympics by studying the effects of firing certain chemicals into clouds with anti-aircraft guns.

SOLID COBS

A former cornfield in Dublin, Ohio, has 109 concrete corncobs, each standing over 6 ft (1.8 m) tall—a tribute to Sam Frantz, a developer of hybrid corn plants.

MINISCULE PARTICLES

Protons, the positively charged particles in the center of an atom, are so small that 500,000,000,000 could fit into the period at the end of this sentence.

SAUSAGE RACE

Miller Park, home of the Milwaukee Brewers baseball team, stages a sausage race during each game. People dressed as a hot dog, a Polish sausage, an Italian sausage, and a bratwurst race each other around the playing field.

BIG DUCK

The Big Duck building located in Flanders, Long Island, is 20 ft (6 m) tall and shaped like a duck!

COLD COMFORT

A warmly dressed chambermaid plumps up the pillows in a room in Eastern Europe's first ice hotel in February 2006. The Balea Lac Ice Hotel is located at the end of a remote valley in the Fagaras Mountains, which are the highest in Romania and lie 186 mi (300 km) northwest of the capital Bucharest.

JUMBO HOME

Architect David Hertz is planning to build a home made out of a scrapped jumbo jet. He paid $110,000 for the Boeing 747-200 and says he will incorporate all 4.5 million parts of the plane in the building in Victorville, California. The jet's wings will be used in the roof and the top deck of the plane will convert into a guesthouse.

▽ WHALE SHARK

This extraordinary whale shark, 45 ft (13.7 m) long, 23 ft 9 in (7 m) in circumference, and weighing 30,000 lb (13,600 kg), was captured after a fight lasting 39 hours on Knights Key, Florida, on June 1, 1912. It was loaded onto a flatbed truck and driven to Miami—a very smelly load!

SHORT RIDE

Even if you don't have sea legs, you should be able to cope with the Kemah Boardwalk Shuttle, a Texas passenger ferry where the ride is just 65 ft (20 m), or .01 nautical miles, and the boat itself is 26 ft (8 m) long! The ferry connects parking lots under a bridge at Highway 146 with the Kemah Boardwalk attractions, and perhaps the biggest surprise is that the ride takes as long as two minutes.

CASH BASH

Some 200 treasure hunters from 15 American states arrived in Woodbury, Connecticut, in 2006 for the Cash Bash, the National Metal Detector Championships. Competitors have half an hour to find and dig up as many pre-planted tokens as possible from a field the size of a football field.

TALL SKIS

The pair of cross-country skis that stand vertically outside the town of 100 Mile House, British Columbia, Canada, are definitely not for beginners. The 39-ft (12-m) aluminum skis and their 30-ft (9-m) poles weigh a combined 1,200 lb (545 kg).

GRAYS ONLY

A horse race run at Newmarket, England, every August is for gray horses only!

BEE-STING THERAPY △

A Chinese man receives a stinging treatment for rhinitis, when two bees are held against his nose until they sting him, at a clinic in the town of Xi'an in China's Shaanxi province. The bee venom is also said to help cure diseases such as multiple sclerosis, arthritis, and rheumatism.

BOULDER TEST

In Tibet, there is an annual stone-carrying contest in which herdsmen hoist 25-lb (11-kg) boulders and then carry them as far as they can, competing for the longest distance.

BEE-WARE

Watch out for the honeybee that hovers around Tisdale, Saskatchewan! For the metal and fiberglass bee is 16 ft (5 m) long, 7 ft (2 m) tall, and has a wingspan of 11½ ft (3.5 m). The town is the honey capital of Saskatchewan and produces 10 per cent of Canada's honey.

100 UP

There are more than 28,000 people in Japan over the age of 100. The number of Japanese reaching this age has almost quadrupled in the past ten years, and 85 per cent are women.

VAST VASE

A hand-thrown pottery vase in East Dundee, Illinois, stands 8 ft (2.4 m) high and weighs 650 lb (295 kg).

LONG FENCE

A continuous fence—known as the "dingo fence"—runs through central Queensland, Australia, for 3,436 mi (5,530 km). It is 5.9 ft (1.8 m) high and is designed to keep sheep safe from Australia's native wild dog.

HOLY HAUL

Every July, 120 men carry a 65-ft (20-m) seven-story tower that weighs four tons and honors St. Paulinus, through the streets of Williamsburg, New York.

CEMENT POTATO

Wearing a top hat and a smile, a 19-ft (5.8-m) cement potato greets visitors to Maugerville, New Brunswick, Canada. It was built in 1969 to promote a roadside vegetable stand.

TINY GALLERY

A tiny art gallery in Buenos Aires, Argentina, has a ceiling that is just 1 ft (30 cm) high. Patrons must put their heads through a hole to see the 27 miniature paintings and sculptures on exhibition.

FUNKY FISH

In a room on a quiet rural homestead in Australia is an amazing collection of stuffed fish. This colorful school comprises an impressive 96 species and belongs to John Kruger (pictured here) from Hervey's Range near Townsville in Queensland.

CANDY COUNTER

A candy store in Littleton, New Hampshire, has a counter that is 111 ft (34 m) long. Run by Jim Alden, Chutter General Store displays 700 jars of sweet treats on its three-tiered counter, including eight different kinds of black licorice.

WORM GRUNTIN'

The town of Sopchoppy, Florida, has an annual Worm Gruntin' Festival, where locals use vibrations of all kinds to lure earthworms out of the ground.

CONVERTED CARRIER

In 2006, the Minsk—a Russian aircraft carrier that had been converted into a floating entertainment center complete with a movie theater and restaurants—was put up for sale in Shenzhou, China.

SOCK BURNING

Every year on the first day of spring, boaters in Annapolis, Maryland, gather for a sock-burning ceremony to celebrate the return of warm weather.

TASTY BUGS ▷

A bug eater in Wageningen in the Netherlands enjoys a tasty morsel. Insect lovers gathered in the Dutch university town in the summer of 2006 to participate in a mass insect-eating attempt. An amazing 1,747 portions of a variety of delicious bugs were eaten.

UNDERSEA RIVER

An undersea river known as the Cromwell Current flows eastward beneath the Pacific for 3,500 mi (5,633 km) along the Equator. It is 190 mi (305 km) wide and reaches a depth of 1,300 ft (400 m) in places. Its volume is 1,000 times that of the Mississippi River.

PET BEDS

A leading British hotel chain announced in 2006 that it was offering pets their own beds. The special pet beds, which measure 2 ft 6 in x 2 ft (76 x 60 cm), were introduced by Travelodge to cater for customers who hate being parted from their cats and dogs.

WRESTLE OF THE TITANS

Since 1357, the city of Edirne in northwestern Turkey has been home to the annual Kirkpinar Wrestling and Culture Festival. This popular traditional event is believed to be the oldest wrestling festival in the world, and features titanic bouts of oil wrestling between hundreds of pairs of men. Olive oil is applied to the body before the wrestling bouts begin. Until 1975, the wrestling bouts had no upper time limit, and were sometimes known to continue for up to two days—now, they last for a more comfortable 30 to 40 minutes.

BURNING AMBITION

Scrap metal worker Eddie Heath of Staffordshire, England, has become a local legend in his home county on account of setting fire to several famous buildings including the White House!

Happily the White House that went up in smoke in November 2006 was only a model that Eddie had built from 2,000 donated wooden pallets and 60 pt (30 l) of white paint. Measuring 60 ft (18 m) wide and 15 ft (4.5 m) high, the impressive structure had no less than 28 windows. It took him eight weeks to create but just minutes to destroy. He said he chose the White House because it is square and simple and everyone recognizes it. This was the latest of Eddie's annual extravaganzas. In recent years he has built and burnt models of Captain Hook's galleon, Dracula's castle, and Big Ben.

The White House (with Eddie on top) and Dracula's castle (above), were both razed to the ground.

Eddie's scaled down version of the White House burns against the night sky.

SHAPELY SUNDIAL

At Roselawn, Indiana, there is a huge sundial in the shape of a lady's leg. The leg, which is properly positioned to tell the time, is 63 ft (19 m) long and was built at the request of the owner of the adjoining nudist resort.

SPOILT FOR CHOICE

Heladeria Coromoto, an ice-cream parlor in the Andean hills of Venezuela, boasts over 800 different flavors. They include smoked trout, pumpkin, black beans and rice, tuna, avocado, rose petal, bubblegum and honey, chilli pepper, corn, beetroot and cream, and fried pork rind.

NO GARBAGE

Hugh and Jo-Ann Robertson of Ottawa, Ontario, Canada, recycle so much that they had only two bags of actual garbage over a four-year period.

DOG PERMIT

According to Oklahoma law, dogs must have a permit signed by the mayor in order to congregate on private property in groups of three or more.

MOUNTAIN CATHEDRAL

In Zipaquira, Colombia, there is a cathedral built into the walls of a salt mine 600 ft (180 m) deep inside a mountain.

RESTROOM ART

The public restrooms inside a replica of an 1880 train station in Yellow Springs, Ohio, show work by local artists. Dubbed the Chamber Pot Gallery, they display 19 bathroom-themed exhibits, including a dress made of pink, blue, and yellow tissues, and a painting where a person's face screams: "Got paper?"

OLDEST CAVES

In 2006, geologists concluded that the Jenolan caves, west of Sydney, Australia, date back to around 340 million years ago, making them the oldest known open caves in the world. They had previously been estimated to be around 90 million years old.

RIVER LOTTERY

In the town of Nenana, Alaska, residents take part in an annual lottery that offers a jackpot of $300,000—to predict the exact moment that the onset of spring will cause the ice on the nearby frozen Tanana River to break.

BAMBOO-CHOO-CHOO

Cambodia has a railroad with trains built mostly from bamboo and scavenged parts.

TOY STORY

Over a period of three months, 40 stuffed animals were removed from power lines and telephone wires in Canmore, Alberta, Canada. The toys were stuffed with metal railway spikes and large stones, and some were mysteriously marked with the number 26.

COVER-UP

Kira, Japan, famous for its recuperative hot spring baths, had its springs dry up in 1980. Townsfolk used boiling tap water to hide the fact for over a decade.

STEELY STRUCTURE

The Golden Gate Bridge in San Francisco, California, has enough steel wires in its cables to circle the Equator 3.5 times.

ICY DIP

Masamitsu Nakagawa (left), a Japanese Shinto priest in his nineties, winces as he bathes in iced water as part of an annual New Year's purification ceremony for good health and happiness at the Teppozo Shrine in Tokyo.

STATUE'S ▷ SOAKING

This huge statue of Bahubali— a key figure in the Jain religion—stands 57 ft (17 m) tall on a mountainside in the town of Shravanabelgola in southwestern India. Devotees of the Jain religion congregate here every 12 years to perform the spectacular ceremony of Mahamastakabhisheka, whereby they anoint the statue by pouring more than a thousand pots containing milk, water, flowers, and orange-colored turmeric over Bahubali's head. This has the striking effect of turning the gray stone statue bright golden orange from head to toe.

SHOE TREE

A giant cottonwood tree, near Middle Gate, Nevada, is hung with hundreds of shoes. Apparently, the first pair were tossed into the branches over 20 years ago by a husband after a fight with his new bride. When they made up, he then threw his own shoes into the tree as an act of union.

DAYTONA'S DOG

After wandering into a cab company office in Daytona Beach, Florida, in 1940, Brownie, a small tan dog, was adopted by the town and became a local celebrity for the next 14 years. Cab drivers bought him an ice cream every day. When he died, there were 75 mourners at his funeral and he is still remembered today by a marked grave in Riverfront Park that is watched over by a topiary Brownie.

SUPER SAUSAGE

A 42-ft (13-m) fiberglass sausage was built in 2001 at Mundare, Alberta, Canada, to promote a local sausage factory. Weighing six tons, it took four years to complete and was designed to withstand 100-mph (160-km/h) winds.

SHELL STATION

The old Shell service station in Winston Salem, North Carolina, is actually shaped like a shell. Based on the company logo, the orange-yellow structure was built in 1930 of concrete stucco over a wood and wire framework. After it stopped selling gas, the station became a lawn mower repair shop but is now the regional office of the Historic Society for the Preservation of North Carolina.

FIDDLE TRIBUTE

A 14-ft (4.3-m) metal fiddle, weighing 500 lb (230 kg), stands proudly at Harvey, New Brunswick, Canada, in honor of famed fiddler Don Messer, who lived in the area.

ENGLISH QUARTER

A little corner of England has been re-created 6,000 mi (9,660 km) away in a suburb of Shanghai, China. Thames Town is a replica of a quaint English community, complete with cobbled streets, red mailboxes and telephone kiosks, mock-Tudor boutiques, a pub, and a fish and chip shop. There is also a magnificent sandstone church, modeled on a Bristol chapel.

POTTER'S MUSEUM

For over 100 years, Potter's Museum of Curiosity was one of Britain's most bizarre attractions. It showed rabbits at school, kittens enjoying a tea party, and a marching band of mice.

However, what made it so weird was that the 6,000 animals on display weren't mere models—they were real stuffed creatures, the work of master taxidermist Walter Potter.

Potter developed a taste for taxidermy in his teens and began by stuffing his own pet canary after it had died. The hobby was popular in Victorian England and in 1861 Potter opened his museum at Bramber, West Sussex, charging two pennies' admission. All of the animals were supplied to Potter by local breeders and farmers—he was at pains to point out that no animal had been deliberately killed for his personal use.

He then arranged them into charming tableaux. "The Rabbits' School" showed 20 rabbits sitting on benches, reading books, and doing their sums. "The Kittens' Tea and Croquet Party" featured 37 ginger-and-white kittens—the ladies decked with jewels, the men wearing cravats—all sitting at a long table eating baked mouse tart. There were also guinea pigs playing cricket.

His collection moved to several different homes before ending up at the famous Jamaica Inn in Cornwall. But, in 2003, Potter's Museum was split up and sold at auction, the scenes raising around $1,000,000.

OF CURIOSITY

A group of mice in one of Potter's tableaux enjoy a game of dominoes around a table.

Squirrels often feature in Potter's tableaux, such as these pipe-smoking friends, seen here enjoying a game of cards.

"The Rabbits' School" features a group of young rabbits at lessons in their classroom.

KILLER ELEPHANT

In Delavan, Wisconsin, known in the 19th century as the circus capital of the world, there is a life-size fiberglass statue of a rearing elephant on Main Street. The statue commemorates the fearsome Romeo, a vicious bull elephant that killed five people over a period of 15 years, came close to demolishing a Chicago theater, and once terrorized the country for three days after escaping.

GOLD BAN

In an attempt to improve the country's image, President Emomali Rakhmonov of Tajikistan announced in 2006 that he was banning state employees from wearing gold teeth.

ICE ANGEL ▷

This photo of an angel in ice was taken by Vicki Whitehill of Alachua, Florida, in Great Smokey Mountain National Park in Tennessee in 2003.

SLUSH RACE

The town of Girdwood, Alaska, hosts the annual "Slush Cup," in which contestants ski downhill and then try to cross a 90-ft (27-m) lagoon of icy water at the bottom of the slope.

TIRE MEN

A group of three tire men—the tallest 25 ft (7.6 m) high and made from 75 tires—stand by the side of the road at Daphne, Saskatchewan, Canada. As well as tires, the sculptures also contain hubcaps and coffee cans.

THICK TRUNK

A giant sequoia tree growing in California has a trunk that is over 102 ft (31 m) in circumference. The tree is 275 ft (84 m) tall and it is estimated that it contains enough timber to make five billion matches.

COLD DIP

At the World Winter Swimming Championships held in Finland each March, swimmers compete in a pool 82 x 39 ft (25 x 12 m) that has been cut from the ice with chainsaws.

BITING LAWS

In Louisiana, biting someone with your natural teeth is considered to be "simple assault," but biting someone with your false teeth is "aggravated assault."

VIRTUAL △ VERSAILLES

Enthusiastic do-it-yourself decorator Adrian Reeman from Southampton, England, has transformed his tiny apartment into a replica of the Palace of Versailles. From the outside it could be any one of the apartments in the anonymous 1960s block he lives in, but inside it is a scene of opulent splendor.

SINGING SANDS

Sand dunes can actually sing! The natural phenomenon can last several minutes and reach 115 decibels. It has been heard at some 35 deserts worldwide and, in 2006, scientists found the explanation. Collisions between grains of sand cause the movement of the grains to become synchronized. The outer layer of the dune then resonates like a loudspeaker cone, the note produced depending on the size of the grain. The most beautiful sounds are said to be in Oman, on the southeast coast of the Arabian peninsula.

HOUSE OF THE FIGURINES

In the French town of Dieulefit, self-taught artist Roland Dutel has designed his "House of the Figurines," decorating the walls and the garden with curious creations made from 150 tons of recycled materials.

Dutel started work on his collection of sculptures, paintings, and mosaics in 1989. He used off-cuts, broken tiles, and rejects from the town's pottery workshops, teaming them with flotsam washed up by the stream that runs past his house together with metal, wood, concrete, and paper, which formed the bizarre faces and figures.

Bizarre Buildings

SODA HOME

This house was built using more than 60,000 soft-drink bottles in the 1950s. It was owned by John Makinen, Jr. of Kaleva, Michigan.

HOLY TREES!

Known as The Hymn House, this home in Herstmonceux in Sussex, England, featured a tree that was trained to grow across the front of the building to form the words "Praise the Lord."

ROCK SOLID

Named "The House of the Odd Rocks," this dwelling was constructed out of 8,246 rocks that had been gathered from 40 states and foreign countries by Frank A. Bissing of Hays, Kansas, in the 1930s.

LOG HOUSE

This unique house on Redwood Highway in Garberville, California, was built in the 1930s by Arthur Johnson, who ran a business building log cabins.

IN DRY DOCK

An old river steamer that ran aground on Sauries Island in Portland, Oregon, in 1936 got a new lease of life when it became a houseboat. The dwelling, which was also used as a dairy farm, sat on the Willameth River in the state.

STUMPED!

This three-bedroomed home was built in and around a huge tree stump in Vancouver, British Columbia, in the early 1930s.

PICKLE FLINGING

In Berrien Springs, Michigan, there is an annual Pickle Flinging contest. The record throw is nearly 300 ft (90 m).

BEST BAGGERS

Store workers from across the U.S.A. compete in the National Grocers Association's Best Bagger Contest. Competitors fill two bags with a selection of grocery items and are judged on appearance, attitude, time, weight distribution, and technique. There are separate categories for paper and plastic bags.

ROAD BOWLS

Competitors in Northern Ireland take part in the sport of road bowls, where they toss an iron ball along a winding country road to see who can cover a distance of 2.5 mi (4 km) in as few throws as possible. Bowls of half a mile are not uncommon.

CHICKEN FESTIVAL

At the 17th World Chicken Festival in London, Kentucky, in 2006, chicken-related events included impersonating a chicken, a wings-eating contest, and dropping eggs without breaking them.

STILETTO SPRINT

A total of 150 women wearing stiletto heels at least three inches high ran 80 yd (75 m) along a cobbled street in Amsterdam, the Netherlands, in March 2006. The winner of the race was 20-year-old Nancy Karels who had never worn high heels before.

STAIR LIFT

Scotland's Ferniehirst Castle has staircases that spiral counterclockwise, giving advantage in sword combat to the left-handed defenders of the property.

URBAN HOUSEWORK

Mark Tilbrook and James Doherty from the U.K. invented the sport of Urban Housework, which includes mop-jousting and riding a vacuum cleaner outdoors downhill in as fast a time as possible.

COLD PLANET

The average temperature of the coldest place on Earth, Antarctica, is about four times warmer than the daytime temperature on Pluto.

ICE RIDE

Competitors from across North America are invited to pedal through ice and snow in Montreal to compete in the Ice Cup, an annual contest exclusively for bicycle couriers.

SMALL OFFICE

There's not much room for a queue at the Post Office in Ochopee, Florida. For the former tool-shed building measures just 62 sq ft (5.75 sq m)—about the size of a child's playhouse.

COMFY CATS

A bungalow in San Diego, California, has been transformed into a cat's dream playground by owner Bob Walker. Cat-themed mementoes adorn the walls, and his feline friends enjoy more than 100 ft (30 m) of specially built runways that snake around the house.

VOLCANIC INN

The Lava-Side Inn, a bed-and-breakfast located near Kilauea, Hawaii, is built on an active volcano. Guests at the $100-a-night establishment, who have included actor William Shatner, must cross a treacherous crust of freshly formed volcanic rock that runs over bubbling lava that has a temperature of 2,000°F (1,090°C). The fumes are toxic and even the cracks in the path are hot enough to cook a potato or melt your shoe.

WEB ART

Will Knight harvests spiderwebs at his farm in Williamstown, Vermont, and sells them as art. He originally got the idea from a Girl Scout manual. He sprays a mist of white paint to identify his chosen web and then sticks it to a board that has been sanded smooth or painted black. Finally, he seals the web in place by lacquering both it and the board. "Spiderwebman," as he is known, even has spiderwebs tattooed on his elbows.

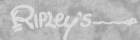

TRAILER HOME

Artist Burke Paterson of Toronto, Ontario, Canada, lives in a loft measuring 850 sq ft (79 sq m), which contains a 19-ft (5.8-m) vintage Airstream trailer! He also uses an old airline food cart for kitchen storage and his liquor cabinet is an old filing cabinet.

REMOTE LOCATION

You can only get to Juneau, the state capital of Alaska, by water or air. There are no roads leading to the city—from anywhere.

UGLY CONTEST

The town of Yellowknife, North West Territory, Canada, stages an annual "Ugly Truck 'n' Dog Contest"!

STAR QUALITY

A single spoonful of material from a neutron star—the burned out and shrunken remnants of a once-functioning star—weighs a billion tons!

BUFFALO DERBY

The villagers of Vihear Suor in Cambodia stage an annual water-buffalo race as part of a festival that honors deceased relatives. In 2006, around 1,000 spectators watched 28 jockeys hang on desperately as the buffaloes, their horns draped with colorful cloths, charged down the course.

QUIET AIRPORT

The Yasser Arafat International Airport in Gaza remains open and keeps its employees on the payroll even though a flight hasn't landed there since 2001.

ARTICHOKE QUEEN

A landmark of Castroville, California, is a steel and plaster artichoke that is 20 ft (6 m) tall and 12 ft (3.6 m) wide and was built by Ray Bei in 1963. The town hosts an annual artichoke festival and Marilyn Monroe was crowned the very first artichoke queen back in 1947.

WEIRD WEEK

Ocean City, New Jersey, stages an annual "weird contest week," with competitions in sculpting French fries and tossing wet T-shirts.

BONE TOWN

Believe It or Not! The original name of Regina, Canada, was Pile 'O Bones!

ART CAR

Richard Moriarty of Newport Beach, California, has a Lamborghini sports car hanging from the wall of his home—as a piece of art!

RAMBLING ROSE

A rosebush in Tombstone, Arizona, spreads over an arbor covering more than 8,000 sq ft (743 sq m). The white Lady Banksia rose, which has a trunk 12 ft (3.6 m) in circumference, was originally brought over from Scotland as a root in 1885.

WHEELS OF FINANCE

Stone wheels, some as large as 12 ft (3.6 m) in diameter, are still used as currency on the South Pacific island of Yap.

SNOWLESS SNOWMOBILES

Fremont, New Hampshire, stages an annual snowmobile race... without any snow. Instead, competitors race their snowmobiles across grass and through water.

ROACH RACE

At the BugFest at Raleigh, North Carolina, contestants wear beards of bees and cockroaches and race in the Roachingham 500. Meanwhile, the Café Insecta offers such delicacies as ant-chiladas and banana worm nut bread.

LANGUAGE CLASS

Southfields Community College, a high school in southwest London, England, has pupils that speak in 71 different languages, including Arabic, Kurdish, Farsi, Kazak, Zulu, Swahili, and Croatian.

LONG JUMP

Owing to the difference in gravity, the men's world long jump record, which is just over 29 ft (8.8 m) on Earth, would be 176 ft (54 m) on the Moon but only 11 ft (3.4 m) on the planet Jupiter.

DARING DIVERS

Each year as part of a local festival, Japanese women dive 30 ft (9 m) beneath the sea without oxygen tanks to find shellfish such as clams, oysters, and lobsters. The Amas, as they are known, have as long as their breath holds—about 1 minute 20 seconds— to prise the mollusks from the rocks. Here, the women are shown making their procession into the sea.

BOTTLE HOUSE ▷

This striking home was built on Cap-Egmont, Prince Edward Island, Canada, by Eduourd Arsenault in 1980. It is made entirely out of glass bottles.

DOUBLE TIME

Churches in Malta have two clocks showing different times. This is to confuse the Devil about the time of the next service.

WEATHER DELAY

The international golf tournament in Castle Rock, Colorado, has been delayed by weather every year for the past 20 years.

WHEELBARROW RACE

The Black Rock Stakes lays claim to being one of the world's premier wheelbarrow races. It takes place at Pilbara, Western Australia, and is run over more than 75 mi (120 km). The wheelbarrows can be modified, but must have headlights and red taillights.

POTATO RACE

In the Millthorpe Murphy Marathon at Millthorpe, New South Wales, Australia, contestants carry a bag of potatoes weighing 110 lb (50 kg) over a course measuring 5,282 ft (1,610 m).

FISH FESTIVAL

In Prairie du Chien, Wisconsin, there is an annual "Droppin' of the Carp" celebration whereby a carp is dropped from a tall crane into the Mississippi River at midnight on New Year's Eve to welcome the New Year.

TOUGH MARATHON

The annual Barkley Marathon in Wartburg, Tennessee—a run of 100 mi (160 km) through rugged woodland that takes 60 hours to complete—is so grueling that only six people have completed it in the past 20 years.

◁ SLEEPING IN THE TREES

Germany's first tree house hotel opened in the village of Zentendorf in the eastern state of Saxony in July 2005. The Tree House offers five wooden rooms that are suspended in the branches of black locust trees, 30 ft (9 m) above the ground. The rooms all come with electric lights, small balconies, and shared bathrooms, and are connected by narrow walkways.

AERIAL BEDS

Paying guests sleep in tree-supported hammocks 30 ft (9 m) in the air at a bed-and-breakfast in Cornwall, England.

TOILET CONTEST

The Montgomery County Agricultural Fair in Gaithersburg, Maryland, stages an annual toilet-decorating contest. The 2006 winners of the $25 grand prize were two Boy Scouts with their Camp Stinkalot Scouthouse. They painted their toilet brown and built an outhouse around it, complete with a plastic vine and fake snake.

TALL SUNFLOWERS

At Goodland, Kansas, stands a huge easel, 80 ft (24 m) tall, and bearing a 32 x 24 ft (9.7 x 7.3 m) copy of Van Gogh's painting "Three Sunflowers in a Vase." The outsize tribute was painted by Canadian artist Cameron Cross and is particularly appropriate, as Goodland is the center of the local sunflower industry.

SHALLOW ROOTS

Although redwood trees can reach the height of a 40-story building, their root systems are only 10 ft (3 m) deep. Instead of growing down, the shallow roots grow out and spread sideways up to 250 ft (76 m) from the trunk.

COW REMEMBERED

A cow that died in 1932 still has its own marble tombstone near the historic barns of the former North Michigan Asylum at Traverse City. Traverse Colantha Walker was a grand champion milk cow, producing 200,114 lb (90,770 kg) of milk and 7,525 lb (3,415 kg) of butterfat in her life. When she died, hospital staff and patients held a banquet in her honor and gave her a ceremonial burial.

COCONUT DELIVERY

More than 10,000 coconuts are delivered daily to the Maa Tarini Temple in Ghatagaon in India's Orissa State by devotees from around the country for rituals and sacrifices to the gods.

SEA DOGS

At the annual LobsterDog Parade in Los Angeles, pet owners dress up their dogs as a variety of sea creatures and seafood, including lobsters, seals, whales, starfish, sushi, and fish cakes.

OLDEST TREES

California's Inyo National Forest harbors the bristlecone pine, believed to be the oldest living tree species. The trees grow only at high elevations and some are thought to be over 4,600 years old.

DIRTY PLAYERS

A player comes up for breath in the U.K.'s first ever Swamp Soccer tournament, held in Dunoon, Scotland, in July 2006. Swamp soccer originates in Finland and is fast becoming an alternative sport, with tournaments taking place worldwide.

HIGH ROLLER

Built in 1991, a double-sized model of a red Rolls-Royce—40 ft (12 m) long, 11½ ft (3.5 m) high and 12 ft (3.6 m) wide—stands at Steinbach, Manitoba, Canada, to emphasize the town's status as the Automobile City... even though there are no Rolls-Royce dealerships in town.

WINDING ROAD

On the island of Maui, Hawaii, the road to Hana is 52 mi (84 km) long and has more than 600 hairpin turns and 54 bridges that have only one lane.

OLD HAM

At the Isle of Wight County Museum in Smithfield, Virginia, there is a 104-year-old ham and a 117-year-old peanut on display. The ham was once insured for $5,000 against fire and theft.

STAY INDOORS

The remote old army outpost of Whittier, Alaska, is constantly battered by biting winds of up to 70 mph (110 km/h). Between avalanches and frequent subzero temperatures, the 180 residents leave home so infrequently that some barely ever put on shoes.

34

Believe It or Not!®

I LOVE SNAKES!

This Thai man is an inhabitant of one of the world's strangest villages—Kok Sa Nga, which means "King Cobra Village," in northeast Thailand. Many of Kok Sa Nga's villagers keep venomous king cobra snakes in wooden boxes under their homes, and every year the village stages a three-day festival celebrating this deadly snake. The entertainment on offer includes men who fight the snakes barehanded and women who dance with the cobra's heads in their mouths.

SPUTNIK RELIC

The most unusual exhibit at the Rahr-West Art Museum in Manitowoc, Wisconsin, is a lump of metal weighing 20 lb (9 kg), which is an exact replica of a piece that crashed into the street outside when the Soviet Union's *Sputnik IV* spacecraft fell to Earth in September 1962. The rest of the seven-ton craft burned up in the atmosphere.

FOOTBALL HOUSE

Dutch architect Jan Sonkie is such a keen soccer fan that he built his four-story house in Blantyre, Malawi, in the shape of a soccer ball.

HANDY SCULPTURE

The brainchild of evangelist Oral Roberts, a huge pair of praying hands guards the Oral Roberts University at Tulsa, Oklahoma. Made of bronze, the massive sculpture is 60 ft (18 m) high and weighs 30 tons.

SPINACH CAN

With a capacity of a million gallons (3,785,000 l), the water tower that is decorated as a spinach can in the town of Alma, Arkansas, lays claim to being the world's largest can of spinach.

SULFUR BLAST

Mount St. Helens in the state of Washington spews out twice as much sulfur dioxide as all of the state's industries added together.

PARTLY SUBMERGED

Measured from its base—on the floor of the Pacific Ocean—to its peak, the tallest mountain in the world is not Everest, but Hawaii's Mauna Kea. This volcanic peak rises to a height of 33,474 ft (10,203 m) from the seabed, but only 13,794 ft (4,205 m) of this is above sea level.

CUBE HOUSE

Designed by Ben Kutner, a bizarre house in Toronto, Ontario, Canada, consists of three green cubes perched at angles above the ground on a single column. A traditional house sits on the ground and the cubes—each 24 sq ft (2.2 sq m) and with around 1,130 sq ft (105 sq m) of floor space—stick out as limbs like the branches of a tree.

GOLFING GILBERT

With a comical face and wearing a Scottish tam o'shanter on his head and plaid pants, a huge golf ball named Gilbert, measuring 6 ft (2 m) in diameter, adorns the town of Gilbert Plains, Manitoba, Canada. The wacky sculpture is made of steel covered with fiberglass.

PEACE SYMBOL

A wooden tomahawk with a 54-ft (16-m) handle and weighing 2,750 lb (1,250 kg) is displayed with a concrete teepee that is 30 ft (9 m) high in Cut Knife, Saskatchewan, Canada, as a symbol of peace and unity between white people and the neighboring Indian reserves.

ROYAL WAVES

The Queen of England is the legal owner of all of the sturgeons, dolphins, porpoises, and whales in the waters within 3 mi (4.8 km) of U.K. shores.

MOTOR CITY

Nearly one quarter of the land area of Los Angeles is taken up by cars, and there are at least half a million more cars in L.A. than there are people—the population of Los Angeles County is 10 million, and there are 10.5 million registered vehicles. And in the city of L.A.—the most car-populated metropolis in the world—there are 1.8 registered cars per licenced driver.

RECYCLABLE BUILDING

Colorado architect Doug Eichelberger built a fireproof insulated barn and stable for his horses, using 80 tons of recyclable magazines for building material.

HIGH FINANCE

An Indian bank set up an ATM machine along a trade route that leads from Lhasa, Tibet, to the State of Sikkim—at an altitude of 13,200 ft (4,025 m)!

HUMAN DANGER

Despite the number of rat-infested slums in the city, only around 300 New Yorkers are bitten by rats in an average year. However, some 1,500 citizens are bitten annually by fellow New Yorkers!

CRAZY RADIO

Nearly 12 million listeners tune in to Argentina's "Crazy Radio" each day. The show is broadcast from José Borda mental hospital in Buenos Aires and features interviews with the patients.

RADON RELIEF

Every year, thousands of people seeking relief from chronic illnesses visit mines in Montana that are filled with radon, a radioactive gas.

▽ GRAB THE GRAPES

Steve "The Grape Guy" Spalding successfully caught an astonishing 1,203 grapes in his mouth in the space of 30 minutes in Sydney, Australia, in November 2005. The grapes were thrown from a distance of 15 ft (4.6 m). Steve has also caught a grape that was dropped from a height of 900 ft (274 m), and once managed to catch 116 grapes in his mouth in three minutes.

PASSPORT MOUNTAIN

Every day, more than three million passports are checked at airports and border crossings throughout the world. If all these passports were stacked on top of each other, they would form a column higher than Mount Everest.

SPRAY-ON SISTINE

The famous Sistine Chapel has been re-created in a rundown building in Iowa. Graffiti artist Paco Rosic studied the real Sistine Chapel in Rome before practicing painting sections of it upside down in his garage at home. He then spent four months—and $10,000 on spray-paint cans—lying on his back on scaffolding painting a half-scale replica of Michelangelo's fresco on the ceiling of the former Waterloo antique store.

SCARY MONKEY

There are so many wild monkeys causing problems on India's Delhi Metro rail line that officials now use a trained black-faced langur monkey to scare the others away.

MAGIC MUSEUM

Among the exhibits at the American Museum of Magic at Marshall, Michigan, is the custom-made milk can into which a handcuffed Harry Houdini crawled before being thrown into the Detroit River. The museum was started by Bob Lund, who went without a car and ate peanut butter sandwiches for years just so that he could collect more magicians' artifacts.

HIMALAYAN RAILWAY

At its highest point, the Himalayan railway from Beijing, China, to Lhasa, Tibet, reaches an altitude of 16,640 ft (5,072 m)—that's higher than any mountain peak in Europe and more than 656 ft (200 m) higher than the Peruvian railway in the Andes.

SPIT The PIT

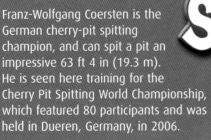

Franz-Wolfgang Coersten is the German cherry-pit spitting champion, and can spit a pit an impressive 63 ft 4 in (19.3 m). He is seen here training for the Cherry Pit Spitting World Championship, which featured 80 participants and was held in Dueren, Germany, in 2006.

GIANT YO-YO

A working yo-yo at a museum in Chico, California, weighs 250 lb (113 kg), is 50 in (127 cm) high, 31½ in (80 cm) wide, has a diameter of 5½ ft (1.7 m), and a 75-ft (23-m) string. An 80-ft (24-m) crane is needed to operate it!

UNDERWEAR PROTEST

Every year, villagers from Veracruz, Mexico, hold farmers' rights protests in Mexico City—dressed only in their underwear!

PLANE LANDMARK

Visitors to Milwaukie, Oregon, have grown accustomed to seeing a grounded World War II B-17G airplane by the roadside. Between 1947 and 1991 it served as the state's most unusual gas station and it is now linked with an adjacent restaurant where visitors can buy souvenir Bomber placemats.

DUNG ISLANDS

Peru's Guano Islands had accumulated piles of dung hundreds of feet high by the time people began harvesting it for use in gunpowder and fertilizer in the 19th century.

CONCRETE HAVEN

Mike Mercier's home in Auburn, Maine, and absolutely everything inside it, is built entirely of concrete, including the walls, floors, furniture, and countertops.

GEM PHONE

A Swiss-manufactured cell phone that has diamonds as control buttons went on sale in 2006 for a cool $300,000. The menu navigator on the Black Diamond Smartphone is a 0.25-carat diamond, and more diamonds decorate the titanium body. Also, the phone offers a touch-sensitive keypad and changes color from silver to black when not in use.

BRAINY COLLECTION

A collection of more than 8,000 preserved human brains is maintained in a World War II bomb shelter beneath the Runwell Psychiatric Hospital in Essex, England. The brains have been collected over the past 40 years and are available for scientists to study for research into Alzheimer's, schizophrenia, and other diseases that affect the brain.

COCONUT MYSTERY

As many as ten coconuts have been discovered on the beaches of Tiree, a small remote Hebridean island off the northwests coast of Scotland. Experts are mystified as to how the coconuts got there but one theory is that the exotic fruits may have been carried to Tiree on the Gulf Stream waters from the Caribbean.

This sculpture, handmade from bronze and stainless steel, contains 920 parts—page 56

Mark Jenkins' plastic wrap figures mysteriously appear all over the streets of Washington, D.C.—page 50

A mind-boggling work of art in Sydney had visitors seeing spots before their eyes—page 47

CURIOUS CREATIONS

DRIFTWOOD HORSES

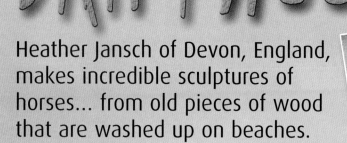

Heather Jansch of Devon, England, makes incredible sculptures of horses... from old pieces of wood that are washed up on beaches.

She had the idea for creating driftwood artworks when her son, looking for wood to light a fire, chopped a piece of ivy that had grown round a fencing stake. He left behind a section that she thought would make a good horse's torso for the copper wire sculpture on which she was working. She makes both small and life-size equine sculptures. Her larger sculptures have a steel frame, which is coated with

Each of Heather's sculptures can be months in the making. Sometimes they are left incomplete while Heather searches for the right pieces of wood to complete the jigsaw.

fiberglass to roughen it up and stop the wood from slipping, as it would do on bare metal. When Heather is happy with the position of the pieces of driftwood, they are tied with wire and then screwed together to hold them in place. The animals' hooves are made from old copper immersion heater tanks. As she usually places her finished works in natural, outdoor environments, such as fields, they must be self-supporting and sturdy enough to cope with high winds without falling over. And for exhibitions, they need to be able to withstand being lifted by crane. Heather's biggest problem is a lack of driftwood. Her full-size sculptures require a number of pieces from which she selects the best. She often has to travel miles to find suitable specimens.

Heather finds the driftwood for her sculptures on beaches after high tides and storms.

GHOST SHIP

When a 29-ft (8.8-m) yacht sailed from Fair Isle, Shetland, to Newcastle upon Tyne, England, in July 2005 (a journey of 330 mi/ 530 km), there was something missing— a crew. For this was the Ghost Ship, the brainchild of Boston, Massachusetts, artist Chris Burden, who wanted to create a crewless, self-navigating yacht. Built in Southampton, England, the boat was controlled via onboard computers but, just in case it ran into trouble, it was shadowed by an accompanying support vessel throughout the five-day voyage.

CHOCOLATE BUST

New York artist Janine Antoni made a series of self-portrait busts in soap and chocolate. For her chocolate creations, she chisels cubes of chocolate with her teeth. Antoni once used the brainwave signals recorded while she dreamed at night as a pattern for weaving a blanket the following morning. And for a 1992 exhibition she washed her long hair and then mopped the floor of an art gallery in London, England, with it!

MIGHTY MURAL

Since the 1970s, thousands of artists have contributed to a huge mural on the banks of a river at Pueblo, Colorado. The mural, which officially measures 2 mi (3.2 km) long and 58 ft (18 m) high, contains portraits of the likes of Elvis Presley, Andy Warhol, and Bob Marley, and contributors are invited to add to it each year.

EMPTY FEELING

British artist David Hensel was surprised when his sculpture was rejected by a leading art show—and even more so when its empty plinth was accepted and displayed on its own! The judges at the Royal Academy's Summer Exhibition thought the statue—a laughing head—and plinth were separate works. And they much preferred the plinth, complete with its piece of wood sticking up that was meant to keep the head in place.

△ PAVEMENT PICASSO

British artist Julian Beever creates incredible 3-D chalk drawings on flat city sidewalks. Known as the "Pavement Picasso," he has chalked pictures in America, Europe, and Australia, including a swimming pool so lifelike that shoppers swerved to avoid it and Coca-Cola bottles that appear to spring out of the ground. In a street in London, England, in 2006, the artist starred in his own work by posing against a wall (perched on a ledge he had drawn), while waiting to be rescued from a burning building by Batman and Robin!

PAPER SHIP

Jared Shipman of Roseville, California, built a 320,000-piece model, 9 ft (2.7-m) long, of the USS *Nimitz* out of paper.

FAKE COLLECTION

Christophe Petyt of Paris, France, founded L'Art du Faux, a collection of more than 3,500 fake masterpieces. He has 82 artists working for him re-creating old masters. Visitors to Petyt's exhibitions have included Arnold Schwarzenegger, Frank Sinatra, and La Toya Jackson.

AMPHIBIOUS TRAILER

From 1989, Rick Dobbertin of Syracuse, New York, spent 4½ years (14,000 man-hours) turning an old milk trailer into a 32-ft (10-m) long stainless steel amphibious craft in which he hoped to circumnavigate the Earth over land and sea. He didn't quite achieve his objective, but he did manage to travel more than 33,000 mi (53,100 km) on land and a further 3,000 mi (4,828 km) on the ocean, tackling seas that swelled up to 18 ft (5.5 m) in the process.

SHARK WATCH

The Pentagon is hoping to use remote-controlled sharks as possible spies. U.S. engineers have created a neural implant—a series of electrodes embedded into the brain—that is designed to enable the signals of a shark's brain to be manipulated remotely. They plan to test the device on blue sharks off the coast of Florida.

BLIND DEVOTION

For more than 30 years, John Cook has created masterpieces in wood. But the Tennessee man never gets to see the finished product—because he is blind. Although he lost his sight to glaucoma as a child, Cook uses a measuring stick and gauge blocks with brail marking to produce beautifully intricate furniture. Each cut he makes is steady, deliberate, and perfect. "My hands are my eyes," he explains.

▲ EXPENSIVE BOOT

This giant boot was made from $6 million of discarded bills.

WOODEN 'GATOR

In 2005, Michael Smith of Baton Rouge, Louisiana, made a solid toothpick alligator from about three million toothpicks! He has also made a wearable hat, a saxophone, a fully functional briefcase, and delicate butterflies—all from common toothpicks.

TALL TOPIARY

In 1983, Moirangthem Okendra Kumbi began turning a Duranta hedge plant into a giant topiary. The plant, which he calls "Sweetheart," now stands a huge 61 ft (19 m) tall in Manipur, India. He spends five hours a day clipping, feeding, and watering his creation.

TURKEY SOUNDS

U.S. artist Jay Jones created "audio sculptures" by playing the sounds of gobbling turkeys to Christmas shoppers in West Yorkshire, England.

EDIBLE EXHIBITION

A show at an art gallery in Brighton, England, gave visitors a chance to eat the exhibits in 2005. "The Lost Apple Field" presented 700 varieties of apples to highlight how people have lost touch with traditional farming.

BATTERY-POWERED

Scientists at Japan's Tokyo Institute of Technology have invented an airplane powered solely by 160 tiny AA batteries. The 97-lb (44-kg) plane, with a 100-ft (30-m) wingspan, flew 1,283 ft (391 m) in one minute during tests in 2006 in what was thought to be the world's first household battery-powered takeoff.

STEAM GRAMOPHONE

Music-lover and steam-train enthusiast Geoff Hudspith from Dorset, England, has created what he claims is the world's first steam-powered gramophone... just so that he could play his collection of old 78 rpm records. It took him four years to build but cost him less than $200 because he used scrap metal.

MINI MASTERS

At the Smithsonian Institute in Washington, D.C., a mini art exhibition featured 1,122 tiny artworks measuring an average of 3 x 4 in (7.6 x 10 cm).

CHAMBER MUSIC

An American firm has invented a new iPod accessory that combines the portable music player with a toilet-roll holder so you can enjoy your favorite tunes while in the bathroom.

▽ Brush Strokes

Calligrapher Zhang Kesi writes the Chinese character "Long" (dragon) on a banner measuring 190 ft (58 m) long and 92 ft (28 m) wide in China. Kesi used a brush 18 ft (5.5 m) long and 6 ft 9 in (2 m) in diameter. The total length of the character stroke is 469 ft (143 m).

Cartoon Mania

CARTOON MANIA HAS GRIPPED MANY RIPLEY'S FANS OVER THE YEARS. AT THE HEIGHT OF THEIR ENORMOUS POPULARITY IN THE 1930s, ROBERT RIPLEY'S BELIEVE IT OR NOT! CARTOONS HAD MORE THAN 80 MILLION READERS DAILY.

FRANK S. NAROKI FROM CLEVELAND, OHIO, COLLECTED ENOUGH BELIEVE IT OR NOT! CARTOONS FROM 1929 TO 1932 TO WALLPAPER HIS ENTIRE BEDROOM. THE LAST THING HE SAW AT NIGHT AND THE FIRST THING WHEN HE AWOKE, HIS COLLECTION OF BELIEVE IT OR NOT! CARTOONS UNDOUBTEDLY GAVE HIM A NEW TOPIC OF CONVERSATION OVER BREAKFAST EVERY MORNING!

UNBELIEVABLE DUMMY

Walter Cunningham, seen here in 1944, made his ventriloquist's dummy out of papier-mâchéd Ripley's *Believe It or Not!* cartoons, and used the dummy in his act for more than 30 years.

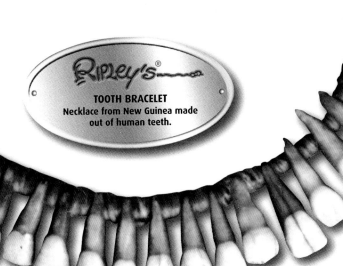

TOOTH BRACELET
Necklace from New Guinea made out of human teeth.

HUMAN EXHIBIT

A student in Yorkshire, England, turned her own grandmother into an art exhibit in 2006! Janis Rafailidous flew 80-year-old Athena over from her home in Greece and placed her in a mocked-up kitchen in a Leeds art gallery as a living sculpture. There, visitors watched Athena tidying up, preparing food, and even doing some knitting.

BARBIE MUTILATOR

There is a good reason why San Francisco artist Sue Wandell is known as the "Barbie Mutilator." Wandell produces works of art by chopping off the heads of Barbie dolls and replacing them with household objects. Among her creations are "Hammerhead Barbie" (where the doll's head is replaced by that of a metal hammer), "Vanity Barbie" (who has a mirror for a head) and "Bar Fly Barbie" (whose head is a removable pouring top for bottles of alcohol).

COLD COMFORT

A company in Alabama has developed a talking refrigerator magnet that berates dieters when they open the fridge to snack!

HORNET MOUNTAIN

In 1999, Yoshikuni Shiozawa of Nagano, Japan, created a model of Mount Fuji 12 ft (3.6 m) high by joining together 160 hornet nests. The finished sculpture contained no fewer than 160,000 hornets.

SAND PAINTING

In September 2005, more than 200 people made a sand painting measuring 46 x 52 ft (14 x 16 m) of "Fun in the Sun" at Jersey, Channel Islands, U.K. Half a ton of sand was mixed with poster paint to create 17 different colors. The dyed sand was then sprinkled onto hardwood sheets over areas of the design that had been covered with glue.

MINUTE FLAG

Jang-Bae Jeon and Carlo Foresca, students at the University of Texas in Dallas, have created a likeness of the American flag so small it would take 14 of them to span the width of a human hair. Using nanotechnology, they made an image of the flag—complete with all 50 stars and 13 stripes—that is just seven microns tall, compared to the 100-micron width of a human hair.

ASH FOREST

As part of a degree show at Camberwell College of Arts in London, England, student Emma Fenelon glazed five ceramic trees with human ashes. She had advertised on the Internet for volunteers to donate the remains of their "loved ones" for the project.

CANDY-WRAPPER ▷ COUTURE

Klavdiya Lyusina, from the village of Tsaryov in Russia, proudly models the skirt, jacket, headscarf, and bag that she made herself, out of candy wrappers. Klavdiya has been making clothes and accessories from these bright wrappers for the past 20 years.

STATE PAINTER

Artist Scott Hagan of Belmont County, Ohio, traveled 65,000 mi (105,000 km) through the state using 645 gal (2,445 l) of paint and 100 brushes to paint the state logo on 88 different barns in celebration of the Ohio bicentennial.

Ripley's — Believe It or Not!®

MUD ART

HOT ICE

Scott Wilson of Cary, North Carolina, has created an ice cream that is made with three kinds of peppers and two types of hot sauce. The product, Cold Sweat, is so hot that customers must sign a waiver before tasting it.

REPLICA ARK

Inspired by the biblical story of Noah, Dutchman Johan Huibers spent 15 months building a wooden ark 230 ft (70 m) in length that he planned to fill with farmyard animals, and sail to several cities in The Netherlands.

ROBOT CONDUCTOR

In 2004, a humanoid robot 23 in (58 cm) tall conducted the Tokyo Philharmonic Orchestra in a performance of Beethoven's 5th Symphony.

CHOPPER MOWER

C.G. Mouch of Brusly, Los Angeles, fitted the front end of a 750cc Honda motorcycle to the rear end of a lawn mower to create a "chopper mower" so that he could mow in style at speeds of up to 10 mph (16 km/h)!

Artist Angela Findlay from London, England, certainly gets her hands dirty in the name of art. She paints pictures with mud taken from the banks of England's Severn River. Angela collects mud in buckets before taking it back to her studio to mix with sand and acrylic paints. She then paints onto large canvases with her hands and fingernails.

ORIGAMI EXPERT

Devin Balkcom, a student at Carnegie Mellon University in Pittsburgh, Pennsylvania, developed a robot that can do origami, the ancient Japanese art of paper sculpture.

JUNK CREATIONS

Freeman Loughridge of Ardmore, Oklahoma, uses discarded junk to create quirky sculptures. Bicycle parts and springs form the basis for a flowering garden trellis, while an old army helmet has been converted into a flamingo! Loughridge says of his whimsical creations: "I'm very serious about not being serious."

FLOWER POWER

In September 2005, a bouquet of more than 150,000 roses was created at a shopping mall in Frankfurt, Germany.

ROBOTIC TASTER

Japanese engineers claim to have developed a robotic wine taster that is capable of distinguishing between 30 different varieties of grape!

CHIN POWER

Owen Orthmann of Minnesota, paralyzed from the neck down, modified a crossbow so that it can be easily loaded, aimed, and fired without the use of arms or legs. Instead he fires it with his chin.

BUTTON COUTURE ▷

In 1936, Owen Totten of Mount Erie, Illinois, modeled a suit that he'd covered with 5,600 buttons—no two of which were alike.

▷ ART AWASH

Volunteers stand at the water's edge and read newspapers to form a "human sculpture" on Manly Beach, Sydney, Australia. Artist Andrew Baines called for men, women, and children on September 2, 2006, to meet him at the beach at daybreak to form this sculpture. Baines said his live work had been inspired by a revelation as a child on the London Underground at rush hour, where he faced a sea of "corporate battery hens."

ILLUMINATED SLIPPERS

Trips to the refrigerator for a middle-of-the-night snack could be safer thanks to U.S. inventor Doug Vick who has devised a pair of slippers with lights. The slippers have powerful flashlights in the toes that shine a beam of light for distances of up to 25 ft (7.6 m). When the slippers are removed, a timer means that the light stays on long enough to enable the wearer to climb back into bed!

GUIDO'S HANDICRAFT

Italian artist Guido Daniele has given a new meaning to finger-painting. Instead of working on canvas, he uses pencil and watercolors on human hands to create incredible portraits of animals and birds such as cheetahs, elephants, crocodiles, and toucans. Daniele, who used to paint human bodies for advertising campaigns, takes up to ten hours to produce his handicraft. This means that his models not only need big hands but a lot of patience as well.

EYEBALL MOUSE

Chinese high-school student Zhou Chen of Nanjing has invented a special computer that can be operated by the user simply moving his or her eyeballs. The "eyeball mouse," as he calls it, enables users to click and, for example, open a website just by looking at the screen and moving their eyes.

SCRABBLE SCULPTURE

Scottish artist David Mach created a sculpture of a woman 8 ft (2.4 m) tall from 4,200 regular Scrabble tiles. The sculpture, entitled "Myslexia," was displayed in Sussex, England, in 2006 and the letters on the tiles were calculated to be worth more than 76,000 points!

MIGHTY MOUSETRAP

Students at the Art Institute in Fort Lauderdale, Florida, built a mousetrap 12 ft (3.6 m) long and weighing more than 600 lb (270 kg).

SAVED DISKS

Artist Tom Dukich of Spokane, Washington, saved on-line software disks for 10 years—enough to fill a 30-gal (115-l) garbage can—then created a giant sculpture out of them.

SPOTS BEFORE THE EYES!

In August 2006, the New South Wales Art Gallery in Sydney, Australia, played host to a mind-boggling work of art that had visitors literally seeing spots before their eyes. Australian artist Nike Savvas created the piece, entitled "Atomix—Full of Love, Full of Wonder," from more than 50,000 polystyrene balls. The balls vibrate with the wind from ten fans to represent the hot shimmering colors found in the Australian outback.

EAGLE-EYED

Nuclear scientist Bob Gibb and engineer Tom Chapman of New Brunswick, Canada, have developed special sunglasses that help golfers locate their lost golf balls.

PICK OF THE BUNCH

San Franciscan artist Steven J. Backman, 40, goes through more than 10,000 toothpicks a year creating his world-renowned sculptures.

Where did your fascination with toothpicks come from?

66 When I was about five years old I made a DNA molecule from beans and toothpicks for a science project. I have a lot of patience when I work now, but I didn't back then— I got frustrated and hit it, and got a toothpick lodged in my hand. That's where it all began! 99

What is the most famous piece you have made?

66 An exact replica of San Francisco's Golden Gate Bridge, made 20 years ago. It's 13 ft long, and took 30,000 toothpicks, perfectly suspended without any cable or wire. It even lights up! It took about 2½ years. 99

Do you have any other favorites?

66 My replicas of San Francisco cable cars, my abstract sculptures of masterworks such as the Mona Lisa or public figures such as President Bush... but above all, a 4½-ft-long radio-controlled yacht, covered with fiberglass resin for water resistance so it actually floats in water. It's my pride and joy—it was valued at $25,000 but I wouldn't sell it for a million dollars. 99

How does your work differ from that of model-makers?

66 Some people create big objects, but I create fine art. People don't always take it seriously because I use toothpicks and not bronze or plaster, but I want to create pieces—like my 2,330-toothpick interpretation of Rodin's The Thinker—that can be compared to Picasso or Rembrandt! 99

Do you wake up every morning and think: toothpick?

66 I'm most creative when I'm asleep! I dream about things, and often get up in the middle of the night and start working on them. 99

What helps you to concentrate while you are working?

66 I used to work 24 hours straight without a break. These days I do about eight or ten hours a day. I work in total silence, not even a radio or a phone. I like to be alone. 99

What kinds of toothpicks do you use—and do they cost you a fortune?

66 I have a contract with a supplier—each piece I make generally requires at least 400 to 1,000 toothpicks. I use mainly blanks, which don't have the tapered ends. They're stronger. And lots of glue! 99

What toothpick challenge awaits you?

66 The hardest piece I made was the Empire State Building, with 7,470 toothpicks, because it was hollow. But the biggest challenge would be to make something life-sized. I want to make a car that will actually operate. 99

You have a motto— what is it?

66 It's 'The Essence of Patience'—to sit for hours on end you need extreme patience. Ironically, outside my work, I'm the most impatient person in the world—I don't even like to wait in line! 99

LARGER THAN LIFE

London-based Australian sculptor Ron Mueck creates hyper-real sculptures of human figures on a mind-blowing scale. These works are part of his 2006 exhibition at The Royal Scottish Academy in Edinburgh, Scotland, entitled "A Girl" (baby) and "In Bed." Before becoming a sculptor, Mueck had a 20-year career as a puppet-maker and puppeteer in Australia.

BALLOON SCULPTURE

New York balloon artists Larry Moss and Royal Sorell used 40,781 oblong balloons to create a huge soccer-related sculpture in which the goal, the players, and even the grass were all made of balloons! It took 640 man-hours to make. The players were 40 ft (12 m) tall and dressed in the colors of the national teams of Belgium and The Netherlands, the host nations for the 2000 European Soccer Championships.

JET CHAIR

Giuseppe Cannela of Bedfordshire, England, successfully attached a jet engine to the back of his mother-in-law's wheelchair to reach speeds in excess of 60 mph (97 km/h)!

BRANCHING OUT

British artist Tim Knowles encourages trees to draw! He attaches pens to a thin branch, places a blank canvas at the end, and allows the wind to do the work.

DOG ON DISPLAY

For Vancouver's first Sculpture Biennale exhibition in 2006, passersby were encouraged to deposit random artistic items on shelves around the city. The objects placed included feathers, shoes, tree branches, and, briefly, a Chihuahua!

SNOW SHOW

At the National Screen Institute Film Festival held in Winnipeg, Manitoba, Canada, the audience sat outside in –22°F (–30°C) weather watching movies projected onto a giant block of snow!

CEMENT BOAT

A group of students from the University of Nevada spent a year working on an eight-man canoe made out of cement. The boat actually floats!

METAL CHEESE

Los Angeles sculptor Bruce Gray created a 25 x 43 x 29 in (64 x 110 x 74 cm) slice of cheese—in welded aluminum! "The Big Cheese," which has metal bubbles of various sizes, featured in the 2004 season finale of HBO's *Six Feet Under*.

FISH ART

Artist Carol Hepper of South Dakota creates sculptures using up to 200 dried fish skins! She collects the skins from fishing trips and fish processing facilities.

PLASTIC WRAPPER

People walking the streets of Washington, D.C., never know what they're going to find next.

It could be a parking meter dressed as a lollipop, a baby up a tree, a translucent dog on the shore, or a man buried head first in a utility box. These and many other strange sculptures that have cropped up around the city are the work of local street artist Mark Jenkins. Mark works primarily in packing tape and plastic wrap to create clear, lifelike molds. He first tried the technique at school when he covered a pencil in plastic wrap and tape, made an incision, and removed the pencil.

Twenty years later, in 2003, in a moment of boredom, he made a ball from clear tape. He went on to wrap the contents of his apartment before making a cast of his own body, which he placed in a dumpster.

Moving to Washington, his tape men soon began to spring up all over the city. Sometimes they were transparent, other times he would dress them in old clothes for added realism.

He has also created tape babies and animals, and has perched them in trees, on monuments, and with abandoned shopping carts.

IN DEPTH

What is your favorite piece of work?

"Right now, it's making the tape horses. They're fun to put out in nature and also in the city. I've been having a good time using them to turn trafficic circles into merry-go-rounds."

Have you had any mishaps or "sticky moments" while creating a piece?

"I think about the physics of what I'm doing to make sure things—including me!—don't fall down from high places. I have specially customized tools to hang things from street lamps and trees."

What is the most challenging thing you dream of taping?

"I'd love to make a cast of Abraham Lincoln's head from Washington, D.C.'s Lincoln Memorial—every time I go I think how cool it would be to have it sitting in my living room when my friends come round. But the authorities won't let me get up there."

What is the worst reaction you've had to your work?

"Usually people don't know it's me—I'll put a black bag over the piece while I'm working, then whip it off and be gone in seconds. But once a guy saw me pulling a pair of legs out of a garbage bag and looked at me as if to say 'That doesn't look good!' —he didn't stick around!"

What will you do next?

"I'm working on a series called 'Legos'—fusing two bodies together to make creatures with two sets of legs and no heads running around the city. As long as I come up with new ideas that amuse me, I'll carry on."

PAPER HOUSES

Sherry Browne, an artist in Charleston, South Carolina, makes sculptures of houses and historical forts out of toilet paper!

PUMPKIN CARVER

Hugh McMahon of New York City makes his living sculpting fruits and vegetables. He charges $1,000 for a carved pumpkin or watermelon.

SUDOKU PAPER

A British company has catered for the craze in Japanese Sudoku numerical puzzles by producing special toilet paper with individual puzzles on each sheet!

FLASHY EARRINGS

Inventors in California have developed earrings that flash in time to the wearer's heartbeat.

MEAT ART

A 2006 exhibition in Ghent, Belgium, featured a coat made of beef steaks, along with a tent of bacon, and sleeping bags made from steaks. Artist Jan Fabre worked through the night to turn 220 lb (100 kg) of steak, 33 lb (15 kg) of minced meat, and a few miles of Parma bacon into art for his Temples of Meat exhibition. But the exhibit could be displayed only for three days before it began to rot. It was not the first time that Fabre had worked with meat. In 2000, he covered the columns of Ghent University in strips of bacon.

MEMORABLE KISSES

Artist Tino Sehgal created a show at the Art Gallery of Ontario in Toronto, Canada, in 2006 where pairs of dancers copied great kisses from the history of art. Visitors came into the gallery to find the dancers performing kisses as depicted by the likes of Rodin, Munch, and Klimt.

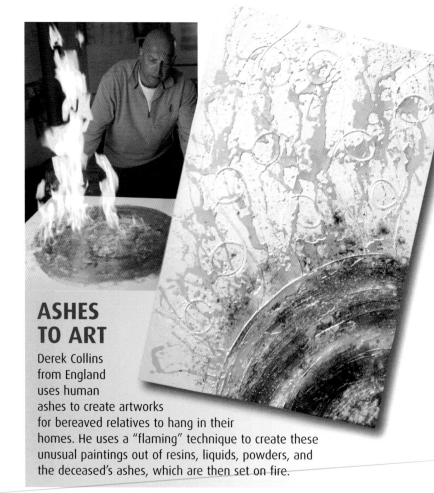

ASHES TO ART

Derek Collins from England uses human ashes to create artworks for bereaved relatives to hang in their homes. He uses a "flaming" technique to create these unusual paintings out of resins, liquids, powders, and the deceased's ashes, which are then set on fire.

CHAIN REACTION

People are amazed when they see Wayne Simmons' ornate wooden carvings of eagles, bears, and pelicans. All the more so when they learn that whereas other artists choose more delicate methods of working, Simmons of Louisa County, Virginia, carves his sculptures of animals and birds using a chain saw!

PAINTS PANTS

Rachel Kice, an artist from Nashville, Tennessee, has made a career out of painting other people's pants. Kice gives the pants highly individual designs to transform ordinary clothes into fine-art pieces.

BABY BOTTLES

Steve Klein of Encino, California, produces hand-blown miniature wine bottles that are just over 1 in (2.5 cm) high. Each bottle is filled with 0.025 fl oz (0.75 ml) of wine, then corked, sealed, and labeled.

◁ BUTT PAINTING

Stan Murmer, an artist from Virginia, is the pioneer of "butt painting," which involves him sitting in paint and stamping his butt on a canvas to create images. He has created butt-print tulips, butterflies, and parrots by this method, among other things, and, believe it or not, he has actually sold some of his work.

COMMUTE SUIT

To counter the heat wave that swept England in the summer of 2006, performance artist Liam Yeates invented a "commute suit" designed to make travel on the London Underground more bearable. The suit had colored spring-mounted balls to keep fellow commuters at least 6 in (15 cm) away, and a bowler hat with a flashing yellow light on top. Yeates also incorporated various gadgets useful for subway travel, including a fan in a briefcase, a built-in water bottle, and perfume bottles sewn into the shoulder pads of the suit to hide the smell of sweat on a particularly hot day.

TINY TESTAMENT

Using microlithography, three scientists at the Massachusetts Institute of Technology created a Bible measuring less than 0.2 sq in (1.3 sq cm) on a silicon tablet.

Tractor Art

Australian artist Ando, who was trained as a mining engineer, has created a vast artwork of a smiling stockman that covers 1½ sq mi (4 sq km) of the Mundi Mundi Plains in New South Wales. Using a tractor to expose the red earth, it took Ando a year to create the artwork. The portrait is visible 1.2 mi (2 km) from above.

TURBO BEETLE

Ron Patrick wasn't content with quietly customizing his Volkswagen Beetle. He wanted something more dramatic, more explosive.

The 49-year-old California-based car computer designer wanted the wildest street-legal ride possible and spent four years making his creation safe to drive. He made several versions out of Styrofoam to get the layout and lighting right. The car has two engines—the production gasoline engine in the front driving the front wheels and the jet engine in the back. He says: "The idea is that you drive around legally on the gasoline engine and when you want to have some fun, you

Ron's jet engine once belonged to a navy helicopter, but has been converted for use in his Beetle.

The Beetle retains its original 90 horsepower engine in the front of the vehicle, but has a 1,350-horsepower jet engine fixed to the rear.

spin up the jet and get on the burner." The jet shoots the VW's speed from 80 to 140 mph (129 to 225 km/h) in less than four seconds! He chose a Beetle "because it looks cool with the jet." The air for the jet enters through the two side windows and the sunroof,

prompting Patrick to concede: "It's a little windy inside but not unbearable." In fact, he is so pleased with his

design that he is currently planning to add two jet engines to his wife's 40 mph (64 km/h) scooter.

The jet burner is particularly eye-catching late at night, which is usually when Ron tries it out.

HAVING A BALL

Danny O'Connor, an artist from Lexington, Massachusetts, creates art using recycled objects, including Scotch tape and old record albums. But his favorite medium is a ball and over the years he has amassed no fewer than 22,000 discarded balls. One of his exhibits featured 17,000 found balls—tennis balls, footballs, squash balls, golf balls, beach balls, basketballs, and soccer balls—all arranged in a circle.

PUB PITCH

Pub landlord James Banbury is so keen on soccer that he covered the interior of the Old Swan at Kibworth, Leicestershire, England, with turf for the 2006 World Cup. He laid turf on one of the bars, painted pitch markings on the grass, and turned the fireplace into a goal, complete with chalk-drawn goalposts and crossbar.

LONG CIGAR

Cigar makers in Tampa, Florida, have rolled a cigar that is 101 ft (31 m) long and weighs 53 lb (24 kg). It took Wallace and Margarita Reyes and their workers more than 75 man-hours over several weeks to craft the supersized smoke.

TOP MOSAIC

In celebration of the town's 950th anniversary in 2005, artists from Landesbergen, Germany, used more than 2¼ million bottle tops to create a mosaic that measured 325 x 209 ft (100 x 64 m). The mosaic was so big it had to be laid out on a soccer field.

STAMP HEAVY

In June 2006, artists Dmitry Shagin and Maksim Isayev delivered a postcard in St. Petersburg, Russia, that was 50 ft (15 m) long, weighed more than 123 lb (56 kg), and bore no fewer than 198 stamps!

ARCTIC BEER

A brewery in Greenland is producing beer by using water melted from the Arctic ice cap. Owners of the Inuit brewery—situated in Narsaq, a settlement 390 mi (628 km) south of the Arctic Circle—claim that the water is 2,000 years old and free of minerals and pollutants. The first consignment of the beer (which has 5.5% alcohol) is bound for the Danish market.

BARKING BELL

Gerrit Bruintjes of Oldenzaal, The Netherlands, has a doorbell that barks like a dog in memory of the family's German Shepherd that died a few years ago. It is so realistic that tax inspectors have twice ordered Bruintjes to get a dog licence because they think he has a dog in the house!

TINY FIELD

Using nanotechnology, a German scientist has created a soccer field so tiny that 20,000 of them could be put onto the tip of a single human hair! The minute creation even has all the details and markings of a real field.

HUMAN SCULPTURE

Mark Ho's handmade sculpture of the human body is made from bronze and stainless steel and stands 17 in (43 cm) high. Made from 920 different parts, including 101 pieces in each hand, it weighs 13 lb (6 kg). It took Mark six years working on a prototype before he was happy with the final product. All joints are adjustable, which allows the figure to adopt an infinite number of positions.

INVERTED CHURCH

Visitors to Vancouver, Canada, in the summer of 2006 were stunned to see an upside-down church buried in the ground on its spire. Measuring 20 x 22 x 9 ft (6 x 6.7 x 2.7 m), it was made from steel, glass, and aluminum, and is called "Device To Root Out Evil." It is the work of New York-based sculptor Dennis Oppenheim.

ROBOT BARMAN

Students from the Technical University of Darmstadt in The Netherlands have created a robot that they claim can pour the perfect pint of beer! The robot, Hermann, is designed to pour the frothy German wheat beer at exactly the right angle.

FRIED FLAGS

Art student William Gentry of Clarksville, Tennessee, staged an exhibit of dozens of deep-fried American flags to protest against obesity. The flags were fried in peanut oil, egg batter, flour, and black pepper.

BIG BOOT

Igor Ridanovic of Los Angeles, California, has created the "Mono Boot," an extra-wide ski boot that holds both feet!

PLASTIC FANTASTIC

In a 2006 contest to make ingenious items from Tupperware, Evelyn Tabaniag of the Philippines designed a blue Tupperware evening bag, complete with lace lining and beaded bracelets for handles. And Stella Filippou from Greece modeled a Formula One race car entirely out of Tupperware items. The wheels were made from jello molds and potato mashers.

CONVERTED TROUGH

A 14-year-old Swiss boy has built a functioning submarine out of an old pig trough and other bits of farm equipment. Aaron Kreier has been working on the pedal-powered craft for four years and in July 2006 took it on a successful 15-minute maiden voyage.

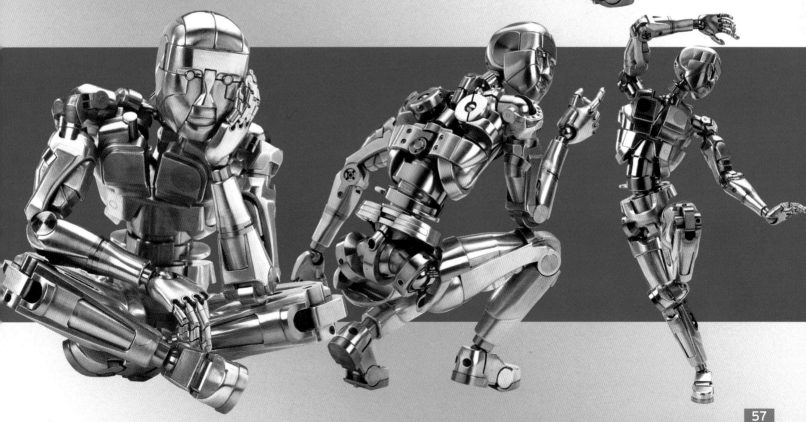

SNOW VILLAGE

A group of 200 Swiss enthusiasts built an igloo village 200 ft (60 m) wide, complete with snow church and piazza, on a frozen lake in 2006. Led by Lars Kienitz, they took 12 hours to build 100 igloos, many with kitchens, fireplaces, and ice sofas.

SOAP STATUE

New York artist Gary Sussman carved a scale replica of the Statue of Liberty, 12 ft (3.7 m) tall—out of soap. Sussman has also made a giant sculpture of Uncle Sam from a 5,000-lb (2,270-kg) block of soap.

COCKROACH BROOCH

A new creepy fashion accessory now on sale is the giant Madagascar hissing cockroach. About 3 in (7.6 cm) in length, it is adorned with colored crystals that are glued in place on its hard outer shell. A small clasp attached to a silver chain allows the insect to roam around the wearer.

AUTO ROBOT

Blacksmith Sage Werbock from Hulmeville, Pennsylvania, has built a robot made entirely of welded car parts. The arms are made from shock absorbers, the chest from a speaker, and the feet from brake pads. The robot weighs more than 200 lb (90 kg) and is 6 ft 9 in (2 m) tall. Werbock used his own body as a template, holding pieces of metal up to his arms and legs to get the proper ratios for his droid.

EIGHT-MILE SCARF

Helped by more than 1,000 volunteers, German woman Elfriede Blees knitted a scarf 8 mi (13 km) long to commemorate the 2006 World Cup. The scarf, which featured the flags of all 32 nations competing in the soccer tournament, used some 70,000 balls of wool worth around $30,000.

BUTTER FIGURES

For an exhibition at the Pennsylvania Farm Show, sculptor Jim Victor spent a week in a refrigerator carving 900 lb (400 kg) of butter into models of two life-size cows and the late chocolate magnate Milton Hershey! Victor, from Conshohocken, Pennsylvania, has also made pigs, a tractor, and a Harley-Davidson from chocolate, and dinosaurs and cars from cheese.

△ CAN DO

In 2006, 55 cities built 500 structures in the Canstruction competition. Works of art, such as this frog, were made from up to 20,000 full cans of food. A variety of can sizes and shapes were used, with the product labels serving as the color pallet. Other materials permitted included clear tape, magnets, elastic bands, and wire.

LEONARDO DA VINCI IN NAILS ▽

Albanian artist Samir Strati, 40, spent almost a month creating a huge 3-D nail mosaic portrait of Leonardo da Vinci using some 500,000 industrial nails. His work, measuring an impressive 86 sq ft (8 sq m), was displayed at the International Center of Culture in the Albanian capital Tirana, in August 2006.

SECRET GARDENING

Members of the Guerilla Gardening Movement in England secretly plant gardens and shrubbery in run-down urban areas under cover of darkness.

TREE MESSAGES

Artist Antje Krueger held an exhibition in Berlin, Germany, that consisted of notes and messages that had been put up on trees and lampposts in her neighborhood.

Way to go!

K. Sudhakar from Hyderabad, India, designed his first bicycle at the age of 14, before going on to create 150 different types of cars, dune buggies, and go karts, such as the camera, cricket ball, cup and saucer, and helmet. He has also designed more than 30 different bi- and tricycles, including a bicycle measuring only 6 in (15 cm) high, and a tricycle 41 ft 7 in (12.7 m) tall. All his models are fully working.

HAMBURGER

TOILET

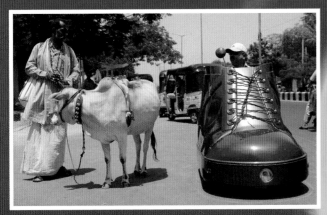
SHOE

TRICYCLE

BED

CRICKET
BALL

RESEARCH COUP

A flock of 20 pigeons wearing cell phone backpacks were employed to monitor California air pollution in 2006. Each pigeon carried a cell phone with a satellite tracking chip and air pollution sensor, enabling data on air quality to be transmitted via text messages. The birds also had miniature cameras tied around their necks to record aerial pictures of environmental black spots.

BLINKING MOUSE

Dmitry Gorodnichy, an inventor from Ottawa, Canada, has developed a computer mouse controlled by nose movements and blinking. He calls the nose-steered mouse a "nouse" and blinking the left or right eye twice takes the place of left or right mouseclicks.

TIRE TREE

British sculptor Douglas White has created a 16-ft (4.8-m) palm tree made from blown-out truck tires in the middle of a rainforest in northern Belize.

OUTSIZE COW

Harvey Jackson spent over 18 months and 220 gal (833 l) of paint creating a 220 x 56 ft (67 x 17 m) mural at Gillette, Wyoming. It depicted a tractor, a train, and a cow, representing the town's major industries. The cow alone is larger than George Washington's face on Mount Rushmore.

CHEESE CHURCH

In Edam, The Netherlands, there is a 1:10 scale model of the town's great church made out of 10,000 balls of Edam cheese.

FINGER PAINTING

Elizabeth McLeod and Amanda Riley, both ten from Snelville, Georgia, created a giant finger painting that measured 3,100 sq ft (290 sq m).

BATHROOM PLAY

A play in Sao Paulo, Brazil, in 2006 was staged in a theater bathroom! Only 30 audience members could fit inside the bathroom and they had to stand during the half-hour show.

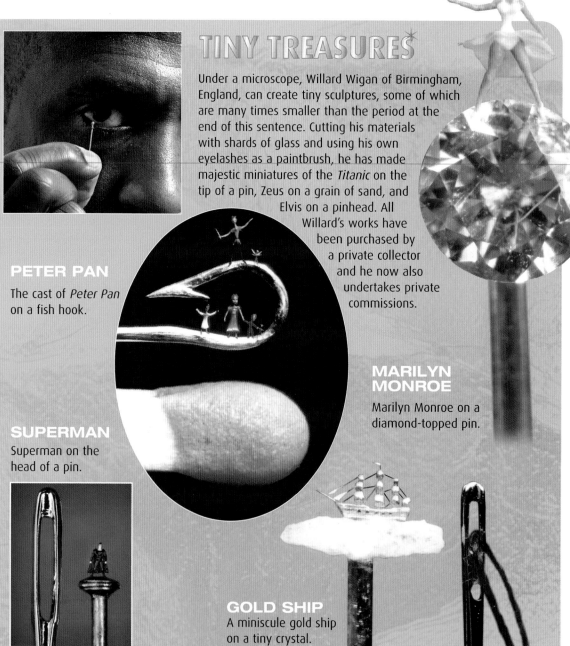

TINY TREASURES

Under a microscope, Willard Wigan of Birmingham, England, can create tiny sculptures, some of which are many times smaller than the period at the end of this sentence. Cutting his materials with shards of glass and using his own eyelashes as a paintbrush, he has made majestic miniatures of the *Titanic* on the tip of a pin, Zeus on a grain of sand, and Elvis on a pinhead. All Willard's works have been purchased by a private collector and he now also undertakes private commissions.

PETER PAN
The cast of *Peter Pan* on a fish hook.

SUPERMAN
Superman on the head of a pin.

MARILYN MONROE
Marilyn Monroe on a diamond-topped pin.

GOLD SHIP
A miniscule gold ship on a tiny crystal.

SHEDBOATSHED

British artist Simon Starling won the 2005 Turner Prize for converting a shed into a working boat and then back into a shed! He found his wooden shack in the Swiss town of Schweizerhalle and, after turning it into a boat, he paddled 7 mi (11 km) down the River Rhine to Basel, where he rebuilt it. In a previous artwork he used the waste water produced by a self-built electric bicycle during a ride across a Spanish desert to create a cactus painting.

PETITE PICASSO

Phoenix Perego of Ormond Beach, Florida, sees her paintings sell for anything between $50 and $100. And that's no mean feat considering she is only 2½ years old! She has created more than 15 works and, according to her father, who is himself a professional artist, she likes to paint in her diaper.

ICE CARVING

Residents of Arlberg, Austria, created a near full-size replica of their town hall out of 176,500 cu ft (5,000 cu m) of snow and ice. Led by sculptor Christoph Strolz, volunteers spent hundreds of hours painstakingly carving out the 46-ft-high, 65-ft-long (14 x 20 m) building on the side of a mountain.

MINI MOBILE

Jan Krutewicz of Munster, Illinois, built a working telephone that is smaller than a human thumb.

STONEHENGE REPLICA

When he died, Al Sheppard of Hunt, Texas, was cremated and had his ashes spread about the half-sized replica of Stonehenge that he had built on his property.

EGGSCLUSIVE ART △

Many years of training have enabled Wang Jinyi from Tianjin, China, to develop his considerable skill in egg carving. He carves a variety of subjects ranging from characters in ancient Chinese legends to the mascots for the Beijing 2008 Olympics.

ROME RECREATED

Using 10,000 tons of special river sand imported from The Netherlands, 60 artists created sand sculptures depicting the glory of Ancient Rome. Among the 200 sculptures at the exhibition, which opened in Brighton, England, in summer 2006, were the Pantheon, the Colosseum, and Emperor Augustus.

NOTE HUNTERS

Davy Rothbart of Ann Arbor, Michigan, is the editor of the magazine *Found*, which prints letters, photos, drawings, and notes that he and others have found on the ground.

BEACH SCULPTURE

In 1991, a sand sculpture an astonishing 16.4 mi (26.4 km) long was built by more than 10,000 volunteers at Myrtle Beach, South Carolina.

HEAVY EGG

Twenty-six chocolate makers took eight days and used 50,000 chocolate bars to make an edible chocolate egg that measured 27 ft 3 in (8.3 m) tall, 21 ft (6.4 m) wide and weighed 4,299 lb (1,950 kg). Metal scaffolding with wooden panels was used to create a "shell" to support the egg, which went on display at Englewood Cliffs, New Jersey.

CARTON CARTOGRAPHER

Skip Hunsaker of Coos Bay, Oregon, created a topographical map of his home county using cigarette cartons! A specialist in unusual materials, he also made miniature poodle figures from myrtlewood nuts.

FALLEN HOUSE

There is something strange on the roof of Austria's Viennese Museum of Modern Art—an upside-down house. In fact it is a sculpture by Erwin Wurm and, although it is supposed to look as if the house has fallen from the sky and landed on the museum, it actually took two large cranes to lift it into place.

Ripley's Believe It or Not!

DUCT LOVE

Something to Do, a band in Waukesha, Wisconsin, won $2,500 in a songwriting contest by writing a love song about duct tape!

PENNY PILE

Artist Gerald Ferguson created a work of art at a gallery in Halifax, Nova Scotia, Canada, that consisted of a pile of one million pennies worth $10,000.

CARDBOARD PIANO

Researchers in a Swedish packaging company have made a working grand piano out of cardboard.

⚠ HEART-SHAPED TREE

This romantically shaped tree was photographed growing out of solid rock in Manitoba, Canada.

⚠ ROTTEN ART

Rotten tomatoes, moldy bread, and decomposing fruits formed the centerpieces of an art exhibition in England in January 2000. The exhibits were the work of Canadian artist Michael Smietana who wanted to highlight the amount of food wasted globally.

PIPE MUSIC

Mike Silverman of Walnut Creek, California, makes music playing a galvanized steel pipe that is 7 ft (2.1 m) long and fitted with a bass and cello string.

GINGERBREAD HOUSE

A gingerbread house standing over 67 ft (20.4 m) tall was designed by Roger Pelcher in Bloomington, Minnesota, in 2006. It took a team of builders nine days to create the cookie domicile, which contains 14,250 lb (6,464 kg) of gingerbread, 4,750 lb (2,155 kg) of icing, and more than one ton in candy embellishments.

POTATO LONGHOUSE

Over a layer of glue and cardboard, Washington State artist Marilyn Jones created an authentic-looking model of a longhouse from steak fries, shoe-string potatoes, hashbrowns, and instant mashed potato.

FLORAL SCULPTURE

A floral sculpture measuring 249 x 86 ft (75 x 26 m) and resembling a strip of Aspirin tablets was constructed in one week by nearly 2,000 people in Jakarta, Indonesia, in 1999.

GUM ARTIST

In 2004, German artist Heidi Hesse made a life-sized Humvee sculpture 16 ft (5 m) long from gum balls!

CHEESY PERFUME

The British makers of the pungent Stilton blue cheese have launched their own perfume, Eau de Stilton. It claims to "re-create the earthy and fruity aroma" of the cheese "in an eminently wearable perfume."

VARNISHED GOURDS

Larry Ray of Gulfport, Mississippi, paints and sculpts gourds. His beautifully decorated creations are finished with two coats of varnish and one coat of paste wax.

GINGERBREAD TOWN

Sven Grumbach re-created the entire town of Rostock, Germany, out of gingerbread. The 4,300-sq-ft (400-sq-m) model was made using 1,760 lb (800 kg) of flour, 705 lb (320 kg) of honey, 880 lb (400 kg) of almonds, 175 lb (80 kg) of raisins, and 2,400 eggs.

FAVORITE VIEW

Artist William A. Bixler of Anderson, Indiana, created 5,000 paintings—all of the same scene, a swimming spot on the Brandyvine River.

⚠ SECRET HEART

A heart-warming surprise greeted loggers (and their young helper) when they cut down this tree to find a perfect heart within its trunk.

CUDDLY CAR

Art student Lauren Porter has created a sports car you could pull over very smartly in—a Ferrari knitted from wool! Lauren, from Hampshire, England, spent ten months making the full-size replica for her honors degree project using 12 mi (19 km) of yarn. Supported by a steel frame, the red bodywork consists of 250 squares of garter stitch. The windows are V-shaped stocking stitch and the Ferrari horse badge is hand-embroidered.

FIZZY MONSTER

At the 2006 Kentucky Art Car Weekend, Lewis Meyer decorated the front of his Nissan truck with a sea monster made out of soda bottle caps.

FLOATING BED

Dutch architect Janjaap Ruijssenaars has spent six years developing a floating bed that hovers 15¾ in (40 cm) above the ground through magnetic force. Magnets built into the floor and into the bed repel each other, pushing the bed up into the air. Thin steel cables tether the bed in place. The bed, which was inspired by the cult film *2001: A Space Odyssey*, has a price tag of around $1,500,000!

THE CANDY MAN

Jason Mecier is a celebrity portrait artist with a difference. Whereas other artists depict the rich and famous in traditional paints, San Francisco-based Mecier creates celebrity mosaics from household odds and ends or food products. Starting out with beans and noodles, he has progressed to doing candy portraits of, among others, Pamela Anderson, Christina Aguilera, Dolly Parton, and the Spice Girls. He has re-created Martha Stewart entirely out of vegetables, Demi Moore from dog food, Marilyn Manson in yarn, Mariah Carey in her favorite make-up, Billy Bob Thornton out of cigarette cartons, and Sigmund Freud from tablets and pills.

"Washington" is covered in about 60 dollar bills. His collar is studded with U.S. quarters.

Banknote Sculptor

Justine Smith collects banknotes from around the world to produce sculptures and collages.

The 36-year-old British artist, based in London, England, has made currency sculptures of animals and plants, including an orchid from Iraqi dinars; a calf from wire, plaster, paper, and dollar bills; dollar dogs; and the "EU Ewe," a sculpture of a sheep with its fleece made from $2,000 worth of Euro notes. She has designed a gun from U.S. dollars, a big dollar sign from hundreds of quarters and, pursuing the message of the power of money, she has produced a series of word collages from banknotes.

Justine makes flowers out of bank notes.

UV TATTOOS

This ultraviolet tattoo is the handiwork of Richie Streate, a Californian tattoo artist who specializes in UV tattoos. The tattoos are completely invisible in regular light, once the scarring heals after about a year, but come to life under UV light used in clubs and bars.

HOPPING MAD

A company in Los Angeles developed a motorized pogo stick powered by a single two-cycle engine that gets 30,000 hops to the gallon.

RECYCLED PURSES

Saroj Welch of Louisiana crochets recycled plastic grocery bags into purses, then donates the proceeds to charity.

SALVAGE SHIP

The USS *New York*, a transport ship, is being built with 24 tons of steel salvaged from New York City's World Trade Center buildings.

SMALL WRITING

A.B. Rajbansh of India handwrote the U.S. Constitution in a 124-page book that measures only ¾ in (2 cm) in height.

TINY GUN

Mark Koscielski, a gunshop owner in Minneapolis, Minnesota, has created a double-barrel shotgun the size of a credit card.

PLANE LAMPS

Designer John Erik of Montreal, Canada, makes furniture and lamps out of discarded airplane parts, including engine turbines.

WASTE MAN

British sculptor Antony Gormley has created a sculpture 82 ft (25 m) high called *Waste Man* in Margate, England. The figure is made entirely from waste materials, including chairs, wardrobes, pictures, old rope, and toilet seats.

SHINY SHOES

Berlin artist Cihangir Gumustukmen uses recycled tin cans to make shoes. Whether they are slippers, sandals, stilettos, or platform shoes, he can create them to form works of art.

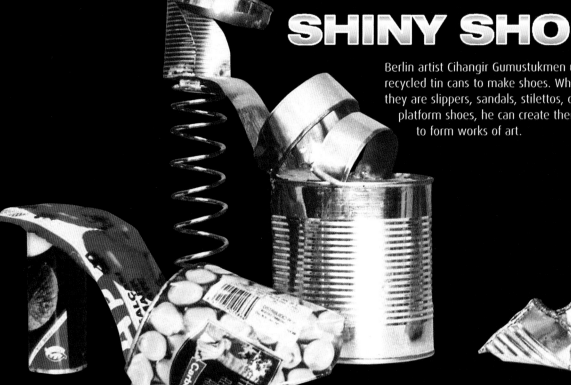

LONG BIBLE

A Bible written on a piece of silk 16,427 ft (5,007 m) long—that's about 3 mi (4.8 km)—was exhibited in Beijing, China, in 2006. The longest Bible in the world, it consists of 50 volumes written in 900,000 Chinese characters and is perfect in every detail.

LIGHT AIRCRAFT

Alexander van de Rostyne created the Pixelito, a tiny helicopter that is controlled by infrared light. The invention, which was displayed in Brussels, Belgium, weighs a mere ¼ oz (6.9 g).

COW PARADE

A 2006 Cow Parade in Lisbon, Portugal, featured a herd of life-size fiberglass cows over which artists painted colorful, individual designs.

△ GILLETT'S GULLET

Chris Gillett took a photograph of every meal he ate for a year! He took a digital photo of every breakfast, lunch, dinner, and snack he devoured in 2005—a total of 2,550 images. He then arranged them in a 16-ft (4.8-m) collage and exhibited them at a gallery near his home in Wiltshire, England. He said he got the idea after sending his wife a photo of a burger he ate in Los Angeles.

FEMININE ROADSTER

Anita Dugat-Greene of Belton, Texas, has turned her 1997 Ford Taurus into a monument to women. The car is covered in thousands of buttons, numerous images of the Virgin Mary, and multicultural Barbie dolls.

CAR COFFIN

Jose Gomez of Ilhavo, Portugal, built a wooden replica of his Mercedes 220 CDI car. He plans to be buried in it!

CARD SIGN

In July 2006, Bryan Berg of Spirit Lake, Iowa, used 500 decks of playing cards, 1,800 poker chips, 800 dice, and several tubes of Superglue to build a replica of the "Welcome to Las Vegas" sign. It took him 450 hours—that's nearly 19 days.

BREAD STATUE

Chilean artist Constanza Puente made a life-size statue of herself out of bread. When she placed the sculpture on a Santiago park bench in 2006, it quickly proved popular with pigeons.

SWEET CAR

The tastiest sight at the 2006 Baton Rouge, Louisiana, Art Car Parade was Amy James's OREO Speedwagon. It was a Ford Contour decorated with 30 bags of Oreo cookies.

COLORFUL SARI

A silk sari made in India has no fewer than 164,492 colors. The Seven Wonders of the World were brought to life on the border of the sari, which took 15 weavers more than 45 days to complete.

STRAW CHURCH

Farmers Will Morris and his son Tim spent two days creating a straw replica of an English village church in 2006, only for vandals to burn it down. The model of St. Mary's Priory Church in Deerhurst, Gloucestershire, stood 40 ft (12.2 m) tall, weighed 30 tons, and was made from 110 bales of straw.

ICE TOWER

Using 45 tons of ice, ten carvers spent 1,440 man-hours creating an ice sculpture that measured 40 ft (12.2 m) tall in Dubai in 2006. The sculpture is a mini version of the Burj Al Alam, which, when completed in 2009, will be one of the world's tallest commercial towers.

POPCORN MICKEY

Sculptors have created a giant model of Mickey Mouse as the Sorcerer's Apprentice... out of popcorn. The model, which stands 19 ft 8½ in (6 m) tall, was created at Disneyland's California Adventure Theme Park using prefabricated blocks of popcorn that were glued together.

TROLLEY RESCUER

British sculptor Ptolemy Elrington rescues supermarket carts that have been dumped in rivers and lakes and turns them into beautiful water wildlife creations. He saws up the carts and welds them into new shapes at his Brighton studio. Each sculpture takes him up to three weeks to complete. Among his works are a frog with bulging eyes (made from the cart's wheels), a dragonfly with a 6-ft (1.8-m) wingspan, and a kingfisher perched on top of a discarded trolley.

DUAL PURPOSE

John and Julie Giljam of South Carolina made an amphibious motor home. The diesel-powered Terra Wind can reach speeds of more than 80 mph (130 kmph) on land and seven knots on the open water.

TV TREE

Lithuanian artist Gintaras Karosas has built a sculpture from around 3,000 old TV sets donated by the public. The sculpture, which looks like a tree when viewed from above, spans an area of 33,745 sq ft (3,135 sq m) and used 64,583 sq ft (6,000 sq m) of polythene, 7,535 sq ft (700 sq m) of bitumen cover, 3,178 cu ft (90 cu m) of wood, and 132 gal (500 l) of paint.

BEAD WATERFALL

To depict the annual salmon spawning, Bill and Clarissa Hudson constructed a cascading waterfall made from around 180,000 glass and crystal beads. The waterfall, which took two months to make, first went on display at Juneau, Alaska, in 1998.

△ GREAT BALL OF STAMPS!

Fred W. Miller from Newark, New Jersey, made this 8½-lb (3.8-kg) ball from 75,000 used U.S. stamps in the 1940s. It measured an impressive 8 ft 9 in (2.7 m) in circumference.

CAR-COVERED CAR ▽

Installation artist James Robert Ford, based in London, England, spent three years creating this eye-catching car, which he completed in October 2006. For the work, James covered a Ford Capri with no less than 4,500 Matchbox® toy cars. He named it "General Carbuncle."

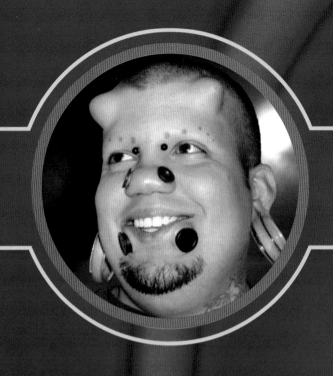

Louis Sanchez has already had six procedures on his implanted silicone horns—page 79.

Kam Ma endured nine hours of piercings, only to have the 1,015 rings instantly removed—page 97

Lee Redmond's 33-in (84-cm) fingernails have not been cut since 1979—page 75

LONG-ARMED RESCUE

When two dolphins at an aquarium in Fushun, China, became sick after chewing plastic, the only man who could save them was Mongolian herdsman Bao Xishun, who is 7 ft 9 in (2.4 m) tall. He was able to use his 41¾-in (106-cm) long arms to pull the dangerous shards of plastic from the animals' stomachs.

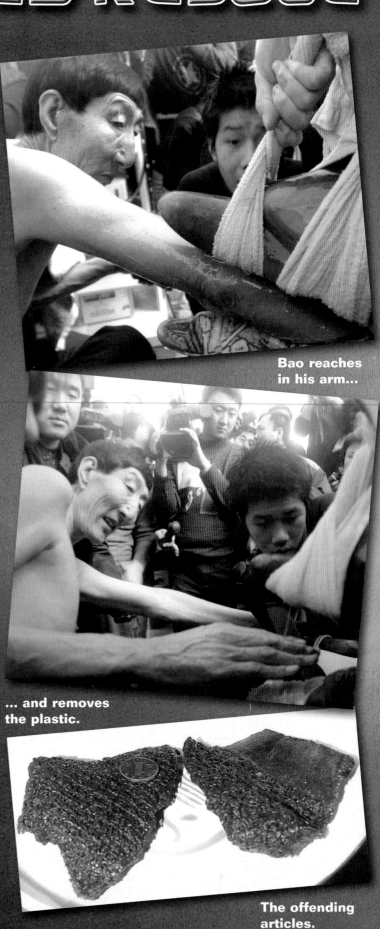

Bao reaches in his arm...

... and removes the plastic.

The offending articles.

Bao Xishun meets the dolphins.

RIPLEY'S RESEARCH

Born in 1951 in Inner Mongolia, China, Bao Xishun was of normal height until he hit the age of 16, when he experienced a sudden growth spurt, reaching his present height seven years later. Unusually for somebody so tall, he does not suffer from any known growth disorder. He's just very, very tall!

Bao reached his great height by the age of 23. His legs are almost 5 ft (1.5 m) long!

The dolphins suffered depression and loss of appetite after nibbling plastic from the edge of their pool. Veterinarians failed to remove the debris with surgical instruments, because the dolphins' stomachs contracted in response to the tools. The arms of ordinary people were unable to reach the plastic, so the Royal Jidi Ocean World aquarium sought the help of Xishun. With the dolphins' jaws held back by towels so that he could stretch in without being bitten, Xishun successfully removed the biggest pieces of plastic. The dolphins were able to digest the few remaining smaller pieces and were expected to make a full recovery.

LUCKY ESCAPE

In May 2006, a 79-year-old Indiana woman lost control of her car and drove straight through a house and out the other side before striking a tree. She survived, but with serious injuries.

FIRST BIRTHS

In both 2004 and 2005, Terri and Mike Gavel had the first baby of the year at Sturdy Memorial Hospital in Attleboro, Massachusetts. Rory Ann was born at 12.16 a.m. on January 2, 2004, and her sister Kelsey arrived at 9.37 p.m. on New Year's Day 2005.

BULLET SLOWED

Near Tampa, Florida, in May 2006, Robin Key survived a .38-caliber gunshot through the windshield of her minivan when the bullet came to rest in her lap after being slowed by hitting her seat belt and bra strap.

HANGOVER CURE

After having too much to drink, a man from Rogers, Arkansas, fell asleep in his driveway and was run over by his wife! Kristine Bolson was returning home after midnight when she heard a loud cracking sound as she turned the car into the driveway. Her husband, Richard Gonzalez, was taken to hospital with minor injuries.

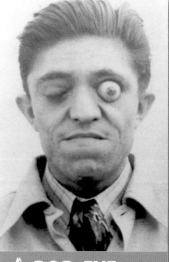

△ POP-EYE

Avelino Perez Matos, of Baracoa, Cuba, had the ability to dislocate each of his eyes out of their sockets whenever he chose.

REMARKABLE RECOVERY

Brian Paolo of Cheshire, England, woke from a coma after his life support was switched off on February 4, 2006—and ten days later gave his daughter away at her wedding. Doctors had given up on him, but were astounded when, after the machine was switched off, he began to breathe on his own.

EYE-MAZING

Jalisa Mae Thompson is a high-school student from Atlantic City, New Jersey, with an unusual talent. Since the age of nine, she has been able to roll her tongue and "pop" her eyeballs almost out of their sockets! Jalisa won the Funny Face Contest at the Ripley's Museum in Atlantic City in 2006, and now has her photo displayed there. She says she enjoys popping her eyes because of the surprised and shocked reaction she gets from most people.

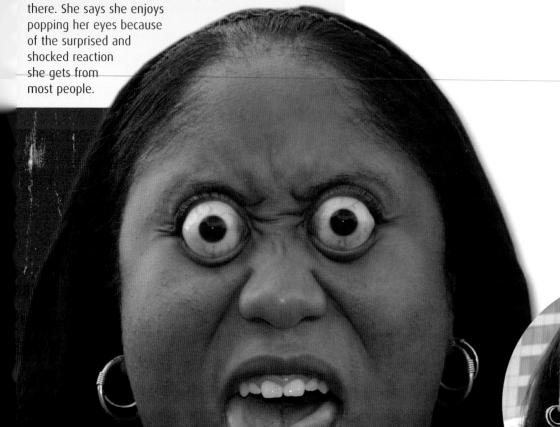

HIDDEN BULLET

After years of suffering headaches and nosebleeds, an 83-year-old Russian man finally found what was causing them—a bullet had been lodged in his head for 63 years! Mihail Kabalin was shot by the Germans during World War II, but doctors failed to remove the bullet. In 2006, they finally extracted the bullet, which measured 1 in (2.5 cm) long, through Kabalin's nose. He plans to have it made into a pendant.

LIGHTNING STRIKE

English teenager Karla Pope was lucky to be alive after a lightning bolt tore through the roof of her home in Chippenham, Wiltshire, in July 2006 and struck the metal-framed bed in which she was sleeping. The colossal current blew a hole measuring 2 ft 6 in (76 cm) across in her bedroom ceiling, but even though Karla was touching the metal frame at the time of the strike, she escaped with only minor burns to her hands.

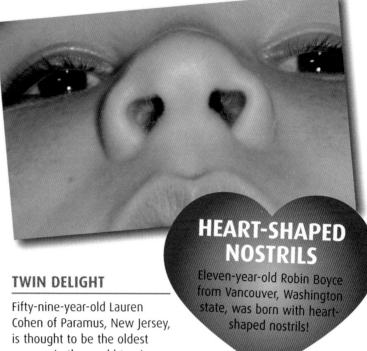

HEART-SHAPED NOSTRILS

Eleven-year-old Robin Boyce from Vancouver, Washington state, was born with heart-shaped nostrils!

TWIN DELIGHT

Fifty-nine-year-old Lauren Cohen of Paramus, New Jersey, is thought to be the oldest woman in the world to give birth to twins. Her babies, Gregory and Giselle, were conceived using donor eggs and were delivered by emergency cesarean section at a New York hospital in 2006. Mrs. Cohen lost 33 pt (16 l) of blood during the delivery.

HEARING RETURNED

A 72-year-old man who had been deaf for 15 years suddenly got his hearing back on a 2006 skiing trip. Derek Glover, from Lincolnshire, England, was descending from 7,000 ft (2,135 m) in a cable car when his ears popped and he was hit by an "incredible wave" of noise. It is thought that the return of his hearing was due to a sudden change in air pressure.

EXTRA CLAWS

A "mutant" crab with three pincers was caught off the coast of Cornwall, England, in 2006. Crabs can regrow lost or damaged limbs and claws, but experts believe this 8-in (20-cm) long edible crab's ability to regenerate lost limbs became confused and, rather than replacing a missing set of claws, it managed to grow an extra pair instead.

REST IN PEACE

In May 2006, a man was charged with breaking into a funeral home in Canton, New York, and falling asleep in a coffin. Investigating a broken window, the wife of the funeral director saw some discarded clothes on the floor of the casket display room and two knees sticking out of a coffin.

EMERGENCY CALL

Truman Duncan of Cleburne, Texas, lost his legs when a train ran over him on June 25, 2006, but he was able to remain conscious long enough to make an emergency call for help on his cell phone.

SMALL PROBLEM

A Filipino judge was sacked in 2006 after admitting that he regularly consulted with three imaginary dwarves! Judge Florentino Floro from Manila said he often conversed with his three invisible friends, who were named Armand, Luis, and Angel. The judge also claimed that he was psychic.

LENGTHY PONYTAIL △

Yam Narayan Bhandari of Nepal has not cut his hair since 1949, when he was three years old. A devout Hindu, Bhandari has decided that cutting his hair would show religious disobedience—it is now an astonishing 9 ft 7 in (2.9 m) long.

AUTISTIC STAR

Jason McElwain overcame his autism to become probably the most famous basketball player in America for a few days in February 2006. McElwain, who didn't begin talking until he was five, was too small to make his high-school team in Rochester, New York, but because of his passion for the game he was appointed manager. Impressed by his dedication, coach Jim Johnson decided to put the 18-year-old on court for the last few minutes of the final home game of the season, and McElwain responded by scoring 20 points in four minutes to send the crowd wild. Within two months McElwain had agreed to allow Columbia Pictures to produce a film of his remarkable story.

FACE ▷ TRANSPLANT

In November 2005, Isabelle Dinoire received the world's first partial face transplant in a 15-hour operation in Amiens, France. Isabelle had been severely disfigured after being bitten by her dog in May 2005, and agreed to the idea of a face transplant immediately. After waiting six months for a suitable donor, she had the ground-breaking surgery and is now doing well and able to smile again (right).

CLOSE CALL

Glenda Clarke was in the restroom of a New York City nightclub in April 2006 when a gunfight started outside. She escaped unharmed after a bullet tore through the door, grazed her scalp, and came to rest in her thick hair.

SIDE EFFECT

A Scottish grandfather suffering from a rare disease found an unexpected side effect to his treatment—it made him look 20 years younger! When 62-year-old Reggie Myles of Clackmannanshire was struck down by the genetic disorder porphyria cutanea tarda, his mop of grey hair fell out and his weight plummeted from 230 lb (104 kg) to just 98 lb (44 kg). But after his treatment, his hair returned in a dark brown shade and most of his wrinkles vanished. And now he's often mistaken for his sons!

PENCIL PIERCING

Eleven-year-old Ben McKinley, of McComb, Mississippi, survived falling off a balance beam and landing on a pencil that pierced his chest and heart.

SPEARED BY FISH

While fishing off Bermuda in 2006, Ian Card was impaled on the bill of a 14-ft (4.3-m) blue marlin that leaped over his boat. The 800-lb (363-kg) fish hit Card with such force that its 3-ft (90-cm) spear went through his chest and knocked him into the sea. As the fish dived, forcing Card underwater, he was able to push himself off the razor-sharp bill and swim to the surface with blood pouring from his chest wound. He was rushed to King Edward VII Memorial Hospital in Bermuda where he underwent emergency surgery. Doctors said that he would have died had the bill struck him a fraction of an inch to either side.

THREE-WAY TIE

In 2002, in a general election in Comal County, Texas, County Judge Danny Scheel received 18,181 votes, State Senator Jeff Wentworth got 18,181 votes, and State representative Carter Casteel also got 18,181 votes!

◁ AWESOME ACUPUNCTURE

Wei Shengchu stuck 800 needles into his head during a self-acupuncture performance in Chongqing, China, in January 2007. An acupuncturist and cosmetic doctor from Guangxi Zhuang in southern China, Wei had previously inserted 1,790 needles in his face.

Fantastic Nails

On a whim back in 1979, Lee Redmond of Salt Lake City, Utah, decided to stop trimming her fingernails. She intended cutting them once they started twisting but somehow the idea of keeping them intact just grew and grew— and so did her nails.

Lee used to soak her nails in a frying pan of warm olive oil once a week— until they got too big to fit in the pan.

They now measure an incredible 33 in (84 cm) long! And she says they would be even longer but for the fact that they broke once when she stepped on them. She concedes: "It's pretty bad when you're stepping on your own fingernails!" The great-grandmother admits that opening doors is not easy, nor is putting on a heavy winter coat. "By the time you thread the nails down through the coat, it's a tough job." Redmond is so attached to her nails that she even turned down $100,000 to part with them. "People always ask me, 'Don't they get in your way?' I say, 'No, they get in everybody else's way but mine. I'm used to them being in my way.'"

THE FUTURE'S ORANGE

Since the age of three, Gemma Williams from Rochdale, England, has suffered from a rare form of dyslexia that meant she could only read and write upside down and back to front. She would astonish friends and family by reading a book or magazine upside down and she even turned her computer screen upside down so that she could read the words. But when she was 17, experts found that, whereas her brain was confused by the glare from plain white paper, the information became clear when viewed through an orange filter. She can write normally on orange paper and read anything through an orange filter. She even hopes to take her driving test—provided she can wear orange glasses.

HEAD DRILL

In 2003, Dr. Keith Sivertson of Shoshone, Idaho, saved Ben King's life by using a $300 power drill to bore a hole in his head. King sustained a head injury after falling down a flight of stairs and, with no neurosurgeon available at his local hospital, Dr. Sivertson made the decision to relieve the growing pressure on King's brain by using the best tools at his disposal.

FIRE REUNION

Allen O'Neil, a firefighter from Long Beach, California, treated a woman for smoke inhalation and, upon hearing her name, realized he had helped deliver her as a baby 20 years earlier!

SLEEP-COOKING

A former chef who cooks meals in his sleep is receiving medical help amid fears he could burn down his house. Robert Wood of Fife, Scotland, gets up four or five times a week and heads to the kitchen where he has made omelettes, stir fries, and chips without waking up.

BLADDER GROWTH

Scientists at Wake Forest University, North Carolina, have grown human bladders in a laboratory and have successfully implanted them into patients who require new bladders.

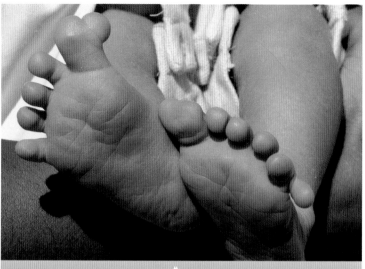

DOUBLE DIGITS △

In December 2006, a baby boy named Lakshya was born in Nadidad, western India, with 25 fingers and toes. Lakshya has six fingers on each hand, six toes on his right foot, and seven toes on his left foot.

MAMMOTH ▷ MUSTACHE

Ram Singh Chauhan from the Indian state of Rajasthan proudly displays his impressive mustache. At 6 ft 5 in (1.96 m), it is longer than Ram is tall. It's not surprising that his favorite saying is "a man is incomplete without a mustache."

IN A TWIST

Matt Suter was picked up and carried nearly a quarter of a mile by a tornado—yet he survived with nothing worse than a scalp wound. He was in his family's trailer home near Fordland, Missouri, in 2006 when it was hit by the twister. Propelled by 150-mph (240-km/h) winds, he was hurled up into the air and thrown over a barbed wire fence before landing in a field.

SUICIDE ATTEMPT

In 2006, a man in Portland, Oregon, survived a suicide attempt in which he shot 12 nails into his head with a nail gun.

LONG TONGUE

Annika Irmler from Hamburg, Germany, has a tongue that measured an incredible 2¾ in (7 cm) in length when she was just 12 years old, in 2001.

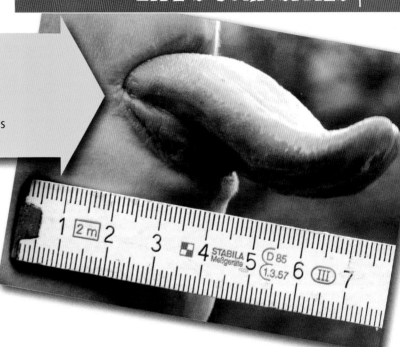

DOUBLE TRAGEDY

In August 2006, two brothers were killed in separate motorcycle accidents on the same stretch of road in Butler, Pennsylvania, within two hours of each other. The second was heading to the scene of his brother's accident.

CHARMED LIFE

Mark Cook really does lead a charmed life. The 35-year-old electrician from Oban, Scotland, has cheated death time and time again. He has been involved in two motorbike accidents, has plunged into the sea from a pier, and emerged from a car wreck in which he and his wife were nearly crushed when a truck fell onto their vehicle. Then, in January 2006, he fell 25 ft (7.6 m) down an elevator shaft and came within inches of being impaled on a spike. His family calls him a cat with nine lives.

UP TO SCRATCH

In 2006, Harold Gray of Beaufort, South Carolina, won $100,000 on a lottery scratchcard—just 20 days after winning $250,000 on another. And what's more, he used to live on Lottery Lane!

HOLY TOOTH

A Phoenix, Arizona, dentist claimed that an X ray of one of his patients taken in December 2004 revealed an image that looked like Jesus. The patient described himself as a devout Christian, but said he had never before seen Jesus in a dental X ray.

SAVIOR SAVED

In 2006, a teenager who saved the life of an apparent stranger in a restaurant in Buffalo, New York, was amazed to discover that it was a woman who had done the same for him in 1999. Volunteer firefighter and boy scout Kevin Stephan, 17, rushed to perform the Heimlich maneuver when he saw Penny Brown choking on her lunch, and only learned afterwards that she was the nurse who had got his heart beating again following a baseball accident seven years earlier.

11-STORY FALL

In July 2006, four-year-old Hasim Townsend of Albany, New York, survived falling 110 ft (33.5 m) from an 11-story window, bouncing off a metal awning before hitting the ground.

IN LUCK

In the 2004 Spanish Christmas lottery, which had prizes totaling $648 million, the jackpot was shared by 195 winning tickets that were sold in the Catalan town of Sort, which means "luck" in the northeastern region's language.

FAVORITE TRACK

Jesse Maggrah, 20, was listening through earphones to heavy metal music while walking on Canadian Pacific Railway tracks near Red Deer, Alberta, in April 2006, when he was hit from behind by a train traveling at 30 mph (48 km/h). Believe it or not, he survived!

PIGEON POOP

On March 13, 2006, part of a roof collapsed on a house in Peoria, Illinois, from the weight of so much pigeon excrement!

TWINS REUNITED

Twin Chinese sisters, separated and abandoned in their homeland, were reunited in America after their adoptive parents met by chance on an Internet site. When Diana Ramirez of Miami, Florida, wrote about her daughter Mia Hanying's forthcoming birthday on an Internet site for parents who had adopted from the Chinese orphanage, the message was seen by Holly Funk of Chicago, Illinois. Mrs. Funk wondered whether there was a connection with her own three-year-old daughter Mia, and sure enough it turned out that the two Mias were sisters.

MILK DIET

An 88-year-old Indian farmer from the state of Rajasthan fathered a child in 2006—by drinking up to ¾ gal (3 l) camel's milk a day. Virmaram Jat claimed the milk was an aphrodisiac, and as a result the price of camel's milk in India doubled overnight.

REAL CORPSE

For more than 20 years, Florida criminology course tutor Sue Messenger had planted cardboard skeletons riddled with fake bullet holes at mock crime scenes. But in 2006, her students from a Fort Lauderdale high school got the shock of their lives while combing Holiday Park for clues. They stumbled across the real corpse of a homeless man in his fifties.

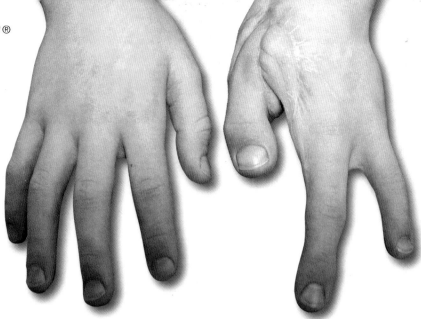

TOE TRANSPLANT △

Gaeton Foos from Rochester, New York, lost two fingers and a thumb on his left hand in an accident when he was just three years old. When Gaeton reached the age of six, surgeons from the University of Pittsburgh Medical Center transplanted one of his big toes onto the hand to act as a thumb.

DOGGED ▷ DEVOTION

Michael Monkeymeat from New York City has had his body tattooed at locations all across the globe since the age of 13. The tattoo of a paw print on his left hand was actually applied using ink that included the ashes of Michael's dead dog.

FAMILY BUSINESS

When an adopted Iowa woman tracked down her biological mother, she was stunned to learn that they had once worked together. Michelle Wetzell, who was adopted when she was four days old, discovered that her real mother was a former colleague at a beauty salon in Davenport.

EAR REATTACHED

Doctors reattached a seven-year-old boy's ear after it was retrieved from the stomach of a Doberman Pinscher that had bitten it off. Brandon Olivas of Whittier, New Jersey, was attacked by two dogs in 1987, and his right ear was bitten off and swallowed by the Doberman.

TORTOISES SEPARATED

A pair of conjoined tortoises born joined at the belly were successfully separated at an animal hospital in Tempe, Arizona, in 2004.

SEVERED HAND

When farmer Gerhard Frank accidentally sliced off his hand while splitting logs in Steeg, Austria, in 2006, he calmly packed it in his chilled lunchbox, climbed in his tractor and drove 3 mi (4.8 km) home. There, his wife put the severed hand in the fridge and it was later successfully reattached at Innsbruck Hospital.

LATE DELIVERY

A postcard that a mother mailed to her son in 1948 was finally delivered 58 years later—after the town's postmaster bought it on eBay. Judy Dishman, from Spiceland, Indiana, bought the postcard because she liked the local view but when she saw it was addressed to 82-year-old Charles Rose, she delivered it. The card turned out to be from Rose's late mother, Dollie.

CHOCOLATE DIP

A man was trapped waist-deep in a tank of thick chocolate for two hours in 2006. Darmin Garcia accidentally slid into the hopper at a chocolate factory in Kenosha, Wisconsin, and firefighters had to thin the chocolate with cocoa butter before they could free him.

THREE ANTLERS

John Moore of Crestline, Ohio, bagged a three-antlered deer on the opening day of the state's 2004 hunting season.

IMPLANTED HORNS

Among a variety of unusual facial modifications, Louis Sanchez III's silicone implanted horns are probably the most extreme. So far, Sanchez, from Phoenix, Arizona, has had six procedures on his silicone horns, and he hopes to have more.

METHANE BLAZE

A fire started at a New Zealand hospital in 2006 after a patient broke wind. The fire was caused by methane in his flatulence igniting a spark from the electrical machine that was being used to remove his hemorrhoids.

RING FOUND

Diane Kurtz of Hartford, Connecticut, lost her engagement ring down a drain and had it returned to her 15 years later by a sewage treatment plant worker.

AN UNUSUAL TALE ▷

Nepalese teenager Ram Kumar Ghimire was born with a 3-in (7.6-cm) tail. His mother, who said she had a dream while she was pregnant predicting that her baby would resemble the tailed Hindu god Hanuman, cut the tail soon after Ram's birth. It is now a shorter 1½ in (4 cm) in length and looks rather like an orange has been stuck in the small of his back.

HAPPY ENDING

A pregnant woman who fell 10,000 ft (3,050 m) in a 2005 skydiving accident gave birth to a healthy baby boy eight months later. When both her parachute and the reserve failed to open on her first solo skydive, Shayna West of Joplin, Missouri, spiraled out of control and landed face first in a parking lot at 50 mph (80 km/h), breaking her pelvis, five teeth, and shattering several facial bones. She had to have 15 metal plates inserted in her face. She hadn't known she was pregnant at the time.

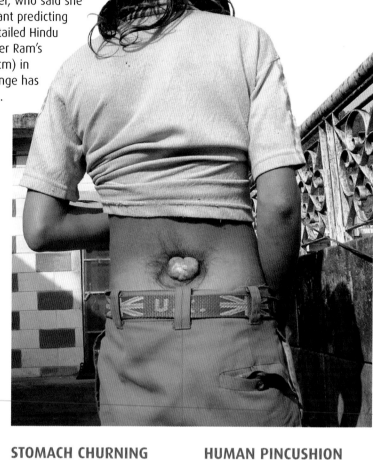

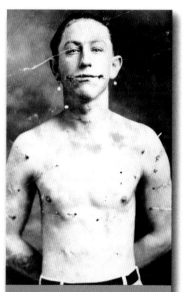

△ PAINLESS PINS

In the 1930s, B.A. Bryant was able to stick a hundred pins into his body without feeling any pain. He performed his feat at the Ripley's Believe It or Not! odditorium in Dallas, Texas.

STOMACH CHURNING

Matt "The Tube" Crowley, a pharmacist from Seattle, Washington, swallows 7 ft (2.1 m) of tubing through his nose, pours over a gallon of liquid into the tube, and then extracts it after it reaches his stomach. Even more shocking, fans drink the fluid after he's finished! Crowley can also use sheer lung power to blow up a hot water bottle until it bursts.

WEIRD HEIRLOOM

The Peavy family of New Hampshire has passed down a mummified baby as a family heirloom since its discovery in a relative's home in 1947.

HEALED HEART

When Adrian Reid, aged two, of Akron, Ohio, suffered burns after accidentally spilling hot coffee on himself, the blister on his chest healed in the shape of a heart directly above his heart!

HUMAN PINCUSHION

Under his stage name "Happy the Human Pincushion," Dave Haskell of Chicago, Illinois, inserts spears, hooks, and other objects into his skin. He also lifts and pulls weights from his various body piercings.

STRUCK TWICE

Lightning has struck twice in the case of Florida construction worker Emory Johnson. In 1986, he was hit by a bolt as he sat in his truck, then, in 2005, he was working outside at Spring Hill when lightning hit him again. He said afterwards: "There was a loud bang, and it felt like I was burning inside, and I passed out."

SPECIAL DATE

Dean Stephens and his daughter Brylee of Victoria, Australia, were both leap-year babies born on 29 February—that's odds of one in two million!

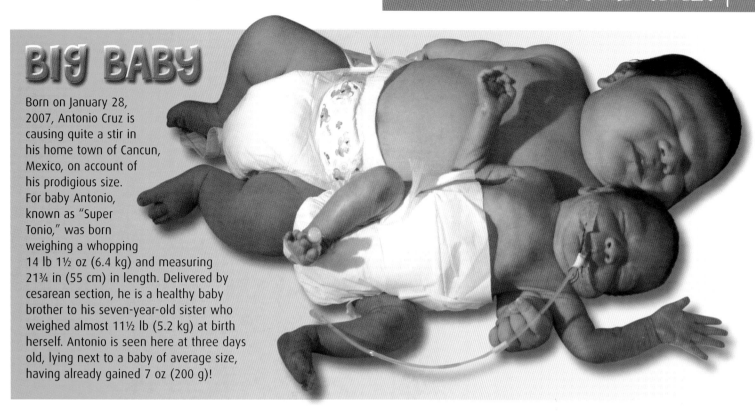

BIG BABY

Born on January 28, 2007, Antonio Cruz is causing quite a stir in his home town of Cancun, Mexico, on account of his prodigious size. For baby Antonio, known as "Super Tonio," was born weighing a whopping 14 lb 1½ oz (6.4 kg) and measuring 21¾ in (55 cm) in length. Delivered by cesarean section, he is a healthy baby brother to his seven-year-old sister who weighed almost 11½ lb (5.2 kg) at birth herself. Antonio is seen here at three days old, lying next to a baby of average size, having already gained 7 oz (200 g)!

MAD MAX

Runner Max Springer from Knoxville, Tennessee, competes in track-and-field meets and runs marathons even though he's 92!

ROBOT CLONE

Hiroshi Ishiguro of Japan created a robot duplicate of himself so that he could teach his classes from a remote connection!

GROUPER'S REVENGE

A 42-year-old diver shot a large grouper fish with a spear gun in 25 ft (7.6 m) of water off the Florida Keys in September 2006, but then drowned when the fish darted into a hole in a coral rock, entangling the man in the fishing line that was attached to the spear. The grouper had managed to wrap the spear line around the diver's waist and when it sped into the hole the man found himself effectively pinned to the bottom of the ocean.

BROWN SNOW

On February 16, 2006, brown snow fell across most of the state of Colorado. A wind storm in northern Arizona probably kicked up dust, which then fell with the snow.

SNAKE BITE

A man crashed his car in Naples, Florida, in 2006 after the pet snake he had wrapped around his neck suddenly bit him. The man was seen climbing out of the car and wrestling with the snake before driving off.

POLICE LEMMINGS

When a suspect ran straight off a 50-ft (15-m) cliff in Princeton, West Virginia, in July 2006, two police officers jumped over the edge to make an arrest. Only the suspect was seriously injured.

NERVOUS ROBBER

A 60-year-old man who robbed a bank in Troy, Michigan, in 2006 emerged from the bank with his haul of cash, spotted a passing police car, and promptly fainted.

RAMU, THE WOLF BOY ▽

Found in 1954 in Lucknow, India, when he was seven years old, Ramu was believed to have been raised by wolves for the previous six years of his life. Stories of the found "wolf boy" reached his parents, who identified Ramu and said that he'd been snatched from his mother's lap by a wolf when he was a baby, and they'd believed him to be dead. Ramu made only animal noises and initially ate only raw meat and fruit. He was not interested in the company of other humans, but when taken on a visit to a zoo became very excited by the wolves, lending weight to the belief that he'd somehow lived with wolves while he was missing. Ramu stayed at Lucknow hospital for another 14 years until his death in 1968.

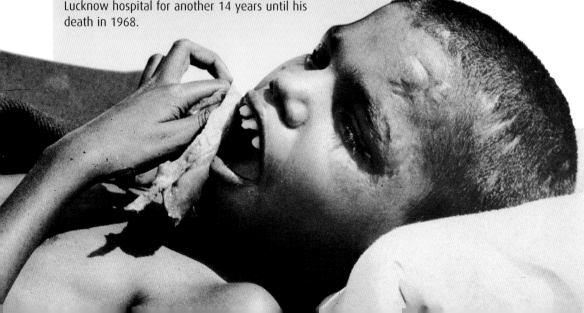

HITZ MISSES

At age 14, George Hitz sent a postcard with an incorrect address to California from his home in DeLand, Florida. That was in 1956—and it was returned by the Post Office 50 years later!

TONGUE SWALLOWER △

Nicole Shaffer from Cocoa, Florida, has an extraordinarily long tongue, which she can also "swallow!" Because Nicole is missing a small skin flap at the back of her throat, when she points her tongue backwards, it travels along the roof of her mouth and goes down her throat, as if it has been swallowed. After accomplishing her feat, Nicole immediately retrieves her tongue without any difficulty.

FLAT DADDIES

Although serving in Iraq or Afghanistan, members of the Maine National Guard are never far from their families. In fact, they ride with them in cars, sit at the dinner table, visit the dentist, watch soccer games, and even go to confession—all as life-size cutouts! As part of its family-support program, the National Guard has produced a series of Flat Daddies and Mummies. Photos of the service personnel in uniform from the waist up are enlarged and printed and the families then glue them to a $2 piece of foam board. Kay Judkins, whose husband Jim is a minesweeper mechanic in Afghanistan, says of her cutout, which she calls Slim Jim: "I prop him up in a chair, or sometimes put him on a couch and cover him with a blanket. The cat will curl up on the blanket, and it looks kind of weird. I've tricked several people by that. They think he's home again."

SNAIL NAIL!

Bud Hart of Placerville, California, coughed up a rusty nail in February 2006—35 years after it had been embedded in his lung! The nail had pierced his body while he was mowing the grass and remained there until he coughed it up after brushing his teeth.

AMAZING TAIL

An Indian man is being worshiped because he has a tail 13 in (33 cm) long! Because of the tail—caused by a congenital defect—villagers believe that Chandre Oram, from Alipurduar in West Bengal, is an incarnation of Hindu monkey god Hanuman. Oram, who has refused all offers by doctors to have the tail removed and who also loves climbing trees and eating bananas, said:

"People have a lot of faith in me. They are cured of severe ailments when they touch my tail. I believe I can do a lot of good to those who come to me with devotion."

Long Nose

A building worker from the city of Artvin in northeast Turkey has a nose to beat all rivals. Mehmet Ozyurek's impressive olfactory organ measures an astonishing 3½ in (8.8 cm) from bridge to tip.

WHIRLWIND TOSS

While four-year-old Grace Hove of Trenton, North Dakota, was hopping on a trampoline on May 7, 2006, a whirlwind picked her up and tossed her over 25 ft (7.6 m) into the air! Grace survived with a broken arm and pelvis, and lots of bruises.

SKIN DISORDER

Despite being born with a rare and fatal skin disorder called Harlequin Ichthyosis, a disease that causes skin to develop into a hard shell, Ryan Gonzalez of San Diego, California, is now a successful young triathlete.

PARALLEL LIVES

When long-lost New York sisters Peggy Lill and Gladys Nohlquist found each other after 79 years in 2006, they discovered that they had led remarkably similar lives. Since being separated at an orphanage in 1927, both were raised on farms, both went back to school in middle age and became nurses, both were married twice, and both had five children—four girls and a boy!

DIGGER HERO

In July 2006, 45-year-old Colin O'Neill of Bury, England, lifted a three-ton backhoe digger off 14-year-old neighbor Jon-Ashley Entwisle and held it for 20 minutes until paramedics could rescue the boy.

UNUSUAL REPTILES

Fred Lally of West Fork, Arkansas, is an avid collector of mutant reptiles. He has been catching, selling, and exhibiting reptiles since he was a child and has provided a home for albino turtles and snakes, two-headed reptiles, and conjoined turtles, including one with two heads and six legs.

FINAL STRUGGLE

In a desperate attempt to land a 150-lb (68-kg) catfish, a Hungarian fisherman drowned when he was dragged into the Szamos River in Hungary because he refused to let go of the line. It is thought he died after hitting his head on a rock. When the man's body was found, he was still clinging to his rod with the 4-ft (1.2-m) monster catfish hooked on the end.

MINIATURE MAN

Although he was born in 1992, Khagendra Thapa Magar of Baglung, western Nepal, stands just 20 in (51 cm) tall and weighs less than 10 lb (4.5 kg). His mother said he didn't start moving around until he was eight and his physical growth stopped at the age of 11.

BEAR CRAWL

Five members of a family in southern Turkey get around by walking on all fours in a "bear crawl." Some scientists believe they could be evidence of backwards evolution.

Three sisters and one brother from the large 19-member Ulas family have only ever walked on two palms and two feet, while another sibling only occasionally manages a form of normal human walking. Although all five can

stand up, it is only for a short time and with both knees and head flexed.

Unlike gorillas and chimpanzees, who walk on their knuckles, the affected Turkish siblings, who are all aged between 18 and 34, use their heavily callused palms as heels, keeping their fingers angled up from the ground. Their quadrupedal gait has never before been reported in anatomically intact adult humans. Their language is also primitive. They cannot count from one to ten and do not know in which country they live. However, the four sisters can do needlework.

Their mother said they started walking at ten months, but began using their hands and never walked normally after that time.

RIPLEY'S RESEARCH

Many scientists have concluded that the affected members of the Ulas family walk on all fours owing to a congenital brain defect, which has stunted their development. As a result, they found balancing on two legs difficult and perfected the bear crawl as a substitute for bipedality. However, Uner Tan of Turkey's Cukurova Medical School argues that the family have reverted to an instinctive behavior deeply encoded in the brain, but abandoned in the course of evolution. He calls the process backward evolution.

The Ulas family show attributes of our apelike ancestors, before the switch to upright walking.

FOREIGN ACCENT

Waking up following a stroke in 2006, an English woman found that her usual Newcastle accent had been transformed into a mixture of Jamaican, Canadian, Italian, and Slovakian. Linda Walker, 60, from Newcastle upon Tyne, was thought to be suffering from Foreign Accent Syndrome, an illness recognized since World War II whereby patients speak differently after a brain injury. Researchers have discovered that patients with the syndrome have suffered damage to tiny areas of the brain that affect speech. The resultant elongated or clipped vowels make it sound as if they are speaking in a foreign accent.

THE WOMAN WITH HALF A BODY

Born with sacral agenesis—a rare condition that left her without a pelvis and part of her spine—Rosemarie Siggins from Pueblo, Colorado, had both of her legs amputated as a result of her illness when she was just two years old. Despite the incredible challenges posed by this, Rosemarie, now in her thirties, has had two successful and ground-breaking pregnancies and is now the proud mother of Luke, born in 1999, and Shelby, born in 2006. Shown here with Luke and husband Dave, Rosemarie moves herself around with her hands, and often on a skateboard. She describes her condition in her own way: "If you take a Barbie doll and remove its legs, the region you are left with is what I have. I have all the female working organs—the only reason I sit shorter is because I'm missing four sections of my spinal column."

UNLUCKY STRIKES

Mrs. G. Patterson of Baltimore, Maryland, and her two daughters all had their homes hit by lightning on the same day—March 17, 1996.

BOTTLE VOYAGE

A bottle dropped into the sea by a four-year-old girl in England was washed ashore six months later in Australia—9,000 mi (14,500 km) away. Alesha Johnson launched the bottle, which contained her name and the address of her nursery school in Lancashire, in July 2005 and, in January 2006, it was found by a boy in a boatyard near Perth.

MUSICAL URN

When Winona, Minnesota, musician Roger Busdicker died in 2006, his ashes were put in his clarinet! His family decided that the ebony and silver clarinet that he had played for the last 50 years was the ideal resting place for his cremated remains, and what didn't fit in the instrument itself went into the lining of the case.

BEAR ATTACK

Bill Murphy of Alaska survived being attacked by a grizzly bear in September 2003, then bound his wounds with duct tape, rode his all-terrain vehicle 15 mi (24 km) to his truck, and drove himself another half-hour to the hospital.

BIG BABY

A 14-lb (6.3-kg) girl born at a Brazilian hospital in 2006 is so large that her feet reach over the edge of the crib. Isabel Vitoria Ribeiro measured nearly 2 ft (60 cm) long at birth.

ICE BITE

When Hungarian skater Ani Zoltany fell through ice and into a freezing lake in February 2006, she survived by holding on to the broken ice with her teeth for ten minutes. She had been practicing on Lake Velence when the ice cracked and, as frostbite set in her hands, the only way she could keep her head above water until help arrived was to grip the ice with her teeth.

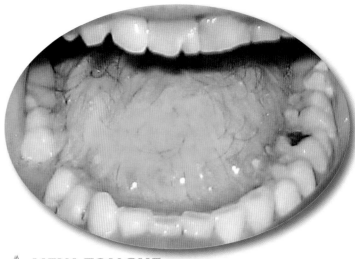

△ NEW TONGUE

A Polish man has a new tongue—made using tissue taken from his buttocks. After 23-year-old Jarislav Ernst from Gliwice had his old cancerous tongue removed, doctors collected skin, fat, and nerve tissue from his buttocks, and modeled that into a new tongue, which they then sewed into his mouth.

THREE ACES

Playing at a course in Edinburgh, Scotland, golfer Stewart Sneddon hit a hole in one at the same hole on three consecutive Saturdays in 2006. Each time, he aced the 147-yd (134-m) 13th hole with an eight-iron, beating odds of two trillion to one!

SLEPT ON

John Betteridge of Quispamsis, New Brunswick, Canada, fell victim to an electrical fault that sent 7,200 volts surging through his home, exploding lamps and appliances. His son, John Jr., slept through the ordeal unharmed—in a metal bed.

◁ LIGHTNING LADY

They say that lightning never strikes twice—this is certainly true in the case of 84-year-old Christine Moody from Somerset, England, who has actually been struck no less than four times! Christine suffered her first shock in 1980 while she was having a cup of tea in a hotel; the second strike happened 22 years later when she was at a friend's funeral; the third when she was walking down a street near her home six months later; and the fourth while she was lying in bed in December 2004. Luckily, Christine was not seriously injured by any of the strikes, but they have left her "allergic" to electricity and she experiences pain if she gets too close to electrical appliances.

HORNED MAN

This photo was sent to Robert Ripley in the early 1940s, shortly after Ripley published a cartoon showing a man with a horn growing from his head. The sender said that it shows a man who lived in China in the late 1930s.

COTTON-PICKING ▷ DELIGHT

Double-thumbed cotton picker R.L. Stubblefield from Italy, Texas, had two thumbs on his right hand, which enabled him to pick an amazing 300 lb (136 kg) of cotton a day during the 1930s.

AN ILL WIND...

After repeated hurricanes pounded the Florida coast in 2004, Joel Ruth examined the beach and found 180 Spanish silver coins that dated back about 300 years and were worth $40,000.

PREMATURE DIAGNOSIS

While lying in a morgue in January 2005, hours after being pronounced dead at the scene of a car accident in North Carolina, Larry Green was seen breathing. His condition was upgraded to alive!

LUCKY BALL

Playing at a course in Cleveland, Ohio, in July 2006, eight-year-old Harrison Vonderau hit two holes in one with the same golf ball in the space of 20 minutes!

DOG DRIVER

A woman in Hohhot, China, crashed her car in 2006—while giving her dog a driving lesson. The woman, Li, said her dog liked to crouch on the steering wheel and watch her drive, so she thought she would let it "have a try" while she operated the accelerator and brake.

STONE CAR

The mausoleum of the late Raymond Tse Jr. in Rosehill Cemetery, New Jersey, has a full-size stone Mercedes parked in the back of it.

BEARDED LADY

Grace Gilbert was the famous bearded lady with the Barnum and Bailey circus in the early years of the 20th century. Grace stood 5 ft 9 in (1.75 m) in height and her beard measured an impressive 10 in (25 cm).

HANDY MAN ▷

Shown here in 1946, W.M. Heldman from Sharpsburg, Pennsylvania, had two thumbs on each hand, and three webbed fingers on his left hand. However, these unusual features did not prevent him from using his hands as well as anyone else.

BREATHE IN!

Ed Anato Hayes from Mountain Air, Colorado, performed amazing anatomical feats during the 1930s. Here he is seen displacing his entire abdomen.

LEG STOLEN

Melissa Huff of Arcadia, California, had her prosthetic leg stolen and returned by a burglar twice in the space of five months. She lost her real leg in 2003 when a car hit her on the sidewalk.

TIMELY ARRIVALS

While driving alone on April 21, 2006, Carolyn Holt of St. Peters, Missouri, had a heart attack—and three of the first four people who stopped to help were two registered nurses and a defibrillator salesman.

JANITOR'S LEGACY

When Genesio Morlacci retired, he took a part-time janitor's job at the University of Great Falls in Montana for a short while. And, wishing other people to have the education that he hadn't, when Genesio died at the age of 102, he left a gift of $2.3 million to the university.

LONG NAILS ▽

Marie Brunozzy of Wanamie, Pennsylvania, actually used to bite her nails as a young woman. She did stop, however, and by the time this photograph was taken in 1953, they had grown to 5⅜ in (13.7 cm).

WHICH WAY?

During the 1930s, Avery Tudor from New York City was able to twist his foot completely around to face backwards.

SMASHING TIME

Visiting the Fitzwilliam Museum, Cambridge, England, in January 2006, Nick Flynn tripped on a shoelace, tumbled down a flight of stairs, and smashed into three 17th-century porcelain Chinese vases, worth a total of $600,000. The vases, which had stood on an open windowsill for more than 40 years, shattered into hundreds of pieces and it took six months to repair just one of them.

◁ TWO-MOUTHED FISH

A rainbow trout pulled from a lake near Lincoln, Nebraska, in December 2005 had double the chance of getting hooked—it had two mouths! As he reeled in the 1-lb (454-g) fish, Clarence Olberding noticed that the hook was in the upper mouth and there was another jaw protruding below. The second mouth did not appear to be functional.

MELTED CROSS

Russian teenager Marina Motygina survived a 2006 lightning strike that was so potent it melted a gold cross on her neck. The bolt hit her on the top of her head and seared through her body into the ground, destroying the necklace that she was wearing and leaving burns in the shape of a cross on her neck.

ACCIDENTAL MEETING

Brothers Joe and George Ipser of Cleveland, Ohio, hadn't seen each other in 20 years until they were accidentally reunited at a local hospital on New Year's Eve.

MIGRATION CLUE

Scientists at the University of Massachusetts School of Medicine have determined that monarch butterflies use the angle and intensity of sunlight to set their internal clocks and migrate from eastern U.S.A. to Mexico.

NATURAL DIET

Stranded in the Australian Outback in 2006, Ricky Megee of Brisbane, Queensland, said he survived for three months by eating leeches, frogs, grasshoppers, and lizards.

LOTTO LUCK

In December 2002, husband and wife Angelo and Maria Gallina of Belmont, California, won two separate lottery jackpots of $17 million and $126,000 on the same day—that's odds of one in 24 trillion!

SECRET LANGUAGE

Identical four-year-old twins Luke and Jack Ryan from Cleckheaton, West Yorkshire, England, have developed their own language. The boys chat away to each other using made-up words that their parents struggle to understand.

IMPRESSIVE EAR HAIR ▽

Seen here in February 2002, B.D. Tyagi from Bhopal, India, proudly displays long strands of hair growing from his ears that measured an incredible 4 in (10 cm) in length.

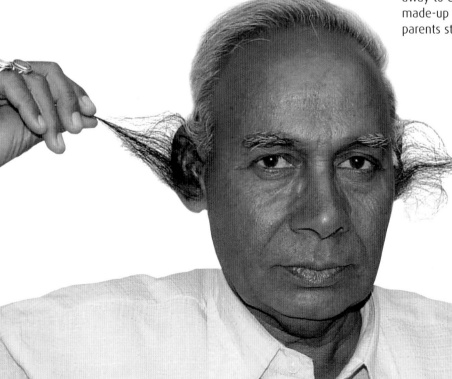

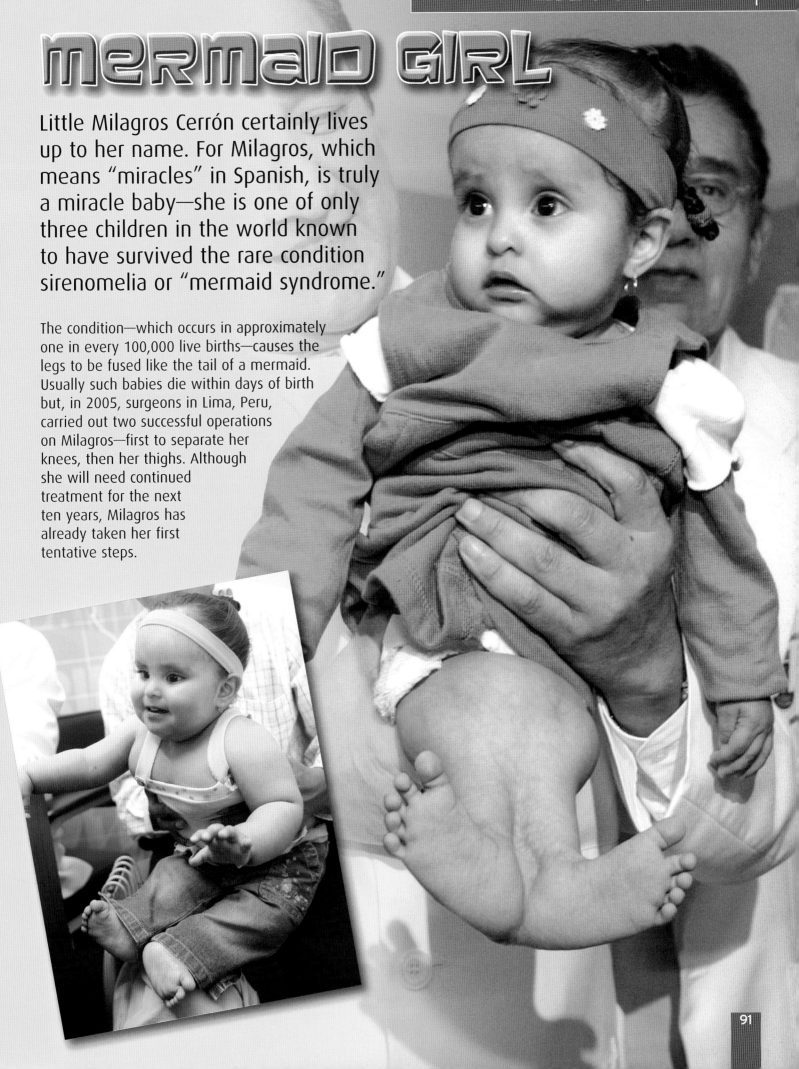

MERMAID GIRL

Little Milagros Cerrón certainly lives up to her name. For Milagros, which means "miracles" in Spanish, is truly a miracle baby—she is one of only three children in the world known to have survived the rare condition sirenomelia or "mermaid syndrome."

The condition—which occurs in approximately one in every 100,000 live births—causes the legs to be fused like the tail of a mermaid. Usually such babies die within days of birth but, in 2005, surgeons in Lima, Peru, carried out two successful operations on Milagros—first to separate her knees, then her thighs. Although she will need continued treatment for the next ten years, Milagros has already taken her first tentative steps.

DEBT REPAID

A man saved by a stranger from drowning in an icy Bosnian river 20 years earlier repaid the favor by donating a kidney to his rescuer. Remzo Pivic kept in touch with the brave rescuer, Ahmet Adulovic, even after the latter emigrated to Canada. And when he heard that Adulovic was suffering kidney problems, Pivic flew to Ottawa to donate the organ as a way to say thank you.

Big Hair

Aaron Studham gives a whole new meaning to having "big hair." The high-school student from Massachusetts has a Mohawk that reaches a magnificent 21 in (53 cm) in height. Taking up to an hour and a lot of hairspray and blow-drying to create, the gravity-defying hairstyle is, according to Aaron, a "real icebreaker with the girls."

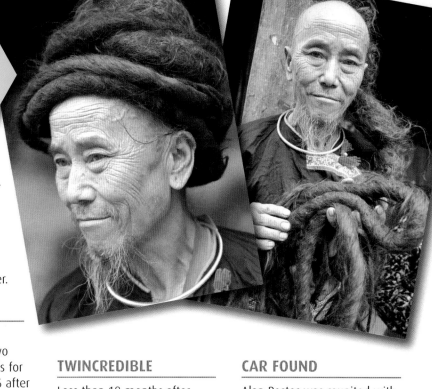

NICE HAT!

This elderly man from a hill tribe living in northern Thailand hasn't cut his hair for more than 70 years. He wears it coiled around his head, which keeps the hair neat and tidy, and his head warm. The incredible long locks are more than 16 ft (5 m) in length.

BUTTER RIVER

A fire at a dairy plant in New Ulm, Minnesota, in December 2005 released a million-dollar wave of melted butter that covered streets, ruined firefighters' equipment, and clogged storm drains.

RING RETURNED

Linda Blardo of Zephyrhills, Florida, lost her high-school class ring at a local swimming spot. Thirty-four years later, the ring was found in a Georgia state park 470 mi (756 km) away from where she lost it.

SWALLOWED NAILS

Doctors in Vietnam removed 119 rusty 3-in (75-mm) nails from a woman's stomach in 2006! The 43-year-old woman had gone to the hospital with severe stomach pains, and X rays revealed the nails and other strange objects.

THREE OF A KIND

English comedian Vic Reeves shares the same real name, Jim Moir, and the same birthday—January 24—as both his father and his grandfather.

A FINE MESS

Matthew Buer of Essex, England, was fined by two different borough councils for littering in February 2006 after French fries that he had been tossing from his car landed in two different boroughs.

AGE GAP

In northern Malaysia in 2006, a 33-year-old man, Muhamad Noor Che Musa, married a 104-year-old woman, Wook Kundor, saying their friendship had turned to love. It was his first marriage, and her 21st.

TWINCREDIBLE

Less than 18 months after identical twin Joanne Johnson married identical twin Richard McGee, she gave birth—to identical twin sons. Experts say the odds of such a thing happening are infinite. And what's more, the doctor at Royal Preston Hospital, Lancashire, England, who told the couple that they were expecting twins, was also an identical twin!

CAR FOUND

Alan Poster was reunited with his beloved car—37 years after it had been stolen. The brand-new Corvette vanished from his New York garage in 1969 but was spotted in November 2005 on a ship bound for Sweden. Although the car was silver instead of blue and lacked a gas tank and radiator, it was worth about $20,000—three times what he had paid for it.

IN NEED OF ▷ A WASH

In September 2006, Luo Shiyuan from a village in Chongqing, China, decided to wash his hair—26 years after the last time he washed it! Shiyuan's hair, which had also not been cut in a very long time, had grown to an impressive 6 ft 6 in (2 m) and his beard was 5 ft (1.5 m) in length. Unsurprisingly, the 80-year-old needed the help of 12 family members and friends to undertake the exercise, which took five hours to complete.

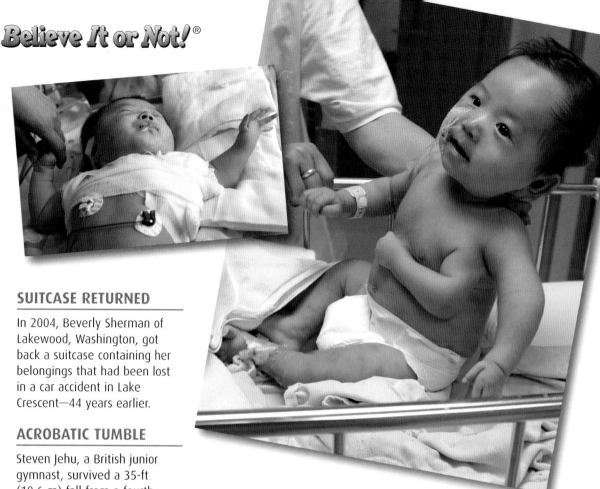

Ripley's — Believe It or Not!®

THREE-ARMED ▷ BABY

When a young Chinese mother, Xu, first set eyes on her new baby, she was amazed to see that the little boy had been born with three arms. Jie-jie was born in Anhui province in April 2006 with two left arms and one right arm. Although they were unusually complete, neither of the two left arms was fully functional and doctors decided to amputate the arm growing closer to his chest because it was thinner and always crooked. This arm was successfully removed in a three-hour operation. Jie-jie will need long-term physiotherapy to build up the strength in his remaining left arm.

SUITCASE RETURNED

In 2004, Beverly Sherman of Lakewood, Washington, got back a suitcase containing her belongings that had been lost in a car accident in Lake Crescent—44 years earlier.

ACROBATIC TUMBLE

Steven Jehu, a British junior gymnast, survived a 35-ft (10.6-m) fall from a fourth-floor hotel window. And he did a somersault on the way down so he could land on his feet.

CHEST IMPALEMENT

While 8½ months pregnant, Jessie Wickham of Ann Arbor, Michigan, was accidentally impaled through her upper chest after falling onto a microphone stand in June 2003. She survived without serious injury and later gave birth to a healthy baby boy.

FATAL FUNERAL

Two people were killed at a funeral in the Dutch town of Vorden in 2006. The victims, who were musicians performing at the funeral of an elderly man, had been sheltering under a tree in the churchyard when the tree was struck by lightning.

SHEEP STRUCK

Croatian shepherd Milan Prpic lost no fewer than 230 sheep during a single lightning strike in 2006. The dead animals represented half his flock.

LOFTY LADY ▷

Yao Defen, from Anhui province in eastern China, stands an incredible 7 ft 8 in (2.36 m) tall. Seen here sitting outside her home with a friend of average size, 36-year-old Defen suffers from agromegaly, a disease whereby a tumor on her pituitary gland caused excessive growth hormone to be produced in her body. She underwent surgery that partially removed the tumor when she was 28, but needs further operations to keep her condition in check.

MACABRE COINCIDENCE

Two women, both named April and with the middle name Dawn, lived in different parts of Fairfax County, Virginia, and dated 22-year-old men. In December 2005, in another amazing coincidence, both women were charged in separate murder-for-hire plots with trying to have those boyfriends killed.

DOUBLE INJURY

Twins Cassidy and Marissa Wiese of Laurel, Nebraska, both had roller skating accidents on the same day that resulted in each breaking their left arm.

MULTIPLE BIRTHS

Angela Magdaleno of Los Angeles, California, gave birth to seven children in just three years. In 2003, she gave birth to triplets and in July 2006, she had quadruplets, bringing her total number of children to nine. The odds of conceiving quads without fertility drugs, as Mrs. Magdaleno did, are one in 800,000.

IRON LUNG

When he died in February 2006, polio patient John Prestwich of Chipperfield, England, had spent more than 50 years breathing with the help of a machine. He contracted polio in 1955 when he was 17 and was left totally paralyzed below his chin. Without the iron lung, which was then fitted to his chest, he would have died in minutes as he was unable to breathe for himself. Despite his incapacity, he went to the top of the Eiffel Tower in Paris, flew in a helicopter, and took a spin on the "London Eye" big wheel in London.

TWO WOMBS

A woman with two wombs in Cariacica, Brazil, gave birth to healthy twin babies—one child from each womb, in May 2003.

ON TIME

There was a timely arrival for Samantha Noble of Florida who gave birth to her third child at 3.33 p.m. on March 3, 2003.

TRAPPED NUT

Doctors feared that 67-year-old Derek Kirchen from Norfolk, England, had lung cancer as he had suffered from pneumonia eight times. But the cause was found to be a cashew nut that had been stuck in his lung for 18 months.

EXTRA HEART

The body of a British tourist who died on holiday in Ireland in 2006 was flown back to the U.K. with an extra heart and pair of lungs. The extra organs were found in a plastic bag stitched inside the man's body.

LATE GRADUATE

Bob Brophy of Hillsboro, Missouri, is blind yet he graduated from college at the age of 72 with perfect grades.

▲ THREE-LEGGED MAN

Francisco Lentini was born in Sicily, Italy, in 1889 with three legs. He moved to the U.S.A. at the age of nine, and became a circus star. Lentini was highly successful, married with four children, and lived to the age of 77, but sometimes used to complain that even with three legs, he still didn't have a pair!

WALLET RETURNED

In 2006, a lengthy 35 years after Gary Karafiat of Naperville, Illinois, lost his wallet in high school, it was returned to him—totally intact!

SAME FISH

In July 2006, English angler Bob Watton from Poole, Dorset, caught the same fish twice within three days—two miles out at sea. The first time he hooked the 11-lb (5-kg) sea bass, his line snagged on a rock and the fish escaped. But three days later—at around the same spot off the Dorset coast—he reeled in a 2-ft (60-cm) bass that he recognized as being the same fish from the distinctive hook and broken line of the previous attempt.

LOBSTER THIEF

A swimmer who lost his wallet on a late-night dip in the sea had it returned a few days later—after it was found in the claws of a lobster. Paul Westlake of Plymouth, Devon, England, thought he had seen the last of his wallet until a deep-sea diver discovered it in the clutches of a lobster on the ocean floor.

MIRACLE BABY ▷

Emylea Tharby, born in London, Ontario, Canada, in April 2005, grew outside of her mother's womb. In a case so rare that only four similar births have been recorded worldwide, baby Emylea developed in mother Lia's abdominal cavity, with her head pressing against Lia's liver and her umbilical cord attached to the outside of Lia's uterus. Although Lia suffered severe abdominal pain during her pregnancy, doctors only discovered Emylea's unusual position during her cesarean delivery.

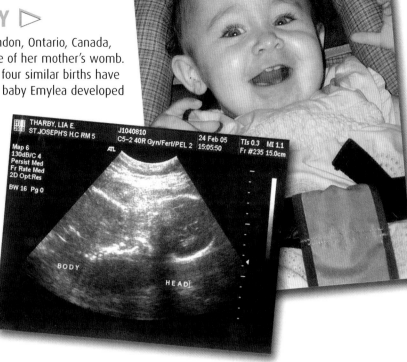

BIT OFF TONGUE

In the course of a disturbance on May 13, 2006, Kaijuan Corbett of Brooklyn, New York, bit off his own tongue and spat it at police officers.

CHIMNEY TUMBLE

Phil Harrison of Yorkshire, England, survived a 30-ft (9 m) fall from a mill chimney in 2006 because he landed in a pile of pigeon poop! Although he broke his neck as he plunged to the basement of the building, the impact was cushioned by a layer of bird droppings 6 in (15 cm) deep.

SOUL SALE

A Chinese man from Jiaxing, near Shanghai, attracted bids from 58 would-be buyers in 2006 when he tried to sell his soul on-line. Taobao, a Chinese Internet auction site, eventually stopped the sale because it needed proof that the seller could actually provide the goods.

FUNERAL SERVICE

Students from St. Ignatius High School in Cleveland, Ohio, have a volunteer pallbearer club that donates its services to nearby funeral homes.

COUGHED UP

Chris Brown of Cheltenham, Gloucestershire, England, finally coughed up a twig 1 in (2.5 cm) long that had been stuck in his lung for 20 years!

CLEVER KOMODO

Flora, a captive female Komodo dragon who lives at Chester Zoo in England, has produced 11 eggs without having had any contact with a male Komodo, ever. Scientists have concluded that her eggs are the product of asexual reproduction—they have developed without being fertilized by sperm in a process called parthenogenesis, a phenomenon that is occasionally reported in vertebrates that have lived without a male mate for an extended period.

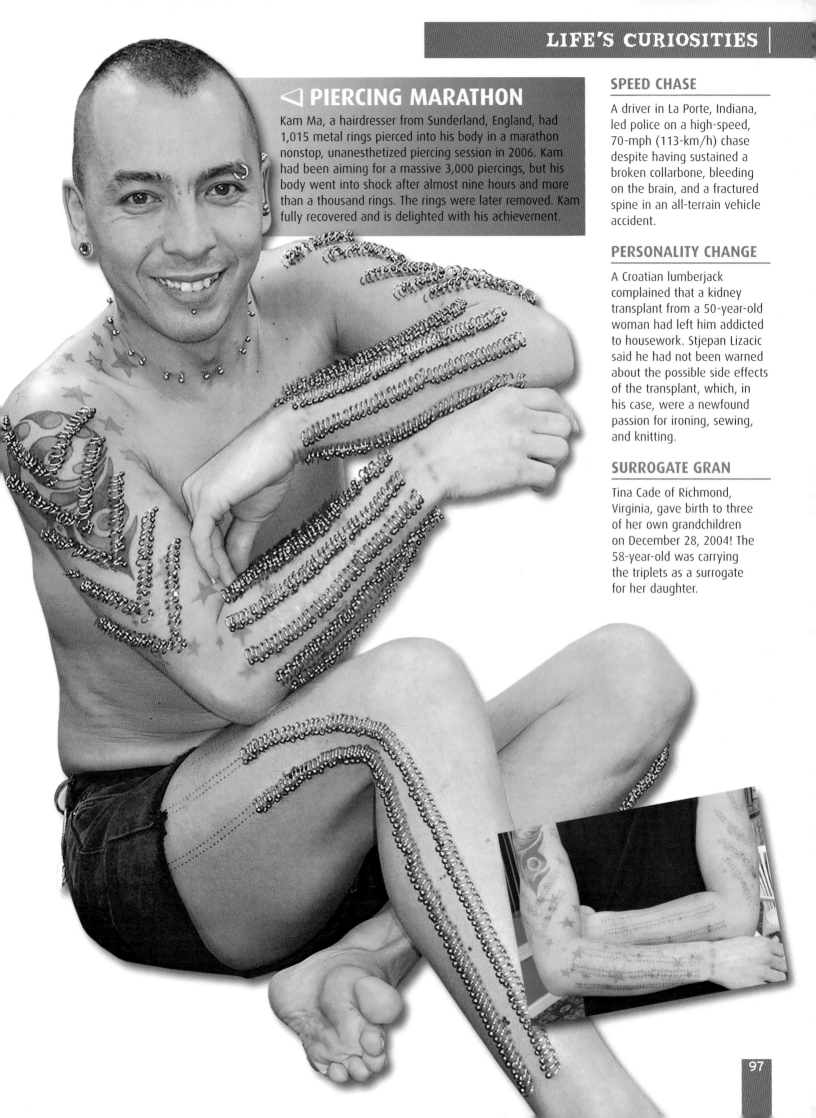

◁ PIERCING MARATHON

Kam Ma, a hairdresser from Sunderland, England, had 1,015 metal rings pierced into his body in a marathon nonstop, unanesthetized piercing session in 2006. Kam had been aiming for a massive 3,000 piercings, but his body went into shock after almost nine hours and more than a thousand rings. The rings were later removed. Kam fully recovered and is delighted with his achievement.

SPEED CHASE

A driver in La Porte, Indiana, led police on a high-speed, 70-mph (113-km/h) chase despite having sustained a broken collarbone, bleeding on the brain, and a fractured spine in an all-terrain vehicle accident.

PERSONALITY CHANGE

A Croatian lumberjack complained that a kidney transplant from a 50-year-old woman had left him addicted to housework. Stjepan Lizacic said he had not been warned about the possible side effects of the transplant, which, in his case, were a newfound passion for ironing, sewing, and knitting.

SURROGATE GRAN

Tina Cade of Richmond, Virginia, gave birth to three of her own grandchildren on December 28, 2004! The 58-year-old was carrying the triplets as a surrogate for her daughter.

Reggie isn't meant to be bald, but has had the hair licked from his head by his mother—page 108

At one year old Rudi the rabbit weighed 22 lb (10 kg), and was still growing—page 111

Pinky loves nothing more than a morning swim in his owner's swimming pool—page 113

INCREDIBLE ANIMALS

Ripley's—Believe It or Not!®
Reality Show

The fur definitely flew during a U.S. TV reality show in 2006, because all the contestants were cats!

Ten cats—all taken from animal shelters or rescue groups—spent ten days in a New York shop window inside a specially constructed house complete with mini sofas, beds, and even a fish tank... with fake fish. There, they completed tasks and were graded on such activities as purring and catching toy mice.

Each day one of the ten was eliminated by public vote.

The show was created by a pet food company eager to promote cat adoption. All of the cats were found homes after their eviction.

Indulge

Indulge

The ten lucky cats lived in the lap of luxury and provided much amusement to passing shoppers.

SNAKE FEET

This snake, found in China and measuring 3 ft (1 m), has two feet-like growths, each of which has five toes.

RAT LOVER

Roger Dier of Petaluma, California, kept 1,300 rats in his one-bedroom home!

GRIZZLY HYBRID

While hunting in northern Canada in April 2006, 65-year-old Jim Martell from Idaho shot a grizzly–polar bear hybrid, the first ever found in the wild. Wildlife officials took an interest after noticing that the bear's white fur was interspersed with brown patches. It also had long claws, a concave facial profile, and a humped back—all characteristics of a grizzly. Genetic tests confirmed that the animal's father was a grizzly and its mother was a polar bear. Previously, the two species had interbred only in zoos.

ANT COLONY

More than 307 million ants were once found in a single colony in Japan. There were 45,000 connecting nests built over an area of one square mile.

FLOOD DAMAGE

A goldfish carried from a garden pond by floodwaters in New Zealand was found alive in a roadside ditch more than a mile away. The fish had been swept from Craig and Julie Struthers' pond by a flash flood in the town of Mosgiel on South Island five days earlier.

FISH FIRE

Kipper the catfish was blamed for starting a fire that destroyed a house in Poole, England, in 2006. During a fight in his tank, water splashed out onto an electric plug, sending a power surge up the tank cable. This burned the tank's plastic lid, which then melted onto a sofa, setting it, and the house, alight.

DEPUTY DOG

In 2006, the sheriff's department of Geauga County, Ohio, unveiled its latest weapon in the war against crime—a 2-lb (900-g) Chihuahua named Midge. Sheriff Dan McClelland plans to train Midge, who stands only 2 ft (60 cm) tall even on tiptoes, as the smallest drug dog in the state.

PET YOGA

Heather Stevens of West Hollywood, California, teaches 30-minute yoga classes that dogs and their owners take together. Stevens, whose clients include poodles, dachshunds, and pointers, says that the classes helped her own aging female dog regain mobility in her hips.

STEALING STARLINGS

Bill Dougherty, a car-wash manager from Fredericksburg, Virginia, was surprised to discover that starlings had been raiding his washing machine, crawling up the change chute to steal quarters!

BEAR WRESTLER

In February 2006, Lydia Angyiou of Ivujivik, Quebec, Canada, who weighed 90 lb (41 kg), wrestled a 700-lb (320-kg) polar bear that appeared on the street where her seven-year-old son and his friends were playing. Seeing the bear begin to size up her son, Angyiou started kicking and punching the animal while a fellow villager fetched a rifle.

◁THERAPY DOG

Hans, the disabled dog, lost the use of both of his hind legs in an accident. Now he is a therapy dog and does his rounds twice a week at Florida Hospital. Complete with personalized license plate, he visits patients who are confined to wheelchairs.

EAGLE SWOOP

Freddie, a Pekingese dog belonging to the Slevin family of Bozeman, Montana, was snatched by an eagle and spent a week in the freezing wilds before he managed to find his way home.

ATHLETIC BEAR

Jennifer Ehrlichman of Hayward, Wisconsin, found a bear hibernating in an eagle's nest at the top of a 45-ft-high (14-m) aspen tree!

TURKEY TERROR

An aggressive 20-lb (9-kg) wild turkey terrorized the residents of Woburn, Massachusetts, in 2005. Many people were afraid to leave their homes, and when the police tried to move it on it kept returning.

BATTERED BY FISH

While Blake Fessenden was riding a personal watercraft on Florida's Suwannee River in 2006, a 4-ft (1.2-m) sturgeon jumped out of the water and hit him with such force that it knocked him unconscious.

TRAPPED CHIPMUNK

In 2003, a chipmunk got trapped in Dixie Goldsby's car while she was camping in Utah and rode with her all the way to California!

PLAN BACKFIRED

A woman in Jacksonville, Florida, set her apartment on fire in 2006 while trying to kill a snake. Finding the snake on her porch, she doused it with petrol and torched it, but in doing so caused $1,000 of damage. The snake got away!

▽ SHEEP SNACK

A python was discovered stuck in the middle of a road in the village of Kampung Jabor, Malaysia, in 2006 after swallowing a pregnant ewe. Unable to move, the greedy snake, which measured 20 ft (6 m) in length, was easily captured by local firefighters. It weighed 200 lb (90 kg) when found—but much of that was its dinner!

CANAL HAZARD

In January 2005, an alligator measuring 12 ft (3.6 m) in length and weighing 400 lb (180 kg) was found living in a downtown Miami canal. It was believed to have grown that big by eating the animals cast into the water following religious voodoo sacrifices.

◁ MIRACLE OF FAITH THE DOG

Faith the biped dog was born in Oklahoma City, Oklahoma, just before Christmas in 2002. Rescued from her guard-dog mother who was going to kill her because of her weakness and deformity, Faith was nursed and nurtured by the Stringfellow family. Over a period of six months, they taught the Labrador–Chow cross how to walk on her hind legs, just like the human members of the family.

JUMBO OPERATION

Dr. William Baldwin, a surgeon at Scarborough General Hospital in Ontario, Canada, performed a nine-hour operation to remove a kidney stone from an elephant.

ELEPHANT ART

An exhibition of paintings by elephants went on display at an art gallery in Edinburgh, Scotland, in 2006. By holding the brushes in their trunks, the elephants—all from Thailand—produced a series of pretty pictures, the best of which was painted by six-ton Paya with what was claimed to be a self-portrait.

△ KANGAROO HORSE

This young foal was born in the early 20th century, without any front legs.

TALENTED TERRIER

Tillie, a Jack Russell terrier from Brooklyn, New York, creates abstract paintings that have been shown in 16 exhibitions. Tillie has sold more than 100 paintings, with the sale proceeds reaching five figures!

PATCHED UP

A snapping turtle hit by a car in Traverse City, Michigan, survived after its cracked shell was fitted with a fiberglass patch at an auto body shop!

IDENTITY CRISIS

J.R. the pot-bellied pig seemed to have suffered an identity crisis in August 2006. The stray was taken to an animal shelter in Shelbyville, Kentucky, after scaring local dogs, but during his two-week stay in a dog kennel he developed canine tendencies, including a sudden taste for dog biscuits!

◁ HOPPING CANINE

In 1932, Nellie, a dog with no front legs who belonged to Dr. P.W. Horner from Elkhart, Indiana, used to move around by "hopping" along, balanced on her hind legs and tail.

Cholla the horse artist

When Cholla stands at his easel and paints, passers-by do a double take—because Cholla is a horse!

Cholla—a 20-year-old quarter horse-mustang owned by Renee Chambers of Reno, Nevada—has been painting for two years and has made quite a splash in the art world. His work has been displayed in several galleries and magazines and he even has his own website. "He loves to do it," says Chambers. "He can be in the back pasture and he sees me bring his easel and he's just right there. He doesn't even have to be called."

"Birds in Flight"

"Horse Jumper"

"Purple Heron"

"Blue Birds"

Cholla paints by holding the brush in his teeth. No one moves the paper or easel. All his owner has to do is put the paint on the brush for him.

"Here's My Pink Bow For You"

105

COLD CAT

A cat in Oklahoma City, Oklahoma, amazingly survived being shut in a refrigerator for four weeks without food or water. His four-year-old owner had put Louis in the fridge in the family barn for safekeeping but the cat's plight was only discovered a month later when the boy's father decided to clean out the appliance and the cat fell out. Louis had lost 7 lb (3.2 kg) in weight but experts agreed that he was lucky to be alive at all.

NIGHT BIRD

The oilbird spends its entire life in darkness. It lives in the caves of South America, venturing out only at night to feed on fruit, and finds its way around by using echolocation in the same way as a bat.

FOOTBALLING ▷ CROCS

Erroberto Piza Rios of Ixtapa, Mexico, enjoys nothing more than kicking a soccer ball around. But the guys he plays with can certainly put in crunching tackles—because they are all crocodiles! He has tamed 47 crocodiles and every one is named after a famous footballer. Their skills include heading the ball and raising their heads to allow the balls to roll down their backs to their tails.

FISH RUN ▷

In April 2006, the 33rd Annual Fisherman's Festival, held in Boothbay Harbor, Maine, featured a codfish relay race, in which Brook Chaney is seen here competing.

BIRD TOLL

In 2006, the Royal Ontario Museum, Canada, staged a gruesome display of around 2,000 birds that had been lured to their deaths by the bright lights of the Canadian city of Toronto. The exhibition was part of a campaign to persuade Toronto office and apartment-building owners to dim their lights at night in order to reduce the number of bird deaths due to collisions with lit skyscrapers. No fewer than 89 different species were scraped off downtown Toronto sidewalks during the 2005 migratory season.

WOOLLY WONDER

George, a merino wether sheep, died at his home in Warren, New South Wales, Australia, in 2006 at the grand old age of 21 years, 5 months and 3 days. He was such a popular character that his owners, Phil and Myra Tolhurst, invited local schoolchildren to attend his 21st birthday party—which featured a poem written in his honor and a cake with 21 candles.

FELINE FORECASTER

Fanny Shields of Baltimore, Maryland, owned a cat named Napoleon that could predict the weather with such accuracy that its predictions were regularly published in daily newspapers.

LUCKY LEAP

A dog survived with only cuts and bruises in 2006 after accidentally running off the edge of a 450-ft (140-m) cliff while chasing rabbits. Russett the Jack Russell terrier was out with his owner Martin Coombes on the Isle of Wight, England, when he suddenly disappeared over the edge of the cliff and landed on rocks down by the sea.

PIG BAN

A Russian farmer was barred from taking his pig into a soccer stadium in 2006 for fear that it could spark a riot. After exhibiting the animal at a Moscow pig show, Vladimir Kisilev was prevented from taking it to the match between Spartak Moscow and St. Petersburg Zenit on the grounds that the home team's fans are referred to as "pigs" by their St. Petersburg rivals.

△ WHAT A CATCH!

In 1934, J.J. Holcomb from Panama got more than he bargained for when he hooked a large sailfish. As he was reeling in his catch, his fishing line snagged around a second large sailfish and Holcombe landed both fish at the same time. His catch had a combined weight of 208½ lb (95 kg).

GLOWING FISH

A Taiwanese company has created a new species of genetically engineered fish that glows fluorescent gold in the dark. Glow-in-the-dark fish are created by injecting a fluorescent protein, which is extracted from jellyfish, directly into the fish embryo. The new rice fish is even more spectacular than previous neon fish because while it glows with gold fluorescence under white light, it is also able to change color under other kinds of aquarium lights.

STAR CHICKEN

Arguably the most famous chicken in the U.S.A. died in February 2006 at the grand old age of 16. Matilda, who lived twice the age of most chickens, had appeared on *The Tonight Show* as feathered assistant to magician Keith Barton of Birmingham, Alabama. She appeared magically from beneath the lid of a closed pan where only an egg yolk had been before.

SHELL SHOCK

In 2006, a pet tortoise accidentally thrown out with the trash survived a nightmare trip through a recycling plant. After taking a ride in a garbage truck and narrowly avoiding being scooped up by a bulldozer, the tortoise was saved as he was about to be thrown into a crusher in Kent, England.

COWCAT

Aptly named because of her extraordinary splotchy cow color markings, Cowcat was a stray before being adopted by Louisa Stroup Nilsson from Devon, England.

DOG WEDGED

After being hit by a passing Peugeot, a small dog traveled nearly 60 mi (97 km) through Northern Ireland one night in November 2005 wedged in the grille of the car. He emerged unscathed, only to be run over again—this time fatally—three weeks later.

EXTRA PASSENGER

A muntjac deer survived a 25-mi (40-km) ride through England in 2004 while stuck in the air-intake slot above the bumper of a Rover car. The driver didn't know the animal was there, thinking he had hit a stone instead.

PET ACADEMY

Viviane Theby of Wittlich, Germany, has set up a talent academy with a difference—all her pupils are pets! Theby has already taught a dog to dance, a chicken to play the xylophone, and a cat to play the piano! The cat, Fuchs, has been so successful that he has sold CDs and given concerts.

HOLY COW

Some 20,000 people from all over southern Egypt came to Mohammed Abu Dif's house in February 2006 to seek blessings from a calf that they believed held religious significance. According to reports, when the calf was born, its skin folds formed the words: "There is no God, but Allah."

LOCUST SWARM

An estimated 12.5 trillion locusts swept across about 198,600 sq mi (514,370 sq km) of Nebraska in 1874.

◁ BALD BABY BABOON

Reggie, a baby hamadryas baboon born in Paignton Zoo in Devon, England, in September 2005, has been attracting a lot of attention because of his unusual haircut. For Reggie isn't meant to be bald, but has had the hair licked from the top of his head as a result of some over-zealous attention and grooming by his mother. Zookeepers were worried that Reggie's family might reject him on account of his appearance, but, happily, he has been fully accepted by his troop.

◁ KISS ME QUICK!

Thai snake charmer Khum Chaibuddee kissed a spine-tingling 19 highly poisonous king cobras at a Ripley's Believe It or Not! museum in Pattaya, Thailand, in October 2006. The cobras were released onto a stage one by one and Khum kissed each snake in turn before moving on to the next, emerging unscathed from his challenge.

MISTAKEN IDENTITY

When a woman in Koblenz, Germany, heard what sounded like a child next door constantly screaming "Mama, Mama," she called the police. But instead of finding a youngster left home alone, they found the cries were coming from the family's talking parrot!

LUCKY CHANCE

A man jumped on the back of a 10-ft (3-m) alligator to save his girlfriend's pet dog as it was being dragged into a lake. Brent Carey was at the park in Charleston, South Carolina, when the alligator leaped from the water and began to drag the dog, Chance, into the lake. But Carey jumped on the reptile's back, grabbed it near its back legs, and persuaded it to free the dog.

ROADKILL ART

Nate Hill of Brooklyn, New York, doesn't believe in letting roadkill go to waste—instead he turns it into works of art. Inspired by a friend who stapled a guinea pig's head to a snake, he sews together paws, tails, and heads of dead animals to create his own crazy creatures.

HiGH-FLAT DiET

There's nothing Arthur Boyt enjoys more than sitting down to a nice weasel casserole, perhaps with a side plate of bat wings. The 66-year-old former taxidermist from Davidstow, Cornwall, England, gets his meat for free by regularly tucking into roadkill.

His freezer is stacked with the carcasses of animals he has found squashed on the road: hedgehogs, cats, otters, even a Labrador. He once brought a porcupine back from Canada! He says: "People are happy to eat an apple that has fallen out of the tree and is lying on the floor, so what's the difference?" Arthur, who has been eating roadkill since he was 13 and has never been ill once, strongly recommends badger sandwiches but was disappointed with giant horseshoe bat ("a bit like gray squirrel, not a lot of flavor") and fox ("a pungent taste that went on and on repeating"). However, his wife Su doesn't share his unusual tastes and refuses to cook them—because she's a vegetarian.

Arthur Boyt prepares an assortment of roadkill creatures for one of his unusual dinners.

WHERE'S GOLDILOCKS?

In what sounds like something out of a bedtime story, a woman in West Vancouver, Canada, arrived home in 2006 to find a bear eating porridge in her kitchen! The bear had broken into an oatmeal container and was enjoying the feast so much that it took the efforts of three police officers to persuade it to leave.

SNAKE'S ALIVE

Jonathan Kent's pet, a 6-ft (1.8-m) anaconda, was found alive and well, crawling through the remains of Kent's California business—that was totally destroyed by fire!

TRAPPED IN SNOW

Guinness, a golden retriever owned by Terry Coward of Barrie, Ontario, Canada, survived being trapped in a snowbank for 11 days after being hit by a car.

RIPLEY'S®

PRETTY POLLY
This two-headed South American parrot was raised domestically in England during the 1990s.

WILD RIDE

A cat that hitchhiked a ride on the underbelly of a sport utility vehicle in 2005 survived a 70-mi (113-km) journey on the New Jersey Turnpike. The cat—nicknamed Miracle—was finally freed when another motorist spotted it through the SUV's wheel well and flagged down the driver. The cat emerged with burned paws, singed fur, and one claw missing.

ALL SHOOK UP

Barney the Doberman pinscher was supposed to be guarding the valuable exhibits at a teddy bear museum at Wookey Hole, Somerset, England. But during a 15-minute rampage in 2006 he inexplicably went berserk, tearing more than 100 of the toys limb from limb and causing $40,000 damage. Among his victims was Mabel, a valuable Steiff bear that had once belonged to Elvis Presley.

THUGS BUNNY ▷

At just one year old, Rudi the rabbit, owned by Erwin Teichmann of Berlin, Germany, weighed 22 lb (10 kg), was 3 ft 1 in (94 cm) in length, had 8-in (20-cm) ears—and was still growing.

SHRINKING FROG

The paradoxical frog of South America is smaller as an adult than as a tadpole. Whereas the tadpole can reach a length of 10 in (25.4 cm), the adult never exceeds 3 in (7.6 cm).

UNDERCOVER KITTEN

Joining the lineup of police and fire officers being recognized for heroism by Brooklyn District Attorney Charles Hynes in 2006 was a cat named Fred! The crime-fighting kitten was given a special award for undercover work that helped trap a bogus veterinarian.

THUMBELINA ▷

Miniature horses usually reach around 34 in (86 cm) in height, and weigh 250 lb (113 kg), but Thumbelina, who was born in 2001 in St. Louis, Missouri, is much smaller than that! Standing 17 in (43 cm) tall and weighing 60 lb (27 kg), she comes up to the shins of normal-sized horses, and lives on a cup of grain and a handful of hay twice a day.

▽ HIGH HORSE

Radar, a Belgian draft horse, owned by Bill Priefert of Texas, stands a colossal 6 ft 7½ in (2 m) from foot to shoulder, weighs 2,400 lb (1,088 kg), and wears a size 9½ shoe. Every day he eats 18 lb (8 kg) of grain and 40 lb (18 kg) of hay and drinks 20 gallons (75 l) of water.

DOGS' DINNER

A restaurant in Denver, Colorado, organizes an annual "Three Dogs Night Out" where dog owners can enjoy a gourmet meal with their four-legged friends.

GREATEST DANE

In 2006, a three-year-old Great Dane called Gibson, owned by Sandy Hall of Sacramento, California, stood an amazing 7 ft 2 in (2.2 m) tall on his hind legs! And his best pal Zoie is a Chihuahua measuring only 7 in (18 cm) tall!

⚠ PIGS IN WATER

Pinky and Perky are two Tamworth pigs that love nothing more than a morning swim in their owner's swimming pool. The pigs live in Worcestershire, England, with farmers Craig and Marjorie Walsh, who first let them swim to stop them getting bored. Now the nautical porkers eagerly look forward to their daily dip.

OWL VISION

Dr. Chris Murphy, a veterinary ophthalmologist in Madison, Wisconsin, performed eye surgery on a blind great horned owl, and then fitted the bird with contact lenses.

MIGHTY CROCS

The Bhitarkanika sanctuary on India's Orissa coast is home to the world's largest saltwater crocodiles. A 2006 census showed that several saltwater crocodiles there have grown to 16–18 ft (4.9–5.5 m), five are up to 20 ft (6 m) long, and three are over 20 ft, including one 23-ft-long (7-m) monster. Saltwater crocodiles can live to 100 years and can devour a human in minutes.

DOGGIE DATING

Dog lovers who are looking for mates for their pets may find a match on a new website. Believed to be the U.K.'s first lonely hearts website for dogs, it also offers canine welfare advice.

RESTLESS DAISY

A female tortoise who decided she wanted a change after 55 years with the same partner made a break for freedom in 2006. Daisy was discovered 12 days later, having ventured nearly a mile from her home in Devon, England—a journey that took her up a steep hill and across a road and tractor trails. It was the first time Daisy had been away from pal Bert since the early 1950s.

SWINGING PARTY

Cheeta the chimp—veteran of a dozen *Tarzan* movies— celebrated his 74th birthday in April 2006, making him the world's oldest living primate.

Cheeta, who is 4 ft (1.2 m) tall and weighs 150 lb (68 kg), was discovered on an animal scouting trip to Liberia, Africa, by a Hollywood animal trainer named Tony Gentry in 1932. Long since retired from acting—his last role was opposite Rex Harrison in *Doctor Doolittle* (U.S. 1967)— Cheeta spends his days at the Cheeta Primate Foundation, playing the piano or painting. His masterpieces have been exhibited in art galleries and sell for more than $100 apiece.

Cheeta is seen here with co-star Lex Barker who played Tarzan in several Hollywood movies in the 1940s and 50s.

A talented artist, Cheeta's work has been exhibited at the National Gallery in London, England.

Cheeta enjoys playing the piano at the Cheeta Primate Foundation in California. It is rare for chimps to live beyond the age of 50 in captivity.

ZAN THE APE MAN

Cheeta in his younger days with co-stars Maureen O'Sullivan and Johnny Weissmuller in the *Tarzan* movies of the 1930s.

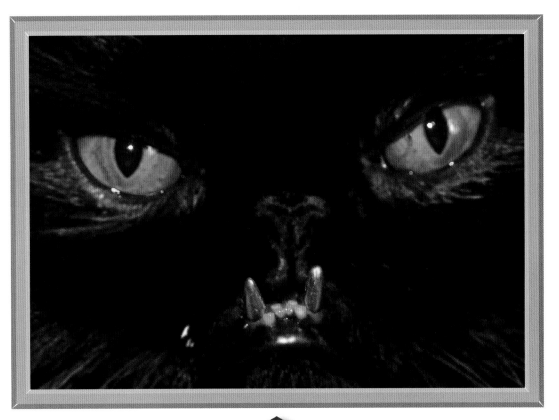

SUFFERED IN SILENCE

A dog with no bark survived after being stuck down a 10-ft (3-m) ditch for a month. Holly, a 12-year-old collie, fell into the ditch in Cornwall, England, after being scared by a thunderstorm and was rescued only when a passerby heard her whimpering.

HOUSE ARREST

After repeatedly attacking people in the neighborhood, Lewis, a cat living in Fairfield, Connecticut, was put under house arrest by police—and was banned from ever leaving the house.

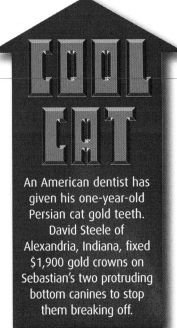

COOL CAT

An American dentist has given his one-year-old Persian cat gold teeth. David Steele of Alexandria, Indiana, fixed $1,900 gold crowns on Sebastian's two protruding bottom canines to stop them breaking off.

EXTRA SHIPMENT

When a business owner from Tampa, Florida, opened a shipment of 400 parrot cages sent from China, he found an additional order that he wasn't expecting—a severely undernourished cat. The female cat tipped the scales at just over 3 lb (1.4 kg) after spending nearly a month trapped in the container.

WANDERING CAT

A cat who wandered away from his Seattle home in 1996 was finally reunited with his family ten years later, thanks to animal care workers in California. Sneakers, a long-haired black tabby, was dropped off at the Sacramento animal shelter in April 2006 by owners who could no longer care for the cat, but an electronic tag revealed that he had actually gone missing a decade earlier—in Seattle, Washington. His original owner, Alison MacEwan, was delighted to have her pet back but remains puzzled as to how Sneakers came to make the 600-mi (965-km) journey south.

◁ TERRITORIAL TABBY

A territorial cat defended his yard in spectacular fashion in 2006 by chasing a wandering black bear up a tree—twice. While Jack, a ten-year-old tabby owned by Donna Dickey of West Milford, New Jersey, stood guard under the tree, the petrified bear clung to the branches. It stayed there for about 15 minutes, frequently looking down at Jack. When it eventually slid down the tree and tried to escape, a hissing Jack immediately gave chase, forcing the bear to take refuge up a second tree until Dickey called the cat home. As the bear ran off into the woods, Dickey summed up Jack's philosophy. "He doesn't want anybody in his yard," she said.

HEAD STUCK

In 2006, a dog spent two hours with its head stuck in a 4-in (10-cm) aluminum pipe before Animal Control in Fort Worth, Texas, freed it by using mineral oil as a lubricant. It is thought the dog had been chasing a squirrel or a rabbit.

DONUT DOG

A donut-loving dog was blamed for starting a house fire in Vancouver, British Columbia, Canada. Investigators believe the dog caused the blaze by jumping up to reach a box of donuts and accidentally switching on the stove.

SHEEP BOOTS

Sheep in Germany have been given miniature PVC gumboots to prevent foot infection. Businessman Wilhelm Fennen started by making the footwear for dogs until a farmer from Hamburg requested some for his flock.

ANGRY SWARM

A teenage driver in Indiana crashed into a hollow tree and stirred up tens of thousands of angry honey bees, creating a swarm that landed her and nine others in hospital. By the time rescuers arrived, a black cloud of insects had engulfed Jacqueline Cossairt's vehicle, forcing firefighters to wear full safety gear during the rescue.

SKIN FEEDER

A Kenyan worm-like amphibian, *Bolengerula taitanus*, has a unique way of feeding her offspring—she allows them to peel off her own skin and eat it!

GLOVE THIEF

Other cats bring home dead birds or mice, but Willy, owned by Jennifer and Dan Pifer of Pelham, New York, collects gardening gloves! His haul from neighborhood gardens was so great that the Pifers took to pinning the stolen gloves on their clothesline with the message: "Our cat is a glove snatcher. Please take these if yours." In the first four months of the 2006 summer, Willy seized at least 25 gloves. In winter, when gardening gloves are thin on the ground, he switches to his off-season prey, dirty socks, which he removes from the family laundry room.

HUNGRY HOUDINI

The latest trick by Houdini, a pet Burmese python measuring 12 ft (3.6 m) long, very nearly turned out to be his last. The snake had such a voracious appetite that when, in July 2006, his regular food, a rabbit, became tangled up with the queen-size electric blanket used to keep him warm, he ate the blanket too! He underwent an operation at a pet clinic in Ketchum, Idaho, where X rays revealed that he had not only eaten the blanket's wires but the heating control unit as well. In fact, the blanket's wiring extended through 8 ft (2.4 m) of the 60-lb (27-kg) reptile's digestive tract.

A Few Too Many

COLLECTIONS

TWO-HEADED TORTOISE

This two-headed baby tortoise was born in South Africa in 2003. Its owner, Noel Daniels, says that both of the tortoise's heads feed on grass, leaves, and other tortoise treats.

FOUR-LEGGED FOWL

An elderly Chinese man from the city of Hangzhou in Zhejiang province found this four-legged chicken while out buying vegetables at the local market.

HOW MANY HORNS?

This hungry five-horned sheep is a popular resident at a zoo in Anhui province, central China.

SNAKE FOR AUCTION

"We" is the unusual name of this incredibly unusual two-headed albino black rat snake. The reptile, which currently resides in an aquarium in St. Louis, Missouri, is being auctioned on-line by its owners in a bid to raise funds for educational programs.

CONJOINED CROCS

Two baby crocodiles at a farm in Bangkok, Thailand, look like they have been accidentally stuck together. In fact, they are conjoined—they both have all their own limbs but are joined at the bottom.

TWO SNOUTS

A piglet with two distinct mouths was born on a farm in the suburbs of the city of Liaocheng in eastern China in 2006.

TWO-NOSED PUP

Duo is a Staffordshire bull terrier with two noses who lives in an animal shelter in Newcastle, England. Given to the shelter by police after apparently being lost or abandoned, Duo has the canine equivalent of a cleft lip. Veterinarians said that they had never before seen a cleft lip to such an extent in a dog.

⚠ LUCKY KANGAROO

A female kangaroo in Hangzhou, China, was the fortunate recipient of an artificial limb in August 2006. After the juvenile animal was involved in an accident, zoo officials contacted a local artificial limb factory, and commissioned a specially designed new back leg for her. She was back happily hopping about in no time.

VAMPIRE FINCH

During times of drought, the sharp-beaked ground finch of the Galapagos Islands (which is also known as the vampire finch), drinks the blood of larger birds.

SURFING MOOSE

In January 2006, a fully grown moose was spotted surfing down Norway's rain-swollen Namsen River on a large chunk of ice!

EMERGENCY LANDING

A snake forced a pilot to make an emergency landing in 2006. Monty Coles of West Virginia was 3,000 ft (915 m) up in his single-engine plane when he saw a 4½-ft (1.4-m) snake looking at him from the instrument panel. As the snake fell at his feet, he grabbed it with one hand while controlling the plane with the other. When the snake then coiled around his arm and started pulling a floor lever with its tail, Coles decided to make an emergency landing in Ohio.

SURPRISE PACKAGE

Dutch customs officials detected a live poisonous snake that was sent by airmail from Hong Kong to the Netherlands in 2006. When they first scanned the package, which was labeled "toy goods," they thought the snake was a rubber novelty, but then they saw it move! It turned out to be a Fea's viper, found in the forests of Southeast Asia.

⚠ FLYING COW

One windy day in Oklahoma in the 1930s, this unfortunate cow was whisked up into a tree by a tornado!

RIVER ORDEAL

A dog that was presumed drowned after falling into an icy river channel that feeds Lake Michigan was found alive 13 hours later. Robert Chavez was walking his German Shepherd beside the Grand River in March 2006 when the dog fell into the channel and through the ice. It saved itself by swimming into a tunnel.

⚠ METAL MICKEY

One of just 12 southern ground hornbills in Britain, this lucky bird was given a new lease of life when keepers at Birdland in Gloucestershire, England, fitted him with a 6-in (15-cm) stainless steel beak in 2006. Metal Mickey, as he soon became known, had broken his beak, and would have starved had it not been for this inventive solution. He is now the proud owner of what is believed to be the first avian steel jaw in Britain.

RAT CATCHERS

In 2006, a Chinese village treated more than 200 cats to a fish dinner to thank them for their hard work. Residents of Sanjiang, in Guangdong province, wanted to thank the cats for eradicating rats from their farms.

COLOR CODE

Con Slobodchikoff, an Arizona professor, found that prairie dogs have very specific verbal calls, including calls that identify a person's height or shirt color.

PENGUIN PULLOVERS △

Chilly penguins are being kept warm and snug thanks to these brightly-colored pullovers, which have been knitted by a group of seniors from New South Wales, Australia. The small, 18-in (46-cm) tall fairy penguins had been hit by oil slicks off the coasts of New South Wales and Tasmania. When they had the spilt oil scrubbed off their coats by rescue workers they lost the natural oils that help them to keep out the cold. The little pullovers are designed to keep them warm while they recuperate.

DOGS REUNITED

In four years British dog lover Jayne Hayes has reunited over 2,500 dogs with their owners via the Internet. Her website receives four million hits a month and has 100 lost or stolen dogs added to its database every week.

GREAT ESCAPE

In April 2006, Rosco, an American bulldog, had had enough of being locked up, so he chewed open the lock on his cage and climbed a 7-ft (2-m) wall topped with barbed wire to escape from the Animal Control Center in Virginia Beach, Virginia.

DOG-EARED PUP

Mongrel puppy "Weasel" didn't have the best start in life. Born with no ears, he was dumped at a police station in south Wales when he was just a few months old. Luckily for the pup a local animal welfare charity took him to an animal hearing specialist who discovered that although skin had grown over Weasel's ears, their inner workings were intact. Workers at the charity, who describe Weasel as "happy, friendly, and really healthy in every other way," were delighted, and Weasel has now been lined up for an operation to maximize his hearing.

CANINE WEDDING

As Bethel Park, Pennsylvania, staged its most eagerly awaited wedding of 2006, there was hardly a dry eye—or nose—to be seen. The bride wore fur, and so did the groom. This was hardly surprising because the groom, Buck, was a Bernese mountain dog and the bride, Peaches, was a collie-beagle-basset mix! Buck was resplendent in a bow tie and Peaches wore a tasteful veil. The ceremony was staged by a local dog club for residents of a retirement home, and had a full supporting cast. The best man was a Shetland sheepdog, the flower girl was a Yorkshire terrier, and the beautiful bridesmaids included a toy poodle and an Irish setter.

DOG JOCKEY

A Jack Russell terrier who lives in Gloucestershire, England, likes to ride on the back of a Shetland pony who is just 37 in (94 cm) tall! Freddie the dog often leaps on the back of his neighbor's pony Daisy for a trot around the farm. His owner Patricia Swinley said: "Freddie is a natural jockey. When he first saw Daisy he rushed across the yard and just jumped straight on her back."

◁ THE BEST OF FRIENDS

Gohan the 3½-in (9-cm) dwarf hamster and Aochan the 3-ft (1-m) ratsnake live happily side by side in a Tokyo zoo. What's all the more surprising is that Gohan—whose name means "meal" in Japanese—was presented to Aochan in October 2005, as his dinner! The ratsnake decided not to eat the hamster, preferring to make friends with him, and the pair have shared a cage ever since.

KITTEN CHARIOT

When a kitten suffered a broken back after being attacked by a raccoon, Dr. Alice Davis of Ashland, Oregon, gave it a new lease of life by fitting it with a wheeled chariot made from a K'NEX™ set.

IGUANA WALK

Robert Garnett from Essex, England, takes his pet iguana for a walk every day.

CLIFF PLUNGE

Pepe the Jack Russell terrier was so intent on chasing a squirrel in 2006 that he dived over a cliff. After tumbling down the cliff, he landed next to the busy Pacific Coast Highway near Los Angeles and narrowly missed getting run over by a big truck. While a passing motorist came to Pepe's aid, his owner, Brandon McMillan, was unaware of the rescue and, scrambling up the cliff in search of the dog, had to be saved by firefighters when the ground suddenly gave way beneath him.

HOOK HORROR

Karen and Phillip Vavro of Butler, Pennsylvania, have a cat named Nippy that swallowed a metal hook, 2½-in (6.4-cm) long, from a Christmas tree ornament. The cat survived when the hook passed through its digestive system 20 days later!

CAT SNATCH

Bamboo, a cat weighing 6 lb 8 oz (2.9 kg) that was owned by Colleen Hamilton of Esquimalt, British Columbia, Canada, survived after being snatched from the back porch by a great horned owl. Bamboo limped home 22 hours later with three broken legs and puncture wounds from the owl's talons. From the injuries, veterinarians concluded that the cat had fallen from a significant height.

Ripley's

HOWLER MONKEY
Five-limbed South American howler monkey, acquired by Ripley's in 2004.

CLEVER CORGI

Tim Pennings, an associate professor of math at Hope College in Holland, Michigan, has a Welsh corgi that "understands" calculus!

SURVIVED AVALANCHE

A Burmese mountain dog named Tiga escaped a Colorado avalanche that killed her owner, and then survived for six days in freezing temperatures before being found alive and well.

GOLD TOOTH

Bosnian dentist Milan Vujnovic gave his pet dog, an eight-month-old Russian terrier called Atos, a gold tooth as a reward for his loyalty.

LAP OF LUXURY

A firm in Essex, England, is manufacturing a temperature-controlled waterbed for dogs. The bed comes with an extra-tough cover.

ARTIFICIAL LEGS

Footsie, a Shepherd-mix dog adopted by Helen DePinto of Ann Arbor, Michigan, was fitted with a pair of artificial hind legs by prosthetic limb specialists Steve Hoover and Kenneth Woodard in 2004. Missing the lower halves of his hind paws, before the fitting Footsie used to have to tuck his two back legs under his backside and scoot along with his front paws.

SNAPPY PETS

Neighbors rarely play with James "Bugs" Brown's pets. For Brown of Tualatin, Oregon, keeps three alligators: Hisser, Chomper, and Snapper.

BRAVE SQUIRRELS

Aaron Rundus, a scientist at the University of California, has discovered that Californian ground squirrels bravely stand their ground when confronted by a rattlesnake. Moreover, the squirrels wave their tales at the rattlesnakes in a taunting gesture that is picked up by the snake's sensitive heat sensors.

ROOF HOME

In 2006, a raccoon made its home on the roof of a 43-story building in downtown Chicago. The raccoon, which was spotted climbing scaffolding on the 36th floor of the Kluczynski Federal Building, was released after being captured with tuna bait.

▽ BABY CHAMELEONS

In August 2006, Charles and Camilla—a pair of veiled chameleons—became the proud parents of no less than 56 healthy babies! It is very rare for such a large number of baby chameleons from one clutch of eggs to survive, and owner Vicky Fox from Dorset, England, had to quickly find homes for the inch-long offspring before instinct kicked in and they became violently territorial at around the age of three months.

SMALLEST CAT

Heed is a tiny cat from the unusual short-legged munchkin breed. His owner, Tiffani Kjeldergaard from San Diego, California, has measured him at just 3 in (7.6 cm) in height and a mere 2.3 lb (1 kg) in weight.

DRIBBLING CROWS

Four carrion crows at Tokuyama Zoo, Japan, use their beaks to dribble a miniature ball toward a soccer goal, sometimes tackling each other for possession before scoring. The zoo is hoping to teach them to pass and take free kicks.

SHEEP-DOG

A sheep belonging to Emlyn Roberts in north Wales, U.K., has started to behave like a sheepdog. The sheep, which was raised with sheepdogs, joins them in herding ducks and likes to be taken for a walk on a leash. She also likes to watch TV and can jump through hoops and slide down a ramp—just like the dogs!

SINISTER STORKER

In 2006, an elderly couple from Potsdam, Germany, revealed that they were being stalked by a stork. Gerhard Schneider told how for weeks a large stork followed him and his wife whenever they left their farmhouse. The bird's campaign of intimidation extended to standing on their car waiting for them and tapping on the windows of their house day and night if they stayed in.

SAVIOR CAT

In December 2005, Tommy the cat called 911 when his owner, Gary Rosheisen of Columbus, Ohio, fell from his wheelchair! Nobody knows how the cat managed to hit the right buttons, but when the emergency call went through to the police, there was no one on the phone. When they called the number back and there was no answer, they decided to investigate. Rosheisen had previously tried to teach Tommy to call 911 but hadn't known if the training had worked.

FROG JUICE

A visit to the frog juice stall at the San Juan de Lurigancho marketplace in Lima, Peru, is not for the faint-hearted. Here, skinned frogs are blended to make a juice drink that is popular among some Peruvians, who believe that it cures a range of common illnesses.

CRAZED CROC

Aggravated by a chainsaw's noise, Brutus, a 14½-ft-long (4.4 m) crocodile living at the Corroboree Park Tavern in Australia's Northern Territory, ran 20 ft (6 m) to snatch the tool from the hands of a terrified worker and smashed it beyond repair.

JET HEALED

When a California gunman took aim at Patricia Maupin, her dog Jet, a five-year-old Australian Shepherd mix, instinctively defended his owner and, leaping in front of Maupin, took three bullets meant for her. While Maupin hailed her dog a hero, Jet was making a steady recovery from his injuries.

PEACEFUL CO-EXISTENCE ▷

A tiger zoo near Bangkok, Thailand, promotes interbreed friendships to an unusual degree. Seen here in 2004, a tigress and a piglet in a tiger-print jacket take a stroll together.

MAGPIE DECOY

To protect their eyes from highly aggressive magpies, Australian pedestrians wear sunglasses or put photos of eyes on the back of their heads to fool the birds!

DRUNKEN PELICANS

Four pelicans were rounded up on suspicion of being drunk in the Los Angeles area in June 2006. Three of the California brown pelicans were found wandering dazed in the streets of Laguna Beach after another pelican struck a vehicle's windshield on a nearby coast road. Experts believed the birds had been eating poisonous algae in the ocean.

SNAKE FIND

A Chinese woman from the city of Xi'an returned to her locked sixth-floor apartment after two months away to find a 5-ft (1.5-m) snake in her bed! The snake was caught and released in hills nearby.

KEEPING MUM

A 14½-ft (4.4-m) hammerhead shark caught near Boca Grande, Florida, in May 2006, was found to be pregnant with a record 55 babies!

NAUGHTY POLLY

Polly the parrot stopped a plane from taking off in 2006 when she escaped from a box on her owner's lap and started pecking passengers. As the aircraft prepared for take-off, Polly proceeded to circle passengers' heads and nibble their shoulders. She was recaptured ten minutes later and the flight—from Alderney in the Channel Islands, U.K., to Southampton, England—went ahead.

◁ MOUSE HITCHES RIDE

This lucky mouse caught a ride with an obliging frog to escape floodwaters in the Indian city of Lucknow in June 2006.

White Mischief

Albino animals are rare and extremely eye-catching creatures, whose unusual appearance is caused by a genetic condition. In some cultures, they are considered sacred; in many others, they have appeared in myths and legends. The animals below are a selection of wild and captive albinos from across the globe.

COLLECTIONS

KANGAROO

BLACKBIRD

CHIMPANZEE

ALLIGATOR

HEDGEHOG

SQUIRREL

GORILLA

MOOSE SUSPENDED

Power crews near Fairbanks, Alaska, found a bull moose weighing nearly 1,200 lb (545 kg) suspended from an electrical pole 50 ft (15 m) in the air!

FISH ATTACK

Marcy Poplett of Peoria, Illinois, was injured and knocked off a personal watercraft on the Illinois River after a silver carp leaped out of the water and smacked her in the face!

FLYING DOG

A Saint Bernard dog survived being thrown from a second-floor window of an apartment in the Polish city of Sosnowiec when it landed on a passerby walking in the street below. The 110-lb (50-kg) dog was apparently pushed out of the window by its drunken owner, but escaped with just a few scratches while the man it landed on was more shocked than physically hurt.

CHAMELEON SNAKE

Scientists in Borneo have discovered a species of snake that has the ability to change color. The venomous water snake's chameleon-like behavior was discovered accidentally by researchers from Germany and Chicago when they put it into a dark bucket and saw it change from a reddish-brown color to almost entirely white.

BEAR BARD

The 2006 Lake Tahoe Shakespeare Festival at Sand Harbor, Nevada, proved a big attraction—to local bears. Raiding the deserted food court, one bear helped itself to a feast of salmon, beef steaks, and cherry ice cream. Another appeared during an actual performance, forcing organizers to tell the audience to stay seated until the animal was chased away.

MYSTERY GUEST

Members of the Leroy family of Washington discovered that a stray dog was opening their car door and climbing inside every night to sleep!

DIED AT 176!

Harriet the Galapagos tortoise, claimed by Queensland's Australia Zoo to be the oldest living animal in the world, died of a heart attack in 2006 at the probable age of 176. Harriet, who spent seven years of her early life in England until the country's lack of sunshine sent her into hibernation, was a sprightly 84 when World War I broke out and 139 when Neil Armstrong set foot on the Moon. Also, for more than a century she was thought to be a male tortoise and was known as Harry.

UNWELCOME VISITOR

When Lori Pachelli heard a knock at the door of her Florida home, she looked out to see an 8-ft-long (2.4-m) alligator on her front porch. While a hysterical Mrs Pachelli phoned her husband, the alligator, which was aggressive and had a bloody lip from banging its head against the door, remained there for about an hour before returning to the lake behind the house.

CUNNING CAT

In 2006, a cat in Porto Alegre, Brazil, adopted a small bird that hurt itself when it fell out of its nest. The pair ate meat from the same plate and the cat even used the bird to help catch other birds!

BLACK (BEAR) JACK

A bear wandered into a Nevada casino in 2006! The Montbleu Resort Casino and Spa promotes itself as a "habitat for everything wild" but hadn't reckoned on the 150-lb (68-kg) bear, who was eventually scared off by employees.

CAT ART

An art gallery in Woodstock, Ontario, Canada, raised money for a local animal shelter by selling paintings made by cats. The collection, entitled Paws and Prints, was achieved by putting paint on the cats' paws and letting them run around on canvases.

⚠ HORN OF PLENTY

Lurch, an African Watusi steer has horns that are 7½ ft (2.3 m) across and 38 in (97 cm) around—and still growing! Lurch, who lives with his owner, Janice Wolf, in Arkansas, is something of a freak, as his parents had normal-sized horns. But his popularity is such that he has attracted visitors from as far afield as Sweden, South Africa, and Ecuador.

NOT CHOOSY

Common toads unable to find a female in the breeding season will try to mate with just about anything—including sticks, water lilies, and goldfish!

QUICK THINKING

Malcolm Locke, aged 12, of Orlando, Florida, survived being dragged into the water by an alligator by punching it on the nose and then swimming away.

MIXED DINING

A new restaurant in China encourages human customers to eat at the same table as their pets! Although the menu is primarily for animals, it also offers drinks and snacks for their owners. The Paradise Pet Club in Shanghai disinfects its dishes three times a day.

Contortionists are able to bend and twist their bodies into extraordinary shapes—page 149

Zhang Yingmin employs an unusual tactic in blowing up balloons—page 133

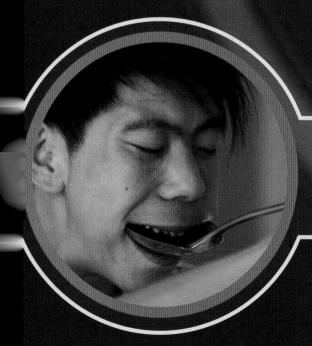

Zhang Dong shows off his skill at inserting a huge spoon into his mouth—page 143

FANTASTIC FEATS

SET IN CONCRETE

In memory of his hero, Harry Houdini, Canadian escape artist Dean Gunnarson freed himself from a locked Plexiglas box filled with two tons of wet cement. He was the first person in the world to attempt such a great escape. Not even Houdini himself had tried it.

The sensational stunt, was timed to take place in Winnipeg at 1.26 p.m. on Halloween 2006 (the exact 80th anniversary of Houdini's death). Gunnarson was bound with several pairs of police handcuffs that were chained and padlocked around his waist and entire body, and tightly around his neck. He was then lowered into the box, the cement was poured in, and the lid of the box was locked tight with six maximum-security padlocks so that he was totally encased in a concrete prison.

To the amazement of the crowd, who could see his every move, Gunnarson escaped from his would-be tomb in 2 minutes 43 seconds. He had to get out before being crushed and suffocated by the sheer weight of the cement. "It felt like being crushed by a boa constrictor," said Gunnarson, who had trained for the death-defying ordeal by wriggling in fast-setting cement. "I could feel it pushing against my ribs and lungs every time I struggled." But he emerged with nothing worse than cement burns.

His inspiration for the stunt came when he escaped while dangling by his toes from a trapeze bar while locked in a straightjacket, 726 ft (221 m) above the Hoover Dam just outside Las Vegas. He learned that some workers had been killed while working on the dam, having been buried alive after falling into wet cement. "I thought to myself, 'What a horrible way to go.'"

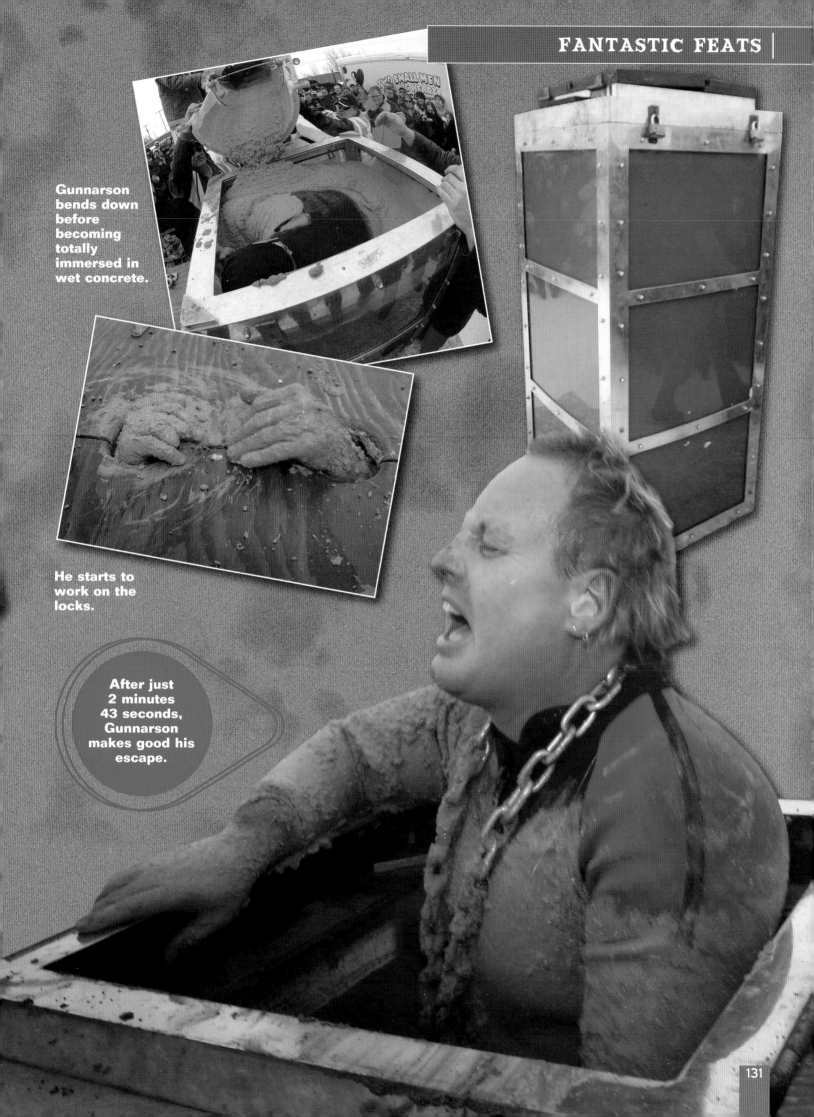

Gunnarson bends down before becoming totally immersed in wet concrete.

He starts to work on the locks.

After just 2 minutes 43 seconds, Gunnarson makes good his escape.

ALCATRAZ SWIM

Fueled by pizza, seven-year-old Braxton Bilbrey of Glendale, Arizona, swam the notoriously difficult 1.4 mi (2 km) from Alcatraz Island to San Francisco in just 47 minutes in 2006.

COMBINE SPEED

In August 2006, 105 combines harvested a quarter section of winter wheat (160 acres/65 ha) near Winkler, Manitoba, Canada, in just 11 minutes 8 seconds.

BIG BUFFET

Diners had an overwhelming choice of food at the Las Vegas Hilton, Nevada, in March 2006 when a buffet was laid out featuring no fewer than 510 different dishes. They ranged from Mongolian chicken and salmon Wellington to crème brûlée and homemade apple pie.

HUGGING SAINT

Mata Amritanandamayi, an Indian humanitarian known as "The Hugging Saint," travels around the world giving hugs—she has given an estimated 26 million hugs during the past 35 years!

SILVER BALL

Stanley Jollymore of Brule Point, Nova Scotia, has spent the last 20 years creating a 77-lb (35-kg) silver ball made from over 139,000 tinfoil cigarette wrappers.

SPOON ENSEMBLE

A street-theater group rounded up 345 spoon players to bash out pub favorite "Knees Up Mother Brown" in Trowbridge, Wiltshire, England, in 2006. The spoons are played by holding two spoons between the fingers of one hand with the bowls facing each other and tapping them against a leg.

⚠ GIANT'S STRENGTH

Eddie Polo, known to all as "Little Giant," drew quite a crowd when he managed to pull this car 100 yd (91 m) along the road in Dover, New Hampshire, in 1937—using only his hair.

BACKWARDS RUNNER

A Brazilian pensioner claimed he owes his health to his unusual fitness regime of running 19 mi (31 km) every day—backwards. Ary Brasil, 69, from Joacaba, has been running since he was 16 but started going backwards only six years ago. "I used to feel a lot of pain in my back and legs," he said, "but I found that by running backwards I felt less out of breath and my muscles got stronger. It's been nine years since I had a cold and I don't even remember the last time I went to the doctor."

GROUCHO GATHERING

The town of Gorham, Maine, achieved an unusual claim to fame in July 2006 when nearly 1,500 people gathered together wearing Groucho Marx disguises! A total of 1,489 residents turned out wearing the familiar glasses, oversized nose, bushy eyebrows, and mustache.

QUICK CARVER

Stephen Clarke of Haverton, Pennsylvania, can carve a face into a pumpkin in less than 25 seconds!

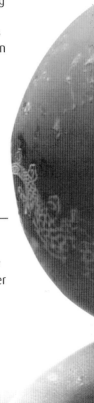

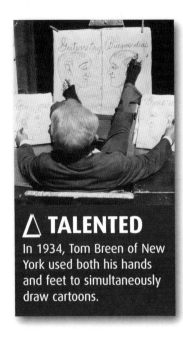

⚠ TALENTED

In 1934, Tom Breen of New York used both his hands and feet to simultaneously draw cartoons.

BARKING BIKERS

At the 2006 Hogs for Dogs charity run at Amherst, New York, Harley-Davidson bikers brought their dogs along for the ride. Some pets sat on the passenger seat, but Beau, Don Wereski's Maltese Yorkshire, rode in a carrier across his chest. "He goes everywhere with me," said Wereski. "He loves the ride."

VAST VERSE

In 2006, a Frenchman produced a poem of epic proportions—nearly 7,600 verses written on a half-mile roll of fabric. Patrick Huet spent a month and a half composing "Pieces of Hope to the Echo of the World" and then a further month copying it on to the material, which was unrolled with the help of a tractor and put on display around a racetrack in southeast France.

HENDRIX TRIBUTE

In May 2006, 1,581 guitarists simultaneously played Jimi Hendrix's "Hey Joe" at the Old Town Square in Wrocław, Poland. The guitarists traveled from Germany, Hungary, the Netherlands, Sweden, and even the U.S.A. to take part.

FAIRWAY TO HEAVEN

Don't tell Tiger Woods, but a Russian man has driven a golf ball over a billion miles! In 2006, cosmonaut Mikhail Tyurin launched the ball into orbit using a gold-plated six iron from a special tee attached to a platform on the International Space Station 220 mi (355 km) above Earth. Scientists say the ball is likely to circle the Earth for up to four years at a speed of five miles per second before falling from orbit and burning up in the atmosphere.

BICYCLE BELLS

Conducted by Jörg Kärger, 500 people played six pieces of music on bicycle bells at the University of Leipzig, Germany, in 2003.

FURMAN'S FEATS

Ashrita Furman, a 52-year-old health-food store manager from New York City, shows no sign of easing up. The man who has climbed Mount Fuji on a pogo stick, somersaulted the entire length of Paul Revere's ride, and ran 7 mi (11 km) in Egypt while balancing a pool cue on his finger didn't stop there. Among other achievements he balanced on a ball at Stonehenge, England, for more than two hours, did 9,628 sit-ups in an hour, and ran 6 mi (10 km) in 1 hour 25 minutes while hula hooping!

EYES AND EARS

Zhang Yingmin from China's Shandong Province, seen here in 2006, has an unusual method of inflating balloons—he blows them up by expelling air from his eyes and ears!

HOOP ENTHUSIAST

Ohio-born mother-of-three Lori Lynn Lomeli is never happier than when surrounded by hula hoops. Introduced to hula hooping at the age of eight, she once made headlines for spinning 82 hoops simultaneously for three complete revolutions in Reno, Nevada.

LITTLE ▷ DRUMMER

Two-year-old American Julian Pavone has already played the drums in front of 30,000 people! According to his father, Bernie Julian, he started playing on a drum kit at just three months. He has even made his own CD.

MILK MACHINE

Joey Chestnut of San José, California, drank a gallon of milk in 41 seconds to qualify for the 2006 Philadelphia Wing Bowl eating contest, and then ate 173 chicken wings to win the competition!

RADIO REV

Jay and Jason Plugge of Sunnyvale, California, have invented a car radio that plays the engine sounds of classic cars and motorbikes, including Ferraris, Corvettes, and Harley-Davidsons from the 1950s, 1960s, and 1970s.

STRETCH SARI

Weavers in India created a silk sari that is 1,585 ft (483 m) long and more than 4 ft (1.2 m) wide. Up to 120 weavers worked 24 hours a day on it for more than 80 days, and the finished article weighed over 125 lb (57 kg).

TEMPORARY PARK

In November 2005, the arts group Rebar transformed a downtown San Francisco parking space into a temporary park. They put coins in the meter and proceeded to position turf, a bench, and a tree to create a green space for two hours. In a previous venture, they spent five days digging a filing cabinet into the New Mexico desert to serve as a library.

INSECT FEAST

To mark Montreal Insectarium's 15th birthday in 2005, the attraction staged an insect-tasting celebration—a six-legged lunch prepared by chef Nicole-Anne Gagnon. The menu included atta ants in a tortilla, roasted crickets served on a cucumber canapé, barbecued locusts, and bruschetta with olive tapenade and bamboo worms.

DOGGIE SURFING

The world's first canine surfing championships took place in California in 2006 at, naturally enough, the Coronado Dog Beach. Riding the waves on custom-made dog surfboards, each surf-loving hound had three chances to impress a panel of professional surfing instructors. The animals were scored on confidence level, length of ride, and overall surfing abilities.

◁ NEWSPAPER MODELS

Zhu Zhonghe from Shanghai, China, at the age of 70, discovered the art of making models created entirely from newspaper. He has made the Eiffel Tower, a Dutch windmill, bridges, boats, and the former residence of the late Chairman Mao Zedong.

SWORD SWALLOWER

Roderick Russell makes a living by inserting blades 24 in (61 cm) long into his esophagus. The average adult esophagus ranges in length from 12 to 15 in (30 to 38 cm), so the Burlington, Vermont, sword swallower, gambles with death every time he performs his routine.

Russell learned the art of sword swallowing in Italy and practiced three times a day for a year before he was ready to perform in front of an audience. The first thing he had to master was the gag reflex. Some swallowers perfect this with an unfurled wire coat hanger or a peacock feather, but Russell used a sword from the outset. He also learned that the esophagus isn't as straight as a sword.

"The stomach is much shallower than it appears," he says, "and it curves to the left. The epiglottis and trachea were surprisingly difficult obstacles for me to push past. I learned to push the epiglottis closed with my hand before learning to control it with the tip of a sword. Then I hold my breath for a split second as the sword glides past the closed epiglottis. Getting past the heart is always a touchy moment. I need to turn the sword a little to the left to get into my stomach."

Russell took up sword swallowing to help audiences realize they could achieve anything they wanted. He describes the art as the Holy Grail of mind over body techniques. So far, the mind is definitely winning, although he does take one precaution. "Before I swallow a sword, I always lick the blade. A dry sword is even more difficult to swallow."

X rays show just how far down Russell has actually swallowed a sword.

ROOFTOP MUSIC

In 2006, three "extreme cellists"—Clare Wallace, Jeremy Dawson and James Rees—set out to play on the roof of every cathedral in England! They visited all 42 Anglican cathedrals in England over 12 days, and were allowed to play on the roofs of 31 of them. Their repertoire included "Up on the Roof" and "Climb Every Mountain."

AIR GUITARIST

After years of mocking air guitarists, Craig Billmeier of Alameda, California, finally realized that they struck a chord with him. And four months and two victories after entering a regional competition, Billmeier (whose stage name is "Hot Lixx Hulahan") was crowned U.S. Air Guitar Champion of 2006. Contestants at air guitar competitions play for 60 seconds while judges mark them on technical ability and stage presence.

△ TWO-HANDED BOWLER

Edward Soloff from Atlantic City, New Jersey, was able to bowl two games in two different bowling lanes simultaneously in 1930. What's more, he averaged an impressive score of 270 points for each of the games.

BAND OF OUTLAWS

A total of 307 children, dressed as legendary British outlaw Robin Hood, gathered at Ravenshead Church of England Primary School in Sherwood Forest, Nottinghamshire, England, in March 2006. The children provided their own outfits, including bows and arrows, and made their green hats in school.

HOGWARTS MODEL

Pat Acton of Gladbrook, Iowa, has created detailed and realistic models of ships, airplanes, space shuttles, and buildings—all from matchsticks. His first project 30 years ago was a country church that took 500 matchsticks and a couple of days to complete. His latest, a model of the Hogwarts School immortalized in J.K. Rowling's *Harry Potter* books, took more than two years and 600,000 matchsticks!

SUPER SMOOTHIE

After 3½ hours of blending, using seven blenders, a store in Kitchener, Ontario, Canada, produced a 25,000-oz (740-l) smoothie in August 2006. The monster drink was sold afterwards in 24-oz cups.

SKETCH SKILL

A group of around 3,000 people collaborated in drawing a giant teapot on a huge Etch A Sketch™ that measured 20 x 35 ft (6 x 11 m) at Boston, Massachusetts, in 2006.

VENDING FUN △

On October 21, 2006, Robert Moore, aged 3, unhappy at his unsuccessful attempts at scooping out a stuffed toy with the machine's plastic crane, decided to go in and get one. He climbed into the stuffed animal vending machine at a small store in Antigo, Wisconsin. Robert was later rescued by the Antigo Fire Department, who broke the lock and passed a screwdriver to Robert, who managed to undo the necessary screws to effect his release!

LENGTHY LECTURE

Botany lecturer Anniah Ramesh of Mysore, India, delivered a talk on "Molecular Logic of Life" in March 2006 that lasted for over 98 hours! He spoke continuously for three days and three nights until aching legs and sleepless nights finally took their toll. He was so tired that he could be seen dozing while writing on the blackboard.

ROLLER RIDERS

Marriage is definitely a roller coaster ride for Don Tuttle and Carol Deeble. The couple from Manchester, Connecticut, were married on their favorite roller coaster, the Comet at Lake George, New York, in 2001, and in 2006 they renewed their vows on it. In all they have ridden nearly 750 roller coasters in 15 countries, and visited Japan in 2005 and South Africa in 2006 to add to their list.

MODEL REBUILT

A detailed plastic model of Australia's Sydney Opera House, which had taken seven years to make but had vanished after appearing at the Washington World Expo in 1974, was painstakingly reassembled in 2006 after being found inside 24 storage crates at a Sydney warehouse. With no drawings or plans for guidance, it took 2,000 hours to rebuild the model, the exercise being described as "like a giant jigsaw."

BALLOON EXPERT

As a boy, Nate Mikulich was fascinated by magic and when, at the age of 13, he met balloon artist Crazy Richard, he became hooked on making animals from balloons. These days, Mikulich of Eastern Michigan is so skilled at the art that he can tie a balloon poodle behind his back in under eight seconds.

WEIGHTY BALLS

In Germany in 2006, Milan Roskopf from Slovakia juggled three shot balls weighing a hefty 22 lb (10 kg) each for 15.8 seconds. He started to juggle balls at the age of nine, moving from small balls to cricket balls, to 2.2 lb (1 kg) balls cast in bronze.

BiG BAND BALL

This giant rubber-band ball was made from more than 175,000 rubber bands in November 2006. Seen here being rolled toward a set of scales, it weighed in at an incredible 4,594 lb (2,084 kg). It was created by Steve Milton from Eugene, Oregon, who spent a few minutes a day, for just over a year, adding bands to his ball. The result reaches 5½ ft (1.7 m) in height, and has a diameter of 19 ft (5.8 m).

Ripley's Believe It or Not!®

OUTSIZE PAINTING

Working for two and a half years and using 100 tons of paint, artist David Aberg produced a painting that measured a staggering 86,000 sq ft (7,990 sq m). The picture, titled "Mother Earth," is a symbol for peace and is so big it had to be created inside an aircraft hangar in Angelholm, southern Sweden.

TRICKY TEXTER

Tell Ben Cook he's all thumbs and he'll probably take it as a compliment. For the 18-year-old from Orem, Utah, proved himself an expert texter in July 2006, by sending a 160-character message in just over 42 seconds at a contest in Denver, Colorado.

BALLOON FEAT

John Cassidy of Philadelphia, Pennsylvania, inflated and tied more than 700 balloons in an hour at New York City in May 2006. Cassidy has also completed 654 balloon sculptures in an hour.

ATV PARADE

Members of Harlan County, Kentucky, ATV club paraded over 1,100 all-terrain vehicles one Saturday in 2006. The parade began in Verda and ended 2 mi (3.2 km) away in Evarts.

TALL STORY

Canadian stilt walker Doug Hunt has taken 29 independent steps on a pair of stilts 50 ft 9 in (15.5 m) tall and weighing a combined 137 lb (62 kg).

PILLOW FIGHT

Nearly 1,000 people lured by Internet postings and word-of-mouth took part in a half-hour outdoor pillow fight in San Francisco on Valentine's Day 2006. Participants arrived with pillows concealed in shopping bags, backsacks, and the like, and within minutes the area around the city's Ferry Building was covered in white down.

DUAL TALENT

Drew Tretick, a graduate of the prestigious Juilliard School of Music in New York City, who now lives in southern California, plays beautiful tunes on the violin—while riding a unicycle!

BUMPER BEACH TOWEL

A gigantic terry-cloth beach towel was unveiled at Hermosa Beach, California, in June 2006. It measured 131 x 78 ft (40 x 24 m) and weighed nearly 1,000 lb (454 kg).

QUICK CLEANER

If you want your windows cleaned quickly, ask Terry Burrows. For at Birmingham, England, in 2005, Burrows cleaned three windows, each measuring 45 in (114 cm) square, and wiped the sill—all in under 10 seconds!

GUITAR SOLO

Apart from a short break every eight hours, Chicago musician Jef Sarver played the guitar uninterrupted for 48 hours in 2006. Sarver, who prepared for the challenge by doing push-ups and sit-ups, played a set of more than 600 songs.

FOIL ART

Pete Schwickrath from Piscataway, New Jersey, makes sculptures from household tin foil, which he then paints. Here, a newly transformed werewolf threatens a young maiden.

SNAKE KISSER

Malaysian snake charmer Shahimi Abdul Hamid kissed a wild, venomous king cobra 51 times in three minutes outside Kuala Lumpur in March 2006. He used agility, skill, and quick reflexes to dodge bites from the 15-ft (4.6-m) snake with only his bare hands to protect him. He was also an hour's drive from the nearest hospital—a daunting prospect considering that a person can be killed with just one drop of cobra venom, and each bite can produce up to 12 drops of poison.

STRAW CHAIN

Brad Mottashed, Evgueni Venkov, and 18 fellow students of Waterloo University, Ontario, Canada, made a straw chain 28,158 ft (8,580 m) long in April 2006 using 50,000 drinking straws.

SNOWBALL FIGHT

More than 3,700 people took part in a mass snowball fight at Houghton, Michigan, in February 2006!

MUTTON BUSTIN'

At just eight years old, Ryan Murphy is already a retired champion. For Ryan's chosen sport is riding sheep rodeo-style, or "mutton bustin'" as it is popularly known. At the 2006 Truckee Rodeo at Sierra, Nevada, Ryan won the title for the second successive year but must now retire because he will soon exceed the riding weight limit of 60 lb (27 kg). The secret of his success is to sit on the sheep backwards so as to get a better grip. Whereas other riders quickly bit the dust, Ryan's individual style helped him to stay on for an unbeatable 22 seconds.

KICK LINE

Over 700 people put their best foot skyward at the Algonquin Arts Plaza parking lot, Manasquan, New Jersey, in August 2006 to form a kick line. As well as dance students, the long line included men in sneakers, women in sandals, and teenage boys in surfer shorts and flip-flops.

FOOTPRINT TRAIL

National Geographic Kids magazine spent 1½ days taping together 10,932 paper footprints that zigzagged 1.8 mi (2.9 km) heel-to-toe along the walls and hallways of its headquarters in Washington, D.C. The footprints had been submitted by children from as far away as Australia, Japan, and Mongolia. One was from a child with six toes!

EYELID FEAT

In 2005, Chinese Yang Guanghe fitted hooks to his eyelids and proceeded to pull a car along a street!

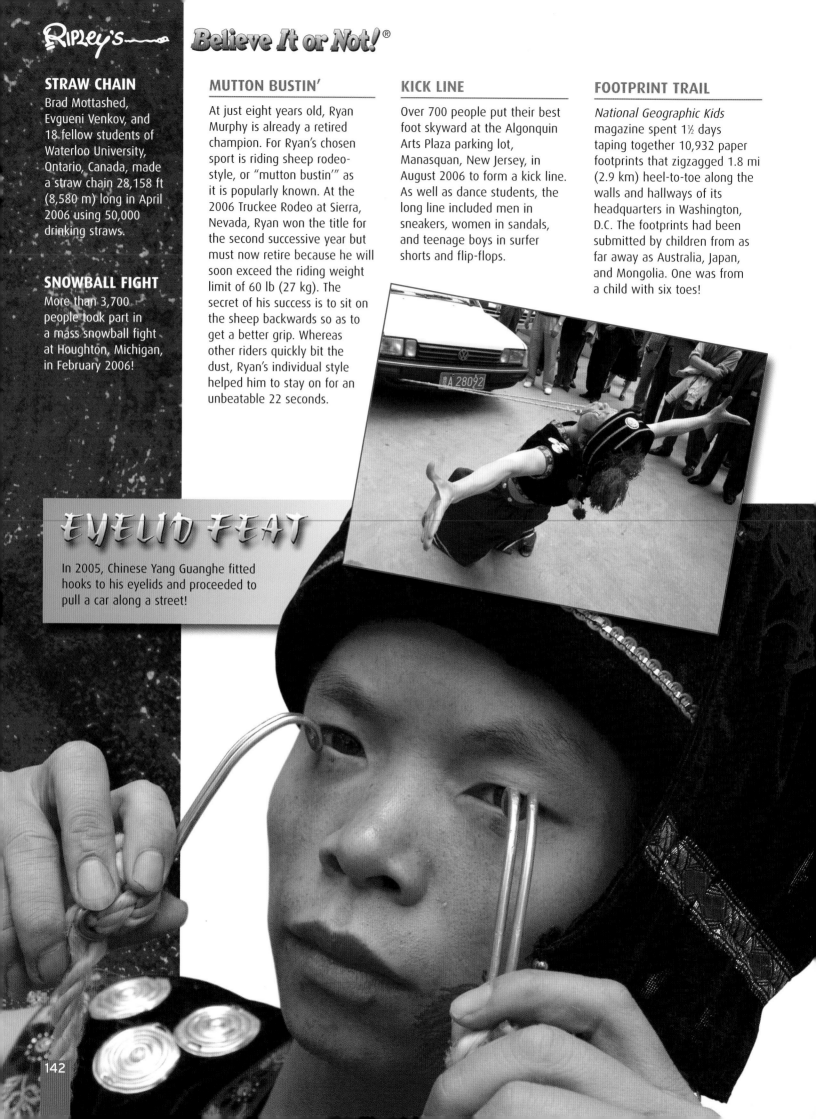

HUMAN FLAG

In May 2006, over 18,000 people gathered in Lisbon's soccer stadium to create a human depiction of the Portuguese national flag.

KAZOO PARADE

In 2006, more than 500 people turned out on the streets of Nazareth, New Jersey, to celebrate the Fourth of July by playing the kazoo.

OLD PRICES

Michael "Mickey" Di Fater of Greenburgh, New York, celebrated his 75th year selling hot dogs by rolling back his prices to 10 cents for a hot dog and a nickel for a soda!

MELON GROWER

Ivan Bright of Hope, Arkansas, devoted the last 30 years of his life to raising huge watermelons, notably a 268-lb (122-kg) Carolina Cross. He died at the age of 92 on August 12, 2006—the 30th anniversary of the Hope Watermelon Festival.

WATER-SKI CHALLENGE

Dirk Gion went water-skiing behind a huge German cruise liner in 2006 to disprove a claim made on TV that the feat was impossible. The 40-year-old stayed upright for more than five minutes.

PENGUIN AIRLIFT

After more than 100 penguins were left stranded on beaches in Rio de Janeiro, Brazil, in 2006, the Brazilian air force and navy transported them safely back to Antarctica. Penguins arrive from the Antarctic on ice floes that melt near Brazil's coast every winter and the flightless birds then find themselves washed up on Rio's beaches. Usually they are sent to local zoos but this time the military intervened.

A REAL MOUTHFUL

In 2006, the city of Nanjing, in eastern China, played host to a TV show that featured people with highly unusual skills. Zhang Dong, shown here inserting a huge spoon into his mouth, was one of the show's participants.

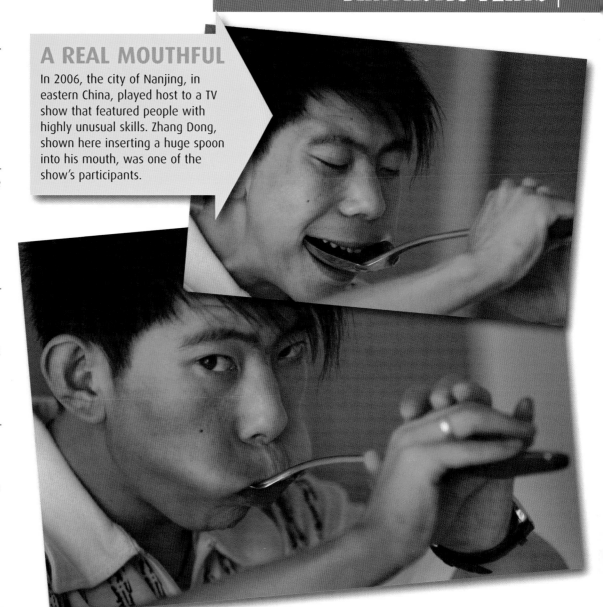

TRUCK DRINK

Rather than drink Milo (a milk beverage with chocolate) from a glass, 620 staff and students at the National University of Singapore decided to drink it from the back of a truck! They drank 92 gal (350 l) of Milo from the truck in 30 minutes.

BABY MARATHON

The city of Cali in Colombia hosted a crawling marathon for babies in 2006—and more than 1,100 babies took part. Infants aged between 8 and 18 months were eligible and they crawled along a 16-ft (5-m) covered track. The winner's prize was a bag full of baby goodies.

ELVIS PARADE

In a variety of sequined jumpsuits, bright pink jackets, and blue suede shoes, 94 sideburned, hip-swivelling Elvises took to the stage at Collingwood, Ontario, Canada, in July 2006 to perform the King's classic hit "All Shook Up."

MASSIVE MURAL

In 2006, Boeing completed a mural on its factory building in Everett, Washington, that comprises more than 100,000 sq ft (9,290 sq m) of pressure-sensitive graphic film. It consists of some 475 sheets, each 60 x 4 ft (18 x 1.2 m) and took over five months to install.

BOWLING MISSION

Larry Woydziak from Lawrence, Kansas, made it his mission to bowl in every county in Kansas that had a bowling alley. He bowled his 79th and final game in the town of Sterling.

BRA CHAIN

Hundreds of volunteers linked together more than 114,700 bras around Paphos harbor in west Cyprus in April 2006 to form a 70-mi (113-km) long chain to raise breast-cancer awareness. Bras were flown to Cyprus from all over the world, including Canada, the U.S.A., Thailand, Brazil, Russia, Iran, and all 25 European Union member states.

BOARD SURFER

A French veterinary surgeon became the first person to cross the shark-infested Indian Ocean on a sailboard.

Raphaela Le Gouvello of Brittany, France, landed on the island of Réunion, off the eastern coast of Africa, in June 2006, having completed a solo 3,900-mi (6,300-km) voyage from Exmouth in Western Australia. Throughout much of the 60-day journey she battled seasickness, strong winds, and rough seas. She made the epic crossing on a simple board—26 ft (8 m) long and 4 ft (1.2 m) wide—named Mahi Mahi. Her board capsized twice, and on one occasion cost her essential supplies of fresh water. Mme Le Gouvello said that although the heavy winds had been a problem, the hardest times were when there was no wind at all. "I couldn't make any progress," she said. "I waited below deck, being tossed around in all directions. It wasn't very comfortable."

When not steering on her eight-hour shifts, she kept herself occupied by listening to music and reading books. She did not fish in case she attracted sharks. Before the trip, she overcame her fear of sharks by diving with them in an aquarium in France.

The tiny cabin—just 2 ft 6 in (76 cm) high—housed a bed, spare sails, food, and communication equipment.

The 46-year-old is no stranger to solo sailboard voyages. She was the first woman to cross the Atlantic and the Mediterranean on a sailboard, and in 2003 she became the first person to cross the Pacific by board.

Raphaela tests her board off Fremantle in Western Australia before setting off on her epic voyage.

SIMULTANEOUS CARTWHEELS

Almost 1,000 people, wearing an array of leotards, T-shirts, and shorts, converged on the Minnesota State Capitol lawn at St. Paul in 2006 to perform an amazing display of simultaneous cartwheels.

SPEEDY HAIRDRESSER

Even at the age of 71, Trevor Mitchell can give a decent haircut in less than a minute. To prove it, in August 2006 he clipped exactly 1 in (2.5 cm) of hair from all over the head of former England soccer manager Kevin Keegan in just 59 seconds.

JONES GATHERING

A small town in North Wales united 1,224 people with the same surname in November 2006. Blaenau Ffestiniog out-performed Sweden, which had previously held an assembly of 583 Norbergs, by inviting anyone around the world with the surname Jones to a 1,600-seater venue. The town was chosen for the gathering because the area boasts the highest concentration of Joneses in Britain.

POLISHED ▷ PICTURES

Mary Scott from Horn Lake, Mississippi, is an artist with a difference, for she paints using bottles of nail polish. Mary has a collection of more than 1,000 colors, and uses as many as 30 bottles of polish to create one painting. She paints with the small brushes that come with the bottles, and has to work rapidly, because the polish dries very quickly.

SKYDIVING DOG

Wearing a specially made harness and a diaper—in case of mid-air accidents—Mindy, a three-year-old Jack Russell terrier, went skydiving in 2006 with the Jonoke Skydive Team in Alberta, Canada. Diving under a canopy strapped to a tandem skydiving master, Mindy made a successful free-fall of 9,000 ft (2,743 m) in 40 seconds. Her owner, Al Christou, said: "She kept looking at us on the way down. When she landed the first time, she was spinning around in circles."

REVERSE SPELLER

Eight-year-old Raghav Srivathsav from Hyderabad, India, has made a name for himself by spelling words backwards. He first started doing this aged three and can now spell 50 words in reverse in under three minutes, and can reverse spell any word or line given to him in just a few seconds.

WATERY CONFERENCE

Wearing full diving gear, a group of 21 Austrian journalists swam 16 ft (5 m) below the surface of the Traun Lake to stage an underwater press conference in June 2006! An underwater flipchart was set up for the presentation and the reporters were given special waterproof paper and pens to enable them to take notes.

NUMERICAL GENIUS

If you give Nishant Kasibhatia a number, he's unlikely to forget it—for 10 years! The 29-year-old Indian man has a phenomenal memory for numbers, having started at the age of 17 by memorizing 100-digit numbers before graduating to 1,000 digits. He can now recite 1,000-digit numbers in reverse order and in 2005 he memorized 200 binary numbers in just over three minutes and recalled them in five minutes without a single mistake.

PIZZA ORDER

Papa John's delivered an order of 13,500 pizzas to San Diego's NASSCO Shipyard on June 8, 2006. To meet the 11 a.m. delivery time, Papa John's used the resources of 15 San Diego restaurants, beginning at 6 a.m., with each making around 56 pizzas per minute throughout the morning—that's nearly one pizza per second! The 2,725 lb (1,236 kg) of cheese needed was the weight of an average family car.

MILK SQUIRTER

An Indian teenager has become a national celebrity for his ability to suck milk up through his nose and squirt it out of his eyes for distances of up to 12 ft (3.7 m). Praveen Kumar Sehrawat, a 16-year-old wrestler from the Delhi region, can also eat 170 chillies in just over five minutes and hammer a nail into his nose without suffering discomfort.

FAST FEATS

David Gonzales performed an astonishing 21 different strongman acts in a single afternoon in Fort Meyers, Florida, in November 2006. Ten of these were completed in less than a minute, including tearing a 1,000-page telephone book in half, bending a steel bar 4 in (10 cm) thick over his head, and standing on his head while holding himself steady with hands resting on glass.

◁ COIN-COVERED CAR

In February 2006, Scott Hampton from Davenport, Iowa, finished covering his Ford car, inside and out, with 30,500 penny coins. Every single penny was glued on, head side up, and covered with two coats of varnish. The car is still fully operable, and catches the sun beautifully as Scott drives around town.

HAIR COLORING

In a period of less than 24 hours in August 2006, hair stylist Amjad Habib of New Delhi, India, colored the hair of 113 women. The marathon exercise included shampooing, coloring, washing, and blow-drying.

TEXAN FRUITCAKE

Gladys Farek, a baker from Cistern, Texas, made a specialty fruitcake in the shape of her home state that measured 5 x 6 ft (1.5 x 1.8 m) and weighed 150 lb (68 kg).

PICTURE MOSAIC

Over eight months, more than 29,000 people of all ages snapped with their digital cameras and cell phones the funniest close-up pictures of themselves and their friends and sent them to a website. The result was unveiled in Milan, Italy, in June 2006—a huge photo collage of 20,400 pictures covering an area of 1,518 sq ft (141 sq m).

EGG HUNT

Over 10,000 children and adults searched for more than 300,000 Easter eggs, weighing a total of more than 12,000 lb (5,443 kg), that were hidden around Stone Mountain Park, Georgia, in April 2006.

CHICKEN DANCE

In an event organized by Texas-based Konrad Bouffard, more than 200,000 people took part in a nationwide chicken dance on July 4, 2006, at 57 minor-league baseball stadiums around the U.S.A.

BIRTHDAY CAKE

To celebrate the 230th birthday of the U.S.A., caterers in Fayetteville, Arkansas, baked a 230-layer cake for the Fourth of July, 2006. The cake, which stood 2 ft (60 cm) high and weighed more than 100 lb (45 kg), took 21 hours to bake.

BASKETBALL STAR

Riley McLincha of Clio, Michigan, is a "drubbler"—he can juggle and dribble three basketballs at the same time!

PENNY PYRAMID

This pyramid is made from 298,318 U.S. pennies and weighs a hefty 1,969 lb (893 kg). Its creator, Marcelo Bezos from Miramar, Florida, has been building the pyramid since 1971, and he plans to continue adding to it until he reaches one million pennies. Each penny is placed individually, and Marcelo uses no adhesives of any kind.

Twists & Turns

Often training from as young as two years old, contortionists bend and twist their bodies into dramatic and unnatural-looking shapes, and, unsurprisingly, spend many years perfecting the art. Medical examinations of contortionists' spines have revealed that it is probably both genes and intensive training that allow them to get into such extreme shapes.

RIPLEY's Believe It or Not!®
SURF'S UP!

Brazilian surfing legend Rico de Souza rode a surfboard that measured an amazing 26 ft 5 in (8.05 m) in length at Macumba beach in Rio de Janeiro, Brazil, in November 2006. It had taken two months to develop a board strong enough to withstand the waves, and the result needed five people to lift it. De Souza managed to paddle the huge board into the sea and to stand up on it, alone, on the crest of a wave, for 11 seconds.

JOGGLERS DUEL

The 2006 Boston Marathon provided a unique spectacle: the first time two jogglers—runners who juggle—had competed head-to-head in a marathon. The combatants were Zach Warren, from West Virginia, an expert juggler who can juggle blindfold and while riding a unicycle, and Michael Kapral, who once ran the marathon in his home city of Toronto, Canada, in 2 hours 49 minutes— while pushing his baby daughter Annika in a stroller. In Boston Kapral juggled three bean-filled balls and Warren juggled three beanbags, never taking more than two steps without juggling. Warren (911th overall) emerged the winner of their personal duel in a time of just under three hours, with Kapral 8 minutes behind in 1,761st place.

GRANDAD'S GRUMBLES

An unlikely Internet hero emerged in 2006—a 79-year-old British grandfather, Peter Oakley. Peter hit the top of the most subscribed list on a popular free video sharing website with his ramblings and grumbles about the modern world. Equipped with headphones and a mike, he posted a series of videocasts, attracting some 30,000 subscribers. He also received more than 4,500 e-mails from fans in Japan, U.S.A., Australia, Germany, and Ireland.

CLOG DANCE

Nearly 500 teenagers from 26 countries donned oversized wooden clogs to perform a modern ballet version of a traditional Dutch clog dance in The Hague in July 2006. The dancers learned the steps in their own countries, which included Canada, Jamaica, Israel, and Finland, before traveling to the Netherlands for the performance.

WORD PERFECT

Mahaveer Jain of Lucknow, India, has memorized the entire *Oxford Advanced Learner's Dictionary*, which includes 80,000 entries in all!

GIANT CROQUETTE

Cooks in Assabu, Japan, made a croquette nearly 7 ft (2.1 m) in diameter. It contained 397 lb (180 kg) of potatoes mixed with meat and onions and, at 705 lb (320 kg), was so heavy that a crane had to lower it into a vat containing 67 gal (252 l) of salad oil. The giant croquette was then cut into 1,300 pieces for visitors to taste.

HAPPY SHOPPER

In 2005, Edd China from Maidenhead, Berkshire, England, built a motorized shopping cart that can hit speeds of 60 mph (97 km/h). China, who has previously built a motorized sofa, shed, and four-poster bed, spent six months designing the cart, which is over 11 ft (3.3 m) tall, nearly 10 ft (3 m) long and 6 ft (2 m) wide. It is powered by a 600cc motorbike engine hidden in a huge shopping bag, while the driver sits in an oversized child seat.

PRIZE PEACH

Paul Friday of Coloma, Michigan, has grown a peach that weighs an incredible 30½ oz (864 g).

LIGHT DISPLAY

October 2005 saw 24,581 jack-o-lanterns lit up on Boston Common, Massachusetts, in a mass gathering of more than 45,000 people.

EXTREME CROQUET

Bob Warseck of West Hartford, Connecticut, enjoys a game of croquet—but not on a conventional lawn. For Warseck is a pioneer of the sport of extreme croquet, which is played through woods, over rocks, up and down hills, and across streams. He and his fellow players have had to design special heavy-duty mallets to cope with the rough terrain.

PAPER FOLDERS

In 2006, a total of 545 nimble-fingered staff and students from the National University of Singapore folded 9,300 origami paper cranes in just one hour.

PREGNANT ROBOT

At Kaiser Permanente Hospital in Vallejo, California, doctors teach students by using a full-size "pregnant" robot patient, Noelle, to simulate giving birth!

CORNY PROPOSAL

When Brian Rueckl proposed to Stacy Martin in the summer of 2006, he did it in style—in the form of a message measuring 4,000 sq ft (372 sq m) tilled in his boss's cornfield near Luxemburg, Wisconsin. The message read "Stacy will you marry me?" and included two intersecting hearts. The unusual proposal required a year of planning and 40 hours of work. Naturally, Stacy accepted.

FISH FEAST

An Irish pub in Boston, Massachusetts, served a portion of fish and chips weighing a colossal 77 lb (35 kg)—34 lb (15 kg) for the cod fillet and 43 lb (20 kg) for the fries.

LONG LUNCH

For one weekend a year husband-and-wife chefs Doug and Helen Turpin find themselves preparing a larger Sunday lunch than usual. They are responsible for "The Long Lunch," an annual barbecue at Warkworth, Ontario, Canada, that stretches on tables 500 ft (152 m) down the village's main street and draws as many as 1,000 people from as far afield as Europe. The Long Lunch is based on a similar event offered by its twin town of Warkworth, New Zealand.

BALLOON HATS

At Hillsboro, Oregon, in 2006, 20 volunteers used air pumps to blow up 7,000 balloons—so that they could be used as hats! Over 1,800 people then gathered for a group photo in the Civic Center Plaza, wearing the inflatable headgear.

NINE-HOUR RAP

In 2006, rapper Supernatural performed a freestyle rap in San Bernardino, California, that went on for an incredible 9 hours 10 minutes! Afterwards, he said that the hardest parts were keeping his breath and pacing himself.

A SKIP AND A JUMP

Kyle Nolte from Fort Smith, Arkansas, is a pogo stick fanatic. Not only can he jump rope while hopping up and down on his pogo stick, but he can also play baseball and hula hoop while pogoing.

PANCAKE FLIP

Nobody tosses a pancake quite like Dean Gould of Felixstowe, Suffolk, England. For Gould, renowned for his dexterity at flipping beer mats, can also toss a pancake 424 times in two minutes. He practiced his new skill with a plate and a Whoopee cushion!

HOOP HEROINE

Betty Shurin of Aspen, Colorado, ran a 6-mi (10-km) race at Boulder in 2005 in 1 hour 43 minutes 11 seconds—while hula hooping. In order to make sure the hoop was never accidentally knocked down, Shurin, who has been hula hooping since 1998, surrounded herself with a "bubble" of friends throughout the race. "I communicated with the bubble and it communicated with me," said Shurin. "For every water station, they would circle around me and hold hands. I had about three inches of mistake room."

BRUSH OFF

As part of a special challenge, at exactly 1.45 p.m. on August 7, 2006, some 32,000 people—both young and old—across New Zealand brushed their teeth simultaneously.

TEAM EFFORT

Thirty students from the Ishii Higashi Elementary School in Japan ran a 31-legged race over 164 ft (50 m) in a time of 8.8 seconds in October 2005.

CAR CRUSH

Twenty-one Malaysian students, all of whom were over the age of 18, somehow managed to cram themselves into a Mini Cooper in June 2006. And what's more they had to do it twice after the TV crew sent to cover the event turned up late!

ROCKET MAN

Thousands of people flocked to the 2006 U.K. Fireworks Championships in Plymouth, Devon, to see 55,000 rockets launched simultaneously. The idea was the brainchild of Roy Lowry who, by using 15 specially constructed frames that were laced with a pyrotechnic fuse and ignited electrically, managed to launch all the rockets in the space of five seconds.

CHOCOLATE ▷ SCULPTURE

The Portuguese village of Obidos, lying 50 mi (80 km) north of the capital Lisbon, fulfilled a chocoholic's dream in November 2006 when it played host to the Chocolate Festival. The festival included an exhibition of chocolate sculpture, which featured this chocolate car and chocolate Marilyn Monroe.

BALLOON MURAL

A mural of the Chicago skyline, 58 x 86 ft (18 x 26 m), made from 70,000 balloons was once displayed in Rosemont, Illinois.

SKIMMING CHAMPION

Dougie Isaacs of Scotland was crowned World Stone Skimming Champion in 2005 at a disused quarry in Argyll. Each of the 220 competitors was allowed five skims using special slate stones. The stone had to bounce on the water surface at least three times and was then judged on the distance it traveled before sinking. Isaacs hit the flooded quarry's back wall, recording a distance of 207 ft (63 m).

CAR HURDLER

This amazing montage of images shows Jeff Clay of Rossville, Georgia, performing the astonishing feat of hurdling lengthways over a car. Clay, who hurdles in the correct style of track athletes, also hurdles cars widthways, and once jumped 101 different cars that were lined up inside a track stadium in 38 minutes flat.

RIVER BATTLE

Snowmobiles are primarily designed for traveling on land in the depths of winter but in 2006, Greg Nielsen covered over 59 mi (95 km) on one—on water in summer. Tackling the Wapiti River, Alberta, Canada, he faced a constant battle to keep water out of the machine. He said: "I just talked nicely to the sled the whole way and hoped the engine held together."

BARE DEVIL

A Nepali high-altitude guide posed on the summit of Mount Everest in 2006—in the nude! After reaching the top of the world's highest mountain, Lakpa Tharke took off his clothes on the icy peak where the temperature was −40°F (−40°C). Lapka, who climbed the mountain as part of a 14-member expedition led by American Luis Benitez, stayed in the buff for three minutes so that his companions could photograph him.

GAS SAVER

A team of engineering students from the University of British Columbia built a vehicle so efficient it could travel from Vancouver to Halifax—the entire breadth of Canada—on just a gallon of gasoline. In tests, it achieved an amazing 3,145 mi (5,060 km) to the U.S. gallon, the only possible drawback being that the futuristic, single-occupancy vehicle requires the driver to lie down while navigating it.

SCROLL DOWN

Jack Kerouac wrote the classic novel *On The Road* in 20 days, typing it onto a single 119-ft (36-m) scroll!

STILT DANCERS

Thirty-four members of the Lieder Youth Theatre Company line-danced on stilts for 6 minutes 15 seconds at Goulburn, New South Wales, Australia, in January 2006.

GENETIC MUSIC

In 2003, composer Richard Krull and researchers Aurora Sanchez Sousa and Fernando Baquero of Ramon y Cajal Hospital in Madrid, Spain, turned DNA sequences into music and recorded a CD.

BURGER QUEST

Retired teacher Bill Bunyan of Dodge City, Kansas, set off in June 2000 with the intention of eating a hamburger in all 105 counties in the state. He completed his journey in Sterling in August 2003 on his 65th birthday in the presence of friends who had been sent hamburger-shaped invitations by his wife Susan.

LETTER WRITER

Whenever he has something to say, Jacob Sahayam of Trivandrum, India, writes a letter to a newspaper. In 2005, he had no fewer than 523 letters published by the editors of various newspapers and magazines, easily beating his previous year's total of 340.

Bottled Cards

Vancouver master magician Jamie Grant has told nobody how he managed to insert an unopened pack of playing cards into this glass bottle.

BRIGHT IDEA

An artist who once tried to leave a tap running for 12 months to highlight water wastage and pushed a monkey nut across London with his nose to highlight student debt came up with a new project in 2006—to leave 100 lightbulbs on for a year. Mark McGowan arranged for the lights—at different locations across London and southeast England—to be left on until August 2007 in the hope of making people aware of the waste of electricity.

HOCKEY TAPE

In June 2006, 12-year-old Ryan Funk of Langley, British Columbia, Canada, assembled a ball out of ice hockey tape that weighed an incredible 1,862 lb (845 kg). The tape had been donated by 19 ice rinks across Canada.

SKATE CHAIN

Some 280 Singaporeans strapped on their wheels, clutched the waist of the person in front, and formed an in-line skating chain that snaked through the streets of Singapore City in August 2006.

QUICK SHAVE

In April 2006, a team of five hairdressers shaved 662 heads in just four hours at Sudbury, Ontario, Canada.

BIG BOWL

In 2004, Australian chefs cooked a 7.5-ton bowl of risotto—a rice dish—that was so big it took paddles the size of oars to stir it!

BUSY BUBBLE

Canadian bubble artist Fan Yang linked 15 pairs of people in a "bubble cage" at the Discovery Science Center in Santa Ana, California, in April 2006. The following month he encapsulated 22 people inside a single soap bubble in Madrid, Spain.

THREE-LEGGED RACE

Ben Scott and Jo Gittens from the Isle of Man competed in the London Marathon three-legged and dressed as fairies! Their legs tied together with a scarf, they got round in an impressive 5 hours 45 minutes.

DRUM BEAT

Col Hatchman, drummer with Sydney, Australia, rock band Dirty Skanks, drums so loudly it is the equivalent of listening to a jet plane taking off 100 ft (30 m) away! In 2006, he recorded a massive 137 decibels, compared to the 85 decibels of busy city center traffic.

TUNNEL VISION

Germany's Christian Adams specializes in cycling backwards while playing the violin. Adams, who has been playing the instrument since 1970, once cycled over 37 mi (60 km) backwards through a Swiss motorway tunnel while playing Bach on his violin.

150-SLICE PIZZA

Mama Lena's Pizza House in McKees Rocks, Pennsylvania, produces a commercially available 53½-in (136-cm) pizza that offers 150 slices, for $99.99. It contains 20 lb (9 kg) of dough, 15 lb (6.8 kg) of cheese, and 1 gal (4 l) of sauce.

CREAM DRESS

Ukrainian baker Valentyn Shtefano created an edible wedding dress for his bride. Made from 1,500 cream puffs, the dress weighed 20 lb (9 kg) and took him two months to complete.

IN DEPTH
THE GREAT ESCAPE

World-renowned escape artist David Straitjacket, 29, from Manchester, England, can release himself from straitjackets, handcuffs, and ropes within minutes. Dubbed the "Modern Houdini," he claims the old master had it easy!

How did you discover your talent for escaping?

❝When I was about seven, me and my cousins played a game tying each other to chairs. I was by far the best at getting free!❞

When did you decide to pursue it?

❝When I was 13 I was a Sea Cadet and we spent a week with the older boys who were going into the Navy. Two 18-year-olds were bullying us, making us wash their dishes! I refused, so they tied me to the sink and left me there. Two minutes later I caught up with them and handed them the rope. They left me alone after that... that was probably when I thought: 'I am going to do this for a job!'❞

When did you get your first straitjacket?

❝About 10 years ago. I was a poor street performer and bought it cheap. It tore in half the first time I used it. I spent the next week rebuilding it to make it strong enough for me.❞

Is your body "different" from everyone else's?

❝I have very nimble fingers which are good for picking locks, but I'm not double-jointed and can't dislocate my joints.❞

What is the most dangerous escape you have attempted?

❝I was in China on a huge lake. It was murky and deep. The Chinese police took me out on a boat tied up with three pairs of handcuffs and about 10 kg of chain with two padlocks. I jumped off, hit the bottom about four meters down, and couldn't see more than six inches. I had no safety divers. It was touch and go.❞

So do you have to practice?

❝Yes! I have a strong working knowledge of locks and cuffs. I fiddle with handcuffs while I'm sitting watching the TV. On top of that, you have to have a natural talent—and a few personal trade secrets!❞

Do you do any mental training—and is it true you don't like enclosed spaces?

❝I'm actually really quite claustrophobic! I train myself to relax. If you panic, you fail. Underwater, you've got three minutes to escape, but if you panic, you run out of oxygen in just one minute.❞

How do you cope with injuries?

❝I carry on. I did a televised escape called 'Barbed Wire' five days after I'd had surgery on my shoulder. I was bruised all over my chest and arm—the make-up department had a field day. I had barbed wire round my neck, attached to a chain between my legs, which led to more barbed wire round my wrists. I was padlocked, handcuffed, and hung upside down by my feet.❞

Are you "the modern Houdini?"

❝I understand people say that as a compliment—but I'm just me. He used to do the straitjacket escape in about 80 or 90 minutes—he'd disappear behind a curtain for that long while the orchestra played, then appear again. If I'm still going at 90 seconds, people get bored! These days we have much shorter attention spans... and better locks.❞

What will you try next?

❝I'm preparing for some big high-risk stunts. One involves the Burj al-Arab building in Dubai, and me training in free-fall parachuting, to give you a clue!❞

HONEY TRAP

Denzil St. Clair of Spencer, Ohio, allowed himself to be covered from head to toe in more than half a million honey bees in June 2006. He wore a mask that covered his nose and mouth, goggles to protect his eyes, and stuck cotton in his ears, but he was still stung up to 30 times. He said afterwards: "It was like being blind, covered with wet towels, and very hot."

YOUNG UNICYCLIST

Whereas other youngsters are into skateboards, 15-year-old Jonny Peacock of Shalimar, Florida, is a budding extreme unicyclist. He can walk on his wheel and twist it 360 degrees, jump off picnic tables on a unicycle, and zigzag between wooden posts. He owns five different unicycles, including one called the "giraffe" with an elongated seat and another called the "impossible wheel" that has no seat at all.

△ EYE BLOWER

In 2005, Yu Hongqua from China blew out candles with his eyes using a specially crafted pair of glasses with air tubes attached.

HUGE UMBRELLA

In October 2005, Sun City Umbrella Industries of Jin Jiang city, China, made an umbrella that was 31½ ft (9.6 m) tall and over 53 ft (16 m) in diameter.

BODY PAINTING

At Sherman, New York, in July 2006, body artists Scott Fray and Madelyn Greco of Reidsville, North Carolina, sponged 337 people in head-to-toe non-toxic washable paint. The volunteers then laid down in a colorful pattern to be photographed from a passing helicopter.

APPLE PICKER

George Adrian of Indianapolis, Indiana, once picked 30,000 apples in one eight-hour day—that's about 1,000 lb (454 kg) every hour!

NOODLE TREE

Workers at a hotel in Bangkok, Thailand, spent 16 hours creating a Christmas tree 17 ft 4 in (5.3 m) tall made entirely from noodles and decorated with colored sugar.

LIZARD BOY

Mukesh Thakore, a 25-year-old Indian man, has eaten more than 25,000 lizards over the past 20 years! He first became addicted to eating the reptiles as a five-year-old when, spotting a lizard in the wild, he popped it in his mouth out of curiosity. Now Thakore, known locally as the Lizard Boy, devours up to 25 live lizards every day for breakfast, lunch, and dinner.

HARPISTS' HUDDLE

A total of 45 harpists (ranging in age from 5 to 55) gathered in the town of Harlech's 13th-century castle in north Wales, to play a concert in 2006. It was the first time so many harpists had played simultaneously in a Welsh castle.

△ TONGUE BURNERY

An Indian performer touches his tongue with fire, apparently without damage, in New Delhi in 2006.

TOUGH GUY

Running through flames, this participant takes part in the 2006 Tough Guy competition held in England. The contest is designed to test physical and mental endurance on an assault course and an 8-mi (13-km) country run. In 2006, a total of 4,515 competitors entered but only 3,235 are recorded to have finished in times that varied from 1 hour 17 minutes to 4 hours.

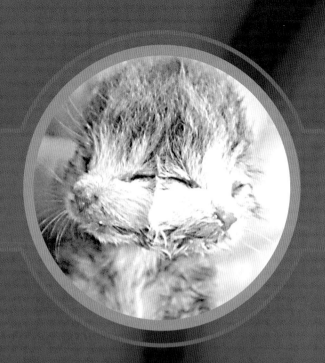

This two-headed kitten had two mouths, two noses, and four eyes—page 173

A statue of Shiva in India reportedly drank 21 pt (10 l) of milk—page 170

Peggy the carthorse regularly joins her owner at the bar of the Alexandra Hotel—page 166

Ripley's Believe It or Not!®
FISHY TALES

Florida-based artist Juan Cabana creates his own fantastic mermaids and sea monsters from fish and animal remains.

He wraps fish and animal skins around steel, plastic, and fiberglass frames, often adding alligator claws for the hands and monkey skulls for the heads. One of his biggest creations—a mermaid nearly 7 ft (2.1 m) long—had the body of a 100-lb (45-kg) grouper.

His interest began several years ago when he acquired an old Japanese-made Feejee mermaid on the Internet auction site eBay. "Just holding the mermaid, I felt the energy and power. I was hooked and decided to continue the tradition of making these creatures." At first he tried to copy the originals, but then developed his own style.

The shape and size of each creature depends on the materials he has available. "I don't kill any fish or animals. I get my fish skins from a local market, where they would otherwise be thrown away. At first I was revolted by handling fish skins but gradually I got used to them. I also had to learn taxidermy."

Each mermaid can take weeks to build. "Rather than looking fresh and alive, my creations are supposed to look old, mummified, and withered, as if they had been found washed up on a beach. I invent a story for each mermaid, saying that I found it on a particular beach rather than just saying I made it."

One of Cabana's mermaids is seen here looking as if it had washed up on a beach.

RIPLEY'S RESEARCH

Tales of mermaids date back centuries. However, the most famous mermaid of all was the Feejee mermaid, brought to New York in 1842 by a mysterious Englishman, Dr. J. Griffin, who claimed it had been caught by Japanese fishermen. In truth, Griffin was an associate of the renowned showman, P.T. Barnum, and the mermaid was nothing more than a monkey's head and body sewn onto a fish's tail. Even so, huge crowds paid 25 cents a head to see Barnum's mysterious mermaid.

161

LIGHTER LIT!

The government building in Astana, Kazakhstan, known by locals as "The Cigarette Lighter" because of its shape, caught fire on May 30, 2006.

HEBREW COIN

After shopping at her local supermarket in Sumter, South Carolina, Lynn Moore noticed something odd in her change. She knew it wasn't a penny, but she was very surprised to hear the news from a coin expert that the coin was probably from ancient Hebrew society, and was minted around 135AD.

HAMSTER HOME

In May 2006, as revenge for a practical joke, Luke Trerice's friends turned his apartment in Olympia, Washington, into a giant hamster cage! The cage featured an exercise wheel that was 6 ft (1.8 m) in diameter, shredded newspaper on the floor, and a huge water bottle. In 2004, Trerice had wrapped the entire contents of a friend's apartment in tin foil!

MISSED MONOLITH

A 44-year-old Australian man was arrested for drunk-driving in March 2006 after asking police the way to Uluru—when he was parked just 330 ft (100 m) from the world's largest monolith with his headlights pointing straight at it. The Uluru landmark, also known as Ayers Rock, rises 1,115 ft (340 m) above the Australian desert and is 6 mi (9.6 km) around.

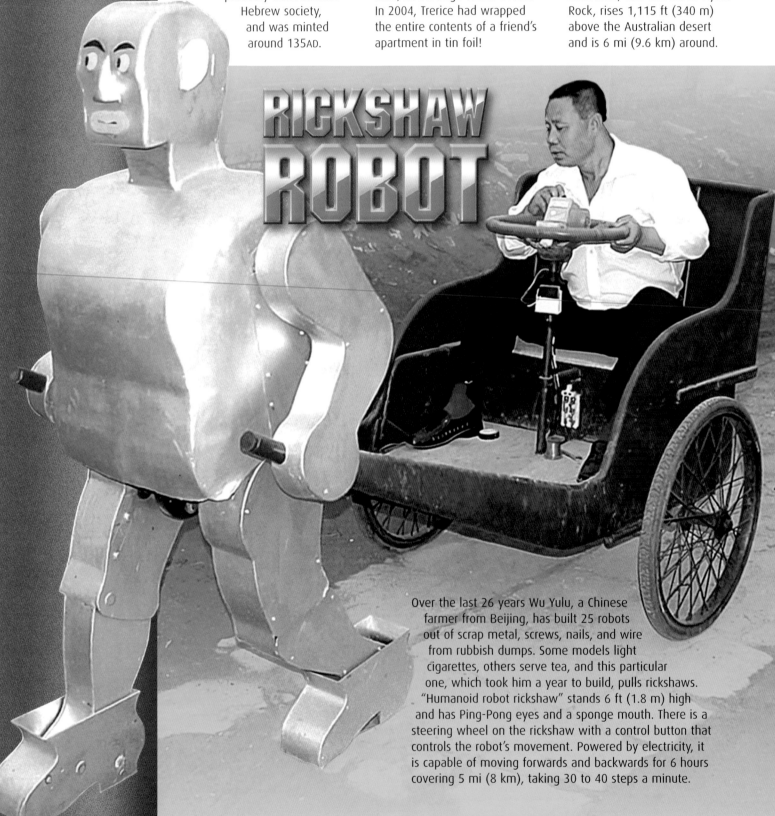

RICKSHAW ROBOT

Over the last 26 years Wu Yulu, a Chinese farmer from Beijing, has built 25 robots out of scrap metal, screws, nails, and wire from rubbish dumps. Some models light cigarettes, others serve tea, and this particular one, which took him a year to build, pulls rickshaws. "Humanoid robot rickshaw" stands 6 ft (1.8 m) high and has Ping-Pong eyes and a sponge mouth. There is a steering wheel on the rickshaw with a control button that controls the robot's movement. Powered by electricity, it is capable of moving forwards and backwards for 6 hours covering 5 mi (8 km), taking 30 to 40 steps a minute.

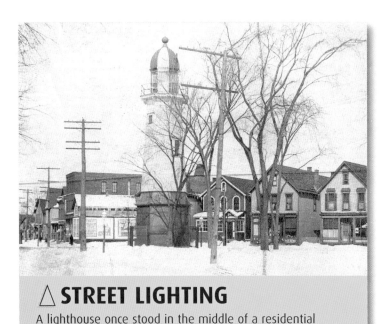

⚠ STREET LIGHTING

A lighthouse once stood in the middle of a residential street in Niagara Falls, New York. It was torn down during the winter of 1933–34.

EMERGENCY LANDING

In September 2006, a light airplane made an emergency landing on a busy street in the heart of Montreal, Canada. The Cessna's engine had cut out during an aerial tour of the city, forcing the pilot to touch down safely on Parc Avenue, a main north–south thoroughfare, in front of dozens of baffled onlookers. The only damage was to a street sign clipped by one of the plane's wings.

PIG PONG

The entire village of Elsa in southern Germany was flooded by pig manure when a storage tank with a capacity of 63,400 gal (240,000 l) burst in February 2006.

SUSPICIOUS MINDS

Texas farmers near the Mexican border have erected ladders to allow illegal immigrants to climb over their fences. The move was designed to stop them cutting holes in the fences, which allowed the farmers' cattle to escape. However, most of the illegal immigrants have apparently been ignoring the ladders because they think it's a trick!

OCTOPUS WRESTLING

Eric Morris of Port Orchard, Washington, regularly wrestles giant Pacific octopuses in Puget Sound and at the World Octopus Wrestling Championships each year in Tacoma, Washington.

BOG JOG

A jogger who took a wrong turn during a 2006 lunchtime run in Florida ended up stuck in a swamp for four days. Training for the Baltimore Marathon, 62-year-old Eddie Meadows left his desk at the University of Central Florida's research park every lunchtime to jog around the campus. But on this occasion he got lost, fell into a bog, and survived only by sipping water from the swamp.

ELDERLY ROBBER

A 79-year-old woman was arrested in Chicago, Illinois, in 2006 after she tried to hold up a bank at gunpoint. Brandishing a toy gun and demanding $30,000 cash, she told the cashier she wasn't able to speak very loudly because she had just come from the dentist.

TREE-MENDOUS OFFICE ⚠

Davison Design and Development, a product design company based in Pittsburgh, Pennsylvania, has provided its employees with a tree house, the insides of a robot, and a pirate ship as creative spaces within which to work, known as "Inventionland." The tree house is actually an area of trees, the first of which is about 20 ft (6 m) in diameter with a tunnel carved into it through which workers pass on their way across a bridge of water to get to the elevated "house" standing 15 ft (4.5 m) high. A porch in the tree house overlooks a lake and a waterfall.

TALES

GOLD DIGGER

...en his gold detector picked ...signal near the front patio ...ome in Montclair, ...fornia, in 2006, 63-year-old Henry Mora started digging. He intended excavating only a few feet but as the detector kept bleeping, Henry kept digging. Eventually, worried authorities were forced to stop him after he created a hole 60 ft (18 m) deep! He admitted he had got "carried away."

CAT KILLER

A woman from Miami Gardens, Florida, had been searching for her one-year-old Siamese cat for two days in 2005 when her son discovered a bulging python slithering in the family's backyard. An X ray on the snake showed that it had indeed eaten a cat.

...man ...d for ...ing in downtown Ottawa, but a judge ruled him not criminally responsible because he suffered from delusions that female celebrities were communicating with him telepathically.

MINNOW MYSTERY

Biologists at the University of Manchester found this duck egg in a small pond in the French Alps. They noticed something moving inside and when they cracked open the shell discovered three live minnows inside! They were baffled as to how the minnows got inside. There appeared to be no crack in the egg.

FLUTE MELTED

A Swedish orchestra playing instruments carved from ice had to abandon a 2006 concert after the flutist's warm breath caused her flute to melt! Tim Linharts had made functioning flutes, violins, and a double bass out of ice for the performance in a large igloo in the town of Pitea.

EXCUSED DUTY

A 103-year-old Canadian woman was excused from serving her jury duty in 2006 because it would have interfered with her afternoon nap. Phyllis Perkins from Saskatoon, Saskatchewan, asked to be excluded on the grounds that she needed her regular daytime doze.

PARKING FINE

A Florida motorist finally paid his parking fine—60 years after getting it. William Fogarty, now 87, received the ticket in Norfolk, Virginia, in May 1946. He bought a $1 money order to pay the fine but forgot to send it off. When he was clearing out an old box in 2006, he found the money order and mailed it.

◁ FAKE CRASH

A California man staged a fake plane crash in his own garden—as a Halloween stunt! Complete with false human legs sticking out the bottom, the scene was so realistic it even fooled the police. Inspired by the TV series *Lost*, Steve Chambers picked up the parts of a G3 Gulfstream jet from the factory in Van Nuys where he works as an aviation mechanic. He sealed off the site with yellow caution tape and added a sign reading: "Do not enter: Under investigation."

WINTER BLUES

In 2006, Dr. Alex Bobak converted the waiting room in his London surgery into a beach to help patients beat the winter blues.

He transformed the space into a Caribbean-style paradise where waiting room chairs were swapped for sun loungers, palm trees, sand, and sun. Several light-therapy lights were brought in to replicate the sun's rays.

HOSPITAL WEDDING

Rev. Don Hoover of Lincoln, Illinois, conducted the marriage of Janel Hoover and Ed Tibbits at the hospital emergency room where he'd been taken after developing severe leg cramps.

ANGER BAR

A new bar that has opened in the Chinese city of Nanjing allows stressed-out customers to unleash pent-up anger by attacking staff, smashing glasses, and generally causing mayhem! The Rising Sun Anger Release Bar employs 20 strong young men as "models" for customers to punch and scream at.

BAR HORSE ▷

Peggy, the carthorse, regularly joins her owner Peter Dolan for a pint of beer and pickled onion potato chips at the Alexandra Hotel in Jarrow, England. She used to be tied up with a long rope outside the pub, but one day followed her owner into the bar and stayed for a drink.

SPLASHED CASH

When Vanisha Mittal married Amit Bhatia in Paris, France, her father, billionaire industrialist Lakshmi Mittal, rented the Tuileries Garden at Versailles and Louis XIV's chateau for a wedding celebration that cost $60 million.

PANCAKE FOLLY

A man from Bensalem, Pennsylvania, who robbed a bank in 2006 and escaped with around $4,000, was caught when he stopped for pancakes. Police said the man might have got away with the raid on a Bank of America branch had he not stopped for a snack at the nearby Sunrise Diner.

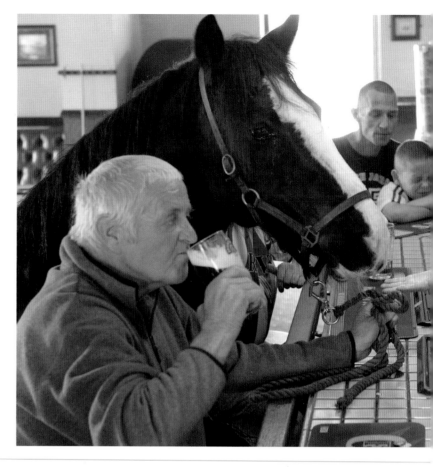

CHEESY ATTRACTION

U.S. Navy Petty Officer Mike Evans opened a bag of Cheetos and discovered a giant cheese snack the size of a lemon. He then donated the cheesy lump to the town of Algona, Iowa, to be used as a tourist attraction.

PET SOUP

A 2006 survey showed that one in three dog owners in South Korea enjoys boshintang soup, which is made from dog meat. It is said to aid stamina and virility.

HEFTY HERO

When a teenage cyclist was trapped under a car in Tucson, Arizona, in July 2006, he was saved by a strong bystander who lifted the car right off the ground. At 6 ft 4 in (1.93 m) tall and weighing 300 lb (136 kg), Tom Boyle raised the Chevrolet Camaro single-handedly, allowing the driver to haul the injured cyclist clear.

KITCHEN TRAP

A Czech man avoided jail for four years by hiding under the floorboards in his mother's kitchen. Police finally caught up with him on a surprise visit to the house when they spotted him trying to slide through a trap door into a vacant cellar.

ALCOHOLIC LAKE

Following a malfunction at a nearby distillery in June 2006, Bracholinksie Lake in Wielkopolska, Poland, was reported to have concentrations of vodka as high as 30 per cent.

◁ CAT WITH 12 CLAWS

This five-month-old cat called Bigfoot from Brooklet, Georgia, has six claws on each of its front feet. It was born of normal parents.

FLOCK OF SEAGULLS

A flock of several hundred gull-like shearwaters crashed into a fishing boat for half an hour off the coast of Alaska in the early hours of August 30, 2006. More than 1,600 bird carcasses were found washed up on the nearby shores of the town of Unalaska over the next two days. Flocks of shearwaters can number a million birds and some species are attracted to lights on boats.

WEDDING FRAUD

A Japanese man and woman were sent to prison in 2006 for falsely claiming that he was of royal descent and for staging a lavish wedding to collect gift money from unsuspecting guests. They had apparently swindled over $25,000 in gift money from 61 guests at their 2003 wedding reception.

BABY NAMES

A Belgian couple expecting their 15th baby put an ad in an Antwerp newspaper because they had run out of ideas for names. Brigitte Dillen and Ivo Driessens had given all of their children names ending in a "y" but after Wendy, Cindy, Jimmy, Brendy, Sonny, Sandy, Purdy, Chardy, Yorry, Yony, Britney, Yenty, Ruby, and Xanty, they were unable to come up with any new suggestions.

TRASH FIND

Dropping off his household trash at a dump site, Michael Hoskins of Danville, Virginia, spotted a pile of old books waiting to be thrown away. Among them he discovered a 188-year-old King James Bible, one of less than half a dozen copies belived to be in existence.

CHARITY RECEPTION

A scorned bride canceled her September 2006 wedding and turned the reception into a charity event. After learning that her fiancé had been cheating on her, Kyle Paxman decided to salvage something positive from the disappointment by inviting 125 women and making the reception at Lake Champlain, Vermont, a charity benefit.

GOLF SHAME

A caddy at a golf course in Long Island, New York, was awarded $34,000 in a sexual harassment lawsuit in 2006 after he was ridiculed by his boss for losing two golf matches to a woman.

ROOSTER SILENCED

In 2006, a Scottish council sought an Anti-Social Behaviour Order on a rooster that crowed too early and too loudly. Since Charlie's crowing apparently exceeded the 30-decibel limit set by the World Health Organization, Borders Council demanded that his owner, Kenneth Williamson, keep the bird silent between 11 p.m. and 7 a.m.

PIECE OF MIND

Sambhu Roy of India survived an electrical accident with severe burns to his skull. His scalp was completely burned and several months later, reportedly, a piece of his skull fell off. The inner covering of the skull was unaffected and new bone had grown and pushed the dead skull out. Sambhu has kept the old piece of skull as a personal trophy.

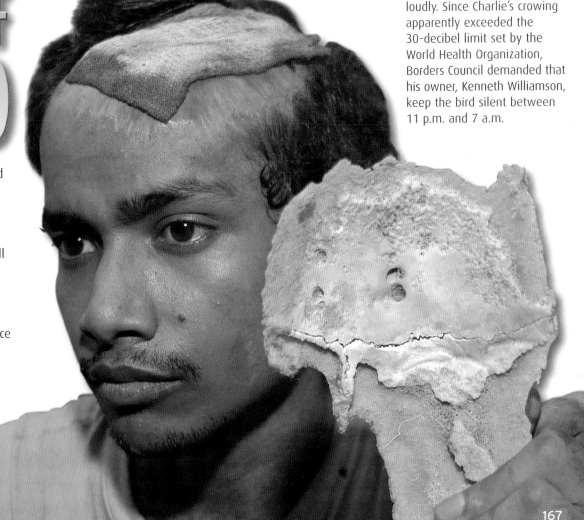

167

MISSING KEY

A locksmith from North Platte, Nebraska, made a key to this man's truck from an X ray that the local hospital made when the man swallowed the key. The new key worked on the first try!

UNUSUAL DIET ▷

R. F. Durga swallowed all of these metal objects, which included a fish hook, three pocket knives, five rifle shells, 17 horseshoe nails, a collection of coins and keys, and various pieces of broken glass. He underwent surgery in 1908 to remove the items from his stomach.

BITING THE BULLET

A 73-year-old Inuit woman was hospitalized in Nome, Alaska, after an abdominal X ray revealed that her appendix was filled with buckshot. Doctors said Inuits hunt so many ducks and geese for food that some of the buckshot remains in the cooked meat and is then eaten and digested.

DRANK COINS

Gigi Florin of Romania was hospitalized after swallowing 120 coins washed down with wine—the result of a bet he made with a friend. He thought the wine would help digest the coins, but then collapsed.

KNIFE SWALLOWER

Mao Kyan from Chendu in China had a 3-in (7.6-cm) knife stuck in his throat for eight months. He had swallowed the knife during a police raid on his flat to avoid being charged with possessing a weapon.

ALIEN VISITOR

When the International Bird Rescue Research Center in Cordelia, California, treated an injured duck in May 2006, an X ray revealed what looked like the face of ET in the bird's stomach. The Center planned to auction the "unbelievable" X ray to raise funds.

CLOSE SHAVE

A 61-year-old Mesa, Arizona, man was shot in the face while sleeping. He didn't realize what had happened until three days later when the bullet showed up in an X ray.

FALL GUY

A retired Polish schoolteacher went to the hospital hoping to be given painkillers to relieve his headache, but instead doctors pulled a 5-in (13-cm) knife blade out of his head. The knife had pierced Leonard Woronowicz's skull when he had fallen over a stool in his kitchen. All he noticed was a small gash on his head, so he put a bandage on it. He wasn't even suspicious when he couldn't find the kitchen knife the following day.

LIFE SAVER

A police officer in Serbia, saved an old lady's life after she accidentally swallowed a set of false teeth while eating a sandwich. The passing policeman thought the woman had choked on the sandwich, but when he squeezed her diaphragm the pair of dentures flew out of her mouth.

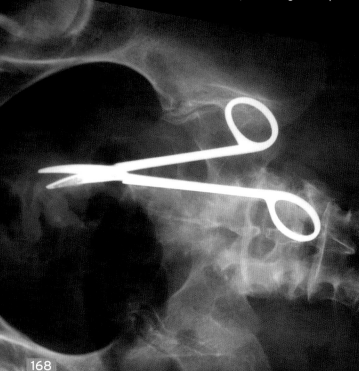

MISLAID SCISSORS

Australian Pat Skinner got a shock when she saw this X ray of her pelvis in 2004. It showed a pair of surgical scissors that had been left inside her body during an operation she'd had 18 months previously.

SNAKE X RAY ▷

In July 2006, a yellow rat snake was found in a chicken coop in Homosassa, Florida, suffering from severe indigestion after having swallowed a golf ball. The snake was taken to Midway Animal Hospital in the town, where it underwent life-saving surgery to remove the offending object—it would not have been able to digest or pass the solid ball, and would have died without the operation.

▽ UNFINISHED OP

Donald Church from Lynnwood, Washington, survived a surgical mishap when a surgical retractor 13 in (33 cm) long and 2 in (5 cm) wide was accidentally left in his body.

△ SEVERE HEADACHE

Isidro Mejia from California had six nails removed from his head and neck after nails from a nail gun were shot into his head in 2004. Five of the six nails were removed in surgery immediately and the sixth was removed from his face when the swelling went down.

TIME CAPSULE

A message in a bottle that had remained hidden in a wall at Quonset Naval Air Station, Rhode Island, for 65 years was finally unearthed in 2006. It had been written in 1941 by two carpenters who were part of a civilian army hired to build military bases in the area. The message asked, "Will this bottle see the sun?" With its discovery came the answer.

BURNING HEART

To demonstrate his love for his girlfriend, Hannes Pisek made a huge heart out of 220 burning candles on the floor of his apartment in Hoenigsberg, Austria. Sadly, while he was collecting her from work, his burning heart set fire to the apartment. He not only lost his home but also his girl who promptly went back to live with her parents.

TONGUE VISION

Although he has been blind since birth, Mike Ciarciello can "see" through his tongue. In 2006, researchers at Canada's University of Montreal mounted a small camera on his forehead, which sent electrical impulses about what it saw to a small grid placed on his tongue. As a result, he was able to walk through a tricky obstacle course without a cane. "It's a concept in which you replace a sense that was lost by another one that is there," explained supervising neuropsychologist Maurice Ptito. "They sense the world through their tongue, and that gives them the feeling of seeing. You don't see with your eyes. You see with your brain."

PARKING ROW

A street parking attendant in Rio de Janeiro, Brazil, was charged in 2006 with sawing a woman in two over a parking space dispute. Police said the man murdered the 51-year-old businesswoman following an argument after she had parked her car in a prohibited spot.

△ IT'S FISH AGAIN!

In 1941, Adolph Flashner was known as "King of the Sea," because he ate fish at every single mealtime, including breakfast. He also claimed never to have eaten meat in his life.

POOR PLANNING

Two thieves from Cincinnati, Ohio, might have got away with stealing a flat-screen TV measuring 55 in (1.4 m) wide from a store in Middletown, Ohio—if only they had brought a bigger getaway car. Instead they made their escape in a tiny Mercury Sable with the TV hanging out of the open rear door, and were quickly spotted by police.

◁ MILK FOR THE GODS

August 2006 saw Hindu temples across northern India thronged with devotees all coming to see statues of the gods Shiva, Ganesh, and Durga purportedly drinking spoonfuls of milk that were offered to them. At the Shiva temple in Lucknow, priest Sudhir Mishra said that 21 pt (10 l) of milk had been offered to a statue of Shiva and that all of it had been drunk by the god. Indian government scientists said that the milk had disappeared because it had effectively been absorbed by the statue, but this did not stop the rush of pilgrims to the temples.

IN DEPTH
STOMACH FOR A FIGHT

Sonya Thomas is America's competitive eating champion, calling herself the Black Widow. She weighs just 99 lb (45 kg), but has managed to put away 46 mince pies in ten minutes and 52 hard-boiled eggs in just five!

How did you start competitive eating?

"I eat more than normal people, so I thought it might be something I'd be good at. I won a qualifier for the annual July 4 contest three years ago at Nathan's Famous Hog Dogs on Coney Island, New York. In the final I ate 25 hotdogs with buns in 12 minutes—a new women's record."

Were you a big eater as a child?

"I was born and grew up in South Korea, and only emigrated to America when I was 26. I didn't eat a lot as a child because we were so poor."

Do you feel ill after a contest?

"No—an average contest consumption will only be about 9 lb of food in 10 or 12 minutes—that's not enough to fill me up!"

Do you have any special training or techniques?

"I do daily aerobic exercise and eat one big, but healthy, meal a day. I drink a lot of water or diet cola with it—maybe 20 glasses—to expand my capacity. And before a big contest, I find out what food it will be and practice eating it at speed."

Why do you call yourself the "Black Widow?"

"Eating contests are traditionally all male, and the Black Widow is a female spider that kills and eats her mate! When I started to rank higher and higher in the contests, the men said: 'How can a little woman do that?' I kept beating them and eventually they respected me."

You are only 5 ft 5 in with a tiny frame—have you got an unusual digestive system?

"Most top eaters are not heavy—skinny people have less fat to restrict the stomach. You need a large throat, or esophagus, to get the food down, a strong jaw for chewy foods, and a big stomach capacity. Mine holds 18–20lb of food."

Is it dangerous—and how do you avoid putting on weight?

"I don't gain weight because I only eat like that once in a while. During contests, there is a danger of choking, but every sport has its injuries. There are always medical people standing by."

What are your favorite contest foods?

"Oysters—46 dozen in 10 minutes. Seafood is the easiest. 11 lb of cheesecake in nine minutes was one I'm proud of, as well as 46 crab cakes in 10 minutes and 162 buffalo wings in 12 minutes."

Is there anything you won't eat?

"I didn't eat any meat until I was 21. I still don't like it much—especially pork. And I don't like anything too unusual, like frogs' legs! But I don't think about how it tastes—I just think about winning."

How long will you carry on—and what would you like to eat next?

"I hold 27 records, but I will carry on as long as my body can do it. I manage a fast food restaurant—perfect for me! But I want to increase my speed. I want to try sushi, and after that noodles—I think they would go down quickly!"

EXTREME HEARTBURN FORMULA

▽ LOST RING

Mrs. Caroline Scufaca of Canon City, Colorado, was understandably upset on losing her wedding ring in 1923. She had to wait 15 long years before the ring turned up in her garden—on a carrot!

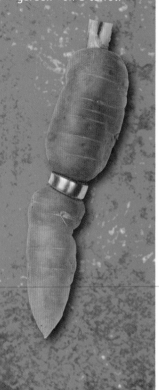

△ TREE TRANSPLANT

This 120-year-old oak tree was one of several large old oaks that were dug up and moved just 500 yd (457 m) from their original home in Spring 2006. A chain store wanted to build on the land in Auburndale, Florida, and had to pay more than $100,000 to have the trees moved under new laws protecting established trees. This tree was the largest to be moved and weighed a colossal 353 tons. It took six weeks to dig out, transport, and move to its new home.

HEARING VOICES

A Japanese man was arrested in 2006 after making 37,760 silent calls to directory enquiries because he enjoyed listening to the "kind" voices of female telephone operators. He made up to 905 calls a day.

INSURANCE CLAIM

English insurance company Norwich Union reached a settlement in 2006 with one of its employees, Linda Riley, over her workplace injuries. Ironically, she had tripped over a pile of claim forms in the office.

WEIRD THEFT

In May 2006, thieves in Germany stole an entire roller coaster! The Big Dipper, weighing 20 tons and worth $25,000, disappeared from a truck that had stopped at a car park on its way to a funfair near Bischofsheim.

TREE DWELLER

An Indian man has spent 50 years in a tree after a row with his wife. Gayadhar Parida, now 84, took to staying in a mango tree after the quarrel and, although he moved trees when his original tree house was destroyed in a storm, he has steadfastly refused to return to the family home in Kuligaon, Orissa. He accepts food offered to him by family members but comes down only to drink water from a pool.

COURT RULING

Believing that posing for photos is sinful, Canada's small Hutterite religious community won a court ruling in May 2006 to acquire driver's licences without identity pictures.

DUNG SOUVENIR ▷

A zoo in Chiang Mai, Thailand, has found a novel way to earn a little extra money, by turning giant panda dung into paper to make souvenirs. Pandas at the Chiang Mai Zoo are fed chopped bamboo and excrete around 50 lb (23 kg) of waste a day, which is primarily composed of bamboo pulp that the pandas cannot digest. This pulp is then turned into paper using traditional papermaking methods.

LITTER SPILL

A major road in California had to be temporarily closed in 2006 after a truck carrying ten tons of cat litter overturned and spilled its load. It took four hours to clean up the mess, spread across two lanes of the Golden State Freeway in Sun Valley.

$10,000 TIP

For Hutchinson, Kansas, restaurant waitress Cindy Kienow, three years of attentive service to a customer paid off in spectacular fashion in 2006 when he left her a $10,000 tip on a $26 dinner— that's over 38,000 per cent of the cost of the meal! Miss Kienow said the regular was always a generous tipper. "He said, 'This will buy you something kind of nice, huh?' And I said, 'Yeah, it will.' I didn't know what to say."

FORGERY FAILED

A man in Thunder Bay, Ontario, Canada, was arrested for forging a prescription in 2004 after the pharmacy staff decided it was too legible and called the police.

GIRL TALK

CNN viewers were able to listen to news presenter Kyra Phillips's private cell phone conversation about her family in 2006 after she forgot to switch off the microphone she was wearing when she went to the washroom. Her thoughts on her "passionate" husband and "control freak" sister-in-law were broadcast live, loud and clear, and drowned out a speech by President George W. Bush.

SKUNK DETERRENT

In order to keep trespassers out of condemned buildings, Richland County deputies in South Carolina use simulated skunk odor as a deterrent.

PILOT STRANDED

Half an hour from the end of a flight from Ottawa to Winnipeg in 2006, the plane's pilot took a toilet break, only to find himself locked out of the cockpit on his return. After he had banged on the cockpit door for 10 minutes, the crew were forced to remove the faulty door from its hinges in order to let him back in.

IN A FLAP

The escape of a chicken from a farm in Nuberg, South Carolina, in 2006 caused widespread damage to an adjoining property. Six large cows on the neighboring farm were spooked by the flapping chicken and stampeded out of their barn, half demolishing the building and knocking down several sections of fence.

BIRTHDAY ESCAPE

In Kolasin, Montenegro, a prisoner broke out of jail in 2006 by overpowering guards and scaling a wall 10 ft (3 m) high... just to wish his girlfriend a happy birthday. After going straight to her house and passing on the greetings, he turned himself in to police. He claimed he had been forced to escape because he hadn't been allowed to use the prison phone.

PERKY PENSIONER

A 75-year-old woman chased after a middle-aged man who stole her purse and when she caught up with him, she gave him $3! Betty Horton of South Salt Lake, Utah, said the man had apologized to her, saying he was broke. So after giving him a sound telling off, she handed him some spare change.

WOW, ALICE!

This kitten with two faces was born in Inverness, Florida, in July 2006. She was inspected by veterinarian Dr. Wade Phillips who reported that she had two mouths, both of which were fully functional, two noses, and four eyes. Her owner, Brandy Conley, gave her two names: "Wow," for everyone's first reaction on seeing her, and "Alice," after rock star Alice Cooper. Sadly, Wow Alice did not survive.

LETTER MANIA

AT THE HEIGHT OF ROBERT RIPLEY'S POPULARITY, HE RECEIVED THOUSANDS OF LETTERS FROM AROUND THE WORLD EVERY WEEK TELLING HIM OF UNBELIEVABLE FACTS THAT THE WRITERS HOPED MIGHT BE INCLUDED IN HIS FAMOUS CARTOON STRIP. OVER A PERIOD FROM 1929-31, MANY OF THESE ARRIVED ADDRESSED IN A HIGHLY UNUSUAL FASHION.

In April 1930 the U.S. Postmaster General said that the Post Office would cease to deliver the coded letters to Ripley because postal clerks had had to devote too much time to deciphering the codes!

LETTERS WERE WRITTEN IN ALL LANGUAGES AND DIALECTS. THEY INCLUDED A LETTER ADDRESSED IN RUNIC CODE—THE LANGUAGE OF THE ANCIENT VIKINGS—AND ONE ADDRESSED TO SIMPLY "BELIEVE IT OR NOT!" WRITTEN IN THE OLD CONFEDERATE CIVIL WAR CODE. OTHERS WERE WRITTEN IN SHORTHAND, NUMERIC CODES, SIGN LANGUAGE, INDIAN SIGNS, AND SOME HAD A RIP ON THE FRONT OF THE ENVELOPE TO INDICATE "RIP"-LEY. SOME BORE ONLY QUESTION MARKS, AND MANY HAD RIPPLING LINES DRAWN ACROSS THEM—INDICATING A "RIPPLY" RIVER.

NEWSPAPER ADDICT

Feng Yi from the southern Chinese city of Hefei has collected more than 800,000 copies of 6,000 different types of newspaper from around the world. He plans to open a museum in his hometown to house his collection.

WIFE SOLD

Unable to settle a $3,500 debt, a Romanian man handed over his wife as repayment instead. Emil Iancu signed a document stating that his wife Daniela would live with elderly creditor Jozef Justien Lostrie. Far from being insulted, Mrs. Iancu was delighted by the new arrangement, as she said she no longer had to tidy up after her lazy husband.

GRAVE CONCERN

In 2006, Yahaya Wahab received a phone bill for $218 trillion from Telekom Malaysia for recent calls that had been made—on the line of his dead father! After initially giving him ten days to pay up or face prosecution, the company agreed to look into the matter.

NUTTY PROFESSOR

In January 2006, a harassed professor of history at a Canadian University offered automatic B-minus grades to any students in his overcrowded class if they would simply go away. Twenty of the 95 accepted.

LUCKY SHOT

A 54-year-old man was shot in the abdomen during a robbery in Bakersfield, California, in February 2006, but during surgery doctors found a tumor that otherwise would not have been identified until much later.

LUCKY BEGGAR

His marriage proposal rejected, an angry lover tossed the engagement ring in a beggar's bowl. The recipient, Tim Pockett, who plays the penny whistle for loose change in Shropshire, England, could not believe his luck when the diamond solitaire white gold ring landed in his collection pot. The spurned suitor had told him: "That will keep you going for a couple of days."

◁ DEAD FAMOUS

In 1960, at the age of 14, Charles Hasley from Bowling Green, Kentucky, started collecting obituaries of famous people, and newspaper reports of their deaths, and has been collecting ever since. All of his clippings come from regional rather than national newspapers, and every one is an original.

MOM ON STRIKE

Fed up with her unruly, untidy children, a single mother from London, Ontario, Canada, announced in September 2006 that she was going on strike. Mother-of-three Roxanne Toussaint erected a tent and a sign on her front lawn that read "Mom On Strike" and refused to do any further housework until the kids signed a written pledge promising to help out more.

IN THE PINK ▷

Brumas, a healthy nine-year-old white cat from Devon, England, has inexplicably turned pink. Brumas went for a stroll one day in 2005 and came home with bright pink fur. He was checked out by a veterinarian, who told his owners that the cat was healthy and that the cause of the color change was not toxic. He also told them that it had not been caused by paint, leaving them mystified as to what had really happened.

GUARD BAIT

After robbing a Jersey City, New Jersey, bank of more than $4,000 in May 2006, a thief slowed down a pursuing security guard by throwing $20 bills to the ground. As the guard stopped to pick up $1,500 in dropped notes, the robber was able to make his escape.

MANY TONGUES

Although it has a population of only 5.5 million, Papua New Guinea has over 700 spoken languages, most of which are entirely unrelated.

DRACOREX HOGWARTSIA

When the children's museum of Indianapolis, Indiana, had the chance to name a newly discovered species of dinosaur, they referenced Hogwarts, the fictional wizard's school attended by Harry Potter.

DUTCH DILEMMA

Police officers from Bristol, England, were forced to learn Dutch in 2006 because three dogs they recruited from Holland did not respond to commands in English.

⚠ FAT FISH

In September 2006, Mr. Zhang caught more than he expected while fishing with friends in Shijiazhuang, Hebei province, China. Dangling from the end of his fishing line was a golden fish which, although only 8 in (20 cm) long, had a huge waistline measuring more than 11¾ in (30 cm). It weighed around 1 lb 12 oz (800 g). Nobody knows the reason for its massive stomach.

HARD KICK

During the 2006 World Cup in Germany, two Austrian men were arrested for placing concrete-filled soccer balls around Berlin with signs that encouraged people to kick them.

TITANIC WEDDING

David Leibowitz and Kimberly Miller of New York City were married in a submersible that was resting on the bow of the sunken *Titanic*.

CIGARETTE BREAK

A hospital patient in Berlin, Germany, was stuck in a broken elevator for more than three days in 2006 after sneaking out of bed for a cigarette. Severely dehydrated, 68-year-old Karlheinz Schmidt was finally found after technicians were called to repair the elevator—80 hours after he first got into it.

Can You See It?

SPECIAL DELIVERY

A chicken named Elvis laid an egg signed by The King in Wiltshire, England, in 2005. The egg marked with a perfect letter "K" left farmer John Warwick wondering "maybe Elvis was reborn as a chicken, you never know."

TOAST KING

Maria Morrow was making toast while listening to the Elvis song "Hunk of Burning Love," when she was stunned to see that the toast had an image of The King imprinted on it. The toast was later sold at an art fair for $200.

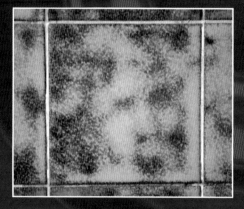

JESUS TILE

This image of Jesus was spotted on the bathroom wall of a house in Essex, England, in 2005. It appeared on one of a panel of randomly patterned tiles in the home of retired city worker, Philomena Risat.

SPIDER-FACE

This spider with markings on its back resembling a human face was found in the city of Wujiaqu in northwestern China in April 2006.

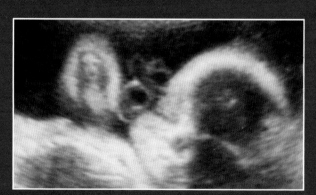

HOLY ULTRASOUND

Studying the latest ultrasound picture of her unborn son, 20-year-old Laura Turner of Warwickshire, England, was amazed to see that it appeared to show an image of Jesus in a shroud.

LITTLE RED ROOSTER

This naturally formed image of a rooster was found in a block of wood about to be used by a wooden stool maker in Shandong province, China, in 2005, which was coincidentally the Chinese Year of the Rooster.

COLLECTIONS

177

HOUND HAIRPIECES

Ruth Regina of Miami, Florida, runs a boutique that sells wigs for dogs whose owners want them to look sexy! Among her most popular lines are the "Yappy Hour" (a fluff of curls) and the "Peek a Bow Wow," which falls down over part of the dog's face, apparently giving a stylish look reminiscent of 1940s movie star Veronica Lake.

SIMPLE EXPLANATION

When water suddenly began spouting from the base of a statue of the late Pope John Paul II in his hometown of Wadowice, Poland, in 2006, people flocked from all over the country to drink from the "miracle fountain." But the suggestion of divine intervention was shattered when city council officials revealed that it was they who had installed a pipe beneath the statue to make it look prettier.

HEAVY SLEEPERS

A pair of Serbian gas station attendants on night shift slept while thieves broke into their office in 2006 and escaped with a safe weighing 700 lb (317 kg). Although the gang had to rip the safe from the wall and drag it out of the building, the theft was not discovered until the morning shift arrived.

EDIBLE WEAPON

In December 2004, a man from Oklahoma was charged with assault after trying to stab another man with a pork chop!

GHOSTLY DRIVER

A Tennessee man was ticketed for five driving violations ten days after he died.

SNAKE STOWAWAY

Like most people returning from vacation, following a 2006 trip to the Philippines, Helga Gurnsteidl from Nuremberg, Germany, put her dirty clothes in the washing machine. When she took her clean clothes out of the washing machine, however, she found a snake in them. The green ring snake—a rare Filipino native—had survived the flight to Germany as well as the spin cycle in the washer.

BOY RACER

An 11-year-old boy from Independence, Missouri, took his parents' 1995 Chevrolet and drove 200 mi (322 km), reaching speeds of 85 mph (137 km/h) before running out of gas and accidentally locking the keys in the car.

DRILL STYLIST

A man in Edmonton, Alberta, Canada, partially scalped his girlfriend by attempting to "style" her hair with a power drill—a technique he said he had learned about on TV.

HEALTH HAZARD

In Greater Manchester, England, in 2006, an office floor collapsed under the weight of a boardroom table during a meeting of 21 health and safety officers.

SHARP SURPRISE ▽

Sarita Bista from western Nepal has defied the laws of nature by pulling small triangular-shaped pieces of glass from her head every day for the past three years. The unusual 12-year-old sometimes loses conciousness when the bizarre process begins, but no serious harm seems to befall her. Her baffled doctors are seeking help from scientists to try to solve the mystery.

OLD NOODLES

Noodles unearthed on an archeological site in Lajia, China, in 2005 are reckoned to be about 4,000 years old. Unlike modern noodles, which are made from wheat flour, these were made using grains from millet grass and are thought to have been buried during a catastrophic flood.

FINGER CLUE

After breaking into a leisure center in Hamburg, Germany, Michael Baumgartner fled when police arrived—but a ring on his index finger caught on a metal fence and tore his finger off. The severed finger was found by police at the scene and matched to his prints on their database.

HOUSE DUMPED

Littering reached a whole new level along a highway in Tampa, Florida, when someone discarded the complete second floor of a three-bedroom, two-bath house beside U.S. Highway 301.

TANK RIDE

In 2006, a man drove a 12-ton tank through the historic town center of Hradec Kralove in the Czech Republic—just to buy his kids ice cream. Miroslav Tucek said he had to use the armored personnel carrier, which he bought from the Czech Army, because his car had broken down. He told police it was too far to walk from his home and he had promised his children an ice cream.

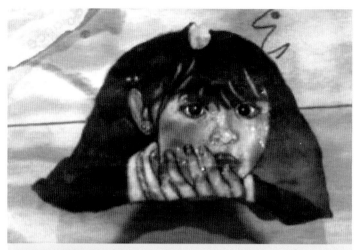

△ SKIN PORTRAIT

This portrait of Sara Fernandez is a painting with a difference, for it has been painted on the surgically removed skin of her mother. Angie Hernandez from Tucson, Arizona, had a tummy tuck in March 2006, and decided to put her skin to this unusual use. The skin, which measures 7 x 9 in (18 x 23 cm), was professionally cured before Angie's brother, Reuben Daniell, painted the portrait. It should last forever.

BLACK AND WHITE TWINS

At odds of around a million to one, these two bonny babies are actually twins. Conceived naturally, Alicia and Jasmin Singerl from Queensland, Australia, have a mixed-race mother and a white father. In most cases, the eggs from a mixed-race woman will be a mix of genes for both black and white skin but, occasionally, the eggs carry genes for predominantly one skin color. This is what happened with the twin's mother—twice over and at the same time!

Dust Artist

Scott Wade doesn't use a conventional canvas for his works of art. Instead, he makes fantastic re-creations of old masters on the dusty rear windshield of his Mini Cooper car.

By using his fingers, paintbrushes, and even popsicle sticks, he has copied in dust such works as Leonardo da Vinci's *Mona Lisa*, Van Gogh's *Starry Night*, and C.M. Coolidge's *A Friend in Need*, which features dogs playing poker.

Scott lives on a 1½-mi (2.4-km) dirt road near San Marcos, Texas. The road is a blend of limestone dust, gravel, and clay, and driving over it produces a fine white dust behind the vehicle. When sufficient dust has collected on the

rear windshield, he uses a rubber "paint shaper" tool to mark out the drawing and then adds the shading with brushes. He achieves the contrast in light and dark gray by varying the amount of dust.

Each picture takes around an hour and he often draws them in three sessions. If he needs more dust, he simply goes for a short drive between sessions. Extra dust and morning dew ensure that the pictures constantly change. However, Scott knows that his dirty car art is only temporary. A heavy shower of rain and it just washes clean away.

Scott re-creates famous portraits and other works of art on his car's rear windshield in Texas.

THE WEIGH INN

In March 2006, the Ostfriesland Hotel in Germany began charging visitors by how much they weigh.

GRAVEDIGGER BURIED

A 62-year-old gravedigger from Nieuwleusen, the Netherlands, had a lucky escape in 2006 after accidentally burying himself. A trailer containing the earth he had removed tipped over and fell back into the grave, knocking him over and covering him completely. Fortunately, a colleague managed to scrape away the soil from the gravedigger's face so that he could breathe until rescued.

JUMBO JAM

A 40-ft (12-m) long water-spewing mechanical elephant weighing 42 tons, as much as seven African elephants, brought the center of London, England, to a standstill in May 2006. The princely pachyderm was part of a four-day street theater performance by a French arts company. The elephant, made largely of wood, consisted of hundreds of moving parts, and was operated by more than ten puppeteers using hydraulics and motors.

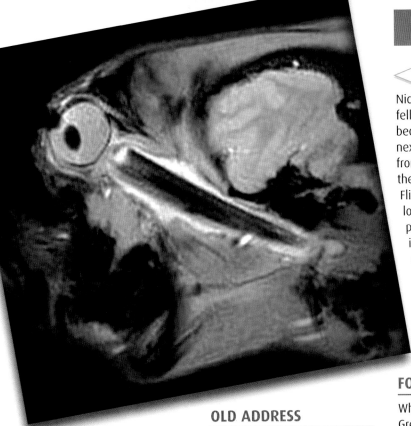

◁IN LIKE FLINT▷

Nicky Killeen's Weimaraner, Flint, fell on a 3-in (8-cm) stick that became lodged behind his eye next to his brain in 2006. Nicky, from Essex, England, didn't see the incident but noticed that Flint's eye was swollen. A local veterinarian initially prescribed the dog anti-inflammatory medication and antibiotics. When the treatment had no effect Flint had a scan, which revealed the large splinter. It had just missed Flint's arteries, eyeball, nerves, and brain. The splinter was removed, and Flint suffered no ill effects from his ordeal.

TOO REALISTIC

Responding to a call from a park ranger reporting a hostage situation, Colorado police arrested a number of suspects, only to discover that they were actors making a crime movie. Larimer County deputies handcuffed crew members and pointed a rifle at actor Chris Borden.

PETITE PUB

Measuring just 8 x 8 ft (2.4 x 2.4 m), the recently opened Signal Box Inn at Cleethorpes, Lincolnshire, England, is not a pub for large parties. A former railway signal box, it has four stools and standing room for another two customers.

OLD ADDRESS

Shot in the head during a robbery, Larry Taylor of Georgia then walked 2 mi (3.2 km) so he could die at his mother's house—only to find that she had moved. Larry ultimately survived the ordeal.

CAR CHASE

The driver of a stolen BMW led police on a 370-mi (595-km) car chase across southwestern Australia, driving up to 110 mph (177 km/h). He stopped only when he ran out of gas.

FOOTBALL FRENZY

When Chicago Bears beat Green Bay Packers 26–0 in their September 2006 season opener, it cost Bears' fan Randy Gonigam $300,000 in free furniture. Gonigam, owner of a Plano, Illinois, store, had offered customers free furniture up to $10,000 a head if the Bears achieved a shutout against the Packers. With 206 customers taking up the offer, it was a good job he had taken out $300,000 insurance to cover himself.

VODKA PIPELINE

In 2004, smugglers were caught bringing vodka into Lithuania from neighboring Belarus through a pipeline that was 2 mi (3.2 km) long.

CAN MOUNTAIN

In 2005, a man in Ogden, Utah, had his house cleaned after amassing 70,000 empty beer cans collected over eight years of living alone.

MIRACULOUS RECOVERY ▷

A dog in California was run over, shot, and frozen—but still lived! Dosha, a ten-month-old of mixed breeding, first ran into trouble when she was hit by a car near her owner's Clearwater home. To put her out of her misery, a police officer shot her in the head and, presumed dead, she was put in a freezer at an animal control center. Then, two hours later, a veterinarian opened the door to the freezer and was amazed to see Dosha standing upright in a plastic orange bag, the equivalent of a human body bag.

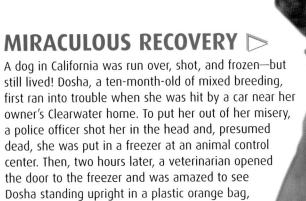

"MINOR" OFFENCE

In May 2006, police in Vancouver, British Columbia, Canada, arrested a 14-year-old boy and two 13-year-olds for robbing seven banks!

GRANNY'S JACKPOT

Just as she was about to run out of coins, grandmother Josephine Crawford won more than $10 million on a five-cent slot machine at Harrah's Atlantic City casino in New Jersey in 2006. Mrs Crawford, a widow, immediately received four marriage proposals while celebrating her good fortune.

HOUNDED OUT

An elderly Polish man was chained up by his wife in a dog kennel for three weeks in 2006 because she was angry with him repeatedly arriving home drunk on vodka. The 75-year-old man had to survive in freezing temperatures wrapped in an old blanket and existing on dog food and water. He was freed only after his drinking friends, concerned by his absence, informed the police.

PILLOW TALK

An Indian man was ordered to leave his wife in 2006 after he said "talaq"—the Arabic equivalent of "I divorce you"— three times in his sleep.

2,000 YEARS ⚠ TOO LATE

A German art student joined the Chinese terracotta army in the city of Xi'an almost 2,200 years too late! Pablo Wendel donned a costume that matched uniforms worn by the soldiers buried in the tomb of Emperor Qin Shihuangdi, who ruled between 221 and 210BC. He slipped past security at the museum and into the pit where 2,000 warriors are on display. Security staff took a few minutes to find him standing still among his fellow warriors.

HOT PANTS

Fleeing after robbing a Bank of America branch in Tampa, Florida, in 2006, a man stuffed the bag of cash down his pants. The chemical dye included in the bag in order to permanently mark thieves then exploded, creating a temperature of around 425°F (218°C)!

GATOR GOD

This alligator belonging to Michael Wilks from Salem, Wisconsin, clearly has the letters "G O D" marked on its side. The letters became visible once the gator reached three years of age.

PORSCHE PRANK

Greg Good, the Carolina Panthers fan who dresses up as Catman at the football team's home games, was excited at the prospect of winning a Porsche in a TV station's competition, but it turned out that the prize was a toy Porsche. When station bosses realized that the on-air practical joke had backfired on them badly, they presented Good with a pickup truck as consolation prize.

DOGGY NUPTIALS

A female Great Dane and male Pug dog had their union blessed by Reverend Charlotte Richards in the petal-strewn Little White Wedding Chapel in Selfridge's department store in London, England, in April 2005. The bride wore a white lace veil and white paw bands.

SURPRISE CATCH

In August 2005, Alan Chaplaski, a fisherman from Stonington, Connecticut, was trawling for shrimp when he snagged a U.S. Navy nuclear submarine 362 ft (110 m) long!

SEEING DOUBLE ▽

Retired lifeguard Michael Morris from Cornwall, England, got more than he bargained for when making an omelette for his lunch one day in April 2006. Cracking a particularly large egg into a bowl (hoping he'd maybe bought a double-yolker), Morris was amazed when a smaller egg fell out. His egg-within-an-egg has been described as extremely rare by experts.

SLIM CHANCE

A prisoner dieted his way to freedom in Australia by squeezing through a narrow gap after losing more than 30 lb (13.6 kg). He had weighed 154 lb (70 kg) when jailed in 2003 but because he had slimmed down to 124 lb (56 kg) in the intervening two years, he was able to escape through a space he had chiseled between the wall and the bars on his cell window.

HIGH DINING △

A group of 22 Belgian chefs took part in an extreme dining experience in Brussels in April 2006. Strapped into racing-car seats, they enjoyed a three-course meal while suspended from a crane 165 ft (50 m) high above the streets of Belgium's capital city.

PINK HANDCUFFS

In 2005, police officers in Maricopa County, Arizona, began using fluorescent pink handcuffs when making arrests!

FAKED DEATH

A woman from Des Moines, Iowa, allegedly faked her own death to avoid paying parking fines. She apparently wrote her own obituary, made to look like a page from the website of the *Des Moines Register*, and forged a letter informing a judge that she had died in a car crash. But she was caught out after she was given yet another parking ticket just a month after her "death."

PIZZA HERO

While dressed in cape and tights as superhero "Luke Pie-Rocker" for his pizza delivery job, Cameron Evans of Minneapolis, Minnesota, foiled a purse snatching in June 2006.

DOG DISTRACTION

Police in Stockton-on-Tees, England, investigated a bizarre burglary in 2006 in which one of the thieves pretended to be a dog. Two men barged into a house owned by a brother and sister in their nineties, and while one of the thieves dropped to his knees and started to crawl around on all fours and bark like a dog, his accomplice grabbed the woman's purse.

PYTHON PACKAGE

Staff at a post office in Mechernich, Germany, were horrified to see a 5-ft (1.5-m) albino python escape from a parcel. The package, labeled "Attention—Glass," had been accepted by the staff and put in the back of the office. But then it started to move and the large snake slithered out of the wrapping.

FAKE FUR

In 2004, a high-tech X-ray machine at Chicago's Field Museum revealed that a mummified cat on display was actually a 2,500-year-old fraud made of cotton and twigs.

PORK TALK

Karim Tiro of Xavier University in Cincinnati, Ohio, teaches a college-level class on the history of pigs in America.

SERIAL OFFENDER

By 2003, Alison Graham of Halifax, Nova Scotia, Canada, had collected 229 parking fines totaling $10,000 in just a couple of years.

FATHER'S FOLLY

Troy Stewart's plan to cure his 10-year-old daughter's fear of heights backfired when he broke his leg as the pair jumped into water from a 15-ft (4.5-m) bridge in Lantana, Florida, in September 2006. While Stewart writhed in pain, the uninjured Meagan cycled home to fetch help.

WINNING BET

When England national soccer team goalkeeper Chris Kirkland made his international soccer debut against Greece in August 2006, he earned his father Eddie $20,000. Eddie had bet $200 at 100–1 in 1997 that his son, then aged 15, would one day play for England's national team.

FOOD HAUL

An escaped prisoner was caught trying to get back into Roane County Jail, Tennessee, in 2005 with four McDonald's hamburgers. The man, who had escaped for only a short time, was found carrying a package containing liquor, prescription pills, clothes, and the burgers.

POISONED PIGEONS

The 2006 city festival at Texarkana, Texas, was marred when more than 25 sick or dead pigeons nose-dived onto downtown sidewalks. They had apparently eaten poisoned corn from the roof of a nearby bank.

COZY COFFIN

Kay Groom keeps a coffin in the spare bedroom of her home in Swaffham, Norfolk, England, and likes to take the mystery out of death by lying in it. Kay, 42, who also has a collection of more than 300 ornamental skulls and admits to being fascinated by death, was measured for the $400 satin-lined pine box a few years ago. "It's the coffin I'm going to buried in," she says. "It's very comfy, although I don't like it with the lid down because I'm a bit claustrophobic. People think I'm mad, macabre, and some think I'm a witch. But I'm not."

This man has passed a rope through his mouth, up through his nose, and back out of his nose—page 193

David Meca swam 21½ hours nonstop from the Spanish mainland to Ibiza—page 200

Whoever consumes the greatest amount of watermelons wins the contest—page 197

MAN IN A BUBBLE

Having previously spent 61 hours inside a block of ice, balanced on top of a 90-ft (27-m) pillar, for 35 hours, and fasted for 44 days in a plastic box, illusionist David Blaine embarked on his latest feat in May 2006—to spend seven days in a gigantic water-filled bubble and then hold his breath underwater for nine minutes, handcuffed to 150 lb (68 kg) of metal chains.

"My only fear is the unknown," said Blaine, before descending into his water-filled sphere.

Blaine said afterwards that the ordeal in the big goldfish bowl was "horrific in many, many ways. Every muscle doesn't just ache, it feels like a sharp, shooting pain—like a knife being stabbed."

Blaine prepared for the stunt by training with U.S. Navy Seals and shedding 50 lb (23 kg) in body weight over the previous few months to improve the efficiency with which his body used oxygen. In the week before the challenge, he practiced holding his breath and refrained from eating any solid foods so that

he wouldn't need the bathroom while inside the 8-ft (2.4-m) acrylic sphere.

Hundreds of people turned out to see Blaine lowered into the tank at the Lincoln Center for the Performing Arts in New York City, wearing trousers, rubber shoes, and a special diving mask. Tubes fed him oxygen and liquid

nutrition to keep him alive, and the water inside his "human aquarium" was maintained at around 97°F (36°C). He said he would try to sleep whenever possible during the week-long performance.

But the final challenge proved beyond Blaine. Two minutes short of his nine-minute goal, after appearing to release his hands successfully, he began struggling to free his feet from the chains and divers had to pull him from the water. Looking shaken and weak, and his skin peeling, he thanked his supporters and headed straight for hospital where doctors tested his physical health. Prolonged submersion in water brings with it a number of hazards, including nerve damage and blackouts, but Blaine's main complaint was a feeling of skin pain "like constant pins and needles."

This was a challenge too far for Blaine, who confessed: "I've never felt this kind of pain in a stunt."

CUTTING EDGE

American magician Matthew J. Cassiere (also known as Matt the Knife) is a skilled fire-eater. He can escape from a pair of handcuffs in five seconds and has escaped from a straitjacket in under 19 seconds.

STUNT KID

In July 2006, 12-year-old Australian motorcyclist Tyrone Gilks landed a jump of 169 ft (51.5 m) on his 85cc bike during a celebration in Butte, Montana, honoring U.S. stunt legend Evel Knievel.

KAYAK MARATHON

In May 2006, 34-year-old Brandon Nelson kayaked more than 146 mi (235 km) in 24 hours on a 2-mi (3-km) course near Lakewood, Washington State. On the way he battled strong winds, broke his custom-made boat, and had to paddle a slower boat for over 5½ hours until his was repaired.

HIGH MILEAGE

Irvin Gordon of Long Island, New York, has driven more than 2.5 million mi (4,023,360 km) in his 1966 Volvo car!

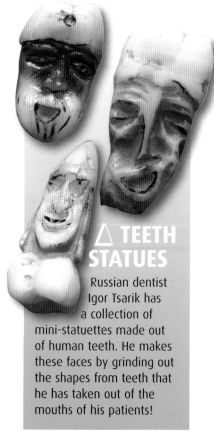

△ TEETH STATUES

Russian dentist Igor Tsarik has a collection of mini-statuettes made out of human teeth. He makes these faces by grinding out the shapes from teeth that he has taken out of the mouths of his patients!

HANG UPS ▽

Johnnie Reick was able to eat and drink while hanging upside down for 1 hour 57½ minutes in Ocean Park, California, in 1930.

△ BALANCING ACT

In 1934, Robert Ripley himself asked a contact in India to look for performers who might come to the U.S.A. to appear at his Chicago Odditorium (a museum), and this is one of the photographs he received.

BASE JUMPER

Thrill-seeker Roger Holmes rode a mountain bike off cliffs 360 ft (110 m) in height in Sussex, England, in 2006—and survived. Holmes, a 37-year-old BASE jumper, was in freefall for two seconds before opening his parachute and landing on the beach 12 seconds later. The term "BASE" jumping is an acronym of the objects jumped from—building, antenna, span, and earth—and Holmes has completed more than 250 jumps in ten countries.

YOUNG BUCK

John Jordan "Buck" O'Neil, who died in October 2006, played in a minor-league baseball game in July 2006— at the age of 94! He had signed a one-day contract to play for the Kansas City T-Bones, the first time he had swung a bat in a game since 1955. A former player and coach, O'Neil said afterwards: "I've been in baseball 70 years—this is how I made my living. And here I am at 94 with a bat in my hand!"

STRANGE JOURNEY

In 2006, Roz Gordon traveled the length of Britain using 73 different types of transport! The 35-year-old landscape photographer from Suffolk took six weeks to make the 1,162-mi (1,870-km) trip from John O'Groats in Scotland to Land's End, Cornwall, England, in 183 stages. Her modes of transport included dog sled, pogo stick, space hopper, camel, unicycle, go-kart, ambulance, catamaran, lawn mower, golf cart, canoe, luggage trolley, pedalo, quad bike, skateboard, tricycle, rickshaw, wheelbarrow, and stilts. She used each method for at least 328 ft (100 m) and a maximum of 50 mi (80 km) and finished the journey with a piggyback from her brother Phil.

STRING STUNT ▽

A Chinese stuntman pulls a rope out of his nose that has passed through his mouth, into his throat, and through his nasal passages.

TIGHT FIT

Wu Xizi, a Chinese contortionist, squeezes his 67⅜-in (1.71-m) frame into a box measuring 23⅝ in (60 cm) long, 11¾ in (30 cm) wide, and 15¾ in (40 cm) high in Nanjing in eastern China on May 22, 2006.

SEVEN UP!

By reaching the top of Mount Everest in 2005, Danielle Fisher had climbed the highest peaks on all seven continents. And she was still only 20! The Washington State University student, who is 5 ft 7 in (1.7 m) high and weighs 130 lb (59 kg), started climbing at the age of 15 when her father took her to climb Mount Baker in northwest Washington. She began the Seven Summits circuit in January 2003 by scaling Mount Aconcagua in Argentina, following that up with Mount Kilimanjaro in Tanzania, Mount Elbrus on the Russia–Georgia border, Mount Kosciusko in Australia, Mount McKinley in Alaska, Mount Vinson Massif in Antarctica, and finally Mount Everest.

JUNIOR SCIENTIST

Maya Kaczorowski of Hamilton, Ontario, Canada, wrote a research paper on headaches caused by ice cream. When she was only 13 years old it was published in the *British Medical Journal*!

◁ REVERSE RUNNING

Swiss runner Rinaldo Inäbnit, 28, was the proud winner of a 7-mi (11-km) run in the Swiss Alps in 2006, but, unusually, he ran the distance backwards. The new sport of "retro-running" is gathering pace in several European countries, with athletes retraining their brains to accommodate their back-to-front coordination. Inäbnit won the race with the aid of a rearview mirror, and told reporters afterwards that his motto is: "Don't look back in anger. We have to move forward backwards."

CROSS-COUNTRY RIDE

A group of about 30 cyclists completed an eight-week cross-country ride from Providence, Rhode Island, to Seattle, Washington, in August 2006 to raise funds for affordable housing. They averaged about 75 mi (121 km) a day on the grueling 3,800-mi (6,115-km) westward journey.

DEEP DIVE

In the Red Sea in 2005, Nuno Gomes, a 53-year-old civil engineer from Johannesburg, South Africa, made a scuba dive to a depth of 1,044 ft (318 m), which is the same height as the Eiffel Tower, including the aerial on top. "I went very close to what was physically impossible," he said. "I knew that I couldn't go another meter deeper. If I'd gone any deeper, it would have meant my death."

SWEET TOOTH ▷

Gamini Wasantha Kumara, 39, from Sri Lanka, lifts one of the fifty 110-lb (50-kg) bags of sugar that he picked up with his teeth during a competition in the capital, Colombo, in 1999. The same strong set of teeth were earlier employed to pull a 220-ton train.

ECONOMY DRIVE

In 2006, John and Helen Taylor of Melbourne, Australia, drove a Volkswagen Golf 18,100 mi (29,129 km) around the world in just 78 days and on less than 24 tanks of fuel. They attributed their achievement to their "relaxed and measured" driving styles.

GREAT ESCAPES

Chicago escape artist and magician Thomas Solomon has escaped from maximum security jails in the U.S.A. and the U.K., from a locked, burglar-proof, titanium steel bank safe under 30 ft (9 m) of water, and from a 20-lb (9-kg) ball and chain at the bottom of the Hudson River. He has also escaped from more than 1,000 pairs of handcuffs and various types of straitjacket.

PANDA ▷ PORTRAIT

Using a single rabbit hair as a paintbrush, Jin Yin Hua took ten days to create a picture of a giant panda on a strand of human hair. His artwork is so tiny that visitors to the Chinese gallery where it was on display had to view it through a microscope. The New York micro-painter also creates portraits of people on single strands of hair. He has carved portraits of the King of Brunei and silent movie star Charlie Chaplin on lengths of white hair.

MINI MONSTER

British rally champion Stefan Attart has given his Smart forfun² vehicle an upgrade, transforming it into an impressive all-terrain 4WD. The chassis has been jacked up to 145 in (368 cm), supported by 26-in (66-cm) wheel rims with a diameter of 55 in (140 cm), achieving a total vehicle height of 12 ft (3.7 m). A massive six-cylinder diesel 5,675cc engine provides the necessary oomph.

SENTIMENTAL JOURNEY

In 2005, British artist Shelley Jacobs embarked on a journey to visit all 288 streets in the U.K. bearing the name "Shelley." She traveled thousands of miles to photograph the signs, and plans to expand her quest to other countries.

NEVER TOO OLD

Edward Nelson of Jacksonville, Florida, aged 67, does pull-ups with a 45-lb (20-kg) plate tied to his waist.

◁ HORNED MAN

Kung Fu practitioner Wang Ying from Jiangsu province, China, discovered a tumor the size of a rice grain on his forehead in 1991, at the age of 59. Fourteen years later, the tumor had grown to almost 2 in (5 cm) in length and measured just over an inch (3 cm) in diameter, and Wang Ying was able to lift 14 bricks with it!

MONSTER DRIVE

Wade Goldberg can drive a golf ball 411 yards (376 m)—and he's only 17. The East Texas teenager produced his monster drive—longer than four football fields—at a junior long driving competition in 2006.

BIRTHDAY JUMP

To celebrate her 90th birthday, Britain's Mary Armstrong chose to jump out of a plane at 12,000 ft (3,660 m). The great-grandmother of nine made her first parachute jump when she was 87 and hopes to be doing it when she is 100.

BLIND FAITH

South African Hein Wagner completed a 24-mi (40-km) cycle race in 2006—even though he is blind. By following a friend with a noise-making device attached to the back of his bicycle, Wagner finished the arduous Constuction du Cap Ninety Niner race around Durbanville in under two hours.

△ PLAYING THE HIGH NOTES

Conservationists cleaning the U.K.'s highest mountain in May 2006 were astounded to find a piano weighing 226 lb (103 kg) on the summit! And it turned out that the piano had been on the 4,409-ft-high (1,344-m) Ben Nevis in Scotland for 35 years, having been carried there by strongman Kenny Campbell in 1971.

LEGLESS HERO

A New Zealander who lost both legs to frostbite climbed to the top of Mount Everest in 2006. Mark Inglis, 47, reached the summit of the world's highest mountain in 40 days even though one of his carbon legs broke during the climb and he had to repair it. Fortunately, he had taken a spare set of limbs and parts in case of an accident. Inglis had lost his real legs below the knees when he was trapped by a storm while climbing New Zealand's highest peak, Mount Cook, in 1982.

Fast Food Eaters

COLLECTIONS

MANGO MUNCH

The only rule of entry for the mango-eating contest is an ability to consume 6 lb 10 oz (3 kg) of mangoes in 3 minutes!

WINGING IT

Competitors in Philadelphia, Pennsylvania's 2005 buffalo-wing eating contest ate up to 10 lb (4.5 kg) at a sitting!

PIG'S FAT SNACK

At the salo-eating contest in the Ukraine, competitor Volodymur Stregalin ate 2.2 lb (1 kg) of pig's fat!

WATERMELON EATERS

Whoever manages to swallow the greatest amount of watermelon in a set time wins this eating contest held in the Chinese city of Zhengzhou.

SHRIMP SUPPER

The winner of the seafood-eating contest in China in August 2005 gobbled up 18 meaty mantis shrimps.

CORNED BEEF AND CABBAGE

Ed "Cookie" Jarvis of New York won a contest by eating 6 lb (2.7 kg) of the combo in 10 minutes.

WHEELCHAIR THRILLS

Tyler Deith of Muskoka, Ontario, Canada, goes to extremes in his quest for thrills—even though he has been confined to a wheelchair since a motorcycle accident in 2002. He once traveled at 50 mph (80 km/h) in his wheelchair while hanging on to the back of a friend's car and has also hung on to the back of moving buses. By way of a change, he rides skateboard ramps on his manual wheelchair, performing a variety of daring stunts.

CRACKING FINALE

For the closing show at the 2006 Pyrotechnics Guild International Convention near Kaukauna, Wisconsin, Dave Carlson pushed a button to detonate 9.8 million firecrackers!

KAYAK KAREN

Karen Richardson of Florida traveled 1,750 mi (2,816 km) to Nashuam, New Hampshire, by paddling a kayak.

WALKING ON EGGSHELLS ▷

In 2005, Zhang Xingquan from northeast China's Jilin province not only managed to pull along a family car using his ear, but achieved his astonishing feat while walking on clutches of raw eggs, none of which broke during the exercise!

CONCORDE TUG

British strongman Dave Gauder once pulled a 101-ton Concorde aircraft a distance of 40 ft (12 m) along the runway at Heathrow Airport, London. He also held back two Piper Cherokee 180 aircraft, one with each arm, to prevent them taking off, and on another occasion he lifted a Volvo estate car weighing 4,180 lb (1,896 kg) off all four wheels.

EYELASH LIFTER

Ashok Verma of Agra, India, can lift heavy objects—using only his eyelashes. He has lifted three 50 fl oz (1.5 l) bottles of Coca Cola with a string attached to his eyelashes and says he can lift an 80-lb (36-kg) stone by the same method. His ultimate goal is to pull a car using his eyelashes.

FLYING JCB

The usual function of a JCB engine is powering a lumbering mechanical digger, but in August 2006 a turbocharged version of the same thing propelled a racing car to speeds of over 350 mph (563 km/h) at Bonneville Salt Flats, Utah. The British JCB Dieselmax, driven by Wing Commander Andy Green, has six gears and reaches 110 mph (177 km/h) in first. It shifts into third gear at 270 mph (435 km/h) and is fitted with a parachute to help it slow down.

BALL JUGGLER

An 11-year-old Hungarian boy, Bence Kollar, juggled a soccer ball an impressive 2,214 times in a Budapest bar in 2006 without the ball once touching the ground.

⚠ CRAZY CAR WRECK

Passersby in a street in Berlin, Germany, were surprised to see this unusual arrangement of cars in July 2005. No, it wasn't a funky art installation, but was the unfortunate result of driving without due care and attention. The yellow VW Beetle drove into the back of the Audi—a move which somehow resulted in the Audi ending up on top of the Beetle!

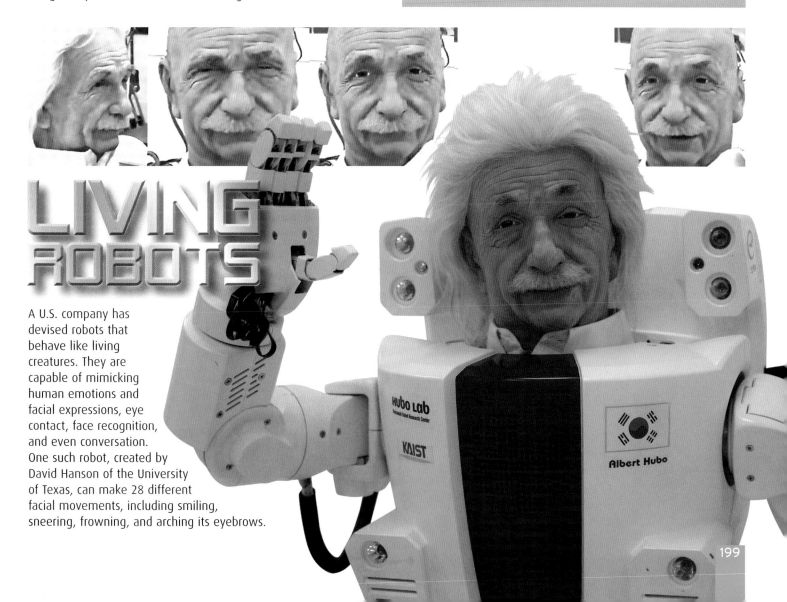

LIVING ROBOTS

A U.S. company has devised robots that behave like living creatures. They are capable of mimicking human emotions and facial expressions, eye contact, face recognition, and even conversation. One such robot, created by David Hanson of the University of Texas, can make 28 different facial movements, including smiling, sneering, frowning, and arching its eyebrows.

BIKE RIDE

Gary Eagan traveled 5,632 mi (9,064 km) from Alaska to Florida by motorcycle in 101 hours, setting a new record certified by the "Iron Butt Association."

BRIDGE JUMPER

In July 2006, Oregon National Guard captain Dan Schilling made 201 BASE jumps in 24 hours off a bridge 486 ft (148 m) above the Snake River Canyon near Twin Falls, Idaho. And the 43-year-old kept jumping even after fracturing his wrist. The feat required the assistance of 15 parachute packers and 25 other personnel, and Schilling admitted: "The difference between life and death on every jump is about two seconds."

FAIR CROSSING

Linda Fair crossed Canada from coast to coast over a period of four years using a dog team and a customized adult-sized tricycle.

FREE FORMATION

A total of 400 skydivers from 31 countries held hands to shape a spectacular midair free-fall formation over Thailand in February 2006.

WOMAN CAGED

A 25-year-old Chinese woman spent a week living in a cage with 300 birds in the spring of 2006. The cage, suspended 12 ft (3.7 m) above the ground, was equipped with a bed and a computer. The woman said she hoped to increase her awareness of conservation by experiencing a caged bird's pain.

OUTRAN TRAIN

Despite having to navigate heavy morning traffic along the 1.5-mi (2.4-km) highway, marathon runner Steve Moneghetti outran a commuter train in Sydney, Australia, in June 2006!

WATER BALLOON FIGHT △

In April 2006, a crowd of 2,921 people launched a staggering 55,000 water balloons at each other during a massive water fight that took place on a beach in Sydney, Australia.

COURAGEOUS CLIMBER

Despite being paralyzed in a mountain climbing accident, Mark Wellman of Truckee, California, has made ascents of the sheer granite faces of El Capitan and Half Dome in Yosemite National Park. A talented wheelchair athlete, he was also the first paraplegic to sit-ski unassisted across the Sierra Nevada Mountain Range.

BOWLED OVER

In June 2006, 40-year-old Dave Wilson of Mason, Ohio, bowled continuously for 102 hours—a period of four days and nights.

EPIC WALK

Canadian Jean Béliveau is halfway through his epic 12-year walk around the world, covering 47,224 mi (76,000 km). The former neon-sign salesman set off from Montreal on August 18, 2000. Traveling alone with a three-wheeled stroller containing food, clothing, a first aid kit, a small tent, and a sleeping bag, he walked through North America to South America before crossing the Atlantic to South Africa and then walking up to Europe. August 2006 found him in Britain. The remainder of his journey will take him through the Middle East, Asia, Australia, New Zealand, and finally back to Canada by 2012. His accommodation has varied from using the tent, staying with friendly families, or sleeping at local police stations and churches. His wife Luce visits him every Christmas... wherever he is in the world.

YOUNG KICKER

Laudon Wilson of Herrin, Illinois, could kick field goals over regulation goal posts at the age of three!

◁ BALEARICS SWIMMER

Spanish long-distance swimmer David Meca arrives at San Antonio, Ibiza, on January 5, 2006, after a 21½-hour nonstop crossing from the Spanish mainland town of Javea—a 64-mile (110-km) odyssey, during which he overcame bouts of vomiting and swarms of jellyfish.

Airbed Spectacular

The waters off Coogee Beach in Sydney, Australia, were the venue in 2006 for a lineup of 863 hot-pink airbeds, all in the shape of giant flip-flops! The event took place on Australia Day (January 26), and flip-flops (or thongs) were chosen as the shape of the airbeds in homage to their status as an Australian fashion staple. In addition, participants maneuvered the enormous line of airbeds to form an outline of Australia.

Ripley's®
STEEL BAR
Steel bar bent by John Brookfield of Pinehurst, North Carolina, with his bare hands.

KARATE DEMOLITION

Fifteen members of the Aurora Karate Club in Ontario, Canada, demolished an entire house in 3 hours 6 minutes 50 seconds!

SKATEBOARD TREK

In August 2006, two months after skateboarding the length of Britain—some 900 mi (1,448 km)—Welshman Dave Cornwaithe set off for an even more daunting challenge—to skateboard 3,000 mi (4,828 km) across Australia. The 27-year-old graphic designer's trek from Perth in Western Australia to Brisbane, Queensland, on the country's east coast took him across hundreds of miles of scorching desert and lasted 90 days. Arriving in Brisbane in January 2007, he said that he'd mostly skated early in the day because it was far too hot during the day to do anything.

MINI MARVEL ▽

Lu Di won admiration at a kung fu school in Songhshan, China, in July 2006 by performing 10,000 push-ups in 3 hours 20 minutes. But what really astounded onlookers was the fact that he was just six years old! The school's president, Shi Yongdi, was so impressed that he decided to waive the boy's tuition fees for the next ten years.

HAiR-RAiSiNG FEAT

Chinese artist Tseng Hai Sun and his partner Brigit enjoy a cup of tea above the harbor in Hamburg, Germany, while hanging from a crane hook by their hair. They were promoting their circus show, which featured the ancient Chinese art of braid hanging—exponents of which were hung by their hair to demonstrate courage.

KEEP FIT

At age 91, Ervin Ashley of Springfield, Oregon, climbed 2,000 steps every day, five days a week, to keep in shape!

TABLE TOPPERS

Sharon Linter, Lorraine Jones, Steve Hammond, and Rhian Jones played nonstop table soccer in aid of a charity for the homeless for an impressive 33 hours 35 minutes at Swansea, Wales, in 2006.

TEENAGE PILOT

Inglewood, California, resident Jonathan Strickland is already an accomplished pilot—even though he is only 14. In June 2006, Jonathan, who has been training to fly since 2003, was flown to Canada, where youngsters can obtain a pilot's licence at 14, compared to 16 in the U.S.A. There, he achieved the unique distinction for someone his age of flying solo both an airplane and a helicopter on the same day.

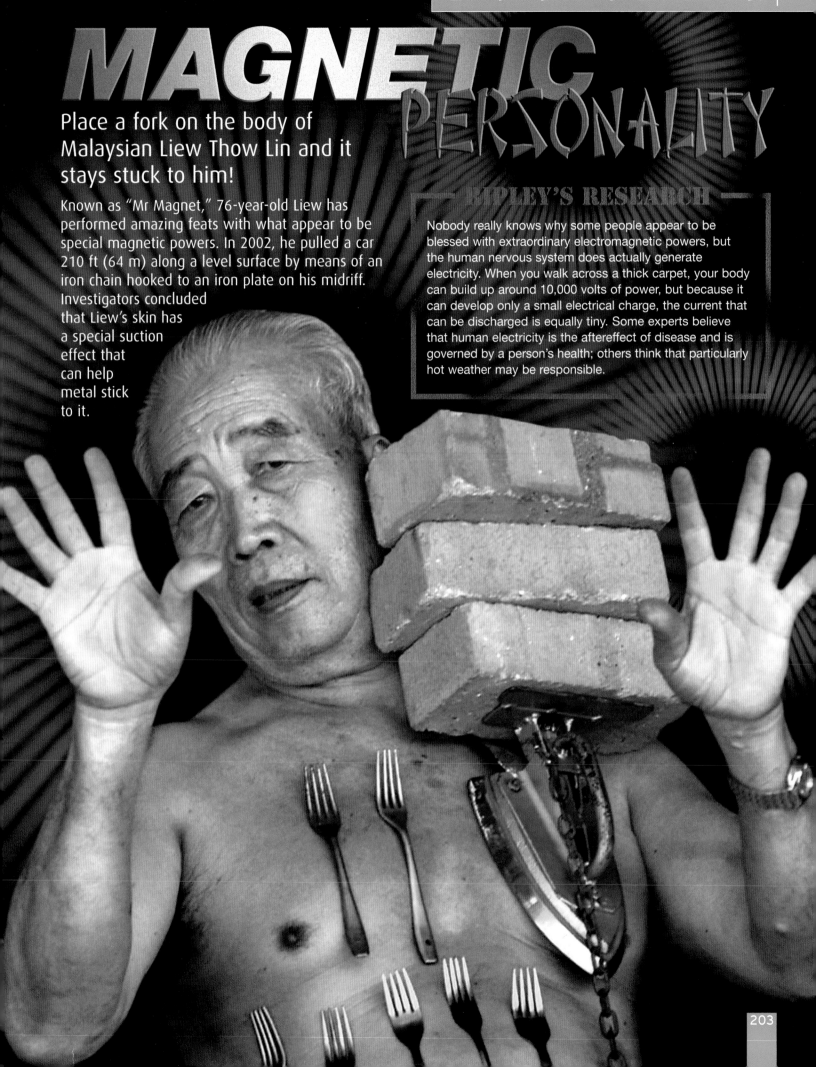

MAGNETIC PERSONALITY

Place a fork on the body of Malaysian Liew Thow Lin and it stays stuck to him!

Known as "Mr Magnet," 76-year-old Liew has performed amazing feats with what appear to be special magnetic powers. In 2002, he pulled a car 210 ft (64 m) along a level surface by means of an iron chain hooked to an iron plate on his midriff. Investigators concluded that Liew's skin has a special suction effect that can help metal stick to it.

RIPLEY'S RESEARCH

Nobody really knows why some people appear to be blessed with extraordinary electromagnetic powers, but the human nervous system does actually generate electricity. When you walk across a thick carpet, your body can build up around 10,000 volts of power, but because it can develop only a small electrical charge, the current that can be discharged is equally tiny. Some experts believe that human electricity is the aftereffect of disease and is governed by a person's health; others think that particularly hot weather may be responsible.

PHIL THE FLIPPER

Show Phil Pfister a car and the chances are he will want to flip it over! For Pfister, born in Charleston, West Virginia, is 6 ft 6 in (2 m) tall, weighs 325-lb (147-kg), and has been named the strongest man in the U.S.A., so flipping cars or pulling two huge 18-wheelers comes naturally.

PULLING TEETH

In summer 2006, Wang Xiaobei, a 72-year-old Chinese grandmother, pulled a four-ton truck, loaded with people, for more than 30 ft (10 m)— with her teeth! In the winter of 2005, Wang had pulled two cars, also with her teeth.

ROAMING PIGEON

When Judy the homing pigeon set off from Bourges, France, on July 7, 2006, she was expected to fly the 596 mi (959 m) back to her owner John Stewart in Northumberland, England, in 48 hours. But she never made it home. Instead, seven weeks later she turned up 5,000 mi (8,047 km) away on the Caribbean island of St. Eustatius in the Dutch Antilles! It is thought that she was blown off course and hitched a ride on a passing ship.

HELICOPTER LIFT ▽

Strongman Franz Muellner from Austria lifted a 4,000-lb (1,800-kg) helicopter on his shoulders for almost a minute at the 2006 Vienna Prater, a famous funfair held each summer between March and October in the Austrian capital.

FIRE-EATER

When his eldest brother suffered serious burns, George McArthur of Bakersfield, California, overcame his fear of fire by eating it! He is a regular fire-eater on the sideshow circuit, where he also swallows swords and devours insects. And at 7 ft 3 in (2.2 m), he lives up to his nickname "The Giant."

SNOW WONDER

Austrian army officer Josef Resnik, 52, skied the Schorshi piste for 240 consecutive hours over ten days in the winter of 2005, taking only short breaks to go to the toilet, eat, and have a warming shower.

DESERT JUMP

Jumping from a ramp 39 ft (12 m) long and 10 ft (3 m) high, 24-year-old Nathan Rennie cleared over 121 ft (37 m) on his mountain bike in the Painted Desert, South Australia, in November 2005.

NATIONWIDE READ

On August 24, 2006, more than 150,000 students right across the U.S.A. read the same book on the same day. The literary event attracted more than 1,200 groups, meeting everywhere from schools to coffeehouses to read the 77-year-old classic *The Little Engine That Could* about a small locomotive that struggles to gets its train over a daunting hill.

FAIR CHALLENGE

Grover and Gamet Castro of Stow, Ohio, have visited every County Fair in the state of Ohio—that's 88 fairs!

AUTOGRAPH HUNTERS

Akram Marufshonow and Musadshon Chornidow, two soccer fans from Uzbekistan, cycled 4,000 mi (6,437 km) across Europe for three months in 2006 to get the autograph of their favorite player—German national team goalkeeper Oliver Kahn.

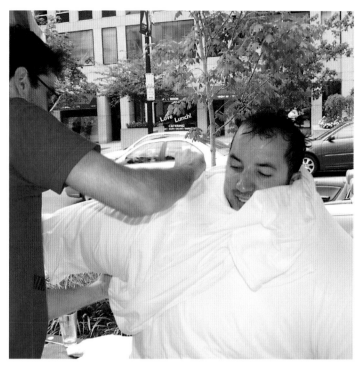

△ TRIAL BY T-SHIRT

David Alexander got a little hot under the collar in 2006, when he put on an incredible 121 T-shirts one on top of another. His friend, Will Sharp, spent almost two hours helping David into the garments, which ranged in size from small to 8XL. Despite sweating profusely in the 93°F (34°C) heat, by the end of the exercise David tipped the scales at 285 lb (130 kg), 75 lb (34 kg) over and above his usual weight.

PAINTERLY ▷ SWIM

Italian painter and long-distance swimmer Alberto Cristini has combined his two passions in life to create the art of "swim painting." Since 1997, Cristini has swum acoss lakes, bays, and seas around the world, including Lake Garda and the Strait of Messina in Italy, English Bay in Vancouver, British Columbia, Canada, and San Francisco Bay, California, painting all the while on a specially created floating easel, which he guides with his right hand and paints on with his left. Cristini says: "I tried to make a fusion between what I do so I invented swim painting."

BACKSACK RUN

With a heavy 40-lb (18-kg) backsack strapped to his back, U.S. soldier Jake Truex of Albany, Oregon, ran 5,468 yd (5,000 m) in just 22 minutes 20 seconds in Hanau, Germany, in February 2006.

SKATING AWAY ▽

Peggy Gray spent a lot of time walking or roller skating upside down near her home in Plainfield, New Jersey, in the 1920s and 30s.

MECHANICAL MARVEL

In 2006, a British mechanic was still working full-time—at the age of 100. Buster Martin actually retired at 97, but three months later he applied for the job maintaining a fleet of plumbing vans because he found retirement boring.

MOBILE THROWER

Finland's Lassi Etelatalo won the gold medal at the 2006 Mobile Phone Throwing World Championships by hurling a scrapped Nokia unit nearly 300 ft (91 m). Around 100 throwers from as far afield as Canada, Russia, and Belgium converged on the competition held in Finland.

Unrattled

On November 9, 2006, American Jackie Bibby, alias "The Texas Snakeman," held a frightening ten western diamondback rattlesnakes 2½ ft (76 cm) long in his mouth for 12.5 seconds!

BIKERS' BURNOUT

By scorching their rear tires simultaneously, more than 260 motorcycle riders staged a mass burnout at Maryville, Tennessee, in August 2006. The bikers performed the burnout by locking their front brakes, gunning the throttle, releasing the clutch and letting the rear tire spin against the asphalt.

DOUBLE BACKFLIP

Riding up a ramp, 23-year-old Travis Pastrana of Annapolis, Maryland, soared into the air on his 200-lb (90-kg) motorcycle and made two complete revolutions to land a double backflip at the 2006 X Games—the first time such a stunt had been performed successfully in X Games competition.

TREE PLANTING

In an attempt to improve air quality in the Philippines, volunteers simultaneously planted more than 500,000 trees on 2,137 mi (3,439 km) of road across the archipelago on August 25, 2006.

AMPUTEE PILOT

Despite suffering 40 per cent third-degree burns and losing his left leg in a 1989 fighter aircraft accident, Commander Uday K. Sondhi of the Indian Navy has retrained as a helicopter pilot. To date, he has flown nearly 2,000 hours.

EVEREST LANDING

In 75 mph (121 km/h) winds, Frenchman Didier Delsalle touched a helicopter down on the summit of Mount Everest in 2005. To make it even more hazardous, Delsalle had no idea whether he was landing on snow-covered rock or merely a lump of brittle ice, which would have instantly given way beneath the helicopter.

TRACTOR TREK

In 2006, a group of 15 vintage tractors, each with a top speed of 30 mph (48 km/h), crossed the width of Australia from Perth, Western Australia, to Cape York, Queensland—that's an epic journey of more than 3,400 mi (5,472 km).

BLIND TEAM

The Seeing Ice Dogs are a hockey team located in Calgary, Canada. The team is so named in honor of the fact that the majority of the players are blind. They use a metal puck with ball bearings inside so that they can follow its sound.

OVERCAME PAIN

In January 2005, a British escape artist who calls himself David Straitjacket escaped from a special high-security straitjacket in Manchester, England. The jacket had loops and buckles designed to be inoperable from inside the jacket, but David managed to extract himself from it in 81.24 seconds, dislocating his right shoulder in the process!

BIKE JUMP

In October 2005, motorcycle stuntman Ryan Capes of Seattle, Washington, became the first person to jump more than 300 ft (91 m) on a bike when he leaped a colossal 310 ft 4 in (95 m). At Ohio Bike Week in June 2006, Capes achieved another landmark jump when he cleared 120 Harley-Davidson bikes. Ramp-to-ramp, this jump measured 187 ft (67 m).

BALANCING ACT ▽

Jewgenij Kuschnow maintains his balance in a headstand for 15 minutes on the roof of a moving car. The journey took place in Munich, Germany, on November 5, 2006.

PRETTY AS A PICTURE ▽

A woman and two children walk in between a painting made by 800 children in Bucharest, Romania, on November 18, 2006. It stretched for an amazing 2.2 mi (3.6 km).

ONE MAN WENT TO MOW ▽

On July 4, 2006, Bobby Cleveland of Locust Grove, Georgia, roared along the Bonneville Salt Flats at a speed of more than 80 mph (130 km/h)... on a lawnmower! The eight-time National Lawnmower Racing Series champion, Cleveland built the specially modified mower from scratch over a period of six months.

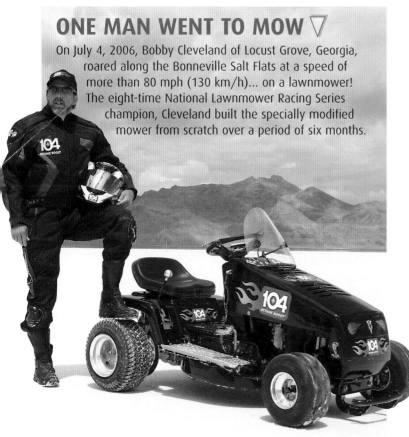

YEARLY DIP

Between 1928 and 2003, Ivy Granstrom of Vancouver, British Columbia, Canada, took a swim in the ocean near English Bay every year on New Year's Day—that's 76 years running!

SKI FANATIC

When he swept down Oregon's Timberline ski area on July 27, 2006, Rainer Hertrich reached the milestone of 1,000 consecutive days of skiing. Since November 1, 2003, Hertrich, from Boulder, Colorado, skied somewhere every day, clocking up 34 million vertical feet (10,363,200 m) in the process. On an average day, he skied 33,000 vertical feet (10,058 m)—that's higher than Mount Everest. He battled through cold, frostbite, rain, and illness, and once hiked up an active volcano in Chile because it had more snow to ski down than neighboring mountains!

GREAT ADVENTURER

Singapore's Khoo Swee Chiow is one of the world's great adventurers. He has scaled Mount Everest twice, climbed a 26,335-ft (8,027-m) peak in Tibet without any oxygen, skied to both the North and South Poles, broken SCUBA diving records, cycled from Singapore to Beijing, and climbed the highest peaks in seven continents.

VETERAN PILOT

Jonas Blanton of Battle Creek, Michigan, is a daredevil glider pilot—even at the age of 84. Blanton has specialized in aerial stunts for more than 60 years and in June 2006, at Whitewater, Wisconsin, he piloted a glider that was towed by a small plane to an altitude of 11,050 ft (3,368 m).

MUSIC DEGREE

Tammie Willis of Richmond, Virginia, received a master's degree in music from Virginia Commonwealth University— the first deaf student ever to earn a music degree there.

SUPERIOR CROSSING

Although he nearly drowned as a child and didn't learn to swim until his late twenties, Jim Dreyer of Grand Rapids, Michigan, is now one of the world's foremost endurance swimmers. In 2005, towing a supply dinghy, he completed a 60-hour solo swim across Lake Superior, battling storms, 15-ft (4.6-m) swells, and powerful rip currents that pushed him off course and increased the distance of his swim from 55-mi (89-km) to 70 mi (113 km). His success meant that he had finally achieved his goal of swimming all five Great Lakes.

COAST TO COAST

In 2006, Ginny Bowman from Rochester, Vermont, teamed up with her 13-year-old son and two of her teenage nieces to cycle across the U.S.A. from California on the west coast to Connecticut in the northeast to raise money for diabetes research. Despite facing temperatures of up to 118°F (47.8°C) and several arduous mountain climbs, they managed to cover an average of 65 mi (105 km) every day.

STEP CLIMB

Medical student Jonathan Hague climbed the 242 steps of Australian landmark Jacob's Ladder no less than 269 times in the space of 24 hours in 2006. Climbing the Perth beauty spot 215 times equates to climbing the height of Mount Everest.

INDIA WALK

In an incredible feat of endurance, Sabalsinh Vala of Toronto, Ontario, Canada, walked 6,200 mi (9,978 km) across India.

WHEELCHAIR STUNT

Trevair Snowden of Gardnerville, Nevada, performs daring stunts in a gas-powered wheelchair. Trevair, who has been in a wheelchair since breaking his back in a snowboarding accident in 1997, races his four-wheeler up a 5-ft (1.5-m) ramp, vaults through the air, lands on a flaming rail, and travels 12 ft (3.6 m) down it on the slide plate—a piece of metal at the bottom of his vehicle. He describes himself as being "like Evel Knievel in a wheelchair."

ALPINE GIFT

Keizo Miura of Japan celebrated his 99th birthday by skiing down the 12,600-ft (3,840-m) high Mont Blanc along with his 70-year-old son Yuichiro.

CARRIAGE PULL

In 2006, a man worried about reaching the age of 60 pulled a carriage 430 mi (692 km) across Hungary in a bid to prove he was still as strong as when he was younger. Fifty-nine-year-old Laszlo Aranyi dragged the 924-lb (419-kg) carriage from Zahony, on the country's eastern border, to Szombathely in the west in 22 days.

DOUBLE ACE

A golfer playing in a weekend tournament at Lubbock, Texas, in July 2006 followed up his first-ever hole in one with another one—on the same hole and using the same club. What's more, Danny Leake, a 53-year-old insurance agent with a 14 handicap, aced the sixth hole with a five-iron on consecutive days.

NET BUSTER

Tom Waite reeled in no fewer than 42 trout in seven minutes while fishing at the State Fair Park in Milwaukee, Wisconsin, in 2006. That means he caught a fish approximately every ten seconds.

MAKING A SPLASH

Swiss businessman Frank Rinderknecht sped across the English Channel in 3 hours 14 minutes in July 2006, in his amphibious sports car "Splash." The car's innovative design enabled it to skim across the surface of the water, but the choppy waters of the world's busiest shipping lane still made the crossing a pretty bumpy ride.

Ripley's Believe It or Not!®

INTERNET TRADER

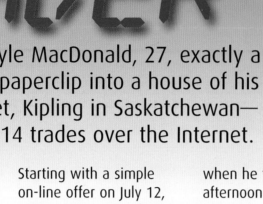

It took Canadian Kyle MacDonald, 27, exactly a year to turn a red paperclip into a house of his own on Main Street, Kipling in Saskatchewan—simply by making 14 trades over the Internet.

Starting with a simple on-line offer on July 12, 2005, two women from Vancouver snapped up the big red paper clip in exchange for a wooden fish pen that one of them had found on a camping trip. MacDonald made swift progress until followers of his adventure despaired when he traded an afternoon with rock star Alice Cooper for a snow globe featuring the band Kiss. But MacDonald knew that Hollywood director Corbin Bernsen was an avid snow globe collector and, sure enough, Bernsen was happy to add the globe to his 6,500-strong collection, in return offering MacDonald a role in his next movie *Donna on Demand*. Finally, the town of Kipling offered to trade a 1920s house for the movie role, which it planned to auction off to promote the area.

fish pen

doorknob

camping stove

electric generator

neon beer sign

snowmobile

Where did you get the idea from?

66 From the children's game "bigger and better." I created a website for the project, and promised to visit potential traders wherever they were— I traded for a pen in Vancouver, a doorknob in Seattle, even a movie role in Hollywood. 99

Why did you start with a red paperclip—and did you always have a house as your goal?

66 It was the first thing I saw when I thought of the idea in my apartment in Montreal. We were renting, and wanted to own a house—it was kind of a joke, but also I figured there didn't have to be an upper limit. 99

Did you think you'd become a global internet phenomenon?

66 No! At first people just thought I was freeloading! I travel all around the country as a trade show representative, so I would make the trades as I went—and gradually more and more people started reading my blog, from as far away as Japan. 99

How did you finally get your house?

66 Director Corbin Bernsen had offered me a speaking part in a film he is writing and directing. He has a collection of 6,500 snow globes, and when I found one featuring the band Kiss, I knew I had something to offer him in return. I then traded the movie role with the town of Kipling, which held auditions for the part. 99

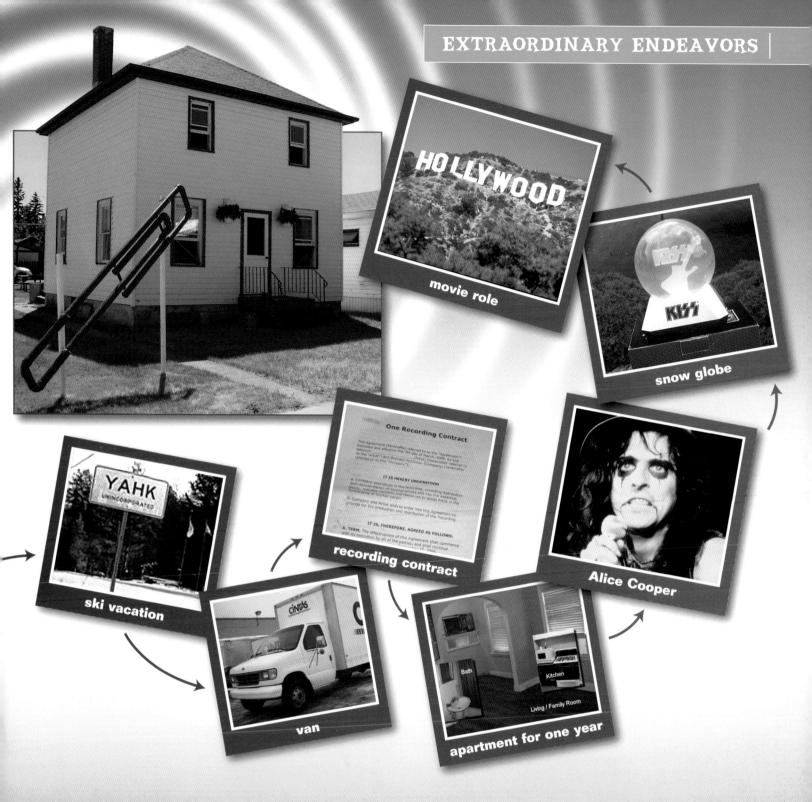

movie role

snow globe

recording contract

Alice Cooper

ski vacation

van

apartment for one year

Who got the role?

❝A local guy called Nolan Hubbard will be in the film *Donna on Demand*—he just blew the crowd away. He was more than ecstatic to get it. He works at a local recycling depot.❞

What was your favorite trade—and which was the riskiest?

❝My favorite was the first trade, the red paperclip for the fish-shaped pen, because if I hadn't made that one, nothing else would have happened. People thought trading an afternoon with Alice Cooper for a snow globe was risky, but I knew I had the trade with Corbin lined up—I left it a week before making the trade to see what people would think, though—they freaked!❞

Were you ever worried it wouldn't work?

❝I was anxious every step of the way. It was stressful—the phone was ringing 20 times a day with people calling from all over the world. I stopped eating and sleeping and regular things like that!❞

What will you do next?

❝I'm writing a book about it all. I don't think I'll be trading again just yet—even for a 'bigger and better' wedding day!❞

How did you celebrate getting your house?

❝We had Saskatchewan's biggest housewarming party ever—several thousand people came to Kipling, which only has a population of 1,140. They're going to put the world's largest paperclip—a giant red one—at the entrance to the town. And I proposed to my girlfriend Dominique—we are getting married next summer.❞

211

SURE TOUCH

Carl Celella of North Greenbush, New York, can easily find any of the 70,000 items in the plumbing department he manages for Home Depot—despite being completely blind.

NOTTINGHAM QUEST

Alex Picker from the city of Nottingham, England, embarked on a six-week trip in 2006 to visit 14 other Nottinghams around the world. He began with Nottingham, in Saskatchewan, Canada, and then visited 11 Nottinghams in the U.S.A.—two each in Alabama, Ohio, and Pennsylvania, and one each in Virginia, Maryland, New Jersey, New Hampshire, and Indiana. Then he flew to South Africa where he paid a visit to the Nottingham Road Village. He also called in on two Nottinghams in Scotland, although both turned out to be just farms.

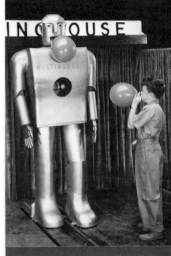

ROBOT BREATH

This robot, built by U.S. firm Westinghouse in 1932, was able to inflate a balloon with its mouth. Westinghouse later created breathing apparatus machines, of which this may have been the forerunner.

SPEED CYCLIST

"Fast" Freddy Markham has designed a bicycle that can travel in excess of 50 mph (80 km/h) over a sustained period of time. The former Olympic cyclist from Soquel, California, covered more than 53 mi (85 km) in one hour at a special challenge in July 2006 in his recumbent bicycle, Easy Racer, and won $18,000 in prize money as a result.

MASS DRIBBLE

More than 1,000 students dribbled a basketball simultaneously at a college in Bendigo, Australia, in 2006. A total of 1,111 people took part, the biggest problem being to find enough balls for them all!

HUDSON SWIM

On July 28, 2004, Christopher Swain of Portland, Oregon, became the first person to swim the 315-mi (507-km) Hudson River. It took him eight weeks to complete the swim.

WING WALKER

An 85-year-old Englishman has developed an unlikely interest— wing walking on an airplane! Grandad Tom Lackey of Solihull, Warwickshire, took up the sport in 2000 following the death of his wife and in 2006 completed his 14th wing-walk when he was strapped to the upper wing of a biplane as it performed a loop and a roll 2,000 ft (610 m) above ground.

GIANT CABBAGE

A gardener from County Durham, England, grew a cabbage almost as tall as him! Frank Watson's prize spring cabbage was 5 ft (1.5 m) tall, 16 ft (4.9 m) round and had more than 100 leaves.

DARING DIVE

Scuba divers Mark Brimble and Jan Burt from the Aloha Dive Center in Limassol, Cyprus, spent 24 hours underwater in 2006 without coming up for any surface breaks.

BULLET BIKE

In 2006, Ironman competitor Greg Kolodziejzyk of Calgary, Alberta, Canada, traveled 650 mi (1,046 km) in 24 hours on his bullet-shaped bicycle called Critical Power. Riding around the track at Eureka, California, he averaged more than 27 mph (43 km/h) on his two-wheeled recumbent bike and didn't get out of the vehicle once during the 24 hours.

CHARITY RIDE

A nine-year-old boy from Calgary, Alberta, Canada, completed a 205-mi (330-km) charity cycle ride to Edmonton over two days in August 2006. Noah Epp learned to ride a bicycle at the age of three and has been going on 10-mi (16-km) rides since he was six years old.

TWO ACES

Marva Ged of Boynton Beach, Florida, beat odds of 67 million to one by hitting two holes in one in a single round of golf.

BALLOON BUFFOON

DIAMOND FORMATION

A team of 85 skydivers teamed up to form a giant diamond in the sky above Lake Wales, Florida, in November 2005. Dropped from an altitude of 24,000 ft (7,315 m), members of the canopy formation branch of skydiving (in which fliers team up to form geometric shapes in the air) quickly assumed their designated positions as their formation descended at a speed of 1,000 ft (300 m) a minute. The skydivers were able to secure themselves to each other by wrapping their feet around the lines of the parachute below them.

KITE CROSSING

Despite failing to cross the Antarctic by kite-powered buggy when he was becalmed by a lack of wind, Britain's Brian Cunningham refused to give up on his quest for adventure. In September 2004, joined by Kieron Bradley and Peter Ash, he crossed the hostile Gobi Desert in Mongolia in a kite buggy, traveling at speeds of 40 mph (64 km/h). The three men made the 625-mi (1,006-km) crossing in 17 days.

LONG MARRIAGE

In 2006, Bill and Eluned Jones of Slough, Berkshire, England, celebrated their 83rd wedding anniversary! Mr Jones was 105 and his wife was 102.

Danish clown Lars Lottrup performed his eye-catching act at the International Clown Festival in Copenhagen, Denmark, in August 2006. A crowd favorite, Lottrup manages to get himself sucked gradually into a giant orange balloon.

SITTING TARGET

Angelo del Monaco of West New York, New Jersey, allowed 128 motorcycles, each weighing up to 800 lb (363 kg), to run over his body in 2006. He lay on the pavement under a 150-lb (68-kg) board, while 13 bikes took turns running over him, one by one, for seven minutes. He said it was the most dangerous stunt he had ever done. "When you jump over cars, you have control. ... But I can do nothing here— my life depends on the motorcycle riders.

SHARP ART ▷

Monks from the Shaolin Temple in China's Henan province are famous for their combination of Zen Buddhism and martial arts. One of their "mind-over-matter" skills is shown here being exhibited at a martial arts show in the city of Xining in Qinghai province, China, in August 2006.

ONE-ARMED GOLFER

Ask golfer Lee Norton his handicap and he'll tell you straight: he can only play with one arm. But Norton, of Greeneville, Tennessee, can hit a golf ball farther with one arm than most people can hit it with two. He lost the use of his right arm in a motorcycle crash in 1987 but refused to be deterred from playing his favorite sport. And in August 2006 he drove a golf ball, one-armed, an amazing 296 yd (271 m).

FAST MOVER

Furniture mover and former wrestler James Clark of Edina, Minnesota, reeled off an incredible 751 push-ups in 30 minutes in August 2006.

STEP MASTER

Indianapolis fireman Jim Campbell climbed more than 106,000 steps on a step mill in 24 hours in August 2006. The feat is equivalent to completing a half-marathon vertically or climbing the steps of the Empire State Building 56 times.

TRICYCLE TREK

Dan Prince of Joseph, Oregon, traveled a distance of 4,250 mi (6,840 km) across the U.S.A. on a 27-speed tricycle to raise awareness of the benefits of gas-free travel.

SCUBA RELAY

Six men and a woman swam the English Channel in 2006 in an underwater SCUBA relay. The British team completed the 21-mi (34-km) journey from Dover, England, to Cap Gris Nez, France, in just over 12 hours. Their biggest worry was huge passenger ferries. Organizer Colin Osbourne said: "When you're under water, you don't know where they're coming from and you think, it's going to hit me!"

IN DEPTH
DIFFERENT STROKES

London-based long-distance swimmer Lewis Gordon Pugh, 37, has conquered the coldest and roughest stretches of water in the world. Known as the "Ice Bear," he can control his own body temperature to battle the elements.

What made you want to swim in extreme conditions?

"My father was an Admiral in the Royal Navy, and he used to read me stories about Captain Cook, Lord Nelson, and Captain Scott. When I was 10 we moved to South Africa and at 17 I had my first swimming lesson—one month later I swam the 7 km (4.3 mi) from Robben Island to Cape Town and barely made it."

You're the first person to complete long-distance swims in all five oceans of the world. What was your longest swim?

"The longest continuous one was the English Channel at 35 km (22 mi). The longest "staged" one, where I swim for a day, sleep, then carry on the next morning, was down the River Thames which was 350 km (217 mi)—I swam the equivalent of half the Channel each day for 21 days. At least the pleasure barges avoided me—but there were lots of jelly fish at the mouth of the river!"

Which were the most dangerous?

"Round the Cape of Good Hope because of the sharks, or inside Deception Island, a flooded volcano in the Southern Ocean. The temperature was 2°C (35°F) and I swam for 30 minutes—the longest Polar swim ever completed."

What are some of the worst obstacles you have encountered on a swim?

"My "big five" predators are the Great White shark, the hippopotamus, the crocodile, the polar bear, and the leopard seal. The least intimidating is actually the Great White—they can come along and look at you, and then speed off!"

How do you prepare for a swim?

"I train physically for power and endurance, but the battle is not in the arms, it's between the ears. I use techniques to turn all my doubt into certainty, so when I stand on the edge of an iceberg and prepare to dive in, I have no doubt that I will get to the other side."

Is it true you can control your body temperature?

"It's done subconsciously. I don't tell myself to start heating up—we believe it's a Pavlovian response to many years of cold swimming. I swim in just trunks, cap, and goggles—no wetsuits. I stand on the edge and look at the cold, and my core body temperature rises from 37°C (98.6°F) to 38.4°C (101.1°F), which is the difference between life and death."

Have you received any serious injuries on a swim?

"So far no. We watch for predators before a swim—I don't get in the water near a penguin because they are the diet of a leopard seal. We've also designed an anti-shark device, which creates a pulse around our boat."

How will you top your achievements so far?

"I never do the same swim twice—the next one has always got to be bigger, longer, harder, colder, rougher! And it has to be a first—I'm a pioneer swimmer. There is better to come!"

BIG MOUTH

Marco Hort from Switzerland stuffed an impressive 264 brightly colored drinking straws into his mouth, beating his earlier best of 259 straws, in Vienna, Austria, in 2006. Marco dislocates his jaw in a painful but necessary maneuver in order to achieve his feat.

◁ MOTORCYCLE MARVEL

Motorcross legend Mike "The Godfather" Metzger executed an incredible 125-ft (38-m) motorcycle jump, which included a backflip, over the top of a fountain at Caesars Palace in Las Vegas, Nevada, in 2006.

SPORTING GRANNY

Spectators at the 2006 World Veteran Table Tennis Championships in Bremen, Germany, were expecting some elderly players, but no one as old as sprightly British grandmother Dorothy de Low—aged 95! Known as "Dotty," she has been playing table tennis for 40 years and has won a number of medals in seniors' competitions.

LOYAL EMPLOYEE

After more than 75 years working for public transit agencies, Arthur Winston retired from the Los Angeles Transportation Authority in March 2006—on his 100th birthday. In his entire career he missed only one day's work—in 1988 when his wife died.

PUZZLE EXPERT

Californian Leyan Lo solved a Rubik's Cube in 11.13 seconds in San Francisco, California, in January 2006. He has even solved the cube blindfolded in less than 1½ hours!

JET SKI JOURNEY

In June 2006, South Africans Adriaan Marais and Marinus Du Plessis set off on jet skis from Anchorage, Alaska, on a 13,000-mi (20,921-km) trip to Miami, Florida. Their route took them down the west coast of the U.S.A., then through the Panama Canal to the east coast. Three years earlier they made a 5,000-mi (8,047-km) jet ski trip along Africa's east coast.

MIRACLE ARROW

Anne Rohner of New Haven, Indiana, shot an arrow that pierced the brackets of an 8-ft (2.4-m) fluorescent tube and came to rest inside the light—all without breaking the glass exterior of the bulb!

CAUGHT SHARK

Melissa Ciolek, 15, of Orleans, Massachusetts, landed an 11-ft (3-m) blue shark, weighing 364 lb (165 kg), single-handedly in 40 minutes off Martha's Vineyard in 2006.

PUSH-UP KING

John Morrow of Ottumwa, Iowa, was sitting in a waiting room at the doctor's office when he read a magazine article about great feats of strength. He immediately set out to surpass those feats and in May 2006 completed an amazing 123 backward-hands push-ups (where the wrist is at a 90-degree angle) in one minute. Morrow says the key to his success is a 40-day fast that he takes each spring.

ACE AT LAST

After 77 years of playing golf, Vivian Barr of Vancouver, British Columbia, Canada, made her first-ever hole in one in 2006—aged 95! Barr, who is also a regular ten-pin bowler, hit her ace with a seven-iron on Point Grey's 114-yd (104-m) second hole.

TOWED TRAILERS

John Atkinson, aged 70, towed more than 100 trailers for nearly 328 ft (100 m) in Clifton, Queensland, Australia, in February 2006. He hitched his Mack prime mover up to 112 loaded trailers, with a total length of 4,837 ft (1,474 m).

△ LONG JOURNEY

This 1919 Studebaker touring car was driven an incredible 520,000 mi (836,859 km) in just 5½ years in the early 1920s. For part of this time it was owned by a transit company and was driven 400 mi (645 km) daily on routes in California.

A Victorian public lavatory has been converted into a 12-seater theater—page 227

Joshua Mueller started collecting Converse shoes in 1991 and now has over 400 pairs—page 222

Gordon du Cane's whopping mouth can easily accommodate an apple—page 242

JET MAN

Yves Rossy really does fly like a bird. The former Swiss military pilot is able to swoop and soar through the skies like a falcon by wearing a pair of kerosene-powered metal and fiberglass wings strapped to his back.

He jumps from a plane at an altitude of around 7,750 ft (2,360 m) and, as his 10-ft (3-m) wings unfold electronically, he becomes a human glider. Then when his four engines are turned on, he is transformed into a jetplane. Not only does he maintain altitude, he can even gain height at the rate of several hundred feet a minute.

In December 2006, Rossy achieved horizontal flight for more than four minutes at a speed of 115 mph (185 km/h). He steers the contraption by shifting the weight of his body and, when the fuel runs out, he lands by parachute. "It is an amazingly good feeling," he says, "like in a dream."

The jetplane is powered by four kerosene engines, each of which develops 49 lb (22 kg) of thrust.

Rossy's "Flying Man" project takes him soaring high above western Switzerland.

MATURE CAKE

Morgan Ford of Tecumseh, Michigan, still has a fruitcake that was made by his great-grandmother, Fidelia Bates, over 120 years ago!

STÜCKE IN THE SADDLE

Since 1962, Germany's Heinz Stücke has ridden more than 335,000 mi (539,130 km) through at least 211 countries and territories on a bicycle he bought at the beginning of his journey.

CONVERSE COLLECTOR △

Joshua Mueller from Lakewood, Washington, started collecting Converse shoes in 1991 at the age of 13. He is now the proud owner of more than 400 pairs, none of which is identical, and he wears at least one or two different pairs every day.

JUGGLING PRIEST

At Fargo, North Dakota, in August 2006, student priest Zach Warren of Charleston, South Carolina, rode a unicycle a mile in just under four minutes while juggling, achieving an average speed of 15.6 mph (25 km/h).

CLUB ADDICTION

Mike MacDougall of North Palm Beach, Florida, fell more than $100,000 into debt by collecting rarely used one-iron golf clubs.

CAGED WRITER

French playwright Norbert Aboudarham lived for a week in a cage at Amiens Zoo while writing a drama about a panda! Composing the play on his laptop, which was hooked up to his cell phone, he sat in a cage furnished with straw and a log alongside neighbors including raccoons and wolves. During his stay, he refused to talk to the public, communicating solely via messages passed through the bars.

MOUSETRAP MANSION

Tim Evans of Brownsburg, Indiana, has a collection of over 1,000 mousetraps in his home.

STORE DWELLER

Skyler Bartels, a student from Drake University, Iowa, spent two days in 2006 living inside a Wal-Mart store. He wandered the Iowa supercenter for 41 hours, day and night, existing solely on Wal-Mart products. He even managed to get a few minutes' sleep, either in a restroom stall or in a chair in the lawn and garden section.

TURTLE TOTAL

Richard Ogust of New York City has a collection of more than 100 species of turtle in his Manhattan loft—that's more than the Bronx Zoo.

PIPE MAJOR

Nick Hudson, a student at Carnegie-Mellon University in Pittsburgh, Pennsylvania, is the only person in the U.S.A. with Bagpipes as his college major.

BIG NOISE

Believe it or not, a company called Hornblasters from Tampa, Florida, installs 140-decibel train horns in cars.

HIGHS AND LOWS

Fran Capo, the world's fastest-talking female, has become the first person to do a book signing at the wreck of the *Titanic*, 12,400 ft (3,780 m) below the sea, some 380 mi (612 km) off the coast of Newfoundland. Fran has previously done a book signing on the top of Africa's Mount Kilimanjaro.

SPECIAL ▷ DELIVERY

Steve Knight from Essex, England, has been collecting old British postboxes for ten years. A true aficionado, he lovingly restores the damaged boxes, and has a collection of more than 80, some dating back to the reign of Queen Victoria.

SPELL IT OUT

Lovestruck Serbian Vujadin Stojkovic hired a fleet of taxi drivers to propose to girlfriend Ivana Novakovic in 2006. He paid each of the 12 cab drivers to paint a single letter of "udaj se za mene," which means "marry me" in Serbian, on the side of their vehicles and then pull up outside Ivana's house. She was so touched by the romantic gesture that she accepted.

MONKEY BUSINESS

Ron Warren of New York City has a collection of around 1,800 sock monkeys.

SCARY GUY

With tattoos covering 85 per cent of his body and many piercings, Earl Kenneth Kaufmann had his name legally changed in 1998 to "The Scary Guy!" Although he spreads a message of peace, he has been banned from two U.S. cities because of the way he looks.

FIAT JAM

More than 750 owners of little Fiat 500 cars positioned their vehicles to form a huge single-model traffic jam at an Italian racetrack in 2006.

LUXURY FACIAL

At a New York City beauty salon, you can get a $270 facial that promises to firm up facial skin by coating it with a layer of caviar.

CASH COMPILATION

Larry Beebe of the U.S.A. has collected banknotes from more than 200 different countries.

GAME GRANDMA

Ohio grandmother Barbara St. Hilaire, 70, who works as a video-game correspondent for MTV, earned her nickname "Old Grandma Hardcore" from playing video games for up to ten hours a day.

FISH FOOD

Visitors to the Kowakien Yunessun spa resort in Hakone, Japan, are offered an unusual treatment for the removal of old or dead skin from their feet. They bathe their feet in a Turkish bath that is filled with Garra rufa fish (also known as Doctor fish or Nibble fish), and the fish happily munch away on the old or dead skin and any other unwanted detritus, to leave the feet clean, refreshed, and revitalized!

PRAYER BEADS

Architect Jamal Sleeq of Kuwait has been collecting precious prayer beads, known in Arabic as *misbah*, since 1979. Today his collection numbers more than 2,000, the majority of which are made from amber. He has been known to fly all the way to Poland or Turkey just to collect one stone. In total he has 56,000 antiques and curios from all around the world, including some 14th-century silverware and 200-year-old carpets.

FROG FRENZY

It all started with the purchase of a small, bright-green china frog in 1979. By 2005, Sheila Crown of Wiltshire, England, had gathered an enormous collection of frog memorabilia comprising a staggering 11,471 pieces. In 1997, Sheila and husband Stephen had moved to a larger house to accommodate her growing collection, but eight years later another house move to a smaller property meant that Sheila had to take a giant leap and sell all of her green friends at auction.

FINAL CUT

Peter Vita of Port Chester, New York, was 12 years old when he began cutting hair and, until his death in 2004, he had been working as a barber for 82 consecutive years.

DUKE DEVOTEE

Jim Duncan of Brownsburg, Indiana, has a collection of more than 4,000 items devoted to the film actor John Wayne.

MAJOR DACHSHUND

An Internet website called "Pets In Uniform" gives you the chance to see your pet dressed as a U.S. Marine or a British General! You simply send a picture of your pet, and three days later a digital download of it in your chosen uniform will be available.

BLACK BELT

Raymond Wood of Hull, England, was given a top martial arts honor in 2006—at the age of 73. A former all-England jujitsu champion, he is one of just six people in the country to be given the coveted Tenth Dan black belt.

BUBBLE KEEPER

Eiffel Plasterer of Huntingdon, Indiana, captured a soap bubble inside a mason jar and kept it intact for almost an entire year.

JUNIOR DJ

At just five years old, Avante Price is a little kid with a big reputation—as a DJ in Chicago, Illinois. According to dad Johnny, who is also a DJ, Avante began scratching out the beats on their home turntables at the age of three, despite having to stand on a piano bench to reach them.

BARBIE GIRL

A collection of 4,000 Barbie dolls—the lifelong passion of late Dutch housewife Letje Raebel—was put up for sale in 2006. She bought her first Barbie for daughter Marina in the early 1960s, but Marina did not want to play with it and left it in the box. However, mom developed the collecting bug, inspired by Barbie's ever-changing wardrobe.

◁ LOST LOCKS

Alan Freed spent 39 years collecting more than 11,000 small padlocks that had become separated from luggage and found inside the airport or on runways at Washington D.C. where he worked. The large dummy padlock made from them all measures 43 x 34 x 20 in (110 x 86 x 50 cm).

LET IT SNOW!

Josef Kardinal from Nuremberg, Germany, is the proud owner of a vast collection of snow shakers that have been gathered from across the globe. Currently standing at more than 7,500 shakers, Josef's collection includes some of the first snow shakers ever produced, made in Austria at the end of the 19th century.

VICTORIAN CAKE

When Vera Howarth of Devon, England, celebrated her 98th birthday in 2006, the cake was even older than she was! The seven-tier fruitcake was made in 1895 (when Queen Victoria was still on the throne) for the wedding of Vera's parents, and the top tier has been kept in the family ever since, to be brought out on special occasions. The cake had yellowed slightly in the intervening 111 years, but still smelled beautiful.

MEDIEVAL ▷ MISSION

Since 1996, Michel Guyot has been building an authentic medieval castle—with turrets, great walls, and a moat—in the forests of Burgundy, France. And he and his 50 helpers have been doing it without any modern power tools, instead relying solely on implements that were available in the 13th century.

IDENTITY CRISIS

A Chinese woman had a mole removed from her leg and grafted on to her face to avoid being mistaken for her twin sister. Xiao Ai from Xiamen City said that after her confused brother-in-law tried to kiss her, she and her sister marked their faces each day so their husbands could tell them apart. Then they decided that the mole would be a more permanent solution.

GIANT ROCKER

When Tom Doxey put his Penrose, Colorado, restaurant up for sale in 2006, it came with an unusual accessory out front— a 9,100-lb (4,130-kg) rocking chair. The rocker stands 21 ft (6.4 m) high and 14 ft (4.3 m) wide, and was built from 12 Douglas fir logs, 25 tubes of caulk, and six gallons of glue by woodworker Dwayne Simmons back in 1990.

QUIET WEDDING

Daisy and John Franko of Springfield, Ohio, were married on February 14, 2006—at the funeral home where they first met!

AIRPLANE MODELER

John Kalusa hand-carved 5,829 model wooden airplanes up to his death in 2003, each built to a scale of $\frac{1}{8}$ in to 1 ft (1.3 mm to 30 cm). His collection is housed in an aeronautical university library at Prescott, Arizona.

BAR TOWEL BOB

Robert Begley has the best collection in Chambersburg, Pennsylvania—bar none. Starting out in 1990, Begley (known to his friends as "Bar Towel Bob") has managed to collect more than 2,300 bar towels, representing 27 different countries.

Tapestry of Love

A woman from London, England, has single-handedly re-created the famous Bayeux Tapestry in a labor of love that has spanned more than 20 years. Annette Banks developed her talent for embroidery as a child. She also loved English history, so her father suggested that she make a replica of the Bayeux Tapestry. When Annette eventually finished her tapestry, it was 51 ft (15 m) long and 23 in (58 cm) wide. After visiting the real tapestry in Bayeux, France, Annette decided to add another 5 ft (1.5 m) to her version, and to make up her own ending.

TOILET ▷ THEATER

Dennis Neale of Worcestershire, England, is the proprietor of a theater with a difference. A puppeteer by trade, he has converted a Victorian public lavatory that he bought in 1999 into a tiny arts venue. The once bleak building now has colorful background scenes on the walls, the urinals have been replaced by a small stage, and the toilet cubicles have made way for 12 audience seats. The wedge-shaped theater measures just 16 x 9 x 6 ft (4.8 x 2.7 x 1.8 m), but has still managed to host drama, puppetry, poetry, music, and even a day of opera. Unsurprisingly, perhaps, the theater is almost always sold out.

BLOOD MONEY

In October 2004, businessman Stephen Son of Los Angeles, California, promised to pay back a finanacial investor with a contract—written in his own blood!

PRISON PAINTER

Donny Johnson, a prisoner serving a life sentence in California, paints as a hobby, using dye leached from candies to make paints and his own hair to make brushes. Twenty of his paintings have sold for $500 each.

HIDDEN SHEEP

Since 1995, James Hartman of Burlingame, California, and his family have hidden over 2,000 tiny plaster sheep all around the world at locations ranging from the Eiffel Tower to Big Ben to India's Ganges River.

BAG MAN

Since 1975, Germany's Heinz Schmidt-Bachem has collected 150,000 plastic and paper bags. He feared that these everyday items would otherwise be lost.

GOLDEN COCKTAIL

Spectators at the 2006 Kentucky Derby were able to order a $1,000 mint julep cocktail—with mint from Morocco, ice from the Arctic, and sugar from the South Pacific, served in a golden cup with a sterling silver straw.

WRONG NUMBERS

The Pierce family of Salt Lake City, Utah, have answered more than 25,000 misdialed phone calls during the past 14 years. They enjoy chatting with each caller and keep a log of each call!

PENNY PILE

John Trembo of Plymouth, Michigan, has a collection of more than one million pennies, weighing more than three tons.

COLORFUL DIET

Soccer fan Scott Campbell took his devotion to new heights in 2006 by vowing to eat food that came only in his club's colors for the whole nine-month season. The Glasgow Celtic club supporter went on a strict diet of green and white foods—mainly chicken, fish, and vegetables.

SWIM TRUCK

Don Underwood of Louisville, Kentucky, owns a 1954 fire truck with a built-in swimming pool that was originally installed to provide mobile swimming lessons for children.

GOLF LINE

Ted Hoz of Baton Rouge, Louisiana, has collected nearly 70,000 golf balls since 1986. If you lined them up side by side, they would stretch almost two miles.

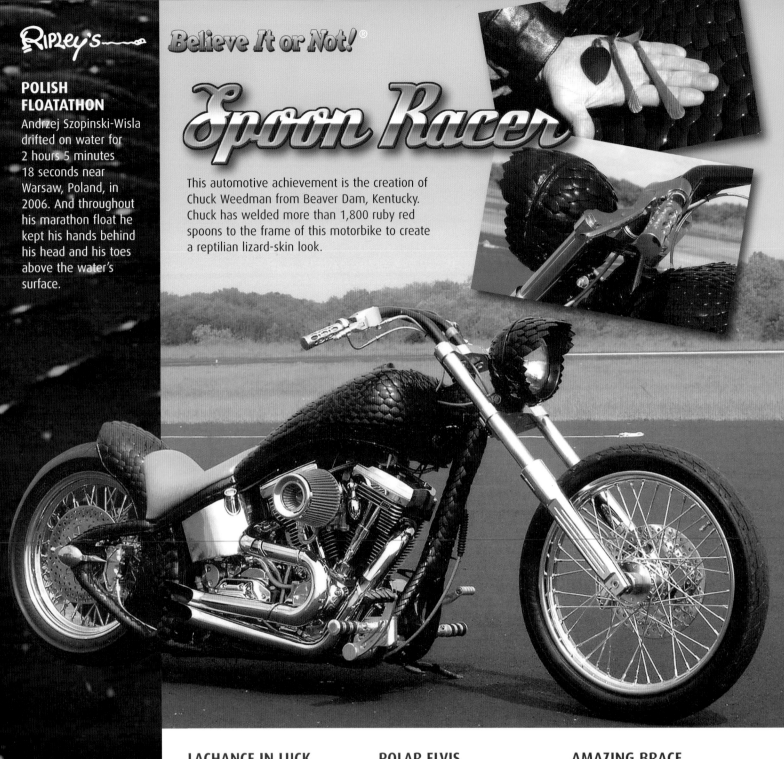

Spoon Racer

This automotive achievement is the creation of Chuck Weedman from Beaver Dam, Kentucky. Chuck has welded more than 1,800 ruby red spoons to the frame of this motorbike to create a reptilian lizard-skin look.

POLISH FLOATATHON

Andrzej Szopinski-Wisla drifted on water for 2 hours 5 minutes 18 seconds near Warsaw, Poland, in 2006. And throughout his marathon float he kept his hands behind his head and his toes above the water's surface.

LACHANCE IN LUCK

After meeting a Belgian woman named Sabine on holiday in Cuba, Marc Lachance of Canada realized he did not have her full name and address. So he wrote to 3,700 Belgian women named Sabine. Eventually, her brother heard about Lachance's search on Belgian radio and, in 2006, the sweethearts were reunited.

POLAR ELVIS

Three British Elvis impersonators walked and skied to the top of the world in 2006. Alex Tate, Jonny Clayton, and Steve Goodair trekked 368 mi (592 km) from Cornwallis Island, off Northern Canada, to the Magnetic North Pole in Elvis-style survival suits, complete with thermal insulation and rhinestones.

AMAZING BRACE

U.S. manufacturer Hasbro has marketed a toothbrush that plays pop songs while you brush your teeth—by transmitting the sound waves along the bristles, through your teeth and jawbone to your ear. The music is stored in a microchip in the brush's handle and plays on a mini-computer at the push of a button.

MALE ▷ KINDERGARTEN

A man tries out a new compass saw at a special kindergarten for men in Hamburg. Women can now leave their partners on weekend shopping trips at the Saturday afternoon men's crèche "Maennergarten" at the Nox Bar. Equipped with tables, couches, comics, games, cards, remote-controlled cars, and plastic toys, men are given a name badge on arrival and for 10 euros can get two beers, a hot meal, and nonstop televised sport.

MOBILE DOCTOR

A New York doctor has opened for consultation in the world's smallest doctor's office—his car. Dr. Safwan Sweidan has installed a desktop computer, a lamp, an Oriental rug, and even fake plants in the front seat of his Chrysler convertible and spends two or three hours every night in the heart of Manhattan dispensing medical advice to passersby.

STICK MAN

You can't beat Peter Lavinger's collection of drumsticks. Ever since he caught a drumstick at a concert in 1980, the New Yorker has been collecting famous drummers' sticks. He has attended thousands of concerts—including The Rolling Stones, R.E.M., and U2—and has built up a collection of more than 1,300 celebrity sticks, nearly all of which are autographed. Each one is valued at over $700.

CHOP SHOP

Customers at Szabolcs Bodnar's barber shop in Budapest, Hungary, no longer expect the traditional scissors and comb. Instead, they have their hair cut with such implements as axes, swords, vacuum cleaners, and irons. Bodnar's chosen method of cutting hair is to place it on a chopping board and strike it with an ax. The hair is then styled using a vacuum cleaner or straightened with an iron. For more energetic customers there is also the option of hanging upside down while Bodnar hacks away with a Samurai sword at such speed that the entire haircut can be finished in seconds!

OLD COACH

Former Welsh international Ivor Powell worked as assistant coach for British soccer club Team Bath in 2006—even though he was 90 years old.

PEEL'S PRIVIES

There's never any shortage of somewhere to sit in Janie Peel's backyard. The real-estate broker from Appling, Georgia, rescues old outhouses that would otherwise have been demolished. Among her growing collection is an ancient two-holer with a tin roof and a metal side that is peppered with shotgun pellets—right where the occupants would have been sitting!

ROCK ARTIST

On September 3, 2006, artist Bryony Graham created a beach sculpture from 30,000 sticks of edible rock candy. It took four hours to assemble the one-ton artwork into a circular mound 20 ft (6 m) across and 2 ft (60 cm) high on the beach at Felixstowe in Suffolk, England. Graham was relieved that it didn't rain for fear that the rock would have dissolved into a sugary mess.

SMALL READ

Neale Albert of New York has a collection of more than 3,000 miniature books. A former corporate lawyer, he began seeking out the books to fill the tiny shelves of the historic dolls' houses that he collected at the time. Among his miniatures is a 30-page, edition of Anton Chekhov's *The Chameleon* with miniscule dimensions of $\frac{1}{24}$ x $\frac{1}{24}$ x $\frac{1}{24}$ in (1 x 1 x 1 mm), which is about the size of a single grain of salt.

COTTON STATUES

Since 1987, Indian sculptor Anant Khairnar has made hundreds of statues of Lord Ganesha, famous personalities, abstract objects, and birds—all from cotton. He uses special chemicals to toughen the cotton so that his statues last for at least 10 years.

DELUXE DOGGY TREATS

Pampered pooches in Taiwan can enjoy top-notch treats in "Dr. Pro," an ice-cream parlor for dogs in the capital city, Taipei. One of a host of specialty stores for pets that have opened recently in the city, Dr. Pro offers a full range of ice-cream flavors with scoops all beautifully presented.

HUGE APPETIZER

A group of 20 Palestinian chefs spent 20 hours in June 2006 preparing a plate of tabbouleh, a Lebanese appetizer, that was 13 x 13 ft (4 x 4 m). The plate of chopped parsley, onion, lemon, tomato, and olive oil weighed over a ton.

CARD DEALER

Walter Cavanagh of Santa Clara, California, has nearly 1,500 valid credit cards, with total credit worth more than $1.7 million. His wallet stretches 250 ft (76 m), weighs about 38 lb (17 kg), and can hold 800 cards. He keeps the remainder in bank safety-deposit boxes. The idea began in the late 1960s when he and a friend made a bet whereby whoever could collect the most credit cards by the end of the year would win dinner. Cavanagh won with 143. He says: "I have a nearly perfect credit score. I only use one card and I pay it off at the end of the month. But you should see the length of my credit report!"

SELF TRIBUTE

British millionaire Scott Alexander has bought an entire town in Bulgaria and plans to rename it after himself.

FAVORITE FOOD

Brenda Lashley of Kenosha, Wisconsin, named her newborn baby Edward Allen Frank after her favorite brand of sauerkraut!

$100 BURGER

Diners at the Old Homestead Steak House in Boca Raton, Florida, can pay $100 for a hamburger made of beef from three different countries. Owner Marc Sherry has created a burger made from cows raised in Colorado, Argentina, and Japan.

△ FLAME FACE

H.H. Getty from Edmonton, Alberta, Canada, was known as "The Fireproof Man" because flames did not pain or blister him. He discovered his "talent" by accident when working on a construction site in the 1930s.

BELIEVE IT OR KNOT!

December 2005 saw workers in the city of Harbin in northeast China take the art of Chinese Knotting to a new level. Exponents of this traditional handicraft make decorative knots as auspicious household ornaments to symbolize such values as happiness and unity—but they are usually no more than a few inches square. However, this gigantic red knot, made to celebrate a snow carving expo in the city, measured an incredible 120 x 80 ft (37 x 24 m) and weighed a colossal 6,175 lb (2,800 kg).

IN DEPTH

GREAT DANE

American runner Dane Rauschenberg, 30, ran a marathon every weekend for a whole year to raise money for charity—even organizing his own race to complete the "Fiddy 2" challenge.

Why 26.2 miles every weekend?

❝My brother dared me to do an event where you run 15 km and then 5 km in one day, and then a marathon the following day. I ended up winning the event! I realized that I only needed a short recovery time between runs—so I decided to set up 'Fiddy 2' and do 52 in 2006.❞

Where were the races?

❝They were all across North America, from Disney World, Orlando, to the Cayman Islands, and a lot near where I live in Virginia. The second-to-last weekend of the year, I couldn't find a race because it was Christmas—so I had to organize my own one in Pennsylvania.❞

How did you choose them, and how did you get to them?

❝I had to finance my travel myself, so many were close to home. But I still completed 85,000 miles of flying and changed time zones 62 times in order to run my 1362.4 marathon miles.❞

Which was the hardest marathon to run?

❝No question—the one in Leadville, Colorado. My average time is around 3 hours 20 minutes—my fastest was Niagara Falls at 2 hours 59 minutes—but Leadville took 5 hours 17 minutes. There was over 12,000 feet of vertical ascension in that race—it was an uphill war.❞

Have you always liked running?

❝I actually don't consider myself a marathon runner—I'm a frustrated swimmer who can't find a pool! I started running in law school because there wasn't a pool nearby.❞

Did you train between races?

❝No. I work about 60 hours a week in patent licensing. Nobody else has ever done this while holding down a full-time job.❞

So how are you able to run marathons so close together?

❝People say to leave a few months between marathons, but I think, why get to your peak and then let it slip? I just maintain it. I am a little more muscular, at 185 lb, than most runners. But I always say I'm just an average runner who happens to be extremely stubborn.❞

What motivated you?

❝I did the first race for L'Arche, a charity which works with mentally and physically disabled people. When I saw what they did, I wanted to run all 52 races for them. I have raised over $30,000.❞

What was the best sight you saw while running?

❝I've run in the shadow of Mount Rushmore, and in view of the Mendenhall Glacier in Alaska. But mostly I don't care about the scenery—the finishing line is the best sight.❞

What will you do next?

❝I would love to do an Iron Man Triathlon, or ultra-marathons. But for now—I'm going to have a rest!❞

UNDERWATER IRONING

A keen exponent of the sport of extreme ironing, whereby competitors press clothing in dangerous environments, Louise Trewavas of London, England, plunged to new depths in August 2006 by taking an ironing board and iron to 452 ft (138 m) underwater at the Red Sea resort of Dahab. After ironing a T-shirt, she had to spend almost another three hours in the water carrying out decompression stops in order to avoid the sickness known as the bends.

CHANNEL PADDLE

In the space of nine days in 2006, Michael O'Shaughnessy of Ponce Inlet, Florida, completed a 64-mi (103-km) paddleboard marathon that took in four countries. First the 49-year-old real-estate broker paddled his way across the English Channel in just over five hours, then he made a 3.00 a.m. start to cross Scotland's Loch Ness in 5 hours 49 minutes, and finally, in a nod to his Irish roots, he crossed the Irish Sea in 2 hours 37 minutes.

STURDY BIKE

Cyclist Reg Blease is still pedaling the streets on his first bike—58 years after he bought it. In that period, the 74-year-old from Greater Manchester, England, has notched up over 300,000 mi (482,800 km)—equivalent to cycling around the world 12 times. The bike has no gears, just one brake, and is built from heavy steel.

FAMILY TATTOO

Father-of-20 Mike Holpin from New Tredegar, Wales, has his family tree tattooed on his back. He started the tree in 1997, adding to it whenever another baby was born—and there's still room for more!

TRICKY TRACK

In 2006, Steve Shanyaski and Richard Connolly created a model racing car track that was enough to drive you round the bend—all 724 of them. Laid out on an airfield in Kent, England, the track had 2,683 straights as well as the 724 curves to make a total length of 3,625 ft (1,105 m). Placed vertically in a straight line, it would be taller than Mount Snowdon, the highest mountain in England and Wales. The track was so long that each lap took 25 minutes.

SWEET ON SUGAR

Phill Miller of Greenfield, Indiana, has a collection of over 6,000 sugar packets from around the world.

KING OF CARDS

LeRoy Gensemer of Exeter, Michigan, has collected over 1.4 million different business cards. To celebrate reaching the million mark in 2002, naturally he had a commemorative business card printed.

NAKED RIDE

Hundreds of cyclists in some 50 cities around the world staged a naked bike ride on June 10, 2006, to protest against pollution caused by cars. Wearing nothing but their helmets, they paraded through venues such as Toronto, Los Angeles, Madrid, Barcelona, Prague, London, Milan, Seattle, San Francisco, and Vancouver.

◁ THEATRICAL DELIGHTS

Dedicated theatergoer Roy Burtenshaw from the city of Bath in Somerset, England, has visited his local playhouse more than a thousand times over a period spanning more than 50 years, and has the theater programs to prove it. A retired printer, Roy has been visiting the Theatre Royal in Bath ever since his father took him to a Christmas pantomime there when he was six years old. At the age of 26, Roy wooed his wife-to-be Sonia (also pictured here) with romantic dates at the theater, and he has seen every show performed there at least once ever since, always sitting in the same seat in the stalls. His favorite shows include *Joseph*, *Blood Brothers*, *Cats*, and *Les Misérables*.

△ MATCH THIS

A total of 6,300 matches were balanced on top of this beer bottle without any artificial supports in the 1930s by a group of friends from Pittsburgh, Pennsylvania.

CHEESY WHIFF

In one year, Alex Johnson, a 17-year-old student at Munising High School in Michigan, collected 3,500 empty bags of cheese-flavored snacks in his locker.

BASEBALL COLLECTOR

John Baker of Gosport, Indiana, has a collection of more than 1,000 old baseball gloves.

BATH FRIENDS

Valli Hammer of Farmer City, Illinois, is never short of company in the bath... because she owns around 2,500 rubber ducks. She began collecting them in 2000 to keep her young son happy at bathtime and now she has rubber ducks from all 50 U.S. states and several foreign countries.

LEGO AIRCRAFT CARRIER ▽

Malle Hawking from Munich, Germany, has made a massive scale model of the U.S.S. *Harry S Truman* aircraft carrier, out of lego. Using more than 300,000 bricks, Malle spent more than a year creating his masterpiece, which boasts electric lights on the flight deck as well as inside the individual aircraft on the deck. It also features movable elevators and radar dishes. The ship's measurements are a whopping 14 ft 10 in (4.52 m) long, 4 ft 6 in (1.37 m) wide, and 3 ft 11 in tall (1.2 m), and it weighs more than 353 lb (160 kg).

KNITTED GARDEN

In some gardens the emphasis is on trees and shrubs, with others the accent is on flowers. However, in a newly unveiled English garden, the overriding theme is wool.

That's because, with the help of more than 300 volunteers, Jane Bolsover of Surrey, England, has knitted a life-sized English garden.

The garden, which is sponsored by the British Hand Knitting Confederation, measures 15 x 10 ft (4.5 x 3 m) and took six months to create. Jane estimates her team made four million individual stitches in that time, knitting together 50 mi (80 km) of wool.

Everything in the garden is hand-knitted (including the wall, pond, and waterfall) and the attention to detail is extraordinary, right down to the flowers, insects, and toadstools, and even the worms and carrots in the vegetable patch.

There is a knitted picnic laid out on a rug on a knitted lawn, next to a knitted path. Among the woolen wildlife are a red squirrel, a robin, a mole emerging from a molehill, a bird at a nesting box, a frog, and a snail. Elsewhere, a woolen dog plays with a woolen ball to the backdrop of "music" from a woolen radio.

It was only when the project was complete that Jane made a startling admission. "I'm one of the world's worst knitters," she said.

A knitted deckchair provides the centerpiece to this amazing woolen garden.

Knitted Garden

◁ GOING OUT WITH A BANG!

American writer and journalist Hunter S. Thompson, author of the famous *Fear and Loathing in Las Vegas*, had his ashes blown sky high amid a spectacular burst of fireworks at his memorial service in Woody Creek near Aspen, Colorado, in August 2005. Thompson's red car is seen here parked in front of the 15-story tower from which the fireworks and his ashes erupted.

NAIL CLIPPERS

Andre Ludwick of Parys, South Africa, has a collection of more than 500 different kinds of nail clippers from around the world. His favorite was handmade by a blacksmith in 1935. The collection started after a visit to Israel in 1971, where Ludwick acquired two nail clippers as souvenirs.

$3,000 TAKEAWAY

A group of curry-mad England soccer fans paid over $3,000 to have a takeout dinner flown out from home to the 2006 World Cup in Germany. Bath restaurant Bombay Nights flew out the meal in an insulated bag to the fans' hotel in Munich.

GOING LOCO

A total of 1,740 students at the University of Guelph in Ontario, Canada, welcomed the new school year in September 2006 by simultaneously doing "The Locomotion."

EGG LAUNCH

The Aerospace Industries Association of America runs a contest for students to build a model rocket that can fly to a height of 850 ft (259 m) while towing two raw eggs, and then parachute the eggs back down to earth—unbroken.

GOLDEN SUM

Cosmetics magnate Ronald Lauder, co-founder of the Neue Galerie, New York, paid an unprecedented $135 million for a painting in 2006. He forked out the staggering sum for Austrian artist Gustav Klimt's 1907 oil-and-gold-encrusted portrait of Adele Bloch-Bauer, the wife of a sugar industrialist.

MARCH OF THE UNDEAD ▷

Every July, the village of Ribarteme in northwest Spain hosts a pilgrimage known as the "Procession of the Shrouds," whereby people who believe they have cheated death during the previous year are paraded through the streets lying in open coffins. This unusual custom, which dates back to the Middle Ages, symbolizes the penitents demonstrating their thanks to God for sparing their lives.

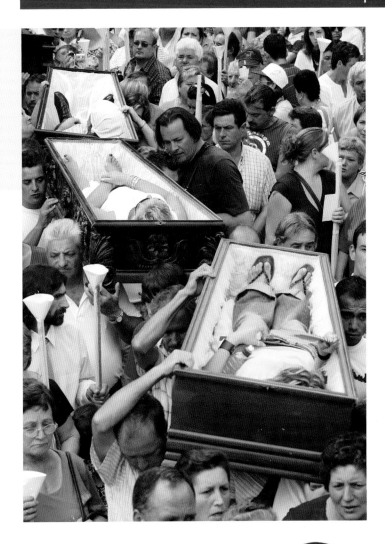

ARROW BIRTHMARK

Adrian Volcu of Richmond Hill, Ontario, Canada, has an arrow birthmark in the iris of his eye.

EARLY BIRD

Jeff Twieden of Seattle, Washington, began waiting in line for *Star Wars: Episode III* at the cinema 22 weeks before the movie's 2005 release!

WEIGHT LOSS

Thai policemen who had waistlines larger than 40 in (102 cm) were ordered to lose weight in 2005 so that they looked good while directing traffic. As a result, more than 80 overweight officers underwent a one-month fitness regime in Bangkok.

DIARY ENTHUSIAST

James Cummings of Knapp, Wisconsin, has a collection of 16,000 diaries, including works by John Quincy Adams, Winston Churchill, and Benjamin Franklin.

FAST-FOOD DIET

For his documentary film, *Supersize Me*, U.S. director Morgan Spurlock ate nothing but McDonald's fast food for breakfast, lunch, and dinner over the course of 30 days.

BOTTLE FIREPLACE

Eric Rayner's family home, near the Russian River in California, has an outdoor fireplace made from hundreds of old bottles.

COLORFUL COFFINS

Artist Alfred Opiolka offers an unusual service to the bereaved and their families in the town of Wertach in southern Germany. He paints coffins in bright colors, often with floral motifs and sometimes decorated with butterfly ornaments, and says that people often find funerals easier to bear when the deceased is lying in a cheerful, brightly painted casket.

SICK BAGS

Feel queasy on airplane flights? Go and see Sweden's Rune Tapper who has 1,079 different airsickness bags from 448 airlines in 131 countries!

CABIN COLLECTOR

James Grisley of Pittsburgh, Illinois, has a collection of around 28 full-size log cabins, ranging from small sheds to large barns, all built in the mid to late 1800s. His interest began in 1976 when a neighbor gave him an old, rundown cabin to use as a toolshed.

RELAXED REPTILES ▷

These lizards have been dressed up and placed in this tableau after being deeply relaxed and hypnotized by a ten-year-old girl in Florida. Lily Capehart discovered her uncanny ability to "hypnotize" lizards when she was just two years old, and has been doing it ever since. Maintaining that all of her lizards are handled with the greatest care and respect, Lily and her parents have created the world of "Lizard-Ville"—a series of images showing the lizards dressed up and placed in whimsical lizard-sized scenes.

DISCO BALL

In Johannesburg, South Africa, in September 2006, the *Citizen* newspaper built an operational disco ball measuring about 12 ft (3.6 m) in diameter and weighing two tons!

BUSY BALLOON

Ralf Schüler from Dessau, Germany, must be really popular at children's parties, because, believe it or not, he has managed to squeeze 23 people inside a latex balloon.

16,000 TIES

Derryl Ogden of the U.S.A. has a collection of more than 16,000 neckties that he has amassed since 1934.

SEAWEED WINE

Marine biologists in Germany make seaweed wine which sells for $28 a bottle.

TAG QUILT

Diana Douglas of Higdon, Alabama, made a giant quilt using 2,591 shirt tags.

CRAZY ERIC

An electrician from France calling himself "Crazy Eric" carries 1,300 objects including screwdrivers, a shaving kit, a fold-up umbrella, spare batteries, and paint brushes in his specially designed outfit.

FISH FAN

In 2006, 98-year-old Constance Brown of Pembroke, Wales, revealed that the secret of her long life was eating nothing but fish and chips. "That's all I eat. I don't eat any vegetables at all," says Constance, who has been frying fish and chips for a living for 80 years.

PLANE AUCTION

An African charter airline bought a Gulfstream jet for $4.9 million... on the Internet auction site eBay.

Wacky Weddings

BUNNY BLISS

Giant rabbits Roberto and Amy got married in Somerset, England, in April 2006. Both bride and groom weigh around 40 lb (18 kg) and are more than 3 ft (91 cm) in length.

CAKE CAPERS

In New York's Times Square in June 2005, 20 brides-to-be dressed in wedding gowns dived into a giant wedding cake to find a $50,000 prize as part of a promotion for a cable channel's TV series *Bridezilla*.

WEIGHTY WEDDING DRESS

In August 2006, Josephine Doherty from Surrey, England, got married in a dress that weighed a colossal 392 lb (178 kg)! The bride took two hours to get into the dress, and its 60-ft (18-m) train took five bridesmaids and eight best men to carry it.

OUT OF THIS WORLD

Russian-born American Ekaterina Dmitriev poses with a life-size cutout of her bridegroom Russian cosmonaut Yuri Malenchenko following her satellite wedding to the Commander of the International Space Station in Texas in 2003. Texan law allows weddings where one party is absent, but this does not usually mean they are in orbit 240 mi (385 km) above the Earth.

COOL WEDDING

A couple adopted drastic methods to avoid getting married in a heat wave that struck southern Italy in 1995. Domenico Manchia from Italy and his French bride Marlene Mulet were wed 18 ft (6 m) under the sea in front of the town of Tavolara in Sardinia.

RUNAWAY BRIDE

Kate Austin and Gordon Fryer had a wedding with a difference when they were married while running the 2006 London Marathon.

IN THE PINK

To raise her profile, 57-year-old Reverend Wendy Saunders of London, England, has gone entirely pink. First she dyed her hair pink, then added a pink jacket, pink trousers, and a pink shirt below her conventional dog collar. To complete the effect, she bought a pink Nissan Micra car. No wonder she is known locally as "The Pink One."

NOISY REJECTS

Believe it or not, China's army turns away recruits that snore too loudly!

24-HOUR RIDE

Mark Brown mangaed to cover a distance of 580 mi (933 km) on a little 50cc scooter at Australia's Le Minz 24-Hour Scooterthon in 2005.

YO, EDDY!

Canadian "Fast Eddy" McDonald is a speedy yo-yo performer who has managed to perform an astonishing 35 separate yo-yo tricks in a single minute, and a dizzying 8,437 loops in one hour.

BASKETBALL MARATHON

Two teams of students and teachers from Japan took part in a basketball game that lasted two and a half days in June 2006. Miyazaki International College beat Miyazaki Municipal University by 5,493 points to 5,432 in the 60-hour marathon.

ROAD FORK

Steve Schreiber planted a sculpture of a 31-ft (9.5-m) high silver fork at the intersection of two roads in Rock City, New York.

FEARLESS GRANDMA

A 92-year-old British great-grandmother rappeled (abseiled) 220 ft (67 m) down the side of an apartment building in June 2006. Doris Long of Hayling Island, Hampshire, completed the daredevil feat in the nearby city of Portsmouth. She said afterwards: "I was swinging like a pendulum. People inside must have thought I was dropping in for tea."

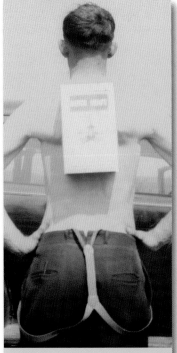

⚠ STRONG SHOULDERS

In the 1940s, Joe Jirgles from Grand Rapids, Michigan, could hold a 1-gal (3.8-l) can of varnish between his shoulder blades. He could also use his shoulder blades to attach himself to a fence so firmly that he could hang in place.

SUPERSIZE SOCCER ▽

Fans warm up with a full-size soccer ball on a giant table soccer game in Berlin, Germany, in 2005. Created to promote the Confederation Cup, which Germany hosted in 2005, the game featured players in the shape of the Berlin Bear—the city's mascot for more than 700 years.

DARING LEAP

Dressed in a dinner jacket and bow tie, Gary Connery from Berkshire, England, performed a daring BASE jump from the rim of the London Eye Ferris wheel on November 29, 2006.

Connery swam up the River Thames in London, England, and climbed onto the wheel's base. Edging his way up the steel frame, it took him two hours to reach the top where he leaped off the 443-ft (135-m) wheel and parachuted safely to the ground as passersby looked on in amazement. He said afterwards: "It's something I've always wanted to do. I'm just attracted to the thrill of jumping off dramatic structures. It's a sheer adrenaline rush." The 37-year-old father of two has previously ridden off an English cliff, 530 ft (160 m) high, on a mountain bike and parachuted from the Eiffel Tower, Nelson's Column, and from inside the top of London's Millennium Dome.

Connery cuts a tiny figure, suspended from his parachute after jumping from the London Eye.

Ripley's Believe It or Not!

A DOG'S LIFE

Eighteen-year-old Aija Gillman of Pinckneyville, Illinois, won a new car after she spent 13 days chained to a doghouse and wearing a dog collar in July 2006, as part of a competition to discourage dog owners from chaining up their pets. Her life was limited to the space accessible within the reach of the chain. She slept in her doghouse, battled boredom by playing in the mud and with her water bottle, and fought off sunburn by rubbing mud on her face. Hygiene was a porta-potty.

MASSIVE MOUTH

At a whopping 11¾ in (30 cm) in circumference, the mouth of university student Gordon du Cane from Wiltshire, England, certainly is something to shout about. It is more than two inches bigger than a baseball, and Gordon can easily hold a whole apple in it, between his teeth.

MOLE MAN

For nearly half a century, 75-year-old William Lyttle of London, England, has been digging burrows beneath his 20-room Victorian house. Known locally as the "Mole Man," it is estimated that, using a shovel and a homemade pulley, he has scooped 120 sq yd (100 sq m) of earth to hollow out a network of tunnels and caverns, some 26 ft (8 m) deep, and spreading up to 60 ft (18 m) in every direction from his house.

OLD CHOCOLATE

A woman from Derbyshire, England, owns a chocolate bar that is 105 years old. Jane Marshall was given the bar, made to celebrate King Edward VII's 1902 coronation, by her grandfather when she was nine.

BIBLE GROUP

Retired Croatian bishop Marijan Oblak has a collection of almost 1,000 Bibles in 250 different languages. He has been collecting Bibles for 20 years and was given some in person by the late Pope John Paul II.

PAPER BOATS

An Indian man has a collection of over 10,000 tiny, handmade paper boats. Shrinath Dixit from New Delhi carves the miniature boats in various colors with glaze and origami papers. They range in size from ⅞ in (2 mm) to 2 in (0.5 cm), so are best viewed under a magnifying glass.

TOP TABLE

In August 2006, 20 people carried a 630-lb (285-kg) pool table almost 3,000 ft (915 m) to the summit of the highest peak in the Brecon Beacons mountain range in Wales.

BRITNEY SANDWICH

In 2006, a sandwich half-eaten by Britney Spears was sold for more than $500. The egg salad sandwich was collected by a waiter after an awards ceremony and put up for sale on eBay. It was bought by on-line gaming company Golden Palace, who also purchased the remains of a corndog that was being eaten by Britney's now ex-husband Kevin Federline.

HEALTHY HOBBY

Huang Chunyi, 94, of Taiwan credits his longevity to his 20-year hobby—collecting photos of beautiful women!

JEWEL BOX

By 2000, Carol McFadden of Oil City, Pennsylvania, had accumulated a collection of more than 30,000 different pairs of earrings.

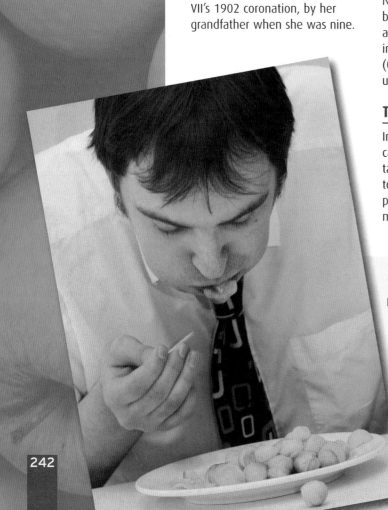

◁ BRUSSELS BONANZA

British office worker Richard Townsend was left feeling a little green when he tried to eat a colossal 44 Brussels sprouts in 60 seconds in December 2006. Using a wooden toothpick to transport the vegetables to his mouth, Richard managed a heroic 37 sprouts before he ran out of time. After his marathon attempt, Richard said that he couldn't face another sprout for a few days, but then popped another in his mouth, saying, "It's a shame to waste them."

SKATER BOYS

In 2005, Moshe Arazi, Aaron Lyon, and David Micley of Newton, Massachusetts, made a skateboard that measured a staggering 30 ft 1 in (9.17 m) in length.

WEIRD TRADITION

Since 1952, fans of ice hockey team Detroit Red Wings have traditionally thrown octopuses on to the rink at the beginning of the play-offs.

ANTIQUE SLEIGHS

Retired teacher Bill Engel of Denver, Missouri, has a collection of more than 80 horse-drawn sleighs, most of them at least 100 years old.

FOOT FUNERAL

Antonio Magistro of Gioiosa Marea, Sicily, held a funeral service for his amputated left foot before burying it in a coffin at the city cemetery.

EXPENSIVE TASTE

New York City's Algonquin Hotel offers a martini cocktail with a diamond garnish at a cost of $10,000.

CODE BUSTER

David Rosdeitcher of Boulder, Colorado, also known as "The Zip Code Man," can identify the location of any U.S. town based on its zip code. He has memorized all 48,000 zip codes in the U.S.A.

DEAFENING DIGITS

When Bob Hatch of Pasadena, California, snaps his fingers, the sound that he makes registers at 108 decibels—that's equal to the sound from a jackhammer or a race car.

LONG BROWS

Leonard Traenkenschuh of Port Townsend, Washington, has eyebrows that are 3½ in (9 cm) long.

BASEBALL COFFINS

Thanks to a Michigan company, U.S. baseball fans will be able to stay close to their favorite teams in the afterlife. Eternal Image announced in 2006 that it would be reproducing the names and logos of all 30 U.S. major league baseball teams on a range of coffins and urns, priced from $600 to $3,500.

CHOPPING-BOARD BELLY

This Chinese chef is seen here displaying great dexterity with two meat cleavers by chopping meat on his stomach in the city of Nanjing in eastern China.

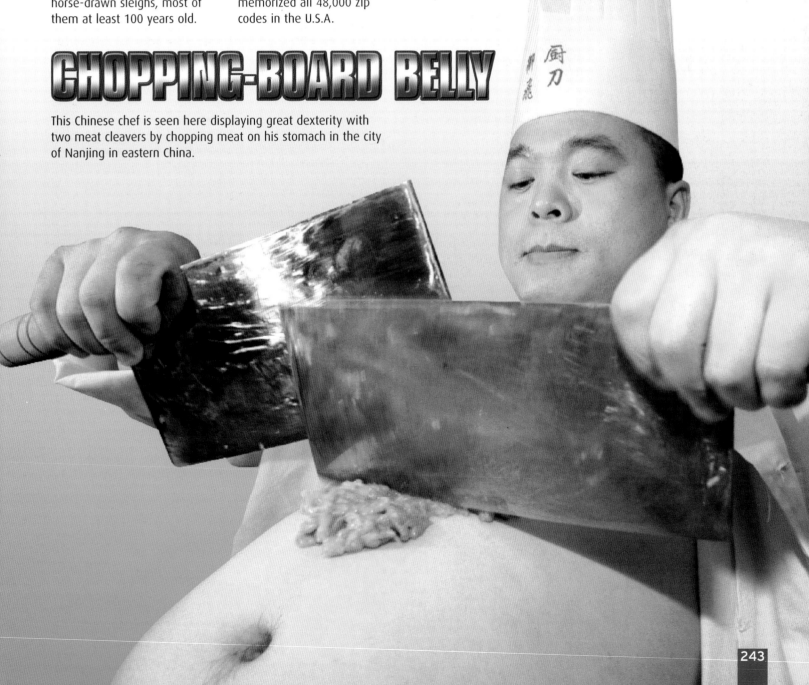

厨刀

DOMINO DAY

A team of 87 builders from 13 different countries took around two months to set up an intricate domino course—and then saw more than four million dominoes toppled in a matter of minutes.

The "Domino Day" challenge took place in the city of Leeuwarden, in the Netherlands, on November 17, 2006. It was created by Weijers Domino Productions, who had designers working on the Domino Day project for almost the entire year. The course comprised 4,400,000 dominoes, took five months to produce, and weighed a total of 77,600 lb (35,200 kg).

Four special builders' challenges were included in the course whereby pairs of builders had to complete key areas of the display while the dominoes were already falling. By the end of the event, 4,079,381 of the 4,400,000 dominoes that had been set up were toppled successfully.

The theme for Domino Day 2006 was "Music in Motion" and nine musical genres, including rock, classical, disco, and hip-hop were represented. The set-up included famous figures, such as Mozart and Britney Spears, as well as pictures, and even a "domino city."

One of the most spectacular sections of the design was devoted to Michael Jackson. A mechanical figure that was part of the display did a moonwalk and, while the soundtrack to "Billie Jean" was played, the dominoes fell to form three impressive figures of Jackson.

More than 250 varieties of dominoes, some with stickers and some painted, were used in the course.

A real flower-power Volkswagen van was hidden inside a domino structure. It took three builders a whole week to wrap the van inside a domino wall nearly 6½ ft (2 m) high.

A member of the international team of builders carefully sets up a part of the course.

One of the builders' challenges incorporated a huge old-style gramophone about 16 ft (5 m) high. During the show a builder had to lie down on the arm of the gramophone to put dominoes onto the record.

I DO... I DO... I DO...

There is no secret to how David and Lauren Blair of Henderson, Tennessee, keep that newlywed feeling alive in their marriage—they simply keep getting married over and over again. In August 2006, the fortysomething couple staged their 90th wedding in 22 years of marriage! They actually had three weddings the first week they were married in 1984. The first was in Topanga Canyon, Los Angeles, which they thought appropriate because they both work in the film industry; the second was a traditional church wedding in Chicago; and the third was in Las Vegas after they picked up a coupon for a free wedding while on their honeymoon. And since then they've tied the knot on a regular basis, including being married in 11 Hard Rock Cafés.

CURRY BATH △

A Japanese health spa is offering the unusual specialty of a communal curry bath to its patrons. The bath, which resembles a green soup, contains a blend of curry spices, including turmeric and red pepper, and is said to improve blood flow, help boost the metabolism, and produce beautiful skin in all who bathe in it.

GIANT GNOME

Artist Maria Reidelbach is dwarfed by her latest creation—a concrete garden gnome that stands 13 ft 6 in (4 m) tall. Chomsky the gnome is part of Maria's *Gnome on the Grange* project, located near Accord, New York.

TWINE BALL

Since 1979, James Frank Kotera of Lake Nebagamon, Wisconsin, has been creating a huge ball of twine. Using leftover twine from a neighbor's bales of hay and working up to four hours a day, he has assembled the "Mr JFK Twine Ball." It weighs more than 19,000 lb (8,600 kg), stands as tall as a person, and is twice as long.

TINNED TREAT

Les and Beryl Lailey of Manchester, England, celebrated their wedding anniversary in 2006 by eating a can of chicken that they had been given on their wedding day... 50 years earlier. They had vowed to keep the canned chicken, which was part of a wedding gift hamper, in their kitchen cupboard as a memento of their happy day in 1956 and promised that they would not eat it until their golden anniversary. And when they finally opened the can, the chicken tasted as good as new. Les said: "I had it with some potatoes and vegetables and it went down a treat."

◁ MUD MUNCHER

For the past 12 years, Bao Bao from Zhengzhou in central China has had a strange compulsion to eat mud. It started one day when, at the age of seven, she was walking along a river bank and thought how she would like to try some mud, and mud has been a staple part of her diet ever since. Yellow mud is her favorite. Bao Bao is estimated to have eaten more than 1.5 tons of mud to date.

WIGGLY FEAST

Eating a handful of worms might not be everyone's idea of a tasty snack, but this man in Madras, India, is loving them! He ate an astonishing 200 worms in a fraction over 20 seconds at a worm-swallowing contest in 2003.

INDEX

ACKNOWLEDGMENTS

FRONT COVER AND TITLE PAGE Ripley's Entertainment Inc.; 8 (t) Reuters/Marcelo Del Pozo, (c) 2daymedia, (b) PA Photos; 9 Jeff J Mitchell/Getty Images; 10–11 (dp) Reuters/Marcelo Del Pozo; 10 (b/l) Reuters/Desmond Boylan, (b/r) Reuters/Heino Kalis; 11 (t/r) Reuters/Albert Gea, (c/r) Reuters/Marcelo Del Pozo, (b/r) Reuters/Albert Gea; 12–13 (dp) Rafa Rivas/AFP/Getty Images; 14 (b) Mark Clifford/Barcroft Media, (t) Reuters/Paul Yeung; 15 2daymedia; 16 (t) Saverkin Alexsander/UPPA/Photoshot, (b) William Thomas Cain/Getty Images; 17 Reuters/Bogdan Cristel; 18 (t) Reuters/China Daily China Daily Information Corp—CDIC; 19 Rex Features; 20 (b) Benguc Ozerdem/Rex Features, (t) Robin Utrecht/UPPA/Photoshot; 21 (t) Rex Features, (c, b) Daniel Graves/Rex Features; 22 Kazuhiro Nogi/AFP/Getty Images; 23 R.Gaillarde/Gamma; 24–25 (dp) Rex Features; 25 Benjamin Stansall/Rex Features; 26 (t) 2daymedia, (b) Vicki Whitehill/Ripley Entertainment Inc.; 27 Chris Hellier/Rex Features; 29 Sam Barcroft/Barcroft Media; 30–31 Junko Kimura/Getty Images; 32 (t) Rejeanne Arsenault/Ripley Entertainment Inc., (b) Reuters/Pawel Kopczynski; 33 Jeff J Mitchell/Getty Images; 34–35 T. Falise/ Gamma; 36 Reuters/David Gray; 37 PA Photos; 38 (t) Louis Lemaire © 2005 ZOHO Artforms, (c) Mark Jenkins, (b) Reuters/David Gray; 39 2daymedia; 40–41 Heather Jansch; 42 (t) Newscom, (t/c) PA Photos; 43 (b) ChinaFotoPress/Getty Images; 45 (b) Rogulin Dmitry/UPPA/Photoshot; 46–47 (dp) Reuters/David Gray; 46 (t) 2daymedia; 47 (t) Ian Waldie/Getty Images; 48 www.toothpickart.com; 49 Jeff J Mitchell/Getty Images; 50–51 Mark Jenkins; 52 (b) Murmur, Stan. Sittin' Pretty [Anthropometric Monotype, Ashley Barlow] 2005, (t) 2daymedia; 53 AndoArt.com; 54–55 www.ronpatrickstuff.com; 56–57 Louis Lemaire © 2005 ZOHO Artforms; 58 (t) PA Photos, (b/l, b/c) Reuters/Arben Celi; 59 Stephen Boitano/Barcroft Media; 60 (fc) Christopher Hall/Fotolia.com, (t/l) David Burner/Rex Features, (t/r, c, b/l, b/r) Courtesy of private collector; 61 UPPA/Photoshot; 62–63 (c) 2daymedia; 62 (t) Philippe Hayes/AFP/Getty Images; 64 Paul Minyo; 65 (t) Gavin Bernard/Barcroft Media, (b) UPPA/Photoshot; 66 Anna Barclay/Rex Features; 67 (b, b/r) Ben Phillips/Barcroft Media; 68 (t) Louis Sanchez III/Ripley Entertainment Inc., (c) www.sunderlandbodyart.com, (b) Rex Features; 70 (b/l) PA Photos, (t/r) ChinaFotoPress/Getty Images, (c/r) PA Photos, (b/r) ChinaFotoPress/Getty Images; 71 PA Photos; 73 (t) Robin Boyce/Ripley Entertainment Inc., (b) Newscom; 74 (b) Wang Xiaocun/CQCB/ChinaFotoPress/Getty Images, (t/l) Denis Charlet/AFP/Getty Images, (t/r) CHU Amiens via Getty Images; 75 Rex Features; 76–77 (c) PA Photos; 76 (t) Sam Panthaky/AFP/Getty Images; 77 (t) PA Photos; 78 PA Photos; 79 Louis Sanchez III/Ripley Entertainment Inc.; 80 (t) Newscom; 81 (t) Reuters/Victor Ruiz, (b) Hulton Archive/Getty Images; 82–83 (t/dp) Nicole Shaffer/Ripley Entertainment Inc.; 82 (fc) Nicole Shaffer/Ripley Entertainment Inc., (b) IB/IHA/UPPA/Photoshot; 83 (b) Reuters/STR New; 84–85 Passionate Productions/Getty Images; 86 Incredible Features/Barcroft Media; 87 (t) De Ville/Rex Features, (b) swns.com; 90 PA Photos; 91 Reuters/Pilar Olivares; 92 PA Photos; 93 (b) CQCB/ChinaFotoPress/Getty Images, (t/c, t/r) Reuters/Str Old; 94–95 (c) Reuters/Nir Elias; 94 (t/l, t/r) PA Photos; 96 (t) Emylea Tharby/Ripley Entertainment Inc., (b/l, b/r) Reuters/Phil Noble; 97 www.sunderlandbodyart.com; 98 (t) 2daymedia, (c) Newscom, (b) David Burner/Rex Features; 99 PA Photos; 100–101 Camera Press London; 101 (t) PA Photos; 102 (t) ChinaFotoPress/Getty Images, (b) Incredible Features/Barcroft Media; 103 (b, t/r) Picture Courtesy of New Straits Times Press Berhad, Malaysia; 104 (t/l) Courtesy of Jude Stringfellow; 105 Renee Chambers www.ArtistisaHorse.com; 106–107 (dp) Reuters/Richard Chung; 106 (b) Reuters/Herb Swanson, (t) PA Photos; 107 (b) Reuters/Richard Chung; 108 (t) Lorna Stroup Nilsson, (b/l, b/c) 2daymedia; 109 PA Photos; 110 swns.com; 111 (b) Newscom; 112–113 (dp) Drew Gardener www.drew.it; 112 (t) Austin Hargrave/Barcroft Media; 113 (t/r, c/r) David Burner/Rex Features; 114–115 (c) Frederic Neema/Gamma/Camera Press London; 114 (b) John Springer Collection/Corbis; 115 (b) Frederic Neema/Gamma/Camera Press London, (t) Painting Displayed at the National Gallery/Camera Press London; 116 (fc) PA Photos, (t) Courtesy of David C Steele; 117 Courtesy of Karl Beznoska; 118 (t/r) ChinaFotoPress/UPPA/Photoshot, (t/c/r) Zhang Yanlin/UPPA/Photoshot, (b/c/r) PA Photos, (b/r) Reuters/China Daily China Daily Information Corp—CDIC, (t/l) AFP Poto/Anna Zieminski, (c/l) Bill Greenblatt/Landov/World Illustrated/Photoshot, (b/l) PA Photos; 119 (t/l) Feature China/Barcroft Media, (b) swns.com; 120 (t) Toby Zerna/Newspix/Rex Features, (b) Rex Features; 121 (t/l, b/l) PA Photos; 122 (t) Sam Barcroft/Barcroft Media, (b) Daniel Rushall/Rex Features; 123 Reuters/Mariano Bazo; 124 (t) AFP Photo/Saeed Khan, (b) Reuters/Pawan Kumar; 125 (t/r) Chris Saville/Rex Features, (b/r) Sipa Press/Rex Features, (t/c) Stewart Cook/Rex Features, (b/c) Richard Austin/Rex Features, (t/l) Chris Martin Bahr/Rex Features, (c/l) Rex Features, (b/l) Hydestile Wildlife Hospital/Rex Features; 126–127 Courtesy of Janice Wolf; 128 (t) Reuters/Alex Grimm, (c) Duan Renhu/Phototex/Camera Press London, (b) Reuters/Sean Yong; 130 (t, b) Spectrum Multi-Media Ltd. Kent Hart—Hart Images www.AlwaysEscaping.com, 131 (t/r) Spectrum Multi-Media Ltd. George Douklias—Winnipeg www.AlwaysEscaping.com, (t/l) Spectrum Multi-Media Ltd. Kent Hart—Hart Images www.AlwaysEscaping.com, (c, b) Spectrum Multi-Media Ltd. George Douklias—Winnipeg www.AlwaysEscaping.com, 132 (fc) Karin Lau/Fotolia.com; 132–133 (dp) Duan Renhu/Phototex/Camera Press London; 134 (t) Newscom, (b) Feature China/Barcroft Media; 135 Roderick Russell/CNY Medical Center; 136 (b) PA Photos; 137 Reuters/Alexandra Beier; 138–139 Reuters/Frank Polich; 138 (fc) Johanna Goodyear/Fotolia.com; 140 Pete Schwickrath/Ripley Entertainment Inc.; 142 Camera Press/Wu Dongjun/Phototex; 143 Reuters/Sean Yong; 144–145 (dp) Richard Bouhet/AFP/Getty Images; 144 (b) Tony Ashby/AFP/Getty Images; 145 (t) Tony Ashby/AFP/Getty Images; 146 (fc) Mary Scott/Ripley Entertainment Inc., (t/l) Mehmet Dilsiz/Fotolia.com, (t/r) Mary Scott/Ripley Entertainment Inc.; 148 (t/l, t/r) Scott Hampton/Ripley Entertainment Inc., (b) Marcelo Bezos/Ripley Entertainment Inc.; 149 (t/r) Reuters/Alex Grimm, (t/l) Reuters/Daniel Aguilar, (c/r) PA Photos, (c/l) Reuters/Mohamed Azakir, (b) Reuters/China Photos; 150 Reuters/Sergio Moraes; 151 Kyle Nolte/Ripley Entertainment Inc.; 152–153 (b,dp) Jeff Clay/Ripley Entetainment Inc., 152 (t) Reuters/Jose Manuel Ribeiro; 153 (t) Jamie Grant/Ripley Entertainment Inc.; 154 PA Photos; 155 Courtesy of David Straitjacket; 156–157 (dp) Reuters/Darren Staples; 156 (t) Camera Press/Zhang Xiangyang/Phototex, (b) Reuters/Kamal Kishore; 158 (t) Brandy Conley/Ripley Entertainment Inc., (c) Stan Honda/AFP/Getty Images, (b) 2daymedia; 159 Stan Honda/AFP/Getty Images; 160–161 (dp, t) Courtesy of Juan Cabana; 162 PA Photos; 163 (l) Davison Design and Development www.inventionland.com; 164 (b) Stewart Cook/Rex Features, (t) The University of Manchester; 165 (t) Nils Jorgensen/Rex Features, (b) Rex Features; 166–167 (t) 2daymedia; 166 (b) William Kennedy/Ripley Entertainment Inc.; 167 (b) Reuters/Stringer India; 168 (t/l) Great Plains Regional Medical Center, (b) PA Photos; 169 (c) PA Photos, (b) Reuters/Anthony Bolante; 170 (b) Reuters/Rupak De Chowdhuri; 171 (t) Matt Cardy/Getty Images, (b) Stan Honda/AFP/Getty Images; 172 (t) The Davey Tree Expert Company, (b) Reuters/Stringer Thailand; 173 Brandy Conley/Ripley Entertainment Inc.; 175 (t) Camera Press/Wu Fang/ChinaFotoPress/Gamma, (b) Charles Hasley/Ripley Entertainment Inc.; 176 (t/r) ChinaFotoPress/Zhao Haijiang/UPPA/Photoshot, (b) Rex Features; 177 (t/l) 2daymedia, (t/r) Camera Press/Wattie Cheung, (c/l) Mark Clifford/Barcroft Media, (c/r) Camera Press/Yang Wanjiang/Phototex, (b/l) Jamie Jones/Rex Fetures, (b/r) Gong Hui/UPPA/Photoshot; 178 Newscom; 179 (t) Sara Fernandez/Ripley Entertainment Inc., (b) Jamie Hanso/Newspix/Rex Features; 180 (t/r, t/c/l) Scott Wade, (t/c/r) Jules Alexander, (b/c, b) Scott Wade; 181 (t/r) Scott Wade, (t/c/l) Jules Alexander, (c) Scott Wade, (b) John McDavitt; 182 Reuters/Stephen Hird; 183 (t) Peter Lawson/Rex Features; 184 (t) Reuters/China Daily China Daily Information Corp—CDIC, (b) Michael Wilks/Ripley Entertainment Inc.; 185 Chris Jackson/Getty Images; 186 (t) Reuters/Francois Lenoir, (b) 2daymedia; 187 PA Photos; 188 (t) Reuters/Sean Yong, (c) Reuters/Gustau Nacarino, (b) Reuters/Stringer Shanghai; 189 Lilli Strauss/AP/Empics; 190 (t, c) Reuters/Brendan McDermid, (b) Reuters/Mike Segar; 191 (t, b) Reuters/Brendan McDermid; 192 (t) Sobchenko Grigory/Itar-Tass/UPPA/Photoshot; 193 (l) Reuters/Sean Yong, (r) Reuters/China Daily China Daily Information Corp—CDIC; 194 (c) Urs Flueeler/epa/Corbis, (b/r) AFP Photo Sena Vidanagama; 195 (t/c, t/r) PA Photos, (b) Rex Features; 196 (fc, t) Sandy Maxwell/John Muir Trust. The John Muir Trust acquired Ben Nevis Estate which includes Britain's highest point at Ben Nevis summit (1334m) in June 2000. www.jmt.org, (b) Chinafoto Press/Gamma; 197 (t/l) Reuters/Gleb Garanich, (b/l) Reuters/China Daily China Daily Information Corp—CDIC, (b/c) Stephen Chernin/Getty Images, (b/r) Reuters/Stringer Shanghai, (c/r) William Thomas Cain/Getty Images, (t/r) Reuters/Adnan Abidi; 198 Newscom; 199 (t) Newscom, (c, b) Courtesy of David Hanson; 200 (b) Reuters/Gustau Nacarino, (t) Ian Waldie/Getty Images; 201 Ian Waldie/Getty Images; 202 (t/r) Kay Nietfeld/AFP/Getty images, (b) Reuters/China Daily China Daily Information Corp – CDIC; 203 Reuters/Bazuki Muhammad; 204 Vladimir Kmet/AFP/Getty Images; 205 (t) Newscom, (b) Giovanni Zardinoni www.studioartezj.net; 206 (sp) Timothy A. Clary/AFP/Getty Images; 207 (b) Reuters/Bogdan Cristel, (t) Reuters/Alexandra Beier; 208–209 (b) Newscom, (t) www.goldeagle.com; 209 (t/l) Courtesy of Trevor Andre Snowden; 210–211 All courtesy of Kyle MacDonald except Alice Cooper—Pictorial Press, and town sign—www.cooperphoto.ca; 212 (b) PA Photos; 213 PA Photos; 214 Gamma; 215 (bgd) Terje Eggum, (t) Investec Asset Management, (b) Terje Eggum; 216 (bgd) Marc Chesneau/Fotolia.com, PA Photos; 217 (t) Ethan Miller/Getty Images; 218 (t) Daniel Graves/Rex Features, (c) Joshua Mueller/Ripley Entertainment Inc., (b) Solent News/Rex Features; 219 Shao Dan/Photocome/UPPA/Photshot; 220–221 Reuters/Yves Rossy; 222 (fc, t) Joshua Mueller/Ripley Entertainment Inc.; 223 (t) Philippe Hays/Rex Features, (b) Sutton-Hibbert/Rex Features; 224 (t) Rex Features, (b) Alan Freed/Ripley Entertainment Inc.; 225 Timm Schamberger/AFP/Getty Images; 226–229 (b) Ben Phillips/Barcroft Media; 226 (fc) Francoise Bro/Fotolia.com, (t) Reuters/Jacky Naegelen; 227 (t) Daniel Graves/Rex Features, (b/r) Ben Phillips/Barcroft Media; 228 Chuck Weedman/Ripley Entertainment Inc.; 229 Reuters/Christian Charisius; 230 (t/l) Reuters/Richard Chung, (b) Gamma/Camera Press London; 231 Courtesy of Dane E Rauschenberg; 232–233 (t) swns.com, (b) Gavin Bernard/Barcroft Media; 233 (b/r) Gavin Bernard/Barcroft Media; 234–235 ICHF www.ichf.co.uk; 236–237 (b) Reuters/Michaela Rehle; 236 (t) Reuters/POOL New; 237 (t) Reuters/Miguel Vidal; 238 Camera Press/ED/DW; 239 (t/l) PA Photos, (t/r) Stan Honda/AFP/Getty Images, (c/l) Helen Jones/UPPA/Photoshot, (c/r) Reuters/Richard Carson, (b/l) PA Photos, (b/r) John Gichigi/Getty Images; 240 (b/l) Courtesy of Edward McDonald, (b/r) Reuters/Fabrizio Bensch; 241 (sp) Winnie Chang/Rex Features, (t) Alisdair Macdonald/Rex Features, (b) Winnie Chang/Rex Features; 242 (b) PA Photos, (t) Solent News/Rex Features; 243 (b) Shao Dan/Photocome/UPPA/Photshot; 244–245 www.dominodomain.com; 246 (b) Imagine China/Barcroft Media, (t) Reuters/Yuriko Nakao; 247 Reuters/Stringer India.

Key: b = bottom, c = center, dp = double page, l = left, r = right, sp = single page, t = top, fc = fly column, bgd = background

All other photos are from the MKP Archives and Ripley's Entertainment Inc.
Every attempt has been made to acknowledge correctly and contact copyright holders and we apologize in advance for any unintentional errors or omissions, which will be corrected in future editions.

The front cover shows eye-popper Avelino Mato of Baracoa, Cuba.

Arran Boyd

KT-446-710

Human Body Encyclopedia

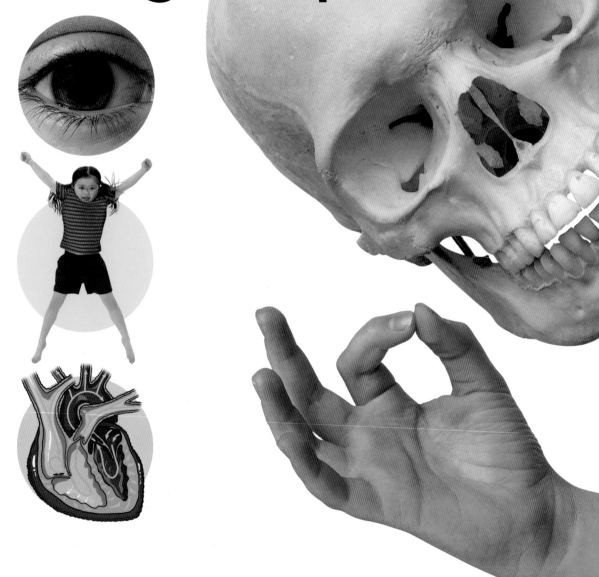

LONDON, NEW YORK,
MELBOURNE, MUNICH, and DELHI

Senior editor Penny Smith
Senior art editor Cheryl Telfer

Editors Ben Morgan, Zahavit Shalev
Additional design Jacqueline Gooden,
Tory Gordon-Harris, Claire Patane, Laura Roberts
Illustrator Peter Bull
Digital illustrator Pilar Morales

Consultants Dr Penny Preston, Dr Frances Williams

Publishing manager Sue Leonard
Managing art editor Clare Shedden
Jacket design Victoria Harvey
Picture researchers Marie Ortu, Rob Nunn
Production controller Shivani Pandey
DTP designer Almudena Díaz

First published in Great Britain in 2005.
This edition published in 2012 by
Dorling Kindersley Limited,
80 Strand, London WC2R 0RL
Penguin Group (UK)

Copyright © 2005 Dorling Kindersley Limited, London

10 9 8 7 6 5 4 3 2 1
002–FD071–Sep/11

All rights reserved. No part of this publication may be
reproduced, stored in a retrieval system, or transmitted
in any form or by any means, electronic, mechanical,
photocopying, recording, or otherwise, without the prior
written permission of the copyright owner.

A catalogue record for this book
is available from the British Library.

ISBN 978-1-4053-9349-2

Colour reproduction by Colourscan, Singapore
Printed and bound in China by South China Printing Co. Ltd.

Discover more at
www.dk.com

Contents

Human body

Skeleton and bones

Moving muscles

Brain and senses

Test yourself with the questions at the bottom of each page...

Circles show close-up images you might not otherwise be able to see.

Coloured discs contain facts about special topics, such as taste.

"Get into it" activity buttons show you how you can try things out for yourself.

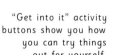

About this book
This book has special features that will show you how to get your hands on as much information as possible! Use the "become an expert" buttons to find out more about a subject on other pages.

You will always find the answers here!

Your amazing body

The greatest machine you'll ever own is your body. It's more complicated than any computer, it lasts for a lifetime, and it's yours for free.

Become an expert…
on the skeleton, pages **12-13** on digestion, pages **82-83**

Body parts
Your body is made up of hundreds of different parts. You probably know the names of the bits you can see, but there are many more hidden deep inside you.

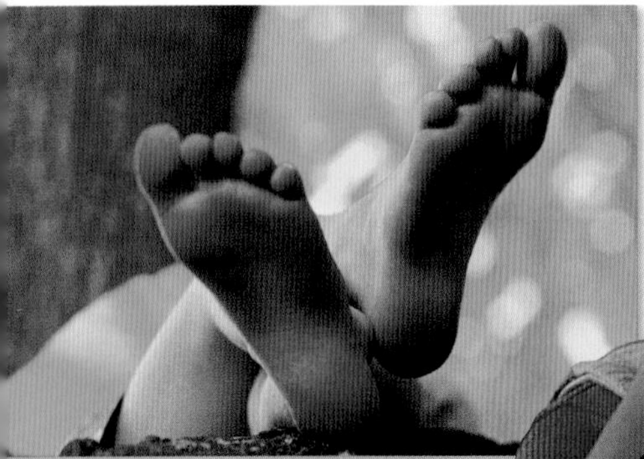

Hair

Forehead

Ears

Eyebrows

Cheeks

Nose

Eyes

Lips

Teeth

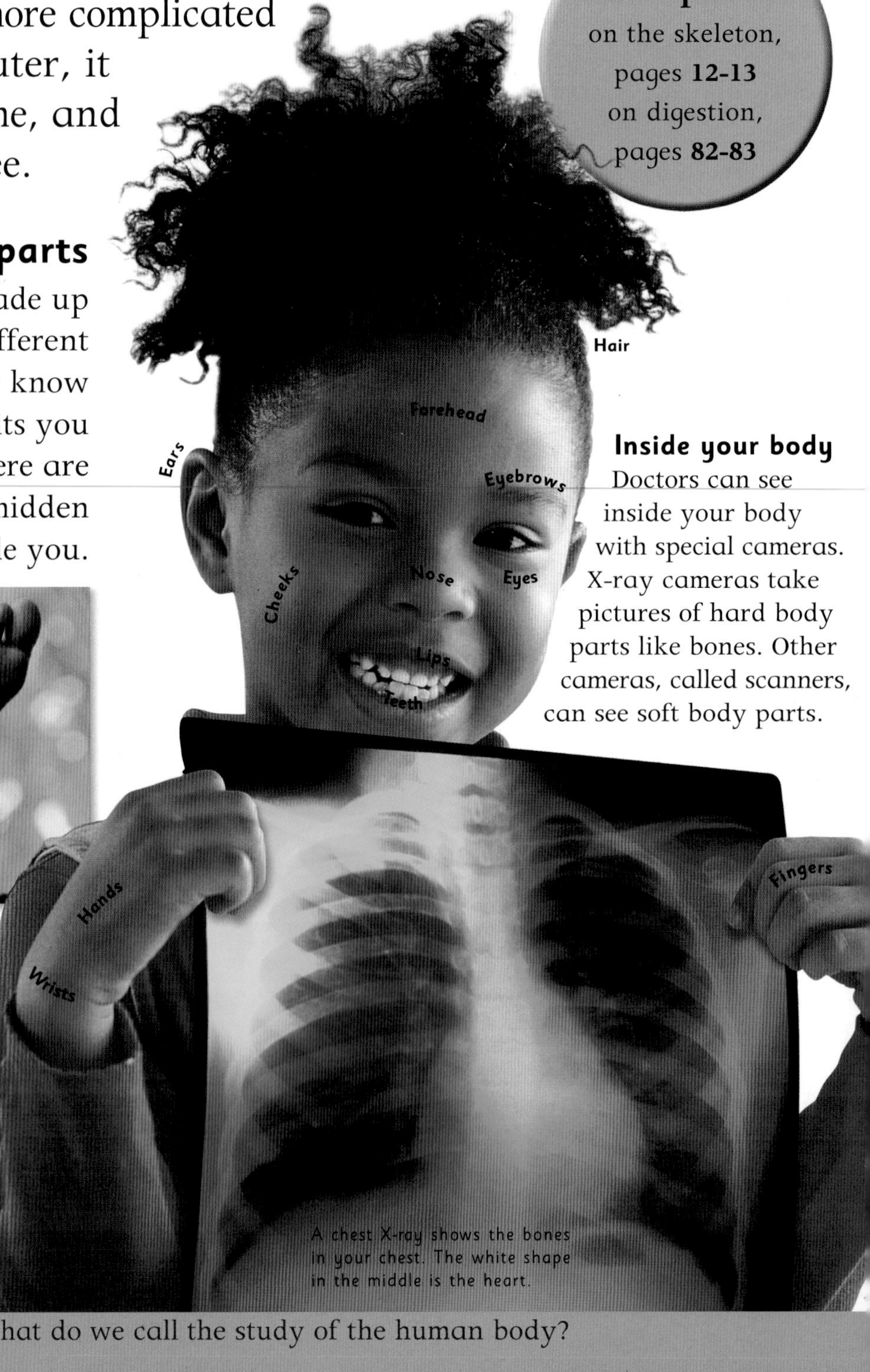

Inside your body
Doctors can see inside your body with special cameras. X-ray cameras take pictures of hard body parts like bones. Other cameras, called scanners, can see soft body parts.

Two of everything
Body parts often come in pairs. You have two feet, two eyes, two ears, two lungs, and so on. This means you have a handy spare in case one of them gets damaged.

Hands

Fingers

Wrists

A chest X-ray shows the bones in your chest. The white shape in the middle is the heart.

What do we call the study of the human body?

Water, water

Water is the most important chemical in your body. About two-thirds of your weight is water.

Curiosity quiz

Take a look at the first few pages in this book and see if you can find these pictures.

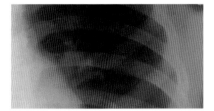

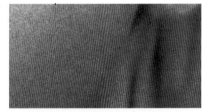

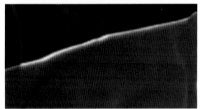

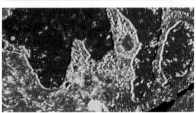

The ingredients

Your body is made of just a few simple chemicals, plus water.

 Carbon is the chemical in diamonds and coal. A fifth of you is carbon.

 Iron makes your blood red. You have enough to make one small iron nail.

 Phosphorus is in the tips of matches, as well as your bones and teeth.

 Sodium and **chlorine** make salt. Blood is one-third as salty as sea water.

 Potassium is used in some types of soap. It's also in your body fluids.

 Nitrogen is important in muscles. It's also the main ingredient in air.

Robot

No substitute

The human body is too complicated for robots to copy. Robots can copy the way we walk, but they can't think or feel like we do.

Chimps have hands like ours.

Compared to chimps, our bodies look almost hairless.

Chimpanzee

Being human

Although we look different to animals, our bodies are similar on the inside. Our closest animal relatives are chimpanzees.

What makes you you?

All human bodies work the same way, but everyone is different. Nobody looks, sounds, or thinks exactly like you. You're different because of the way your genes and experience shape you as you grow up.

Fair skin

Green eyes

Curly hair

Black hair

Freckles

Unique

The shape of your face, the colour of your hair, and many other things make you unique – different from everyone else.

How many genes are there in the human body?

In the genes

Genes are instructions that build your body and tell it how to work. Your genes control many of the things that make you unique, like the colour of your eyes or how tall you'll be.

This girl has a gene that allows her to roll up her tongue. The boy doesn't have the gene, so he can't roll his tongue.

DNA

Your genes are stored in a chemical called DNA, which looks like a twisted ladder with four different types of rung. The rungs make up a four-letter alphabet that spells out your genes, like letters in a book.

There's enough DNA inside you to stretch to the Sun and back 400 times.

DNA can split and copy itself.

get into it

Look in a mirror and see if you can roll your tongue. Don't cheat by squeezing it with your lips. Test your family to see who has the gene.

In the family

Your genes came from your parents. Half come from your mother and half come from your father. If you look like your parents, it's because you share the same genes.

Learning to ride a bike changes your brain and your body.

Changing body

Genes don't control everything – experience also shapes you. If you exercise a lot, for instance, your body gets stronger.

Building blocks

Every part of your body is made of
tiny building blocks called cells, which
fit together like bricks in a wall. Cells
are so small that hundreds could fit
on the point of a pin.

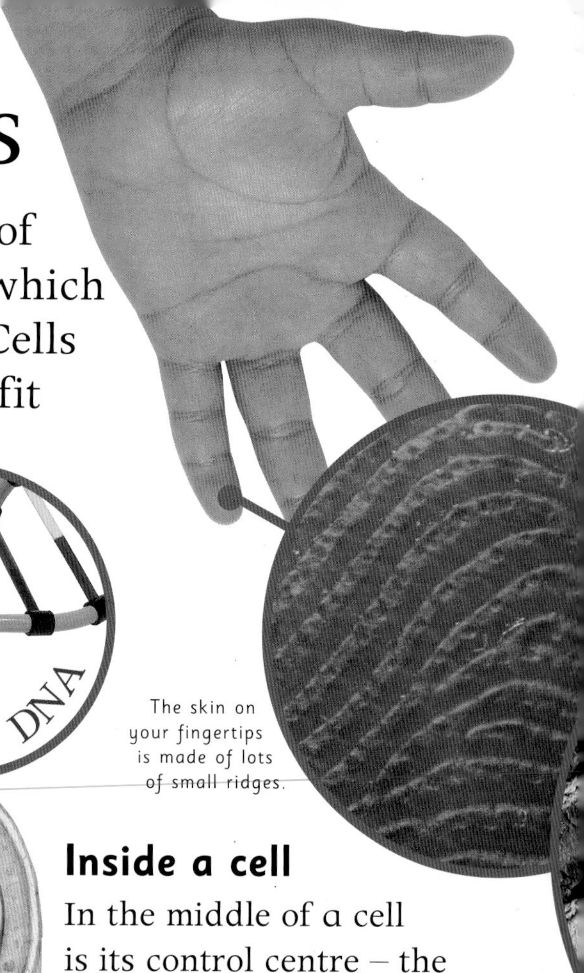

The nucleus
controls the
rest of the cell.

DNA is
stored in
the cell
nucleus.

The inside of
a cell is packed
with a kind of
living jelly called
cytoplasm.

DNA

The skin on
your fingertips
is made of lots
of small ridges.

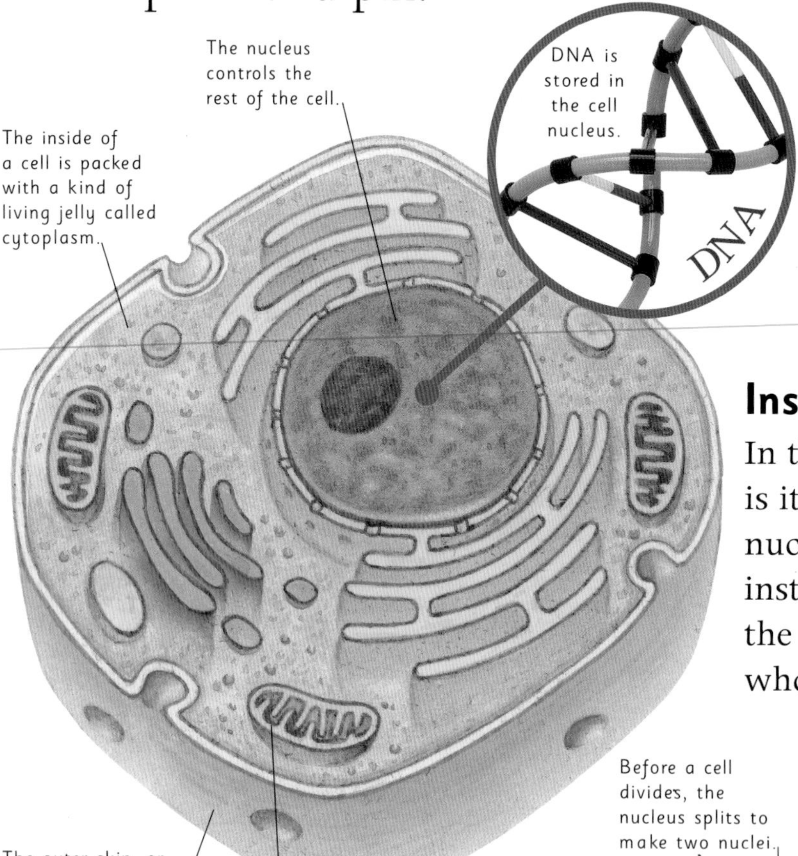

Inside a cell

In the middle of a cell
is its control centre – the
nucleus. The nucleus sends
instructions to the rest of
the cell, telling the cell
what chemicals to make.

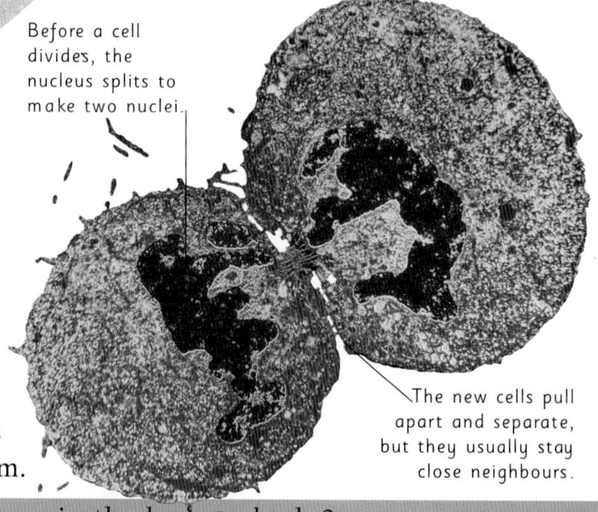

Before a cell
divides, the
nucleus splits to
make two nuclei.

The outer skin, or
membrane, stops
things leaking out.

Tiny generators
provide cells
with power.

Making new cells

A cell makes new cells by dividing.
The two new cells are half the size,
but they soon grow back. Millions of
your cells die every second, but millions
of others divide to replace them.

The new cells pull
apart and separate,
but they usually stay
close neighbours.

How many cells are there in the human body?

How big are cells?

Cells are too small to see with the naked eye, but scientists can photograph them through powerful microscopes. The cells on your skin are about a hundredth of a millimetre wide.

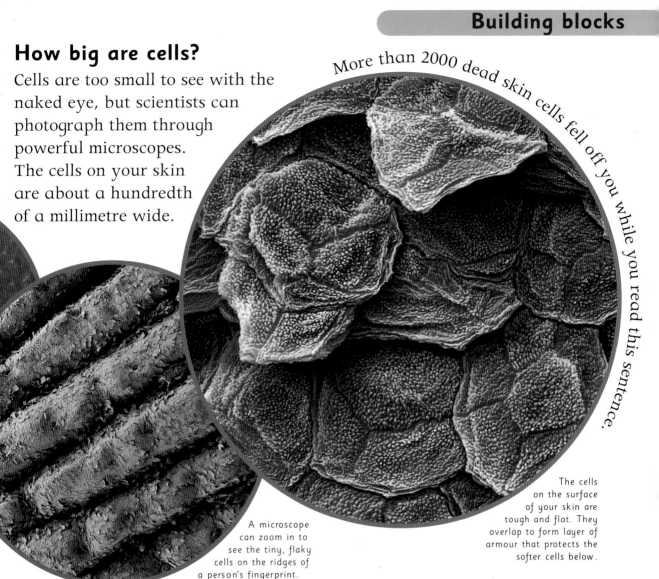

More than 2000 dead skin cells fell off you while you read this sentence.

A microscope can zoom in to see the tiny, flaky cells on the ridges of a person's fingerprint.

The cells on the surface of your skin are tough and flat. They overlap to form layer of armour that protects the softer cells below.

Fat cells are bubble shaped. They store fat under your skin.

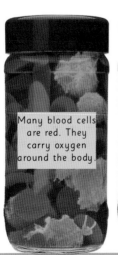
Many blood cells are red. They carry oxygen around the body.

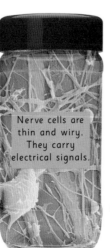
Nerve cells are thin and wiry. They carry electrical signals.

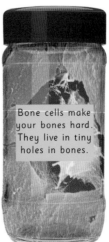
Bone cells make your bones hard. They live in tiny holes in bones.

Cells make tissue

Your body contains hundreds of different types of cells that do different jobs. Cells of the same type usually group together to form tissue. Fat, muscle, bone, and nerves are types of tissue. Blood is a liquid tissue.

Organizing the body

Your cells and tissues are organized into larger body parts called organs. In turn, your organs work together to form body systems.

Systems

Organs and tissues work in teams to carry out major tasks, like transporting blood or processing food. These teams are called systems.

The heart is the largest organ in the blood system. It pumps blood around the body.

Heart   Kidney   Brain

Organs

An organ is a body part that does a specific job. Your heart's job, for instance is to pump blood. Kidneys clean blood.

The tubes that carry blood away from the heart are called arteries (shown in red).

The tubes that carry blood back to the heart are called veins (shown in blue).

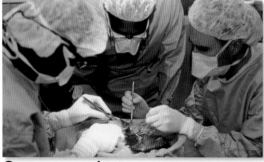

Organ transplant

If a vital organ stops working, doctors may replace it with an organ from another person. This is called a transplant.

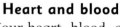

Heart and blood

Your heart, blood, and blood vessels make up the blood system. It transports vital supplies around your body.

Which body system makes your   stomach rumble?

Muscles

Your muscle system is made of tissues that move parts of your body by pulling on them or squeezing them. Your biggest muscles all pull on bones.

Your fingers are moved by muscles in your arm.

Muscles change the position of your skeleton by pulling different bones.

The most powerful muscles are in your legs.

Other systems

Some of your other important systems are shown in this list.

Breathing system: the main organs are your lungs, which take in air.

Hormone system: this uses powerful chemicals to control your body and mood.

Skin, hair, and nails: these form your body's protective covering.

Immune system: this seeks and destroys germs that get into your body.

Urinary system: this cleans blood and gets rid of waste chemicals.

Reproductive system: these are the organs that make babies.

Skeleton

Bones and joints make up the skeletal system, an inner frame that supports the body.

A quarter of your bones are in your feet.

Nerves

Your nervous system carries electrical signals around your body. You need this system to see, hear, think, and react.

Signals shoot along nerves to muscles, telling them when to pull.

Senses, such as touch, rely on nerve cells that send signals to your brain.

Your brain is the nervous system's control centre.

Digestive system

Your digestive organs break down food to provide your body with energy and raw materials.

Your mouth is the first part of the digestive system.

A long, twisting tube makes up your intestines, where digested food is absorbed.

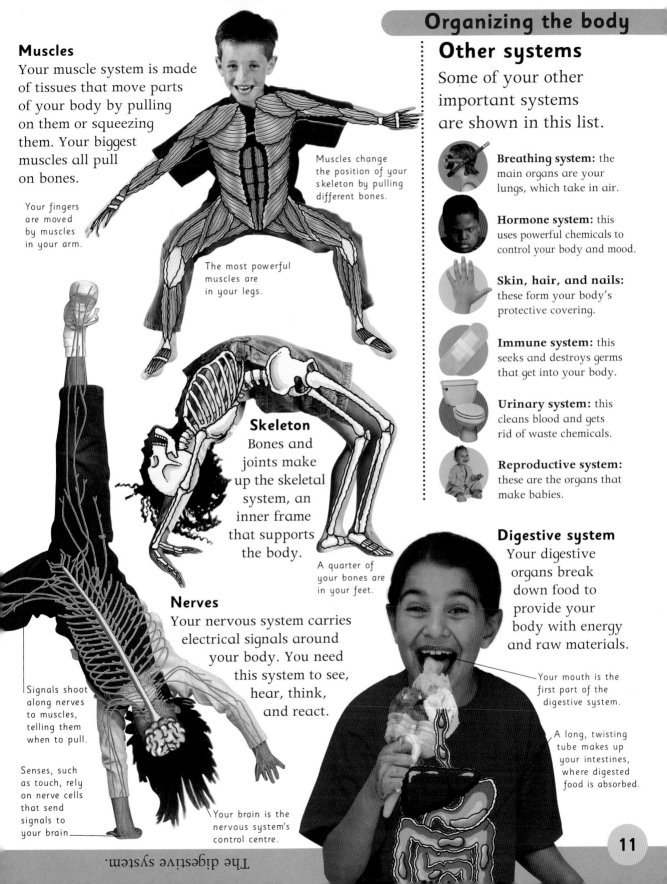

Skeleton

Your bones all join up to make a frame for your body called the skeleton. This protects your insides, and helps you move about.

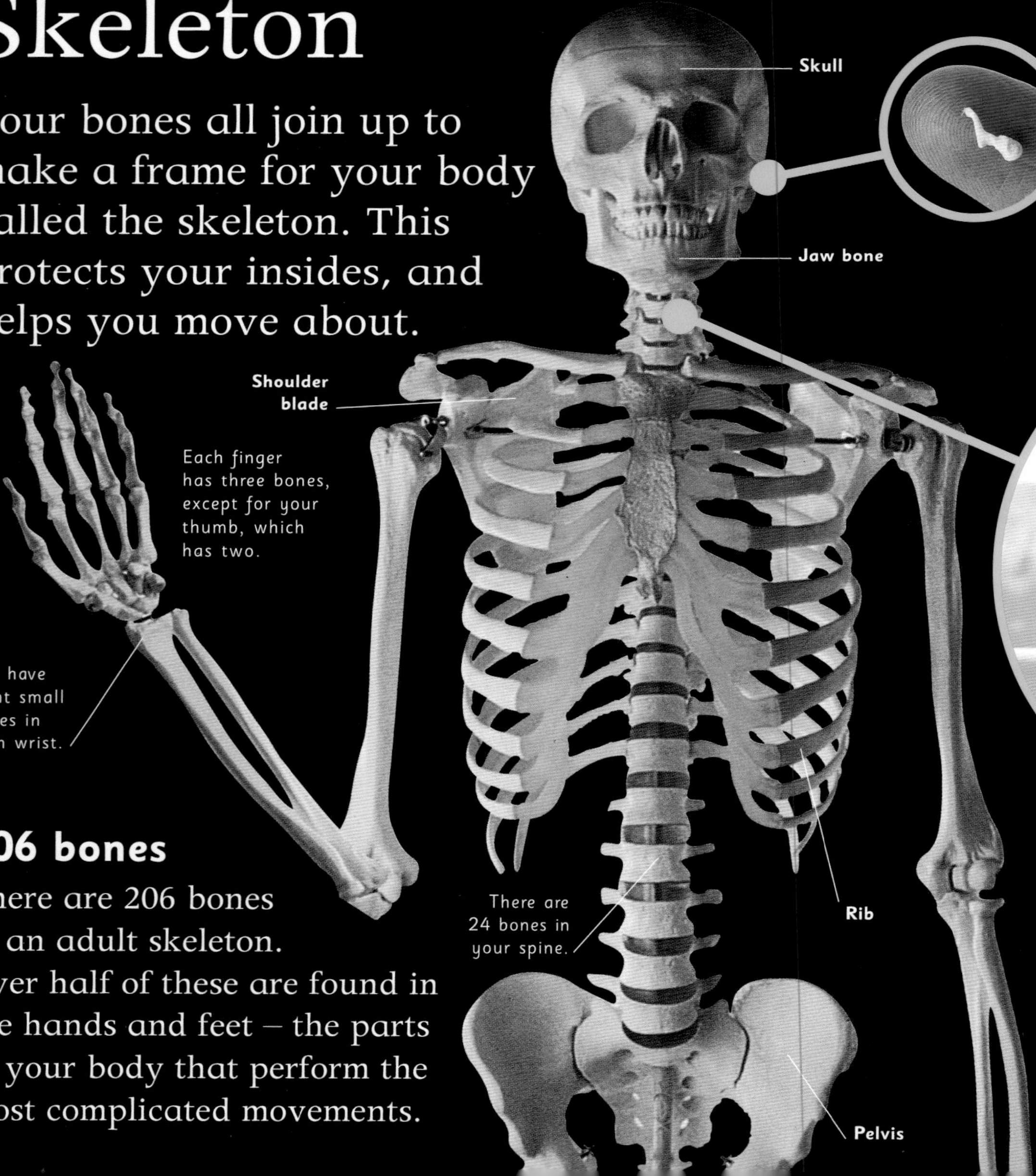

Smallest bone

Around the same length as a grain of rice, this is one of the smallest bones in your body. It lies deep inside your ear.

Skull

Jaw bone

A giraffe's long neck helps it to eat leaves off tall trees.

Neck bones

Did you know that you have seven bones in your neck, the same number as a giraffe? The top one allows you to move your head up and down, the second lets you rotate it from side to side.

Rib

Pelvis

There are 24 bones in your spine.

Shoulder blade

Each finger has three bones, except for your thumb, which has two.

206 bones

There are 206 bones in an adult skeleton. Over half of these are found in the hands and feet – the parts of your body that perform the most complicated movements.

You have eight small bones in each wrist.

How many ribs have you got?

Frogs have very short spines to withstand the strain of the huge leaps they take.

A fish's spine allows it to bend its body from side to side so it can swim smoothly.

Other skeletons

Most animals have a backbone and are called "vertebrates". Animals with no spine, like spiders and bugs, are called "invertebrates".

Snakes are incredibly bendy thanks to many identical vertebrae forming their long spines.

Your tail bone is at the very bottom of your spine.

Thigh bone

Shin bone

Your ankle has three larger bones and four smaller ones.

There are 54 bones in your hands, and 52 in your feet.

The thigh bone is the biggest and strongest in the body.

Long lasting

Bone is a very hard material and one of the last parts to rot away when a body is buried. This woman lived in the Stone Age, 5000 years ago, but her bones have survived until today.

Become an expert...

on bone and cartilage, pages 20-21, on teeth, pages **84-85**

Head case

The most complex part of the skeleton is the skull. It is made of many bones that fit together tightly, to protect the brain and support the face.

The frontal bone forms your forehead.

The cranium is the domed part of your skull!

Helmet
The upper part of the skull is like a helmet that protects the brain. The lower part forms a structure for your facial features to attach to.

Eye sockets are made up of seven different bones.

The front of the nose has no bones.

The brain fills most of the cranium.

Facial features
This image shows the relationship between your skull and face. There are no bones shaping the front part of your nose, your lips, or your ears. Your nose and ears are shaped by cartilage.

Teeth are set into the upper and lower jaws.

Why does a baby have spaces between its cranial bones?

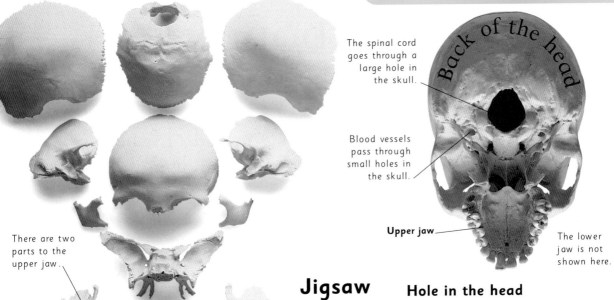

The spinal cord goes through a large hole in the skull.

Back of the head

Blood vessels pass through small holes in the skull.

Upper jaw

The lower jaw is not shown here.

There are two parts to the upper jaw.

The lower jaw is hinged. It is the only skull bone that can move.

Jigsaw

The skull bones fit together like the pieces of a jigsaw. All but one of the bones are locked in place. This makes the skull very strong.

Hole in the head

From underneath you can clearly see the big hole at the bottom of this skull. The spinal cord – which runs down your back – meets your brain here.

Face from the past

Scientists can work out what a dead person's face looked like from their skull alone. They examine the facial bones and build up artificial cartilage, muscle, and skin over them.

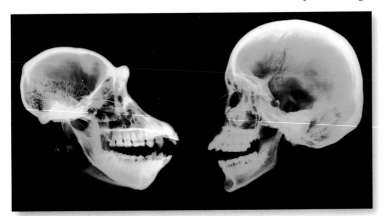

Meet the relatives

Chimpanzees and humans share a common ancestor. However, chimps have smaller brains than humans so their craniums are smaller. Chimps also have a large ridge above their eyes, and a jutting jaw.

So its head could withstand being squashed while it was being born.

Bendy backbone

Your spine is a length of bones running down the back of your body. Without it you couldn't hold up your head and body, or make any sort of movement.

Your spine curves gently, a bit like the letter "s".

The first seven bones are in your neck. They are known as the cervical vertebrae.

The next 12 are called the thoracic vertebrae.

Stack of bones

Your spine contains 24 separate bones called vertebrae. At the bottom are nine more vertebrae. They are much smaller and are fused together.

The thoracic vertebrae form joints with the ribs.

A straight back is actually quite curvy.

The five lumbar vertebrae bear most of your weight.

The five sacral vertebrae are fused together.

The coccyx consists of four fused vertebrae.

Back of spine

Front of spine

The spinal cord goes through this hole.

The fused bones of the sacrum and coccyx don't allow much movement.

Segments of the spine

Each vertebra has a strong, stubby section that supports the weight of your body, and a hole for the spinal cord to pass through.

What is a slipped disc?

Shock absorbers

You twist and bend your spine almost every time you move. Sandwiched between the vertebrae are pads of cartilage to stop them banging and rubbing against each other and getting worn out.

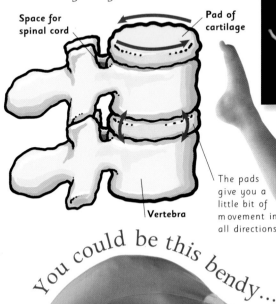

Space for spinal cord

Pad of cartilage

Vertebra

The pads give you a little bit of movement in all directions.

Ribcage

Your thoracic vertebrae connect to your ribs. Together they form a cage around your heart and lungs. Rib bones are curved. They are also thinner and more bendy than the bones in your spine.

A woman's pelvis is shaped differently to a man's. A baby can pass through it when she gives birth.

Pelvis

Reproductive organs and some digestive organs rest in the bowl-shaped hollow of your pelvis. The sacral vertebrae and coccyx form the bottom of the bowl.

You could be this bendy......

The way the back curves means we can't bend as far back as we can forwards.

Bendy backbone

The amount of movement between each vertebra and its neighbours is actually very small, but added together they allow for a large range of movement.

...with a lot of practice!

get into it!
Bend over. Gently feel the bones of your spine with your fingertips. Can you follow them from neck to waist?

17

It's when one of the pads between the vertebrae gets damaged.

Living bone

Their outer surface may be hard
and dry but that doesn't mean
your bones aren't alive. Bones
are always growing and
repairing themselves.

What's inside our bones?

Bone accounts for one
sixth of your body's
weight. Its clever
structure means
it's often
lighter than
it looks.

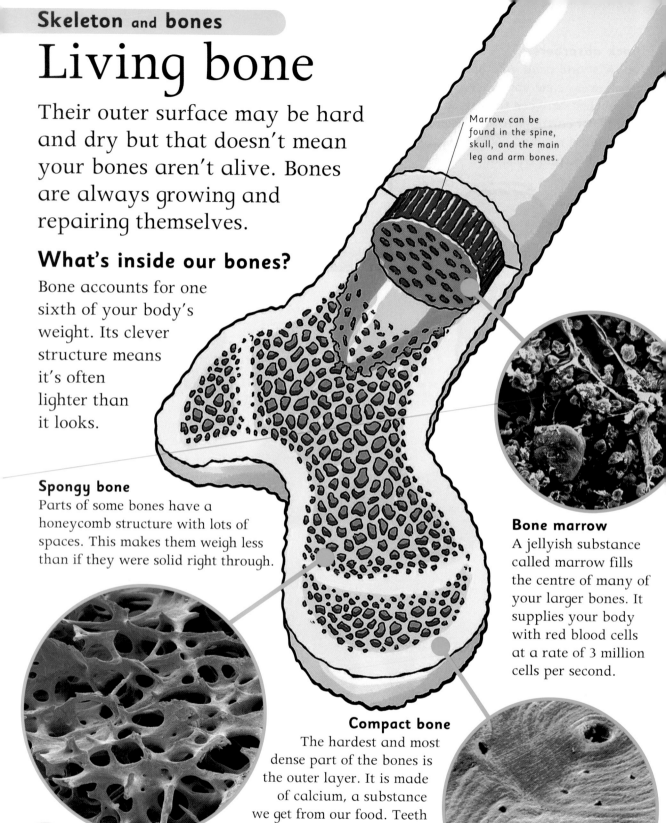

Marrow can be
found in the spine,
skull, and the main
leg and arm bones.

Spongy bone

Parts of some bones have a
honeycomb structure with lots of
spaces. This makes them weigh less
than if they were solid right through.

Bone marrow

A jellyish substance
called marrow fills
the centre of many of
your larger bones. It
supplies your body
with red blood cells
at a rate of 3 million
cells per second.

Compact bone

The hardest and most
dense part of the bones is
the outer layer. It is made
of calcium, a substance
we get from our food. Teeth
are made of calcium too.

What are the most commonly broken bones?

Broken bone

Bones are strong and flexible enough to cope with a lot of pressure, but, as this X-ray shows, they sometimes break. Luckily they can heal themselves.

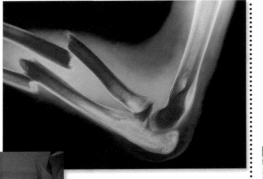

If the broken bone ends have slipped apart they must be repositioned by a doctor before healing begins.

On the mend

New cells form at each end of the broken bone, closing the gap between them. It takes about 6 weeks for this to happen.

Your bones are still growing until your late teens.

Padded clothes help protect bones from sudden impact.

Looking after your bones

Calcium from milk and cheese is needed to build strong bones. Weight-bearing exercise like walking, climbing, or skating helps to strengthen bones.

Curiosity quiz

Take a look through the skeleton and bones pages and see if you can identify where these bony bits come from.

Become an expert... on the skeleton, pages **12-13** on skin and pages **70-71**

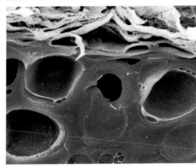

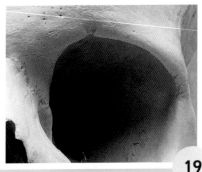

Bone and cartilage

When you were a baby, you were tiny. Slowly, as you get older and bigger, your bones do a clever trick. Not only do they grow, but they also change.

Baby's hand

Making bones

Babies' bones are made out of a soft and bendy material called cartilage. Slowly this hardens and turns into bone.

Baby bones are entirely made of soft, growing cartilage.

Adolescent bones are mostly bone, with a small amount of cartilage.

Adult bones have stopped growing. Most no longer contain cartilage.

Stick out your ears!
Your ears are made of cartilage, not bone. They are strong, but much more bendy than your bony bits.

More, less

You've got more bones than your mum or dad!
You were born with over 300 "soft" bones, but as you get older, many fuse together. By the time you're 25 you'll have 206 fully formed bones.

Cross-section of an ear – the cartilage sits between two layers of skin.

Which foods are rich in calcium, the mineral you need to grow healthy bones?

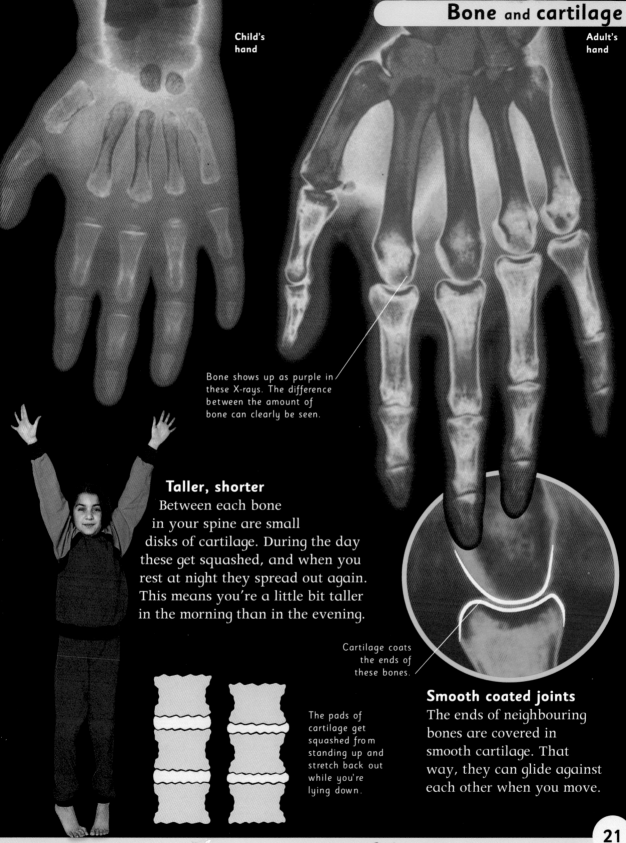

Child's hand

Adult's hand

Bone shows up as purple in these X-rays. The difference between the amount of bone can clearly be seen.

Taller, shorter

Between each bone in your spine are small disks of cartilage. During the day these get squashed, and when you rest at night they spread out again. This means you're a little bit taller in the morning than in the evening.

The pads of cartilage get squashed from standing up and stretch back out while you're lying down.

Cartilage coats the ends of these bones.

Smooth coated joints

The ends of neighbouring bones are covered in smooth cartilage. That way, they can glide against each other when you move.

Milk, cheese, yogurt and ice-cream.

Moving joints

Joints are the places where bones meet. Different kinds of joints allow you to move in different ways.

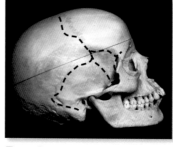

Hinge joint

Your knee can bend in the middle but it can't swing from side to side. This joint has a hinge like the one that allows you to open and close a door.

Knee joint

Fixed joints

The bones that make up your skull start to join up soon after you are born. Once they have fused, none of them allow movement except the hinged jaw joint.

Have you ever used a joystick? That's a ball and socket joint!

Ball and socket

Your hips are ball and socket joints. They allow you to move your legs in all directions and even to turn them.

There are 19 moveable joints in your hand – not counting the ones in your wrist!

What is tennis elbow?

Bendy bits

Different sorts of joints all over your body keep you moving.

 Neck bones feature a pivot joint that allows your head to turn.

 Wrists have a joint that allows them to turn but not to go right round.

 Ankles contain different joints for up and down and side to side movement.

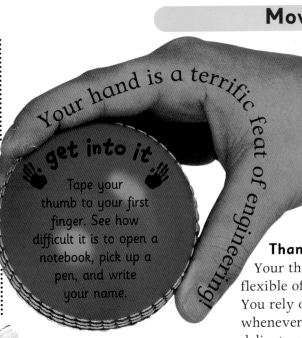

Your hand is a terrific feat of engineering!

get into it

Tape your thumb to your first finger. See how difficult it is to open a notebook, pick up a pen, and write your name.

Thank your thumbs

Your thumb is the most flexible of your fingers. You rely on your thumbs whenever you handle delicate objects.

This woman has stretchy muscles and ligaments that allow her spine to bend further than most people can manage.

Hip hooray

Joints, particularly knee and hip joints, sometimes wear out in old age. When this happens, doctors can remove the worn-out joint and replace it with an artificial one.

Ligaments

Bands of tissue called ligaments act like elastic. They hold your bones together yet still allow you to move.

Ligament

Bone

Your elbows have a hinge joint for bending and a pivot joint so they can turn.

Fabulously flexible

People whose joints are particularly flexible are called "double-jointed". The condition can run in families, but people who are double-jointed must practise if they want to keep their ligaments stretchy.

The name for sore elbow tendons caused by overuse.

The body's muscles

Every time you move, you use muscles. Muscles make you walk, blink, and smile. Some muscles work without you thinking about them, but others need to be told to move. They all work by shrinking, which makes them pull or squeeze.

Pulling strings

About 650 of your muscles are wrapped around the bones of your skeleton. They move your body by pulling on the bones. Together they form the muscle system.

Smooth muscle
This type of muscle makes things move inside your body. It mixes food in your stomach and pushes food through your intestines.

Smooth muscle cells are short with pointed ends.

Heart muscle
When you put your hand on your chest, you can feel your heart beating. Your heart is a strong muscle that squeezes blood around your body.

Heart muscle cells are stripy with oval blobs.

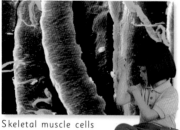

Skeletal muscle
Skeletal muscles pull on bones to change the shape of your skeleton and move your body. These muscles are voluntary, which means you can use thought to control them.

Skeletal muscle cells are long and threadlike.

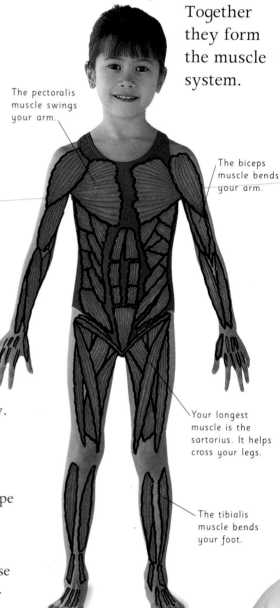

The pectoralis muscle swings your arm.

The biceps muscle bends your arm.

Your longest muscle is the sartorius. It helps cross your legs.

The tibialis muscle bends your foot.

24

What weighs more: all your bones or all your muscles?

Muscle magic

Muscles have hundreds of uses. They make up about a third of your body weight.

 Largest muscle: you use the muscle in your buttock for sitting and walking.

 Fastest muscle: this one makes you blink. It works up to 5 times a second.

 Ear wiggling: a few people can control the muscles around their ears.

 Smile: a fake smile uses different muscles from a real, involuntary smile.

Who's in charge?

You use hundreds of muscles when you run and jump. Your brain controls them all, a bit like a conductor controlling an orchestra. It sends signals along nerves to every muscle, saying exactly when to work and when to rest.

Become an expert ...

on making sounds, pages **64-65**

on how intestines push food, pages **88-89**

Hundreds of muscles work in a carefully controlled sequence when you jump in the air.

Tongue twister

Your tongue is a bundle of lots of muscles that make it super flexible. It can reach anywhere in your mouth to pull and push bits of food. Its acrobatic movements are also vital to speech.

Your tongue contains at least 14 different muscles that make it amazingly flexible.

How muscles work

Muscles work by contracting, which means they shorten. As a muscle contracts, it pulls. The larger the muscle, the more powerfully it pulls.

Working in pairs

Muscles can pull but not push. They work in pairs that pull in opposite directions. When one muscle pulls, its partner relaxes.

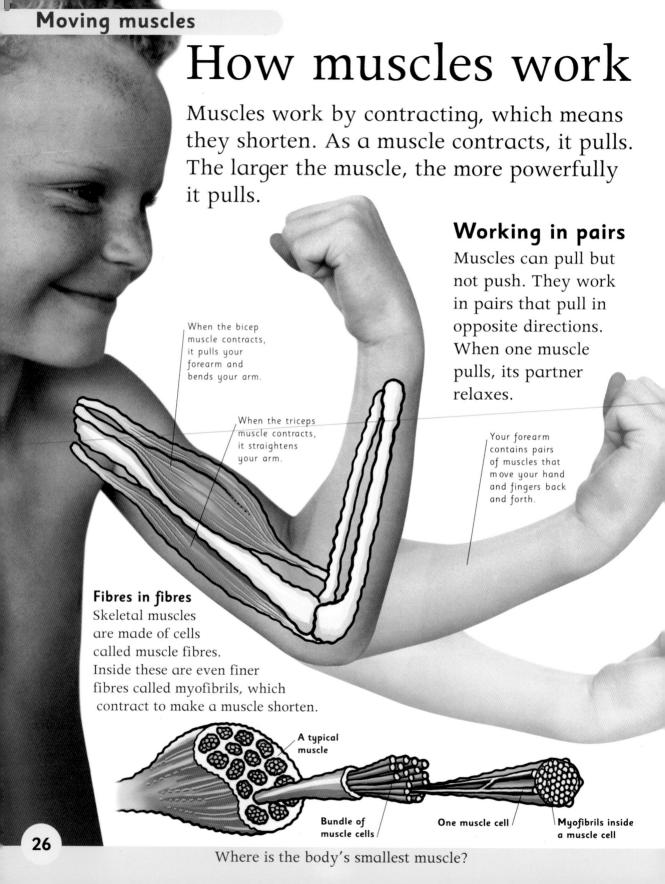

When the bicep muscle contracts, it pulls your forearm and bends your arm.

When the triceps muscle contracts, it straightens your arm.

Your forearm contains pairs of muscles that move your hand and fingers back and forth.

Fibres in fibres

Skeletal muscles are made of cells called muscle fibres. Inside these are even finer fibres called myofibrils, which contract to make a muscle shorten.

A typical muscle

Bundle of muscle cells

One muscle cell

Myofibrils inside a muscle cell

Where is the body's smallest muscle?

Try raising your ring finger with your hand in this position. It's stuck because it's joined to the same tendon as the middle finger.

Middle finger

Ring finger

Tendons

Muscles are fastened to bones by tough bands called tendons. When you wiggle your fingers, you can see the tendons move on the back of your hand.

Making faces

Muscles in your face are attached to skin as well as bone. They pull the skin when you change your expression. You use about 17 muscles when you smile.

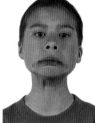

A floppy start

A newborn baby has little control over his head or neck muscles. It takes about a month before it can hold up its head, and six months for strong, steady head control.

No rest

Muscles work all the time. They hold you upright - without them you would flop on the floor. Muscles also work when you are asleep, keeping your body firm and toned.

Getting a stitch

If you run a lot, you may get a pain in your side. This is a stitch. Scientists aren't sure exactly why it happens but it might be because the muscles and ligaments in your abdomen are working too hard.

Muscle power

The more you use your muscles, the better they get. Active games and exercise make your muscles larger, stronger, and more flexible. They also help you keep going without tiring.

Stamina

If you have stamina, you can keep going for a long time without getting tired. Exercise that makes you feel out of breath, like running, improves your stamina.

Flexibility

When you're flexible, your joints and muscles can move freely and your body can bend and straighten easily. Exercise that stretches your body, such as gymnastics or dancing, improves your flexibility.

This contortionist has made her body more flexible by doing exercises that stretch her back.

Strength

Pushing, pulling, and lifting make your muscles bigger and stronger. Bodybuilders lift heavy weights over and over again until their muscles are enormous.

You need strong muscles to win a tug-of-war.

Become an expert ...

on how your heart works, pages **50-51**

on healthy food, pages **106-107**

What happens to muscles if you don't exercise?

Body heat

This picture shows the heat of a man's body. Muscles make heat when they work hard, which is why exercise makes you hot. On cold days, your muscles try to warm you up by shivering.

Muscle food

To build strong muscles, you need a type of food called protein. Meat, fish, beans, milk, and eggs are rich in protein.

Most vegetables don't contain much protein.

Milk

Chicken

Fish

Egg

Beans

Fish is a very good source of protein.

Ways to keep fit

Exercise is very good for your health. As well as making your muscles bigger, it strengthens your heart and lungs.

Walking to school, or going out for walks, builds strength and stamina.

Football is great for improving your flexibility and strength.

Swimming strengthens your heart muscle and builds stamina.

Cycling strengthens your leg muscles and builds up stamina.

Dancing keeps your body supple and helps build strength.

They get small and weak.

Headquarters

The brain is the body's control centre. It is a complicated organ that works very quickly, a bit like a brilliant, living computer.

Sense signals
The cerebrum is the main part of your brain. It gets and stores sense information and also controls your movements.

Cerebrum

Cerebellum

Clever calculator
The cerebrum is also responsible for thinking, speaking, and complicated tasks such as sums.

Your brain stem works at the same rate whether you're awake or asleep.

Brain stem

Muscle control
Your cerebellum helps you to balance and move your muscles. You use this bit of your brain when you dance.

24 hours a day
Whatever else you do, the brain stem makes sure your heart and breathing never stop.

Does your brain hurt when you have a headache?

Skull

In relation to the size of our bodies, humans have the biggest brains of any animal.

Brain

Brain box

Your skull is a bony shell that fits together like a jigsaw around your brain. Shock-absorbing liquid fills the space between the brain and skull.

Curiosity quiz

Take a look through the brain and senses pages and see if you can spot where these come from.

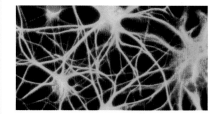

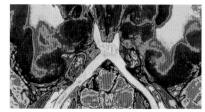

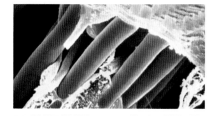

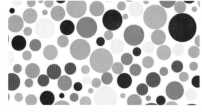

Learning

When you learn to do something you create connections between cells in your brain. Next time you do it the connections are already there so it is easier.

Short-term memory

Your short-term memory only holds information for about a minute. You use it to compare prices when you go shopping, or to remember a name when you meet someone new.

Long-term memory

Your name, phone numbers you know by heart, and skills such as riding a bike can be kept for many years in your long-term memory.

No, your brain can't feel pain but the muscles around your head can.

Network of nerves

All of the body contains nerve cells. These link up to form the network of nerves we call the nervous system. It transports messages between the body and the brain.

Quick as a flash

Nerve cells lie next to one another forming long chains. They pass messages to their neighbours – rather like a speedy relay race – to and from the brain.

A good night's sleep

Your body and brain slow down when you sleep, but they don't stop working. Your brain needs sleep to sort out the events of the previous day.

No need to think

You do some things without needing to think about them. These are called reflex actions and include blinking, coughing, and the knee-jerk reflex.

Your knee jumps forwards even though your brain hasn't told it to move.

Cross your legs and tap just below the knee.

Brain

Spinal cord – the centre of the network

Brain cells viewed through a microscope.

Which is the longest nerve in your body?

Pain-killers

When you get a filling, the dentist gives you an anaesthetic. This drug stops nerves passing on pain messages for a short time.

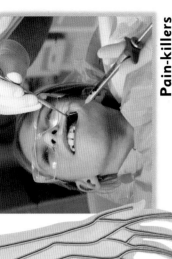

You've got 150,000 km (93,200 miles) of nerves in your body.

Pins and needles

Sitting cross-legged for a long time squashes the nerves in your legs. When you stand up, the nerves start to work again, producing a tingling feeling.

Messages travel faster than a high-speed train.

Messages

Your brain controls your body. It receives messages from all parts of your body and decides what to do.

Walking is the result of your brain telling your leg muscles to move.

Hunger is your stomach telling your brain that it's empty and you must eat.

Needing to urinate is a response to the message that your bladder is full.

Itching is an irritating feeling. Your body reacts by making you scratch.

Pain gets a very quick response. You move away from what's hurting you.

Blinking happens without you needing to think about it.

Breathing is automatic too. It carries on even when you are asleep.

The one running from your big toe to the base of your spine.

33

Touchy feely

Your skin is in immediate contact with the world. Using your sense of touch allows you to tell if something is hot or cold, dull or sharp, rough or smooth, or wet or dry.

Merkel's disk responds to light touch and is sensitive to the texture of things.

Meissner's corpuscle senses light touch.

Things we can feel

Skin is packed with many sense receptors. Each sort responds to different sensations.

Not worth noticing

Although your brain receives messages all the time, it filters out the less important ones. That's why you're not constantly aware of the clothes against your skin.

It feels slimy!....

Warmth is detected by nerve endings quite close to the surface of the skin.

Cold is felt by different sensors to heat. Extreme cold registers as pain.

Deep touch sensors enable you to grip things tightly.

Light touch sensors lie at the root of hairs on your arms and legs.

Vibrations from an electric drill trigger vibration sensors.

Tickly feelings result from a light and unexpected touch.

Sensitive fingertips full of receptors are able to tell coins apart.

Ouch!

The body has its own system of alarm bells. Pain receptors warn us when a part of the body has been hurt or is about to be harmed.

This girl quickly moves her finger away from the thorn to stop the pain.

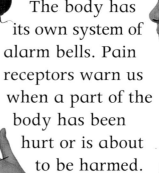

How many touch receptors are in a fingertip

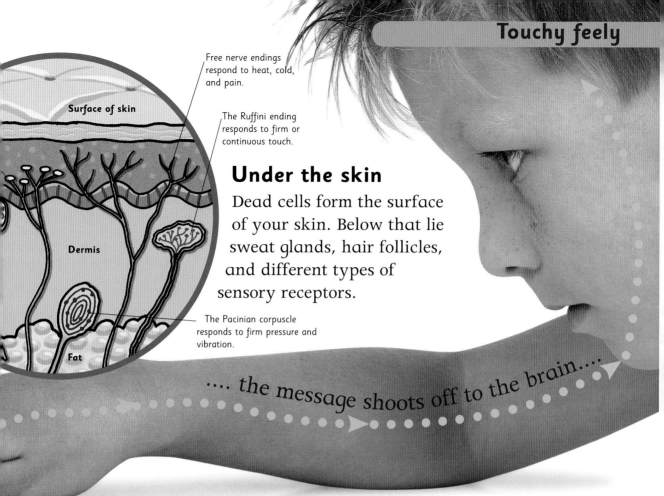

Free nerve endings respond to heat, cold, and pain.

Surface of skin

The Ruffini ending responds to firm or continuous touch.

Under the skin

Dead cells form the surface of your skin. Below that lie sweat glands, hair follicles, and different types of sensory receptors.

Dermis

The Pacinian corpuscle responds to firm pressure and vibration.

Fat

.... the message shoots off to the brain.....

Sensitive bits

Skin contains more touch receptors than any other part of the body. But some areas are more sensitive than others.

Fingertips are packed with sensors, especially light pressure receptors.

Lips have very thin skin which is good at detecting heat and cold.

Toes are very sensitive, but thick skin makes the heel less sensitive.

Reading by touch

Braille is a system that uses raised dots to represent letters and numbers. It was invented so that people with bad eyesight would be able to read by feeling the page with their fingertips instead of looking at words.

Braille was invented over 150 years ago.

B I R D

Get into it
Put one finger in cold water, one in hot, then put both in warm water. The water feels cold to the hot-water finger and hot to the cold-water finger.

35

Taste and smell

We need to eat and drink to survive, but taste and smell are what make these everyday activities so enjoyable.

Taste detector

Your tongue is a big muscle covered in clusters of taste buds. Each cluster recognizes a particular kind of taste.

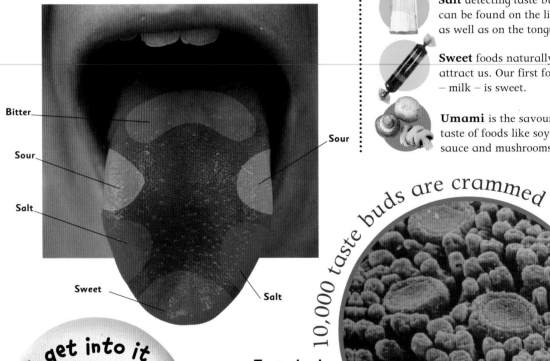

Bitter

Sour

Salt

Sweet

Sour

Salt

Different tastes

There are five types of tastes – bitter, sour, salty, sweet, and umami.

Bitter foods, such as coffee can be bad for you. Most poisons are bitter.

Sour foods include lemon and vinegar. Food that has "gone off" tastes sour.

Salt detecting taste buds can be found on the lips as well as on the tongue.

Sweet foods naturally attract us. Our first food – milk – is sweet.

Umami is the savoury taste of foods like soy sauce and mushrooms.

10,000 taste buds are crammed onto your tongue.

get into it

Try putting sugar on different places on your tongue. It tastes sweeter in some places than others. Now try salt, lemon juice, and coffee.

Taste buds

Saliva in your mouth dissolves your food. The food washes over tiny taste buds between the bumps on your tongue. Taste buds recognize different flavours.

How much saliva does an average person produce in a day?

Runny nose

When you have a cold, tiny hairs in your nose get clogged with mucus. This stops them wafting smell particles deep into your nose and makes it difficult to smell – and taste – things.

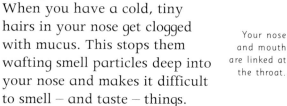

Your nose and mouth are linked at the throat.

Sensitive nose

Much of what we think of as taste is actually smell. The back of your nose is linked to your mouth so you can smell your food as you chew it.

Some noses can recognize 10,000 different smells.

Smell receptors

Special cells deep inside your nose recognize scent particles floating in the air. These cells link directly to your brain.

Look out!

Sight is the body's main sense and the main way we learn about our surroundings. Two-thirds of the information we take in comes from our eyes.

Wandering eyes

Six muscles control each eye. You use both eyes when you look at something, so your eyes move together.

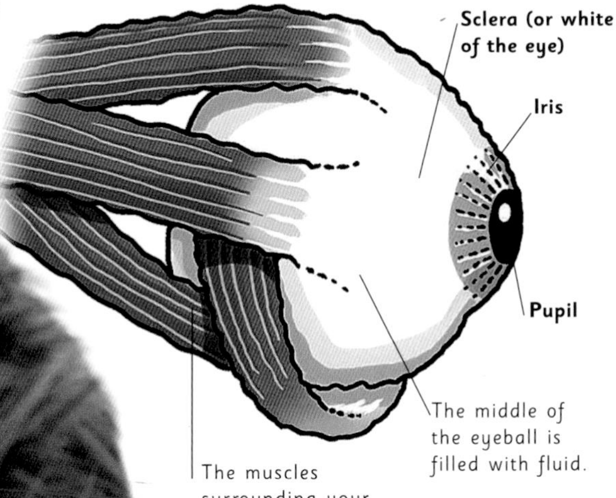

Sclera (or white of the eye)

Iris

Pupil

The middle of the eyeball is filled with fluid.

The muscles surrounding your eyeball make precise movements so you can smoothly track moving objects.

An iris is as unique as a fingerprint

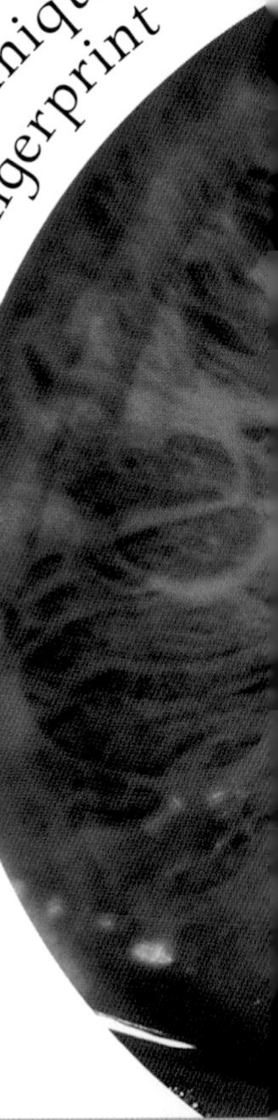

Pupil

Eyelid

Sclera

Iris

At night, our eyes could detect a lighted candle 1.6 km (1 mile) away.

Hidden away

Most of your eye nestles safely in its socket and is protected by pads of fat. On the outside, you can see the iris, pupil, and some of the sclera.

What is the sleep that collects in our eyes?

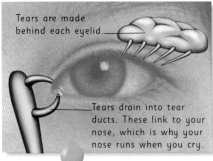

Tears are made behind each eyelid.

Tears drain into tear ducts. These link to your nose, which is why your nose runs when you cry.

Crying

Tear glands behind your eyes produce drops of salty fluid. When you blink, your eyelids sweep this fluid over your eyes to keep them clean. If something gets into your eye, or you feel strong emotions, the drops turn into floods of tears.

Safekeeping

Your eyes are fragile, squidgy balls made of watery jelly so they need to be well protected.

Bone in your skull surrounds your brain and the backs of the eyes.

Eyebrows sit above your eyes and prevent sweat dripping into them.

Eyelids and lashes stop dust entering the eyes and then sweep it well away.

Eye colour

The iris is the coloured part of the eye. All eye colours are produced by one substance, melanin. Lots of melanin results in brown eyes, less means a lighter shade.

Your pupils change size automatically.

Either it's dark or this person has seen something they like.

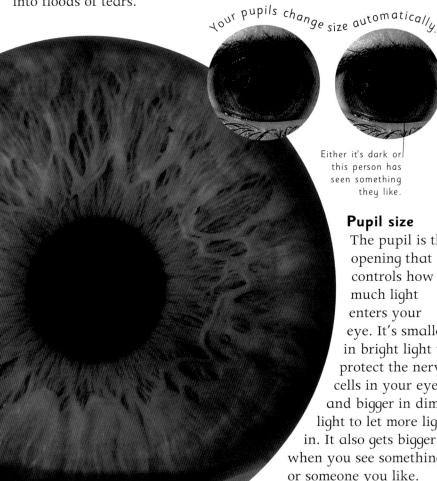

Pupil size

The pupil is the opening that controls how much light enters your eye. It's smaller in bright light to protect the nerve cells in your eye, and bigger in dim light to let more light in. It also gets bigger when you see something or someone you like.

Dust and mucus washed from our eyes as we sleep.

How we see

Inside your eye is a lens like the lens of a camera. Its job is to focus light on the back of your eye so you can see things clearly.

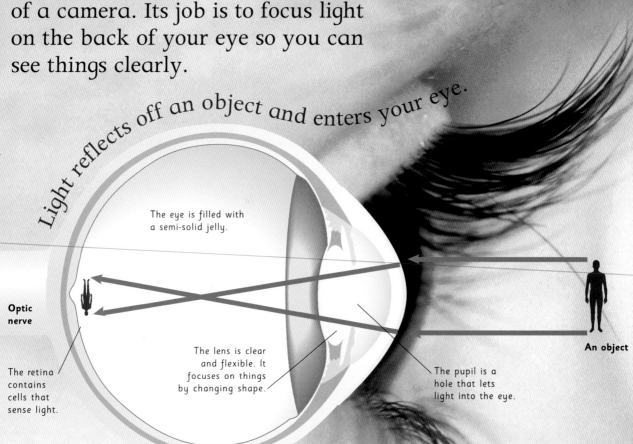

Light reflects off an object and enters your eye.

The eye is filled with a semi-solid jelly.

Optic nerve

The retina contains cells that sense light.

The lens is clear and flexible. It focuses on things by changing shape.

The pupil is a hole that lets light into the eye.

An object

How your eye works

Light from an object enters your eye through the pupil. It passes through the lens, and makes an upside down image on the retina at the back of your eye. Cells in your eye send messages down the optic nerve to your brain. Your brain flips the image back the right way round.

Seeing in colour

Your eyes contain millions of cells. Cone cells give you colour vision but don't work well in dim light. Rod cells work well in dim light but see everything in shades of grey.

What is an eye specialist who tests eyesight called?

Blurry vision

Sometimes an eyeball is the wrong shape. The lens cannot focus light on the retina and everything is blurry. Glasses make the light focus in the right place to make things clear.

Short eyeball

If you have a short eyeball you will have difficulty seeing things close up. This is called long sightedness.

Long eyeball

It is difficult to see objects that are far away when your eyeball is too long. This is known as short sightedness.

Can you see a number? If not, you may be colour blind.

Colour blindness

Some people cannot tell certain colours apart, especially red and green. This is called colour blindness. It is more common in men than women.

get into it

Close one eye and hold a finger in front of your nose. Open that eye and close the other one. The finger appears to move! Each eye sees things differently.

Contact lenses

These work like mini glasses and sit directly in front of the eye. They're a bit fiddly, but once they're in you can't feel them at all.

Glasses bend the light entering your eye so it focuses on the retina.

Contact lenses are made of very thin plastic.

Eye to brain

Your brain works out what you're seeing by comparing the images it gets from your eyes to things you have seen in the past. Sometimes it can be fooled!

Your brain combines images from both eyes.

The yellow areas are the parts of your brain that deal with information from your eyes.

Optic nerve

Eyeball

Your blind spot is the part of the eye that can't see anything. It is where the optic nerve leaves the back of your eye.

What can you see?

The dark blue in these pictures shows how much animals can see clearly. Light blue shows what they can see less well.

Humans have to move their heads to see clearly to the sides or look back.

Tigers see well to the front to help them find and catch their prey.

Zebras keep a look out for movements to the sides so they can avoid attack.

Ducks can see all the way behind them, even while facing forwards.

Chameleons see small areas clearly. They swivel their eyes to see all around.

To the brain

Our eyes swivel around constantly, taking in sights and adjusting to focus on different things. The information they collect travels to the brain through the optic nerve at the back of the eyes.

What is it called when you look at something and think it's something else?

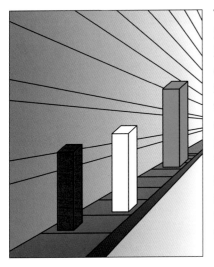

Tallest tower

Does the green tower look taller than the others? That's because it's further along the track and we expect objects further away from us to look smaller. The colours of the towers also affect the size they seem to be. In fact, all the towers are exactly the same size.

Finding your blind spot

Close your right eye and look directly at the star. Slowly bring the book to your left eye. You reach your blind spot when the circle disappears.

Recognizing objects

Your brain is very clever – it can recognize this car from different points of view. A computer would have to be taught that both these pictures are of the same object.

V91 RBW

Certain patterns trick your eyes into seeing movement where there is none.

Do you believe your eyes?

Your brain helps your eyes to understand what they see. Sometimes you see things that aren't actually there...

You see a heart even though the edge of the shape isn't there because your brain uses the information it has to fill in the gaps.

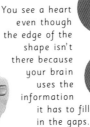

An optical illusion.

Listen here

When you shout you send out invisible sound waves through the air. Your ears pick up the waves and transmit the sound to your brain.

The speed of sound

We don't notice the slight delay between someone's lips moving and the sound actually reaching our ears. It's too fast!

How well can you hear?

Your hearing range is from the highest to the lowest notes that you can hear.

Adults have quite a small range compared to other animals.

Children hear higher notes than adults. Your range shrinks with age.

Cats, dogs, and rabbits can hear much higher notes than people.

Bats have excellent hearing. Their range is five times as large as ours.

Sound travels through the

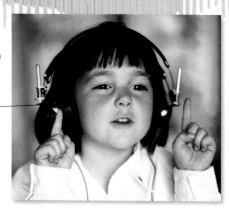

Headphones feed different sounds into each ear so you feel as if you're surrounded by instruments.

Why two ears?

Sounds normally reach one ear first and then the other. This helps our brains work out where sounds are coming from and how far away they are.

Why do we have ear wax?

Outer ear

What we call the ear is really just the part that we can see. Sounds are collected here, and funnelled inwards.

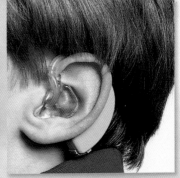

A little help

Partially deaf people may use hearing aids. These make the sounds entering the ear louder and easier to hear.

Middle ear

Sounds arriving here from the outer ear cause the eardrum to vibrate and set off movements in three tiny little bones.

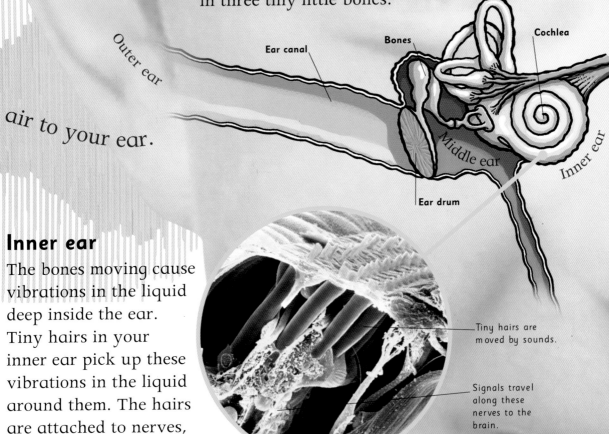

Outer ear

air to your ear.

Ear canal

Bones

Cochlea

Middle ear

Inner ear

Ear drum

Tiny hairs are moved by sounds.

Signals travel along these nerves to the brain.

Inner ear

The bones moving cause vibrations in the liquid deep inside the ear. Tiny hairs in your inner ear pick up these vibrations in the liquid around them. The hairs are attached to nerves, which connect to your brain.

To protect the skin lining the ear canal, trap dust, and repel insects.

Balancing act

As well as hearing, ears help you balance. Sensors in your ears work with those in your eyes, muscles, joints, and feet to let your brain know your body's position.

The three semi-circular canals deal with balance.

Ear hole

Keeping track

Deep inside your ear are three tiny tubes filled with fluid. They detect the movements your body is making and let your brain know about them.

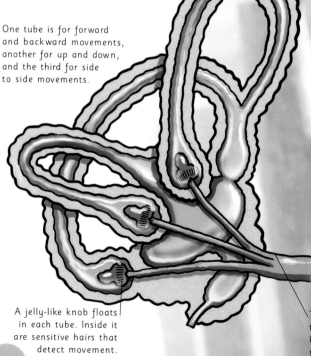

One tube is for forward and backward movements, another for up and down, and the third for side to side movements.

Watch your step!

Keeping your balance while walking along a narrow wall takes a lot of concentration. You are responding to information coming from your eyes, muscles, and ears at the same time.

A jelly-like knob floats in each tube. Inside it are sensitive hairs that detect movement.

The movements travel along the hairs, through a nerve, to the brain.

Can astronauts learn to balance in space?

Motion sickness

Travelling in a car, boat, or plane can make you feel ill. Your eyes tell your brain that you're staying still in the vehicle, but your body says it can feel movement. This confusion is what causes motion sickness.

Basically, your brain is the boss.

The brain

Muscle messages

When you move, sensors in your muscles send messages to your brain. If a movement isn't going right, your brain will make you do things differently.

get into it

First make sure there is nothing unsafe nearby for you to crash into. Then spin round and round and make yourself feel dizzy.

The more you practise the better you will be at balancing.

Why do you feel dizzy?

The liquid in the tubes of your ear is like water in a cup. When you spin, it continues to slosh around for a while even after you've stopped. Your brain gets confused about which way round you are, and you feel dizzy as a result.

Yes, but it can take a couple of days to learn how.

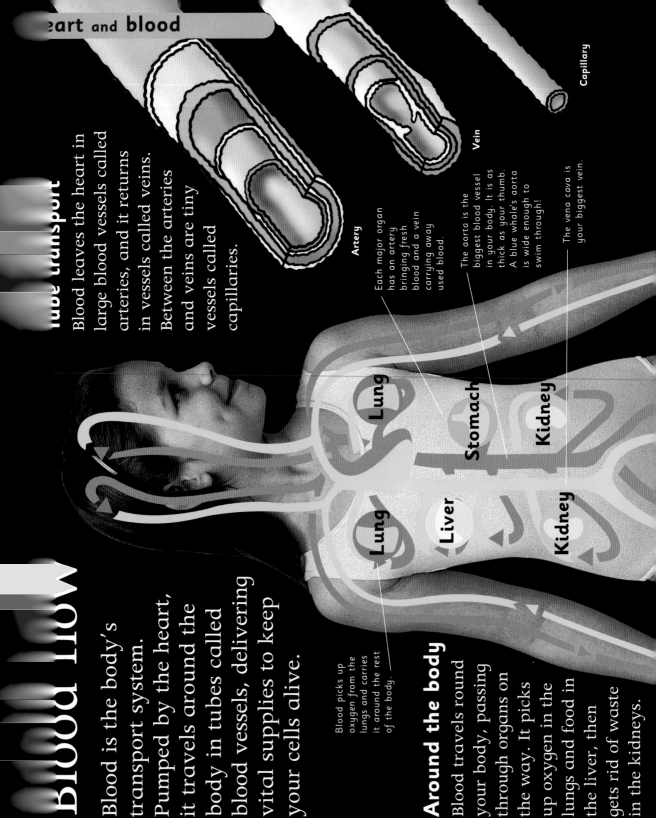

Tube transport

Blood leaves the heart in large blood vessels called arteries, and it returns in vessels called veins. Between the arteries and veins are tiny vessels called capillaries.

Capillary

Vein

Artery

Each major organ has an artery bringing fresh blood and a vein carrying away used blood.

The aorta is the biggest blood vessel in your body. It is as thick as your thumb. A blue whale's aorta is wide enough to swim through!

The vena cava is your biggest vein.

Lung

Stomach

Kidney

Lung

Liver

Kidney

Blood flow

Blood is the body's transport system. Pumped by the heart, it travels around the body in tubes called blood vessels, delivering vital supplies to keep your cells alive.

Blood picks up oxygen from the lungs and carries it around the rest of the body.

Around the body

Blood travels round your body, passing through organs on the way. It picks up oxygen in the lungs and food in the liver, then gets rid of waste in the kidneys.

When you cut yourself, what kind of blood vessel does the blood usually come from?

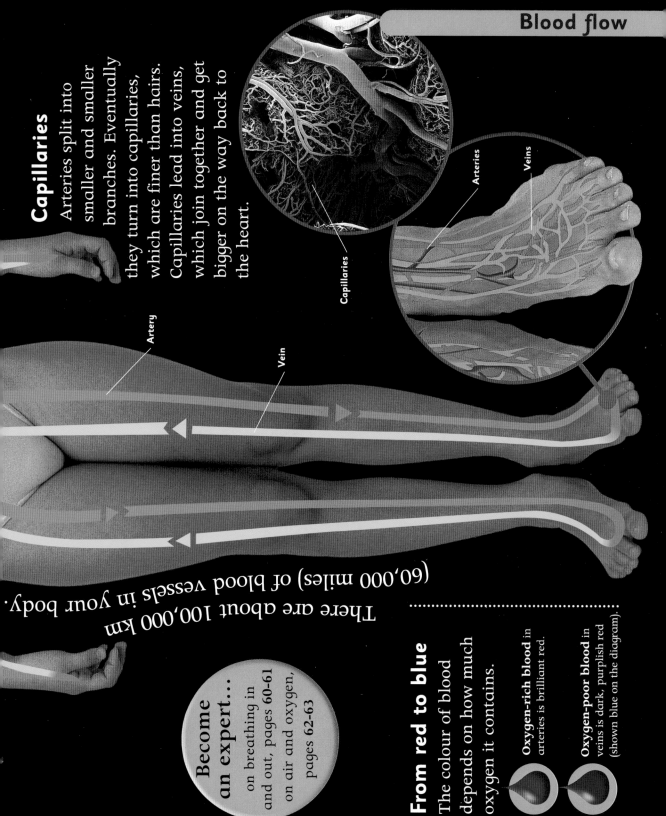

Capillaries

Arteries split into smaller and smaller branches. Eventually they turn into capillaries, which are finer than hairs. Capillaries lead into veins, which join together and get bigger on the way back to the heart.

Capillaries

Arteries

Veins

Artery

Vein

There are about 100,000 km (60,000 miles) of blood vessels in your body.

Become an expert...

on breathing in and out, pages 60-61 on air and oxygen, pages 62-63

From red to blue

The colour of blood depends on how much oxygen it contains.

Oxygen-rich blood in arteries is brilliant red.

Oxygen-poor blood in veins is dark, purplish red (shown blue on the diagram).

A capillary.

Boom boom

Your heart is a pump that pushes blood around your whole body. Each time your heart beats, it squirts out a small cupful of blood and refills for the next beat.

Where is it?

Your heart is in the middle of your chest, squeezed between the two lungs. You can feel its beat just left of the bone in the middle of your chest.

Double pump

Your heart is really two pumps in one. One half pumps blood through your lungs, and the other half pumps blood around the rest of your body.

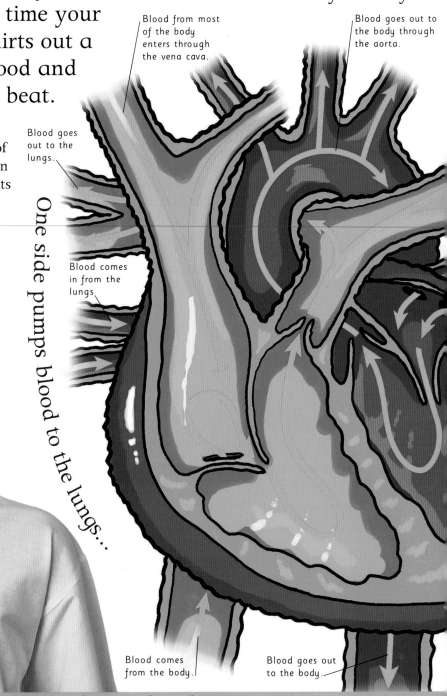

Blood from most of the body enters through the vena cava.

Blood goes out to the body through the aorta.

Blood goes out to the lungs.

Blood comes in from the lungs

Blood comes from the body.

Blood goes out to the body.

One side pumps blood to the lungs...

Vena cava

Aorta

How many times does your heart beat in a year?

One-way system

To keep blood flowing one way only, your heart and most veins contain valves. Your heartbeat is the sound of valves shutting when your heart squeezes.

Blood goes out to the lungs.

Blood comes in from the lungs.

Valves stop blood flowing backwards.

Beating faster

Muscles need extra blood when you're active, so your heart speeds up. It beats about 70 times a minute if you're resting but up to 200 times a minute if you're running.

...and the other pumps blood everywhere else.

get into it

Find your pulse by pressing two fingers on your wrist. You should be able to feel a gentle throb as your heart pumps blood around your body.

Curiosity quiz

Take a look through the heart and blood pages and see if you can spot any of the cells and tissues below.

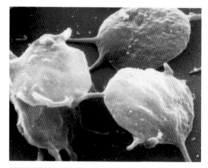

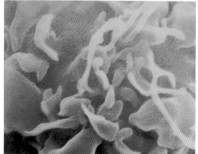

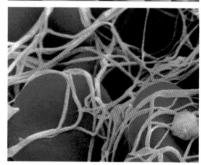

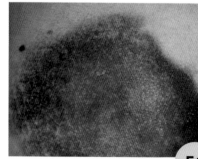

About 40 million times.

All about blood

Blood is a warm, soupy mixture of liquid and cells. The cells carry oxygen and fight germs, and the liquid carries nutrients to body cells and takes away waste.

Main ingredients

Blood contains three types of cells – red blood cells, white blood cells, and platelets. They float in a yellowish liquid called plasma.

One drop of blood contains...
5 million red blood cells, half a million platelets, 7,000 white blood cells, water, sugar, salt, hormones, vitamins... lots more.

Lots of plasma

Yellow plasma makes up more than half of your blood.

White blood cells and platelets.

White blood cells seek out and kill germs. They also eat up the dead cells that they meet.

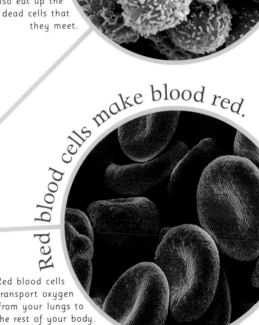

Red blood cells make blood red.

Red blood cells transport oxygen from your lungs to the rest of your body.

Become an expert...

on fighting germs, pages **78-79**
on air and oxygen, pages **62-63**

How long does a red blood cell live for?

Your blood type

There are four main types of blood, called blood groups. Your blood group affects who you can donate blood to.

A People with blood group A can give blood only to people with A or AB.

O People with blood group O can donate blood to almost anyone.

AB People with blood group AB can only give blood to others with AB blood.

B People with blood group B can give blood only to people with B or AB.

Blood bank

One in ten people who go to hospital need extra blood, so hospitals keep a store of blood in a "blood bank". The blood is divided into separate supplies of cells and plasma.

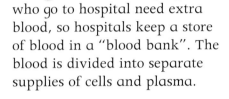

White blood cells and platelets fight disease.

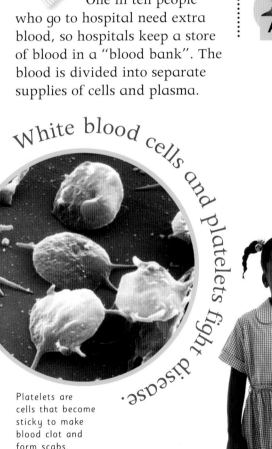

Platelets are cells that become sticky to make blood clot and form scabs.

How much blood?

The average adult has about 10 pints (5.7 litres) of blood, but a newborn baby has only a cupful.

The amount of blood in your body grows with you. By age 10 you have up to 4 pints (2 litres).

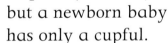

By a year old a baby has more than 1 pint (half a litre) of blood.

About four months.

Blood cells

Nearly half the cells in your body are blood cells. They wear out quickly, so you make three million new ones every second. Most are made in bone marrow, a jelly-like tissue in hollow bones.

Red blood cells

The most common cells in your body are red blood cells. They are circular with dimples in each side. Inside they are packed with a red protein which carries oxygen and is called haemoglobin.

White blood cell

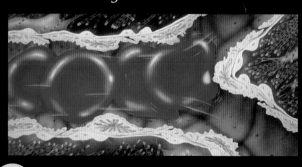

Tiny tunnels

Red blood cells are soft and rubbery so as to squeeze through tiny gaps. In the smallest blood vessels they travel in single file. All the bumping and squeezing eventually wears them out.

Which cells in the human body contain iron?

Stick together

Platelets are tiny fragments of cells that help blood to clot. They cluster around breaks in blood vessels and grow spiky stalks that help them stick together.

Platelets stick together in a blood clot.

This white blood cell eats pus and germs.

This white blood cell crawls between other cells looking for germs.

Soldier cells

There are lots of different white blood cells and they all help guard your body against invasion by germs. Some white blood cells creep along the walls of blood vessels and eat any germs they find. Others make chemicals that destroy germs.

Thicker blood

When people climb high mountains, their bodies make extra red blood cells to help them breathe in the thin mountain air. As a result, their blood gets thicker.

Pupils are normally black but they look red in photographs taken with a flash.

Seeing red

You can often see people's blood in photographs. If you take a picture with a flash, the light reflects off red blood cells in the back of their eyes, turning the pupils red.

Red blood cells.

Bumps and cuts

Blood has the amazing ability to turn from liquid to solid in minutes and so help mend cuts in your skin.

Clotting

The moment you cut yourself, your blood starts turning solid, or clotting. The clot quickly plugs the broken blood vessels and stops them from leaking.

Caught in a net

The chemicals released by platelets cause tangled fibres to form in the liquid part of blood. The fibres trap blood cells like fish in a net, forming a solid plug that gets bigger and bigger.

Tangled fibres trap blood cells.

Platelets in action

Platelets start the clotting process. They change shape to become stickier and cluster around the cut. At the same time, they release chemicals into the blood.

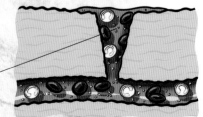

Platelets in the blood start to work as soon as you get a cut in your skin.

How long does a small cut take to stop bleeding?

Bloodsucker

A leech is a kind of worm that bites your skin and sucks out your blood. Leech saliva contains chemicals that stops blood from clotting. As a result, the cut keeps bleeding until the leech is full.

Leeches live in wet, swampy places. They often slip down people's shoes and bite their feet without being noticed.

Vampire bats and leeches can stop blood from clotting.

First aid

A plaster can help a cut to heal by closing the skin and keeping out dirt. Plasters also stop you scratching, which can make a cut worse.

Scabs

When a blood clot dries, it forms a scab. New skin slowly grows underneath the scab, repairing the wound. When the skin is ready, the scab becomes loose and drops off.

Scabs keep out germs while new skin grows.

Bumps and cuts

Painful bumps and cuts are a part of your body's natural healing process.

A graze is a group of tiny cuts. It forms when something rough scrapes the skin quickly.

Blisters are bubbles of liquid that form when skin is rubbed a lot. Don't pop them!

Bruises are patches of blood under the skin. They change colour as they heal.

Black eyes are bruises that form when blood pools under the skin around the eye.

Platelets stick to each other and to other blood cells, causing a clot to start forming.

After a few minutes, the clot is thick enough to stop blood escaping from the wound.

Between three and eight minutes.

Hormones

A hormone is a chemical that changes the way part of your body works. Even tiny amounts of hormones are powerful. Some work slowly over years, but others have instant effects.

The pea-sized pituitary gland is just under your brain.

Main gland
Hormones are made in parts of the body called glands. The most important is the pituitary gland in your brain. Its hormones control many of the other glands.

Growth hormone
Every day, your pituitary gland releases about eight microscopic doses of growth hormone, mostly when you're asleep. This hormone makes your bones and muscles grow.

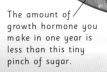

The amount of growth hormone you make in one year is less than this tiny pinch of sugar.

Growing up
Toddlers and teenagers have very high levels of growth hormone, which is why they grow so quickly. Adults also make growth hormone, but the level falls with age.

What carries hormones around the body?

Control chemicals

Hormones are important – they control many body processes.

 Oestrogen is the female sex hormone. It turns little girls into adult women.

 Testosterone is the male sex hormone. It turns little boys into adult men.

 Melatonin helps control the daily cycle of sleeping and waking.

 Glucagon raises the level of sugar in your blood, giving you energy.

 Parathyroid hormone tells your bones to release calcium into the blood.

Sugar control

The hormone insulin helps control the level of sugar in your blood. Some people don't make enough insulin and have to check their blood sugar level regularly. They have a disease called diabetes.

People with diabetes prick their skin to get a drop of blood, so they can check how much sugar it contains.

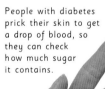

The fright hormone

The hormone adrenaline makes you feel scared or excited. It works in an instant, preparing your whole body for sudden action in case you need to escape from danger.

Your brain becomes alert so you can think quickly.

Adrenaline makes your heart and lungs work harder. Your heart starts to pound and you gasp as your lungs take in extra air.

Glands above your kidneys release adrenaline.

Your hairs stand on end, making your skin tingle.

Adrenaline travels to your arms and legs and prepares the muscles for action.

Become an expert ...
on growing up, pages **102-103**
on sleep, pages **108-109**

Air bags

We have to breathe all the time in order to supply our bodies with oxygen and to get rid of carbon dioxide. We use our lungs to do this.

Prepare the air

Before the air reaches your lungs it travels through your mouth and nose and then goes down your windpipe. It gets warm and damp on its journey.

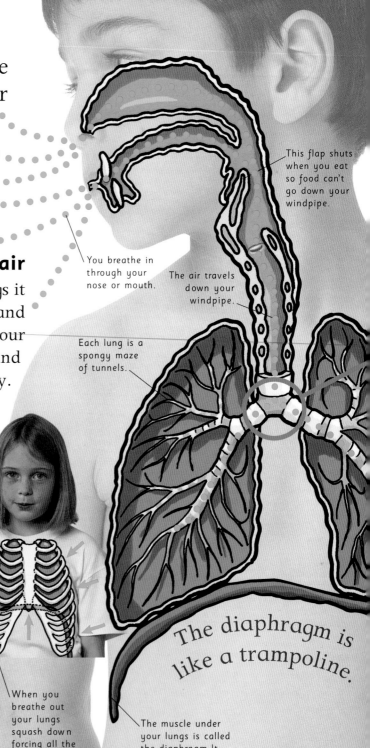

This flap shuts when you eat so food can't go down your windpipe.

You breathe in through your nose or mouth.

The air travels down your windpipe.

Each lung is a spongy maze of tunnels.

When you breathe in, your lungs stretch out and take in lots of air.

When you breathe out your lungs squash down forcing all the air out.

The muscle under your lungs is called the diaphragm. It moves up and down as you breathe.

The diaphragm is like a trampoline.

In and out

Your ribs and diaphragm help you to breathe. Your lungs fill with air when you raise your ribcage, then empty out when you lower it. A muscle called the diaphragm helps you do this.

60

A helping hand

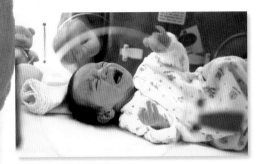

Some newborn babies have trouble breathing. They are put into an enclosed cradle called an incubator. Extra oxygen is pumped into the incubator for them.

The view from the bottom of your windpipe.

Windpipe

Air from your mouth and nose enters your windpipe, which goes down your throat into your chest. Then it splits into two passages — one for each lung.

The alveoli are surrounded by tiny blood capillaries to take the oxygen round the body.

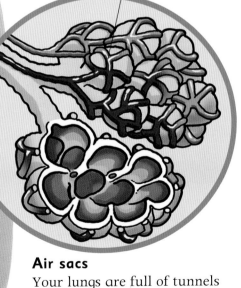

Air sacs

Your lungs are full of tunnels ending in tiny air sacs called alveoli. Here, oxygen from the air passes into your blood. Your blood carries oxygen around every part of your body.

Curiosity quiz

Take a look through these images related to breathing. You should be able to find them all in the next few pages.

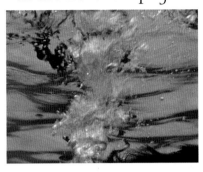

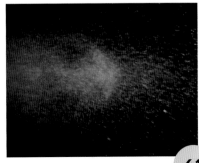

About 23,000.

Air and oxygen

The air you breathe contains a life-giving gas called oxygen. Oxygen helps your cells get their energy from food. They would die within minutes if you stopped breathing.

Oxygen

During the day, trees take in carbon dioxide from the air and give out oxygen.

Oxygen from trees

Trees help to clean the air by filtering out pollution. They also make oxygen, which they release through their leaves.

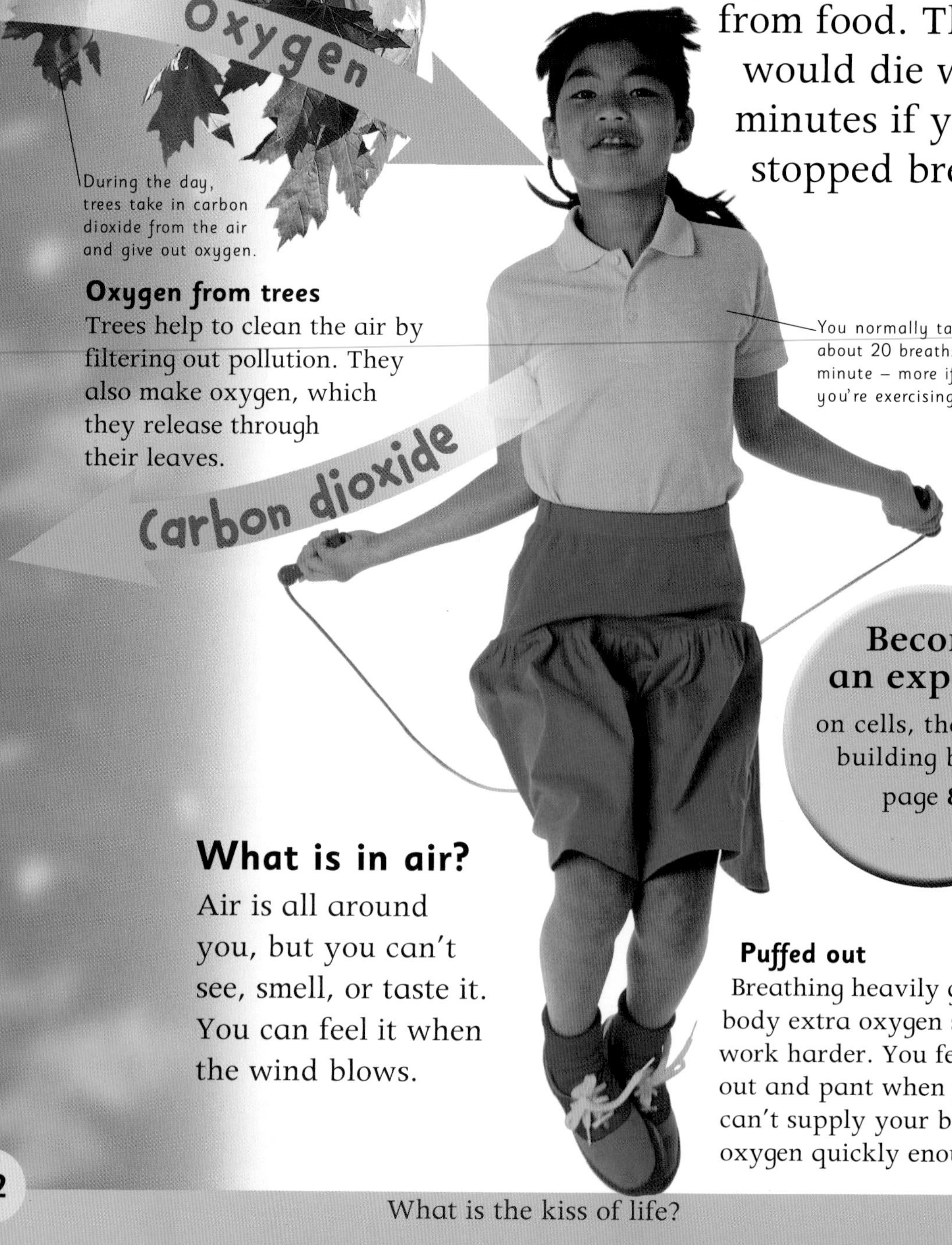

Carbon dioxide

You normally take about 20 breaths per minute — more if you're exercising.

Become an expert...

on cells, the body's building blocks, page **8-9**

What is in air?

Air is all around you, but you can't see, smell, or taste it. You can feel it when the wind blows.

Puffed out

Breathing heavily gives your body extra oxygen so it can work harder. You feel puffed out and pant when your lungs can't supply your body with oxygen quickly enough.

What is the kiss of life?

Airless places

Not every place has air to breathe, so sometimes people carry their own.

 Fires burn up oxygen and produce thick, poisonous smoke.

 Mountain tops have thin air with little oxygen.

 Space and planets near Earth have no air to breathe.

 Water contains oxygen, but humans cannot breathe it.

When you breathe out under water you make bubbles.

Hold that breath!

People can spend a few moments under water without breathing. Most people can manage about a minute, but the world record is around six minutes.

On a cold day you can see the water in your breath turn to steam as it meets the air.

You need to be able to control your breathing to blow up a balloon.

How much puff have you got?

Wet air

Have you noticed that when you breathe onto a window or a mirror it becomes wet? That's because the air you breathe out is slightly damp.

How much air?

You take in about half a litre (0.8 pints) of air with each breath. If you breathe in deeply you can take in about 3 litres (5 pints) in one gulp.

A way of helping someone who has stopped breathing by blowing into their mouth.

Making sounds

Humans can make many more sounds than other creatures. Because the shape of your face affects your voice, your voice is unique.

You can speak, whisper, hum, and shout!

Voice box

Your voice box has two jobs. You use it to make sounds, and to seal off your windpipe when you eat so you don't choke.

Open vocal cords

Closed vocal cords

Vocal cords

Inside your voice box are two flaps called vocal cords. You make sounds by pushing air between them, causing them to vibrate. Fast vibrations produce high sounds, slower ones, low sounds.

Adam's apple

During puberty, a boy's voice box grows bigger, giving him a deeper voice. You can sometimes see it bulging at the front of the throat. It is known as the Adam's apple.

Adam's apple

Air supply

You use the air coming out of your lungs to produce sounds. So it's difficult to speak when you're breathless.

Why do babies and children have higher voices than adults?

Loud sounds

The harder air is forced out of the lungs, the louder the sound. So when a baby takes a big gulp of air you can expect a really big cry!

Do you know a snorer? zzzzz

Shaping words

The air coming from the lungs is shaped by the tongue, cheeks, and lips to form specific sounds.

 Oo is made by pursing your lips and pushing them out.

 Ah sounds are made with a low tongue and a wide open mouth.

 Ee is made by stretching your lips and keeping your tongue up high.

Snoring

Sometimes, when people sleep, the fleshy parts at the back of the nose and throat vibrate as they breathe. This rattling is called snoring. It can also happen when you have a cold.

Didgeridoo

Making music

You control your breath when you speak, but you need really excellent breath control to sing or play a wind instrument.

Become an expert...

on puberty, pages **102-103**
on body language, pages **112-113**

They have shorter vocal cords, which vibrate faster, producing higher sounds.

Ah-choo!

You need to keep your airways clear to breathe at all times. If something gets into your airways you have to get it out pretty quickly!

A sneeze can travel as fast as a car!!!!

Sneezing

Sneezes are a quick way to get rid of unwanted particles that you have accidentally breathed into your nose.

Why do you close your eyes when you sneeze?

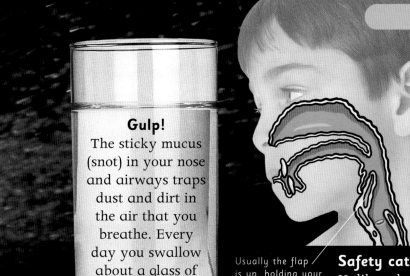

Gulp!
The sticky mucus (snot) in your nose and airways traps dust and dirt in the air that you breathe. Every day you swallow about a glass of the stuff.

Usually the flap is up, holding your windpipe open.

The flap closes when you swallow.

Safety catch

Unlike other animals, human beings use the throat both for eating and breathing. The epiglottis is a small flap of cartilage that shuts off your windpipe when you swallow so food can't accidentally go down it and choke you.

Nose hairs

The tiny hairs in your nose work like brooms to sweep out any particles that you've breathed in. They get trapped in mucus and are swept along to be swallowed down your throat.

get into it

Yawning is catching! Is there anyone nearby? Give a yawn and see if you can start a yawning epidemic!

Coughing

Irritating particles that have entered your throat are thrown out when you cough. Coughing uses your vocal cords, which is why a noise comes out with the cough.

Hiccups

Sometimes your diaphragm suddenly tightens, causing air to rush into your lungs. This makes your vocal cords snap closed with a "hic". Hiccups seem to happen for no reason.

Yawning

Nobody knows why we yawn but we do know one effect of yawning: more oxygen in the lungs. It seems we yawn to perk ourselves up when we're feeling tired or bored.

To stop your eyeballs shooting out of your face with the force of the sneeze.

All wrapped up

Skin covers your whole body. It protects you from germs, water, and sunshine, and helps keep your body at the right temperature.

The skin on your eyelids is the thinnest on your body.

Two layers

Your skin has two main layers. The top one – the one you can see – is called the epidermis. Underneath is the dermis, where there are nerves and blood vessels.

Waterproof seal

Skin stops water getting into your body when you have a shower or go for a swim. It also stops fluids escaping from inside you.

There are flat cells on the surface of your skin. These are made from a tough material called keratin. When the cells die, they dry out and flake off.

Skin cells lower down replace the dead ones that flake off.

Skin is a sort of stretchy overcoat.

Magnified skin flakes

Heavy load

Skin is the heaviest single part of your body. It can weigh as much as a bag of shopping.

House dust

Dust is mostly made of dead skin. Dust mites feed on this skin. They live in beds, pillows, and carpets.

The thickest skin on

Dust mites aren't really this big! They're so small you can't see them.

How many dead skin flakes fall off every day?

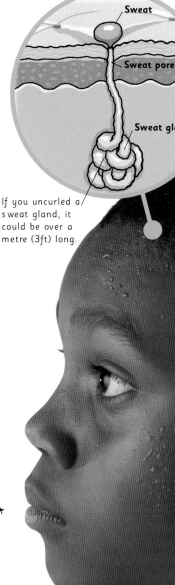

Sweat

Sweat pore

Sweat gland

If you uncurled a sweat gland, it could be over a metre (3ft) long.

Skin colour

The colour of your skin is affected by a substance called melanin. The more melanin you have, the darker you will be. When you are outside in the sun, your body produces extra melanin to protect your skin. This melanin makes your skin darker and you get a suntan.

your body is on the soles of your feet.

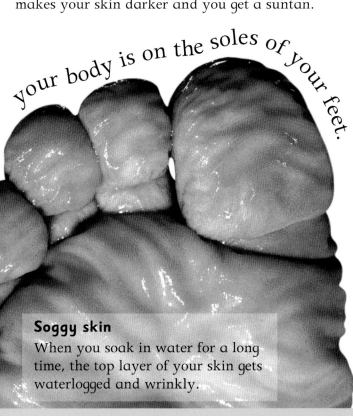

Soggy skin

When you soak in water for a long time, the top layer of your skin gets waterlogged and wrinkly.

Cooling down

When sweat dries on your skin, it helps to cool you down. Sweat comes from coiled tubes under the surface. It gets out through tiny holes called pores.

69

At your fingertips

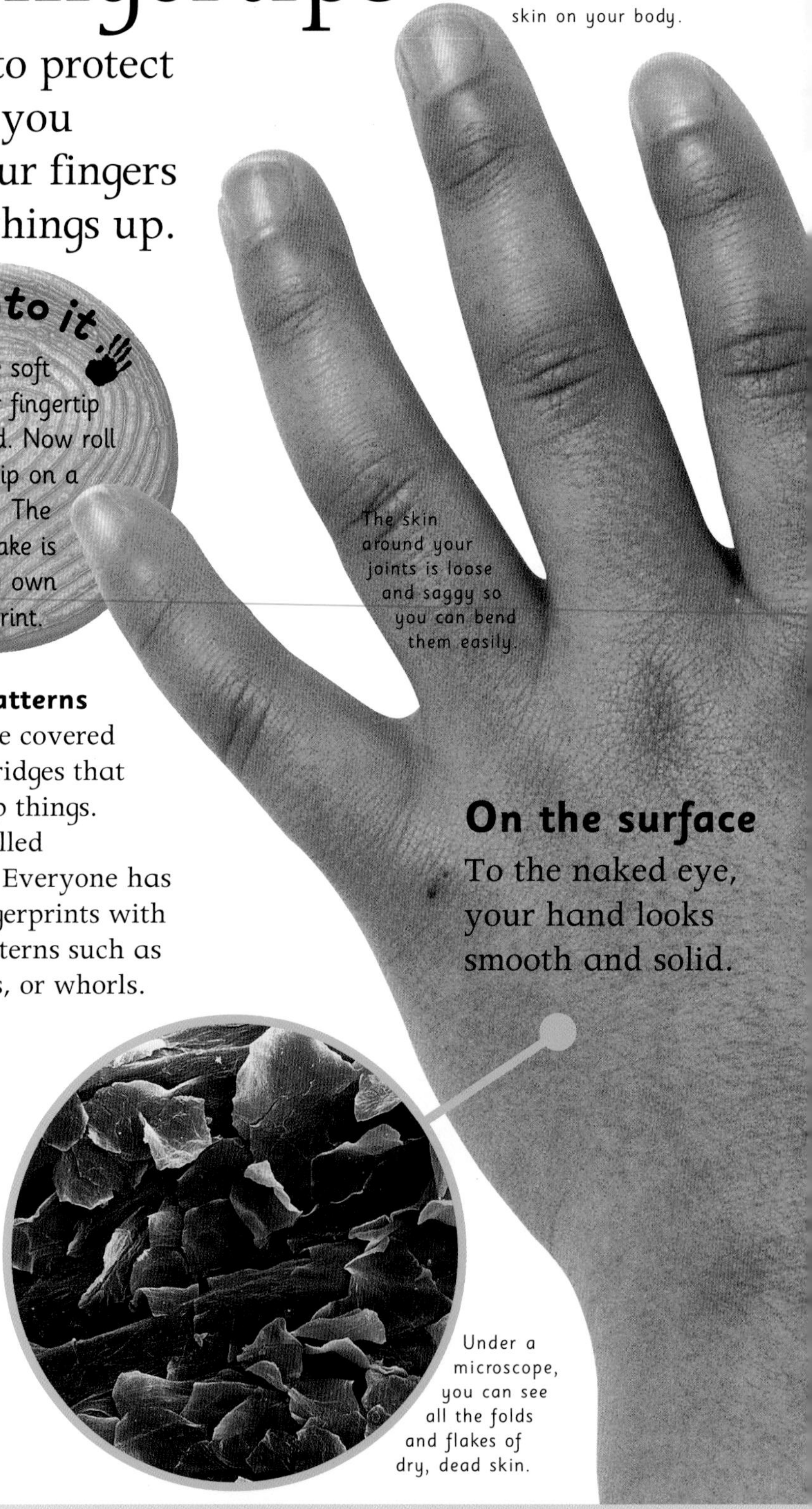

Your fingertips have the most sensitive skin on your body.

Nails work with skin to protect your body. They stop you hurting the ends of your fingers and help you to pick things up.

Arch

Loop

Whorl

get into it

Roll the soft part of your fingertip on an ink pad. Now roll your inky fingertip on a piece of paper. The mark you make is your very own fingerprint.

The skin around your joints is loose and saggy so you can bend them easily.

Fingertip patterns

Fingertips are covered with swirly ridges that help you grip things. These are called fingerprints. Everyone has different fingerprints with different patterns such as arches, loops, or whorls.

On the surface

To the naked eye, your hand looks smooth and solid.

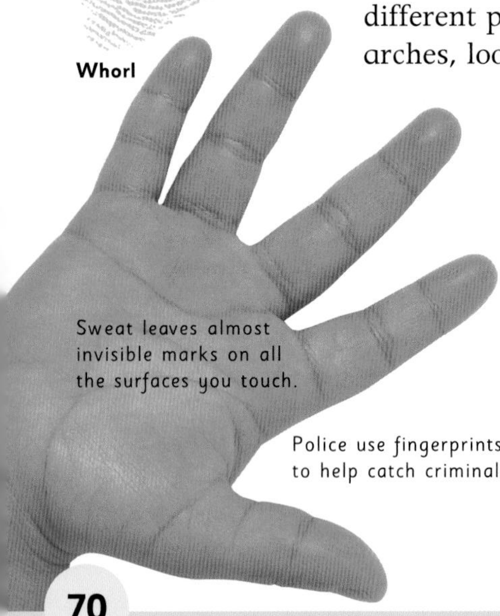

Sweat leaves almost invisible marks on all the surfaces you touch.

Police use fingerprints to help catch criminals.

Under a microscope, you can see all the folds and flakes of dry, dead skin.

Why do you get white spots on your nails?

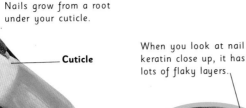

Nails grow from a root under your cuticle.

Cuticle

When you look at nail keratin close up, it has lots of flaky layers.

Fat

Bone

The inside story

Although nails are much harder than skin or hair, they're made from the same basic material. It is called keratin.

Our nails are like animals' claws.

Family connections

Like humans, birds and animals have body parts that are made of keratin.

Claws look like nails, but they are stronger and sharper.

Beaks are very hard so birds can tear food and crack seeds.

Holding on

It would be difficult to hold heavy things if you didn't have fingernails. They help to make your fingertips straight and strong. The other reason you have fingernails is so you can scratch when you're itchy!

Nail growth

Nails start to grow before you're born, and they carry on your whole life. They grow quicker on your hands than on your feet.

Horns contain different kinds of keratin. Rhino horns are made of hair keratin.

These spots mean the new nail has been banged or knocked.

Fairly hairy

Hair is mostly made of keratin, just like skin and nails. You have about 100 thousand hairs on your head and millions more on your body.

Hair grows for up to seven years before it falls out.

Hair close up

Each hair is covered with scales that overlap like roof tiles. This makes the hair strong and protects it. Hair is dead tissue, which is why it doesn't hurt to cut it.

What's your hair like?

Hair grows out of tiny pockets or follicles. The shape of these pockets controls whether hair is straight, wavy, or curly.

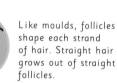

Like moulds, follicles shape each strand of hair. Straight hair grows out of straight follicles.

Slightly curvy follicles produce wavy strands of hair.

Head hair

Lots of body heat escapes from your head, so the hair there is long and thick to keep your brain warm. Fine hairs cover every other part of you except the palms of your hands, soles of your feet, and your lips.

How many hairs do you lose from your head every day?

Smooth surface

Some men lose their hair as they grow older. In fact, the hair still grows, but it is shorter and falls out more easily. A few people are born without any hair at all – not even eyelashes.

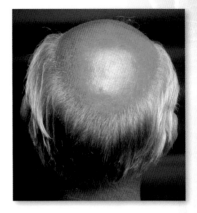

Colour chart

Hair, like skin, gets its colour from a chemical called melanin. If you have no melanin in your hair, it will be white – if you have lots, it will be jet black.

Brrrr...

When you're cold, tiny muscles pull your body hair upright so it forms a fuzzy layer to keep warmth in. When the muscles pull, they make little ridges called goose pimples.

Goose pimple

Follicles that are very swirly in shape produce tightly curled hair.

Good food

If your head is itchy, you may have head lice. These creatures cling to your hair and suck blood from your scalp. When you play with friends, the lice crawl from one head to another. These fussy bugs like clean heads best.

Germs

Your body is a walking zoo. It's covered with bugs that feed and breed on you but are mostly too small to see. Many do no harm, but some, called germs, make you ill when they get inside you.

Viruses spread through the air in coughs and sneezes.

These viruses give people colds or the flu.

Vile viruses

Viruses are the smallest living things on Earth. They break into cells and force them to make new viruses. Viruses can cause colds, flu, measles, mumps, and warts.

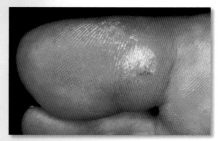

Verucca

A verruca (wart) is a patch of thickened skin caused by a virus. The virus often spreads from person to person in places where people walk barefoot, such as swimming pools.

Become an expert...

on clearing airways, pages **66-67**

visiting the doctor, pages **110-111**

What animal has killed more people than any other?

Beastly bacteria

Bacteria are very common germs that often spread by touch. When bacteria get into cuts, they cause swellings and sores. Certain types cause deadly diseases if they get into your stomach or lungs.

Your hand leaves bacteria on anything you touch

Billions of Bacteria

There are more bacteria on your skin than there are people in the world. Most do little harm, and some actually protect you from other germs. If you touch rotten food or faeces, your hands will pick up more dangerous bacteria.

Big bugs

Creatures much bigger than bacteria or viruses also feed on your body and can make you sick.

 Giardia live in intestines and spread in dirty water. They cause diarrhoea.

 Threadworms live in the large intestine and spread on dirty fingers.

 Follicle mites live in the roots of most people's eyelashes and do little harm.

 Mosquitos suck people's blood and spread germs that cause deadly diseases.

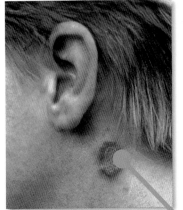

Fungi

Some germs are fungi (related to mushrooms). Tinea (ringworm) is a type of fungus that grows through skin like a plant, sending out long thin shoots.

The tinea fungus grows through your skin like a plant, sending out long thin shoots.

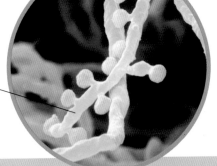

Body defences

Although you can't see them, germs are always landing on your body and trying to get inside it. Your body has lots of clever ways of keeping them out.

Poison tears

Germs that land on your eyes are washed away by tears, which come from glands above your eyes. Tears contain the chemical lysozyme, which kills bacteria by making them burst open.

You make about 1 litre (2 pints) of saliva a day.

Saved by spit

The liquid in your mouth is called saliva. As well as helping you digest food, saliva protects your mouth, tongue, and teeth from attack by bacteria.

Earwax flows slowly out of your ears all the time, flushing out dirt and germs.

Sticky business

Germs get into your lungs when you breathe in. They get trapped in a sticky liquid called mucus, which lines your airways. Tiny beating hairs continually push the mucus up to your throat to be swallowed.

76

Which is your largest defensive organ?

Acid attack

Glands inside of your stomach make acid, which kills germs you've swallowed. Your digestive system then breaks down the germs along with your food.

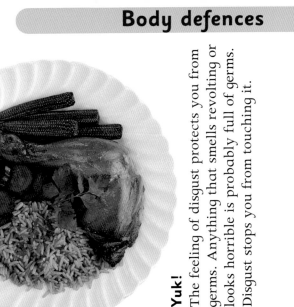

Yuk!

The feeling of disgust protects you from germs. Anything that smells revolting or looks horrible is probably full of germs. Disgust stops you from touching it.

Become an expert…

on eyes, pages **38–39**
on digesting food, pages **88–89**

Slimy guts

The inside of your intestines are covered with slimy mucus, which stops germs from getting into your blood. Your large intestine also contains millions of "friendly" bacteria, which prevent other germs from growing.

Fighting germs

If germs break through your outer defences and invade your tissues, your body fights back. The cells of your immune system hunt and destroy germs. This system also remembers germs and protects you from them in the future.

Antibodies attacking germs.

Killer cells

White blood cells called macrophages kill germs by swallowing them. When a macrophage finds a germ, it stretches out, wraps around the germ, and pulls it inside. Digestive juices then destroy it.

Antibody

Antibodies

Some white blood cells make chemicals called antibodies. These stick to the surface of germs, telling other body cells to attack.

This germ is being swallowed.

This white blood cell is called a macrophage.

Heating up

Your body gets hotter when it fights germs, which gives you a high temperature.

How many tonsils are in your throat?

Lymph system

Fluid continually leaks out of your blood vessels and tissues. It returns to the blood through tubes called lymph vessels. Dotted along these are swellings called nodes, which filter out germs.

Extra protection

Doctors protect you from germs with vaccines. Vaccines contain weak or dead germs that your immune system learns to attack. If the real germ ever gets inside you, your immune system remembers it and attacks very quickly.

Killer milk

Breast milk contains germ-killing antibodies that protect babies from disease. During the first few days of a baby's life, the mother makes a special milk called colostrum, which is packed with antibodies.

The swellings in lymph vessels are called lymph nodes.

Tonsils

At the back of your mouth are several patches of tissue called tonsils. They are full of white blood cells that fight germs in your throat. However, the tonsils sometimes fill with germs themselves and have to be removed.

79

Allergies

An allergy happens when your body mistakes a harmless substance for a germ and overreacts to it. Food, plants, dust, pets, and many other substances can cause allergies.

Who gets allergies?

If you grow up in a large family or on a farm, your immune system will get lots of practice against germs. Some experts think this makes you less likely to get allergies.

Allergens

A substance that triggers an allergy is called an allergen.

Wasp stings can kill people who are allergic to them.

Antibiotic medicines can give allergic people a rash on the skin.

Hair and **skin** from pets can cause an allergy very similar to hayfever.

Moulds grow in damp places. Their powdery spores can cause asthma.

Biological washing powder can cause a skin reaction.

Dust mites

Millions of these tiny beasts, which are smaller than full stops, live in your home. They feed on dead skin. Their microscopic faeces are a major cause of asthma.

Dust mites are related to spiders and have eight legs.

Mouth

What's the most common type of allergy?

Poison ivy

Skin allergies

If you touch a thing you're allergic to, itchy red spots may appear on your skin. Poison ivy plants, make-up, jewellery, and clothes can cause skin allergies.

Skin allergies cause itchy red spots that can look just like a nettle rash.

Pollen

A very common cause of allergy is a powdery dust called pollen which is made by flowers. Pollen floats through the air and enters our bodies as we breathe.

Hayfever can make your eyes swollen, watery, and red.

Food allergies

Foods that cause allergies include strawberries, nuts, seafood, and eggs. These can give an allergic person a skin rash, a runny nose, a sore mouth, nausea, and diarrhoea.

Peanuts can be deadly to people with a nut allergy

Hayfever

People who are allergic to pollen have hayfever. When they breathe in lots of pollen, their noses run and their eyes get sore. Hayfever is worst in spring and summer, when grass flowers release lots of pollen into the air.

Inhalers squirt out medicine in a spray, helping people with asthma to breathe.

Asthma

People with asthma can find it hard to breathe. Their chests feel tight and their breathing becomes wheezy. Asthma can be caused by an allergy to dust mites, cat hairs, or other substances in air.

Digestive system

Food is made up of large, complicated chemicals that your body has to break into small chemicals that your blood can absorb. This process is called digestion.

When you swallow, food passes down a tube called the oesophagus.

Tube journey

Your digestive system is really just a long, tangled tube. Food travels about 9 metres (30 feet) as it passes from start to finish.

Physical digestion

Some parts of your digestive system mash up food physically, just like a food processor does. Your mouth breaks food into chunks. Your stomach then churns these around until they form a slushy liquid.

Become an expert...

on taste and smell, pages **36-37**

on what's in food, pages **106-107**

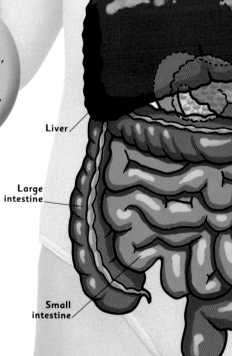

Liver

Large intestine

Venus flytrap

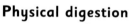

The Venus flytrap catches insects and digests them with enzymes.

Dragonfly

Chemical digestion

Many digestive organs make juices that break down the chemicals in food. The juices contain enzymes, which turn large food molecules into small molecules.

Small intestine

Rectum

Which is longer: your small intestine or your large intestine?

Digesting a meal
A large meal takes a day or more to pass through your digestive system. Different digestive organs make enzymes that work on different parts of the meal.

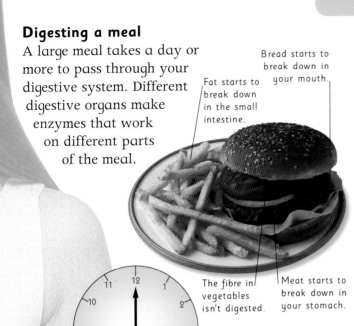

Bread starts to break down in your mouth.

Fat starts to break down in the small intestine.

The fibre in vegetables isn't digested.

Meat starts to break down in your stomach.

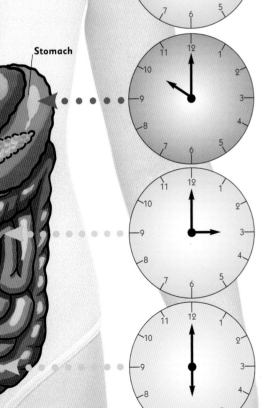

Stomach

6pm
Food gets swallowed 10 seconds after it enters your mouth.

10pm
A meal spends about 4 hours in the stomach, but very rich food can spend twice as long there.

3am
The meal is slowly squeezed through your small intestine, sometimes causing loud gurgling noises.

The next day
Undigested leftovers reach the end of their journey about a day after you swallowed the food.

Curiosity quiz
Take a look through the digestive-system pages and see if you can spot any of the cells and tissues below.

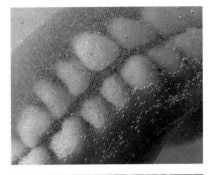
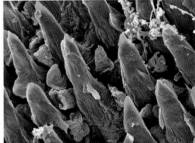

Your small intestine.

Chew it over

We use our teeth to bite off and chew our food. During the course of your life you will have two separate sets of teeth.

First teeth
Your first teeth start to grow when you're about 6 months old. The front teeth usually appear first.

Adult teeth
When you are six your first teeth start to fall out. Adult teeth with deeper roots grow to replace them.

Wisdom teeth
Your back teeth are called wisdom teeth. They appear when you are 17 or older, and sometimes not at all.

False teeth
If you don't take care of your teeth they will decay and fall out. Then you will need false teeth.

Types of teeth

Your mouth contains a selection of different types of teeth. Each type is designed to do a different job.

A child has 20 teeth, an adult has 32.

Molars at the back of your mouth have a flat edge so you can mash your food thoroughly.

Premolars roughly crush and grind your food. They are smaller than molars.

Canines grip and tear food using a single rounded point.

Incisors at the front of your mouth slice up chunks of food.

Roots

Without long roots your teeth might break or fly out of your mouth if you bit down hard on your food. The root is held in place by a kind of cement.

What is another name for your first teeth?

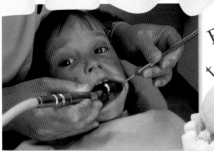

Brush your teeth!

A sticky mixture of food and bacteria builds up on the surface of your teeth if you don't clean them properly. It is called plaque.

Brush twice a day to keep decay away.

Decay

Bacteria in plaque can eat through tooth enamel and attack the blood vessels and nerves deep inside the tooth. This is called decay. It hurts, and the dentist may need to give you a filling.

The sugar in sweets sticks to your teeth, forming plaque. Plaque contains bacteria that causes teeth to decay.

Inside a tooth

Deep inside your teeth are lots of blood vessels and nerves. The nerves mean you can feel heat, cold, and pain.

Enamel

The hardest and toughest substance in your body is tooth enamel. It contains no living cells so it can't repair itself if it is damaged.

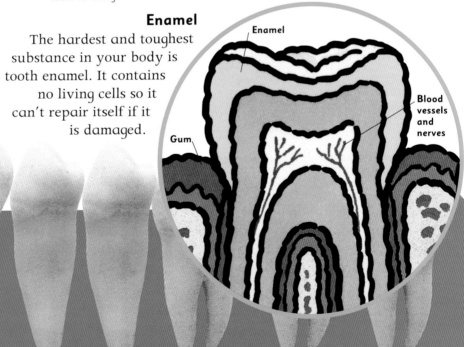

Enamel

Blood vessels and nerves

Gum

Milk teeth or baby teeth.

From mouth to stomach

You start digesting food the moment you bite into it. As your teeth tear the food apart, enzymes in your spit begin to attack it chemically. By the time it reaches your stomach, your meal is unrecognizable.

Get a grip

Your tongue is a super strong, flexible bundle of muscle that pushes food against your teeth as you chew. It has a rough surface for good grip.

Seen close up, your tongue is covered by tiny bumps and stalks that make its surface rough to improve its grip.

Mouth watering

The slimy liquid in your mouth is saliva. It moistens food to make it easier to chew and swallow. Saliva also contains an enzyme that breaks down starch, one of the main ingredients in bread, rice, and pasta.

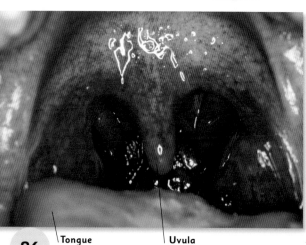

Tongue   Uvula

What is the scientific name for burping?

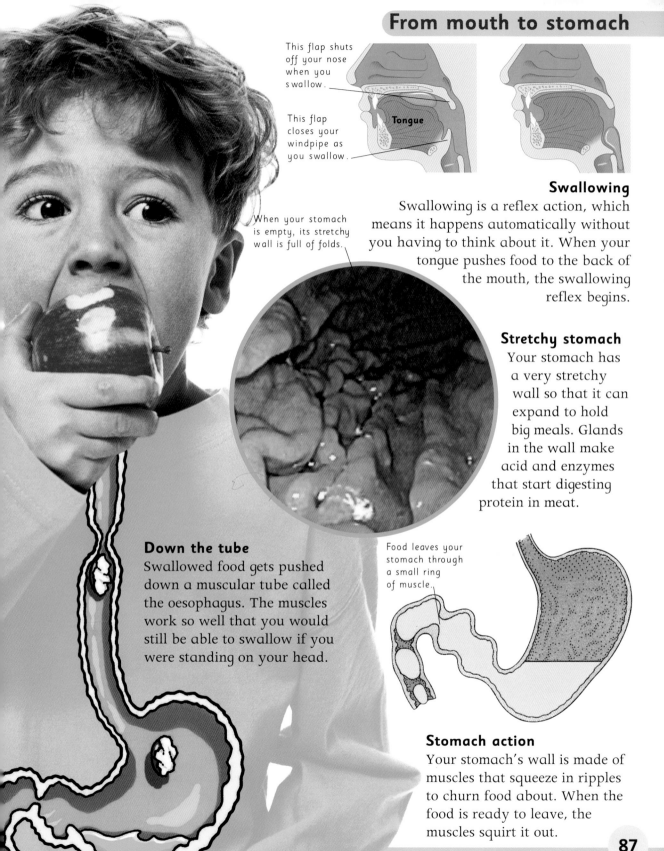

This flap shuts off your nose when you swallow.

This flap closes your windpipe as you swallow.

Tongue

Swallowing
Swallowing is a reflex action, which means it happens automatically without you having to think about it. When your tongue pushes food to the back of the mouth, the swallowing reflex begins.

When your stomach is empty, its stretchy wall is full of folds.

Stretchy stomach
Your stomach has a very stretchy wall so that it can expand to hold big meals. Glands in the wall make acid and enzymes that start digesting protein in meat.

Down the tube
Swallowed food gets pushed down a muscular tube called the oesophagus. The muscles work so well that you would still be able to swallow if you were standing on your head.

Food leaves your stomach through a small ring of muscle.

Stomach action
Your stomach's wall is made of muscles that squeeze in ripples to churn food about. When the food is ready to leave, the muscles squirt it out.

87

Eructation.

Inside the intestines

When food leaves your stomach, it enters a long, tangled tube. This has two parts. The first is your small intestine, which is long and narrow. The second is your large intestine, which is shorter but fatter.

Small intestine

The small intestine finishes off the job of digestion. Digested food soaks through its wall and enters the blood to be carried away.

Finger blobs

Tiny, finger-shaped blobs called villi line the small intestine. They speed up the absorption of food.

Muscles push food through your intestines just like this hand pushes a ball along a stocking.

A squeezing action travels along the intestine in waves.

Pushed along

Your intestines use a special kind of muscle action called peristalsis to move food along. Rings of muscle in the intestines squeeze behind the food, pushing it.

How tall would you be if your intestines weren't coiled up?

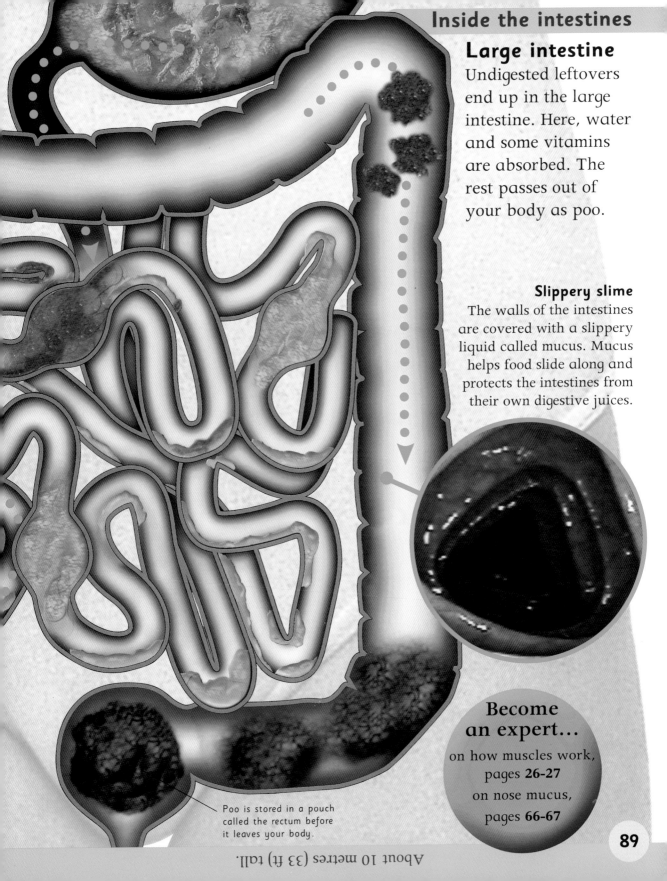

Large intestine

Undigested leftovers end up in the large intestine. Here, water and some vitamins are absorbed. The rest passes out of your body as poo.

Slippery slime

The walls of the intestines are covered with a slippery liquid called mucus. Mucus helps food slide along and protects the intestines from their own digestive juices.

Become an expert...

on how muscles work, pages **26-27**

on nose mucus, pages **66-67**

Poo is stored in a pouch called the rectum before it leaves your body.

About 10 metres (33 ft) tall.

Waterworks

Your body gets rid of waste chemicals and excess water by making urine. Urine comes from two organs called kidneys. They filter and clean blood as it flows through, removing chemicals that your body doesn't need.

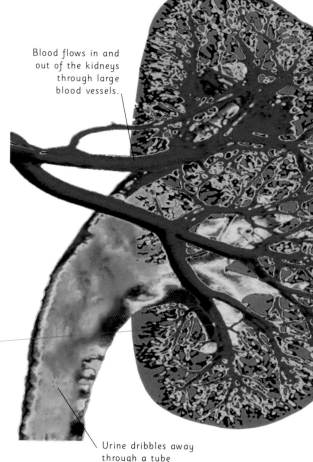

Blood flows in and out of the kidneys through large blood vessels.

Urine dribbles away through a tube called the ureter.

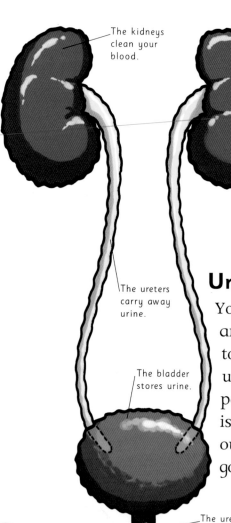

The kidneys clean your blood.

The ureters carry away urine.

The bladder stores urine.

The urethra gets rid of urine.

Urinary system

Your kidneys, bladder, and the tubes connected to them make up your urinary system. The last part of the urinary system is the urethra. Urine comes out of this tube when you go to the toilet.

If you put your hands on your hips and your thumbs on your back, your kidneys are next to your thumb tips.

How long do your kidneys take to clean all the blood in your body?

Inside a kidney

The blood vessels entering your kidneys divide into smaller and smaller branches. These lead to a million tiny filtering units called nephrons.

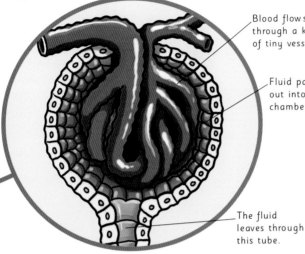

Blood flows through a knot of tiny vessels.

Fluid passes out into a chamber.

The fluid leaves through this tube.

Inside a nephron

As blood flows through a nephron, fluids leave the blood vessel and pass to a long, looped tube. Useful chemicals are then reabsorbed into blood.

Balancing act

Your kidneys keep the water level in your body perfectly balanced. If you drink too much, your kidneys make watery urine to get rid of any excess. When your body is short of water, your kidneys pass less into your urine.

When the water level is low, the pituitary gland releases the hormone ADH.

This part of the brain monitors the water level in blood.

Water disposal

Here's how your body gets rid of water.

Urine makes up more than half of the water that leaves your body.

Breath contains over a quarter of the water your body gets rid of.

Sweat is only about one twelfth of the water leaving your body.

Poo is fairly dry and contains only a little bit of your liquid waste.

A low water level also triggers a feeling of thirst, making you drink.

Water control

Your kidneys work together with your brain to control your water level. When this level is low, your brain releases a hormone that makes your kidneys save water.

ADH travels to your kidneys in your blood.

Your kidneys save water, making your urine stronger.

The stretchy bladder

All day long, a small stream of urine trickles out of each kidney. It collects in an organ called the bladder, which stores the urine until you go to the toilet.

Nappy rash
Babies sometimes get a rash under nappies. This happens when urine mixes with poo and makes the skin sore.

Filling up
Your bladder stretches as it fills up. This sends a signal to your brain, making you want to go to the toilet.

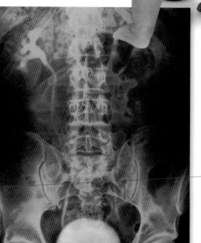

X-ray of full bladder

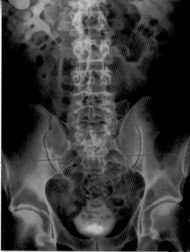

X-ray of empty bladder

Full stretch
An adult's bladder stretches from the size of a plum to the size of a grapefruit and can hold about 500 ml (1 pint) of urine. Your bladder is about the size of an orange when it's full.

The bladder's muscly wall squeezes to push urine out.

Inside the bladder
The bladder has a waterproof lining to stop it leaking. Urine leaves through a tube called the urethra, which is normally kept shut by two muscles.

Grapefruit   Orange   Plum

How much urine do you make each day?

What is urine?

Urine is made of water and waste chemicals. The main waste is urea, which your body makes when it breaks down protein. The colour of urine depends on how much you drink. If you drink lots of water, your urine will turn pale.

The yellow colour comes from a chemical that is made when old blood cells are broken down.

Tubes called ureters bring urine from the kidneys.

Camel urine

Camels can last for months without water so they can survive in the driest deserts. They save water by making thick, syrupy urine that is twice as salty as seawater.

Camels store fat in their humps, which they use for energy.

Bladder control

In young children, the muscles that open the bladder work automatically. As children get older, they learn to control one of the muscles.

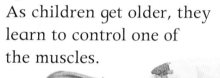

This muscle opens automatically when the bladder is full.

Urethra

We have to learn to control this muscle.

Potty training

Children gradually gain control of their bladder around the age of two, but they still wet the bed at night. By the age of four, most children can stay dry at night as well.

Toddlers have to learn bladder control.

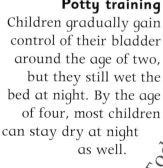

Making a baby

You need a mother and a father to make a baby. The mother's body does most of the work, but the father also has an important job – his sperm joins with the mother's egg and a new life begins...

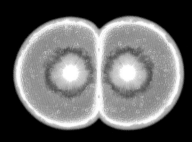

The first cells
After 36 hours, the cell has divided and made an exact copy of itself. These are the first two cells of a baby.

Eggs are the biggest cells in the human body. But they are still very small – ten would fit across a pinhead.

Sperm are amazing viewed under a microscope. They look like tiny tadpoles. You can see their tails wriggling as they swim.

Sperm race
Millions of sperm swim towards the egg cell. Only one sperm can join with the egg to make a new cell.

By the time the baby is born, the fertilized cell will have become 100 trillion cells.

What is another name for the uterus?

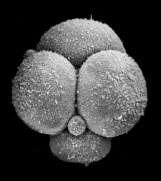

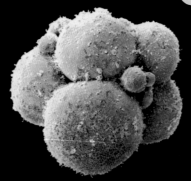

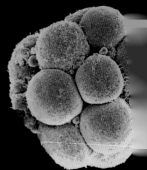

Divide again
You don't grow much in the first few days. The two cells divide to make four, then eight, and so on.

The future you
Each cell is unique to you. Cells are full of instructions about what you will look like.

At three days
The cells have carried dividing. There are nov and they are almost rec plant themselves in the

Where it all happens
The sperm fertilizes the egg in a tunnel, called a Fallopian tube. The fertilized egg moves down the tunnel towards the mother's uterus. The journey takes about five days.

The cells start dividing as they move down the Fallopian tube towards the uterus.

Millions from the travel up towards t

This is the mother's ovary. It releases one egg every month.

This is the uterus. It is about the size of a pear and has muscular walls.

Arriving in the uterus
The ball of cells plants itself in the wall of the uterus. In this warm, dark place the baby will spend the next 40 weeks growing and developing.

Growing in the womb

By eight weeks old, the baby is no longer a bundle of cells. It looks like a tiny person and is called a "foetus". The foetus does not eat, drink, or breathe by itself. All its needs are taken care of by its mother.

Boy or girl?

Parents can find out about a baby's health and sex before it is born. A scanning machine shows the baby on a screen. This is many parents' first sight of their child.

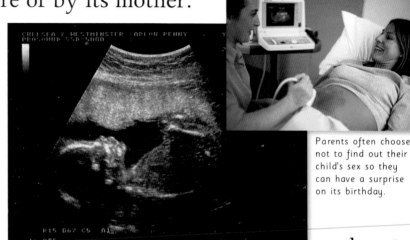

Parents often choose not to find out their child's sex so they can have a surprise on its birthday.

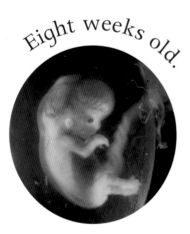

Eight weeks old.

The size of a strawberry
The foetus has eyes, a nose, lips, and a tongue. It lives in a protective bag of liquid and uses its tiny muscles to swim around gracefully.

Sixteen weeks old.

The size of a lemon
At 16 weeks the foetus can make different faces, clench its fist, and suck its thumb. It can hear its first sounds but its eyes are not open yet.

Twenty weeks old.

Food and oxygen from the mother travel through this special cord.

The size of a grapefruit
At 20 weeks the foetus is getting more active. It is still quite small so there's plenty of room to kick around and turn somersaults.

When do we first start to dream?

Twenty-two weeks old.

You might feel the baby move if you put your hand on a pregnant woman's tummy.

Fuzzy foetus

By 22 weeks, the baby is quite well developed but fairly thin. It will spend the next few weeks growing a layer of fat under its skin. It is covered in soft, fine hair.

What's it like in there?

It is quite noisy in the womb with the sounds of the mother's heartbeat and stomach rumbles. The baby can also hear noises outside the womb and loud bangs may make it jump. It learns to recognize its mother's voice long before it is born.

Happy birthday!

At last, after around 40 weeks, the moment comes for the baby to be born. Newborn babies can breathe, suck, and swallow. They communicate by crying if they are hungry or feel uncomfortable.

Before we are born, at about 20 weeks.

Identical twins

Identical twins are made when a fertilized egg splits into two separate cell clusters.

Fertilization occurs when a single sperm fuses with the egg.

The fertilized egg splits into two. We don't know what makes this happen.

Two cell clusters develop into two separate babies.

Non-identical twins

Non-identical twins are made when the mother releases two eggs instead of one.

Each egg is fertilized by a different sperm. Two babies then develop.

Growing up

Identical twins often notice amazing similarities in their taste and behaviour. Sometimes they can even tell what the other is thinking!

Double trouble

There are two different types of twins – identical and non-identical. Identical twins have the same genes. Non-identical twins are like any other brother or sister so only half their genes are the same.

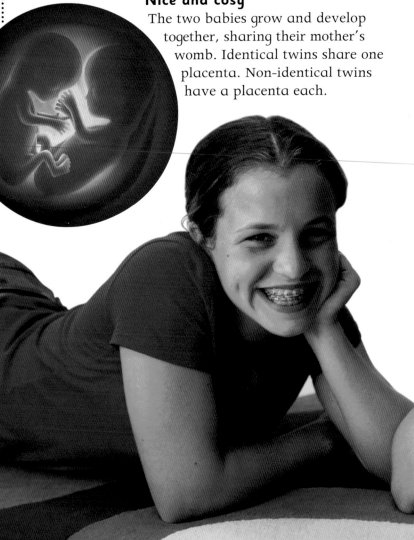

Nice and cosy

The two babies grow and develop together, sharing their mother's womb. Identical twins share one placenta. Non-identical twins have a placenta each.

Do identical twins have exactly the same fingerprints?

Multiple births

Even rarer than being a twin is being a triplet, or even a quadruplet...

Triplets: One in 8,100 natural pregnancies produces triplets.

Quadruplets: It's rarer to be a quad. One in 729,000 pregnancies produces quads.

Quintuplets: Having five children is usually a result of fertility treatment.

Sextuplets: There are currently only around 30 sets of six in the world.

Twins in the family

Once a couple has had one set of twins, they are more likely to have another. Also, if your mother, or *her* mother, is a non-identical twin you may inherit the trait and have twins yourself!

Mirror twins

Some identical twins are called mirror twins. Often, one will be left handed and the other right handed, and their fingerprints appear to mirror each other.

Seven children are called "septuplets". All these children are non-identical.

Record-breakers!

There are presently only two sets of septuplets in the world. These ones are named Kenneth, Brandon, Nathan, Joel, Alexis, Natalie, and Kelsey. They were born in Iowa in America in 1997.

No, because the soft skin on their fingertips was moulded differently in the womb.

The early years

Babies' bodies grow very fast, but their brains develop quickly too. Learning to move around and talk are both huge tasks.

New skills

Children's brains are changing all the time as they learn new skills at an amazing rate.

 Smiling: most babies start to smile at around 6 weeks old.

 Drinking: babies learn to drink from a lidded cup between 6 and 12 months.

 Eating: most babies can feed themselves from a bowl at around 15 months.

 Learning colours: children can name colours by 3 years old.

 Brushing teeth: 5 year olds can brush their teeth without help.

Big head

Babies have enormous heads in relation to the size of their bodies! As you get older, the rest of your body catches up.

Babies' big heads hold big brains! They need them because there's lots to learn.

Your body grows very fast during your first year...

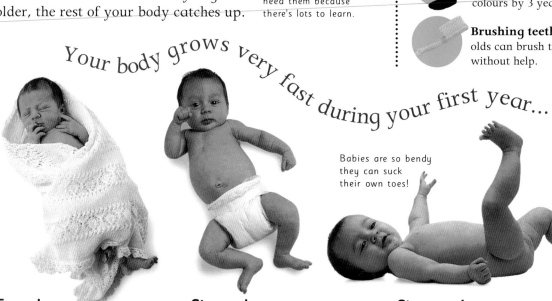

Babies are so bendy they can suck their own toes!

Four days

Newborns spend most of their time asleep. Even when they're awake they don't open their eyes much.

Six weeks

Babies cry when they are cold or hungry. By this age, they start to make cooing sounds too.

Six months

Babies have a lot more control over their bodies now. Their muscles are stronger so they can sit up without help.

When do you reach half your adult height?

Chatterbox
By one year, a baby is trying to speak. By two, children can use 100 different words, and by three most know more than 1000 different words.

Being able to talk makes it easier to play with other children.

...and hardly slows down during your second!

By three, children know the difference between boys and girls.

One year
By this age babies can understand simple words. They also take their first few steps.

Two years
Children this age can walk and run, climb stairs, and kick balls. They are starting to get dressed alone but can't do up buttons, zips, buckles, and shoelaces.

At around two years old.

Growing up

As a child, you learn to walk and talk, run and jump, go to the toilet alone, eat with cutlery, read and write, and even make friends!

Making friends

By five years old, children can form friendships and play together. They start to care what other people think of them.

What can you do?

Do you realize how much work goes into learning all these amazing skills?

Shoelaces: At six years old, most children can do up their own shoelaces.

Riding a bike: At seven, many children can ride a two-wheeled bike.

Reading: Some children learn to read at four, some at five, and some at six!

Writing: You should write fairly clearly by the time you are seven.

As your baby fat melts away, your features become clearer...

You're learning new skills such as skipping.

Sitting still and thinking are skills too.

There's still plenty of time to play after school hours.

Age 4-5

By this age, a child can speak clearly in basic sentences, and knows many thousands of words.

Age 5-6

It's time to learn to read, write, do sums, and maybe even start playing a musical instrument.

Age 7-10

Boys and girls like different things at this age so they have more friends of their own sex.

Why do you grow?

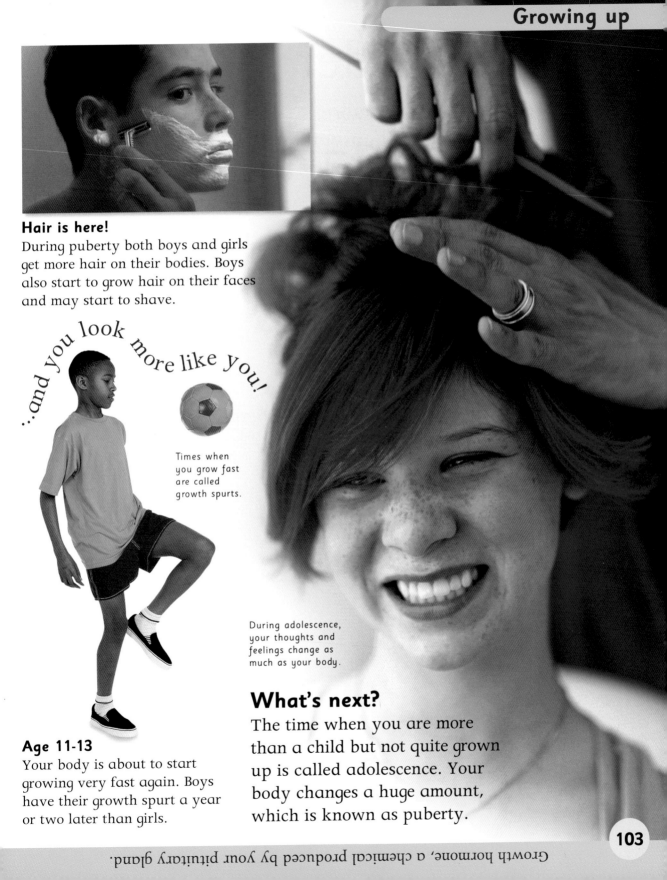

Hair is here!

During puberty both boys and girls get more hair on their bodies. Boys also start to grow hair on their faces and may start to shave.

...and you look more like you!

Times when you grow fast are called growth spurts.

During adolescence, your thoughts and feelings change as much as your body.

Age 11-13

Your body is about to start growing very fast again. Boys have their growth spurt a year or two later than girls.

What's next?

The time when you are more than a child but not quite grown up is called adolescence. Your body changes a huge amount, which is known as puberty.

Growth hormone, a chemical produced by your pituitary gland.

Growing older

Adults keep growing, but more slowly than children. When you get older, your body takes longer to repair itself and replace worn-out cells.

Life expectancy

As a general rule, the bigger a creature is, the longer it lives. So how long do humans live?

Butterflies have very short lives. Many live for only a month or two.

Cats kept as pets live longer than wild ones – up to 15 years.

People can live for 100 years. Women generally live longer than men.

Tortoises can live for 150 years. Some spend a quarter of their lives asleep.

Twenties

During your twenties you are at your peak. Your body has reached its adult size so you don't spend most of your energy on growing.

Thirties

Because they're not growing any more, many people need to eat less so they don't get fat. Most bodies are strong and healthy, but athletes are already past their best.

Brittle bones

With old age, the bones and disks in the spine get weaker and thinner, so people get a little bit shorter.

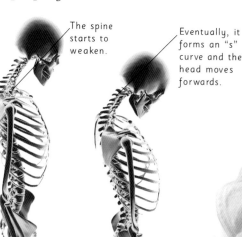

A normal, healthy spine holds the body straight.

The spine starts to weaken.

Eventually, it forms an "s" curve and the head moves forwards.

What is the longest a person has ever lived?

Smile lines

With age, skin gets less stretchy and will not smooth out when you relax your face. This is gives you wrinkles. Many cultures respect wrinkles as signs of wisdom and experience.

Silver surfer

Today people live longer than ever thanks to advances in medicine. A healthy diet, exercise, and a young mind can make old age a happy time.

Middle age

Organs and muscles are starting to get weaker. Skin on the face gets wrinkly, and hair starts to go grey. Women stop having babies.

Old age

Papery skin, weak bones, stiff joints, and bad eyesight are common in old people. Most of the organs including the lungs and heart don't work as well as they used to.

As you get older, your hair contains less melanin – the substance that gives it its colour.

105

Records prove that a French woman, Jeanne-Louise Calment, lived for 122 years.

What's in food?

People eat to get energy.
You need a variety
of foods to keep
your body
in peak
working
condition.

A balanced diet means
eating everything your
body needs.

Proteins
Meat, fish, eggs,
beans, and nuts
contain protein.
Your body needs
protein to repair
its cells.

Carbohydrates
Bread, cereal,
pasta, and sweet
foods are mostly
carbohydrates.
You need them to
give you energy.

Fat
Nuts and dairy
foods, such as
butter and cheese
contain fat. You
only need small
amounts of fat.

Takeaways and
fizzy drinks are nice
as a treat but no
substitute for a
good meal.

Eat your greens
Fresh fruit and vegetables are crammed
with vitamins and minerals. Your body
needs these to stay healthy.

Junk food
Fast foods like hamburgers and
chips contain unhealthy amounts
of fat and salt, and few vitamins.

What is a vegetarian?

Water

Your body is two thirds water, but you're losing water all the time. You could live for several weeks without food but only for about 3 days without water.

You need about six glasses of liquid every day but some of this can come from your food.

Allergies

If your body reacts badly to a certain food and makes you ill, you may be allergic to it.

Wheat isn't good for some people. They cannot eat normal bread.

Nuts can be dangerous – even in tiny quantities – if you have a nut allergy.

Cows' milk doesn't suit some people, but they can drink sheep or goats' milk.

Sunshine food

You need vitamin D for strong bones. It is found in fish and eggs, but your body can produce it when you get sunlight on your skin.

Food gives you energy.

Become an expert...

on chewing food, pages **86-87** on making urine, pages **90-91**

Fuel for your body

An orange gives you enough energy to cycle for 5 minutes. A chocolate bar gives you enough energy to cycle for 45 minutes.

The amount of energy you get from food is measured in calories.

A person who does not eat meat.

Sleep

When you sleep your body rests. Your brain stops dealing with things in the outside world, and uses this time to sort out the events of the day.

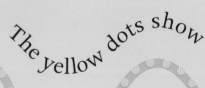

Adults need about seven hours sleep.

A newborn baby can sleep for 20 hours a day. By six months, 15 hours is usually enough.

A three year old needs about 12 hours sleep.

How much sleep?

As we grow older we need less sleep. Young adults need about eight hours, while over 60s may need only six.

Sleep patterns

Throughout the night, you move in and out of shallow and deep sleep several times. As the hours pass, sleep gradually becomes lighter until you wake up.

Time for bed.

The yellow dots show

Awake

Shallow sleep

9   10   11   12   1

Deep sleep

What is insomnia?

Dreaming

Everyone dreams. When you dream, your eyelids flicker. This is called rapid eye movement, or REM, sleep.

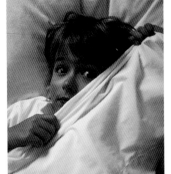

Nightmares

Nightmares are scary dreams that can wake you up and make you feel frightened or sad. During nightmares, people often think they are being chased or bullied.

When you dream anything is... possible!

Everyone dreams, but not everyone remembers their dreams.

K 3215

What dreams mean

People are fascinated by what dreams mean. We don't know for sure but...

Flying can mean that you feel powerful and free of problems.

Being naked sometimes means you are afraid of being weak.

Falling may mean you feel out of control or are scared of losing something.

when you dream.

2   3   4   5   6

Good morning!

Sleep walking

During deep sleep, parts of the brain stay awake. People may talk, or get up and walk around. They usually don't remember they have done this.

109

The medical name for being unable to fall or stay asleep.

Doctors and dentists

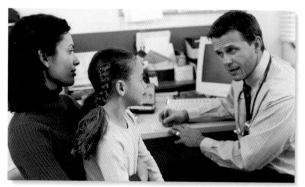

When you are ill you visit the doctor. First, the doctor examines you. Next, the doctor prescribes treatment or medicine to make you better.

The examination

The doctor asks you about your symptoms and then looks at and listens to different parts of your body.

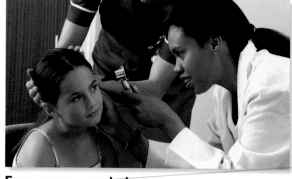

Say "ah"

The doctor uses a stick to hold your tongue down and look at your tonsils. If your tonsils often get infected you may need an operation to remove them.

Ears, nose, and throat

Doctors use an otoscope to examine your ears, nose, and throat. Swelling or itchiness may mean you have an infection.

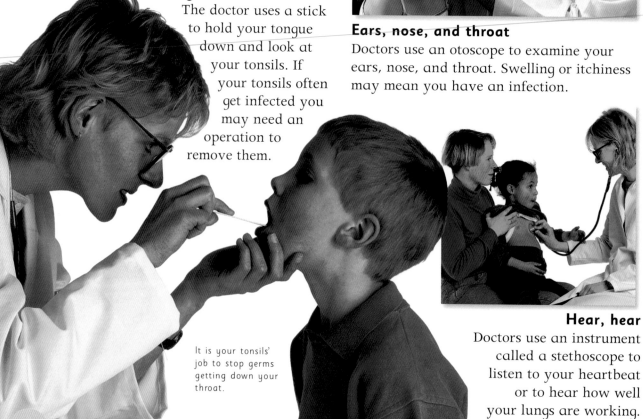

It is your tonsils' job to stop germs getting down your throat.

Hear, hear

Doctors use an instrument called a stethoscope to listen to your heartbeat or to hear how well your lungs are working.

What is a paediatrician?

Tools of the trade

Doctors keep a few simple instruments in their surgeries to help them examine their patients.

A stethoscope allows the doctor to listen to your heart or your breathing.

A rubber hammer is banged against your knee to test your reflexes.

An ophthalmoscope has a bright light for looking at the back of your eyes.

Syringes are used to give people injections to stop them getting some diseases.

Medicine comes from a pharmacy. The doctor just gives you a prescription.

These funny glasses help the optician find out exactly how well your eyes work.

Eye spy

Opticians test your sight and work out whether you need glasses. They test each eye separately because often one can see better than the other. Your eyesight changes so you need to get your eyes tested every year.

Open wide

You can look after your teeth by brushing them, but you should still get them checked twice a year by a dentist. Hopefully, you won't need any fillings.

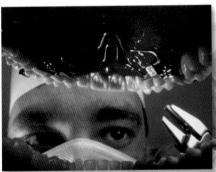

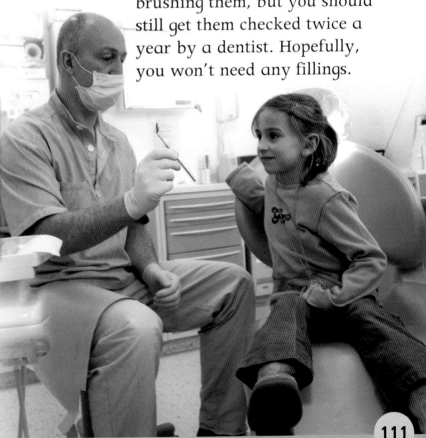

Brace yourself

Orthodontists are dentists who straighten out crooked teeth. They do this by fitting your mouth with braces to push your teeth gradually into the right position.

A doctor who specializes in children's illnesses.

Body language

You don't just talk with words – you also use your hands, face, and body. The look on your face and the way you stand can say a lot about how you really feel.

Personal space

People show how well they know each other by how close they stand or how often they touch. It's rude to stand too close to a stranger but normal to stand close to a best friend.

Only best friends and family can enter the **close intimate zone**.

The **intimate zone** is where people who know you well can stand while talking to you.

The **personal zone** is for people who know you but aren't close, such as teachers.

The **social zone** is where strangers stand while talking to you.

These girls are copying each other's body language.

Copying

Good friends often mimic each other's body language without realizing. They might walk in step, sit or stand in the same position, or copy each other's hand movements.

Who's in charge?

One of the things people signal with their body is whether they're in charge or somebody else is in charge. Leaning forwards or looking relaxed are ways of appearing to be in charge.

This boy's relaxed posture shows he feels very confident.

How does a dog show it knows you're in charge?

Learning gestures

You pick up a lot of your body language from the people you grow up with. Your gestures and the way you sit, stand, and walk are probably similar to your friends and family.

Boys often learn their gestures from older brothers, and girls pick up many of theirs from older sisters.

Open or closed?

When someone feels relaxed or friendly, they have an "open" posture, with arms and legs apart. If someone is nervous or awkward, they have a "closed" posture, with arms and legs close to the body.

Talking to animals

Animals can't understand speech but they often understand our body language. Dogs can sense who's in charge from body language. They need to be treated strictly or will start to misbehave.

Become an expert...
on muscles and movement, pages **26-27**

It lowers its body and tail and flattens its ears.

Use your hands

Most people move their hands as they speak, but what do their gestures mean? Some hand gestures mean the same thing all over the world, but others vary from place to place.

Speak to the hands

Hands seem to have minds of their own. When people talk, their hands move all over the place, even when they're on the phone!

Thumbs up

A raised thumb means "good" or "well done!" in North America. In Germany it means "one", in Japan it means "five", and in the Middle East and Africa it's impolite.

Making a circle

A finger touching a thumb means "OK" in North America, "worthless" in France, and "I want my change in coins" in Japan. In Turkey it can be rude.

Palms together

This is a sign of prayer in Christian countries, but in India it is used as a greeting. Indians place their hands together, make a slight bow, and say *Namaste*.

Shaking hands

Shaking hands is a common greeting in many countries, but there are slight differences. A firm handshake is a sign of sincerity in Europe but is thought to be aggressive in Asia.

In some countries, women never shake hands with men.

In Sicily, this gesture combined with a karate chopping movement means "I hate you so much".

How does a diver say "shark" underwater?

Making a point
Pointing is one of the first hand gestures that people learn, and it means the same thing all over the world. Babies ask for things by pointing at them before they learn to speak.

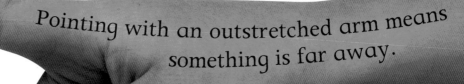

Pointing with an outstretched arm means something is far away.

Become an expert...
on the bones in your hands, page **20-21**

These 26 signs stand for the letters of the alphabet in British sign language.

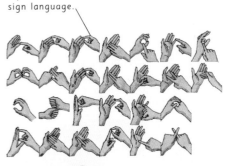

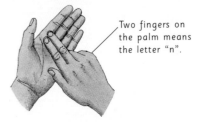

Two fingers on the palm means the letter "n".

Talking underwater

Divers can't speak underwater so they use a kind of sign language instead. They have special signs for marine animals like sharks and turtles.

OK is shown by a finger touching a thumb, making a circle.

Stay at this depth is shown by waving a flat hand from side to side.

Stop is shown by a clenched fist and a bent arm.

Sign language

Deaf people communicate without hearing by reading lips, using facial expressions, or using sign language. Sign language varies a lot from country to country.

By making a shark's fin on the head with one hand.

Express yourself

Your face helps you communicate by showing how you feel. All over the world, people use the same facial expressions to show the six main emotions.

Surprise makes you gasp for breath because the hormone adrenaline makes your lungs work faster.

2 Surprised
When you're surprised, your eyebrows shoot up, your eyes open wide, and your jaw drops. Some people clap the side of their face or cover their mouth as well.

1 Happy
In a genuine smile, the eyes crease and the cheeks rise. A smile means the same thing whether you live in the Sahara desert or Amazon rainforest.

Grumpy or angry people sometimes look red around the eyes.

3 Angry
An angry person's eyebrows move down, their eyes narrow, and their mouth closes tightly. They might also glare without blinking.

How many facial expression are there?

Baby face

Babies communicate with their faces before they learn to talk. They smile, frown, and show all the main emotions.

Babies learn to mirror their parents' smiles from a very early age.

Become an expert...

on how babies develop, pages **100-101**

5 Afraid
Fear raises the eyelids, making the eyes look white. The mouth opens wide in horror, and blood may drain from the face, making the skin pale.

4 Sad
In an unhappy face, the mouth droops, the inner ends of the eyebrows go up, and wrinkles appear above the nose. Powerful feelings of sadness also make people cry.

6 Disgusted
Wrinkles across the nose and narrow eyes are signs of disgust. The sight of disgust in someone's face can make you feel disgusted too.

About 7000.

Amazing facts about YOU!

Skeleton and bones

Without a skeleton to hold you up, you'd collapse on the ground like a heap of jelly.

 Your smallest bone is the stapes in your ear, which is smaller than a rice grain.

 Weight for weight, bones are stronger than steel or concrete.

A baby has more than 300 bones but adults have only 206.

Muscles and movement

Muscles move your body by pulling bones. You use hundreds of them when you walk.

 Every hair in your body has a tiny muscle that can pull it upright.

Your strongest muscle is the masseter (jaw muscle), which closes your mouth.

You use more muscles when you frown than when you smile.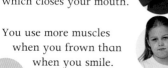

Brain and nerves

Your brain is the body's control centre. Signals zoom to and from the brain along your nerves.

 Nerves carry signals at up to 400 kph (250 mph).

 Your brain is made of about 100 billion tiny cells called neurons.

 The left side of your brain controls the right side of your body and vice versa.

 The human eye can see a candle flame at night from 1.6 km (1 mile) away.

 When you're bored, the pupils in your eyes get smaller.

Heart and blood

Your heart pumps blood around your body. It works nonstop without getting tired.

 Your smallest blood vessels are ten times thinner than a hair.

 Your body contains enough blood vessels to circle the world twice.

Breathing

Lungs take air into your body so that life-giving oxygen can enter your blood.

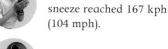 Laid out, the inside of your lungs is a third as big as a tennis court.

 The fastest recorded sneeze reached 167 kph (104 mph).

 In one day you breathe in enough air to fill 33,000 drink cans.

Skin, nails and hair

The tough, protective surface of your body is almost entirely dead.

 Every four years you shed your own body weight in dead skin.

 You have about 5 million hairs, but only 100,000 are on your head.

The thickest skin on your body is on the soles of your feet.

Fighting disease

Germs are always trying to get inside you, but your body fights back.

 Lassa fever is a very dangerous disease. It kills about a fifth of its victims.

 Bacteria are so small that a thousand could fit on the head of a pin.

 The world's most common disease is the common cold.

 Cancer happens when your own cells multiply out of control.

 When you recover from an infectious disease, your body becomes immune to it.

Digestive system

Digestion turns food into simple chemicals that your body can make into new cells or use for fuel.

 The food you eat in a year weighs as much as a car.

 You make enough spit in your lifetime to fill two swimming pools.

 Your digestive glands start working as soon as you smell or see food.

 Your tongue senses five tastes: salty, sweet, sour, bitter, and savoury.

 The smell of poo comes from a chemical called skatole.

Each hair on your head grows for about 3 or 4 years and then falls out. A new one grows in its place.

Urinary system

Urine gets rid of chemicals that your body doesn't need.

 You will make enough urine in your lifetime to fill 500 baths.

 Asparagus can turn your urine green. Blackberries can turn it red.

Reproduction

The reproductive organs create new people from tiny specks of matter.

 The most babies born to one mother is 69. Most were twins, triplets, or quads.

 The first quintuplets known to have survived infancy were born in 1934.

Growth

As you grow you slowly change into an adult, but it takes a long time!

 The fastest-growing part of a baby's body is its head.

A girl is about three-quarters of her adult height at 7 years old.

A boy is about three-quarters of his adult height at 9 years old.

Through the ages

The human body is so amazingly complicated that it's taken doctors at least 4000 years to figure out how it works. Their discoveries have led to many new ways of curing illness.

460–377 BC

The Greek doctor Hippocrates is sometimes called the father of medicine. He was one of the first people to realize that diseases have natural causes and cures.

Before the time of Hippocrates, many people thought that diseases were punishments sent by the gods.

250 BC Egyptian doctors cut open corpses to find out how the body works.

100 BC Chinese doctors discover that blood travels around the body in cycles.

1290 Spectacles are worn for the first time in Venice, Italy.

1350 Rats spread bubonic plague in Europe, killing a quarter of the people.

1500 A Swiss pig farmer performs the first Caesarian section on a living person.

1596 The Italian scientist Galileo Galilei invents the thermometer.

1684 Dutch microscopist Antony van Leeuwenhoek discovers blood cells.

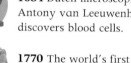
1770 The world's first comfortable false teeth are used in France.

1796 English surgeon Edward Jenner discovers how to make vaccines.

1816 The stethoscope is used for the first time.

What life-saving antibiotic did Alexander Fleming discover?

The Italian scientist Lazzaro Spallanzani ate his own sick over and over to find out how the stomach works.

 1818 James Blundell carries out the first blood transfusion.

 1852 Doctors use bandages soaked in plaster to make casts.

 **1853** Scottish doctor Alexander Wood invents the syringe.

1895 Wilhelm Röntgen accidentally discovers how to take X-rays of bones.

 1928 An English scientist discovers antibiotics – drugs that kill bacteria.

 1953 Scientists work out the structure of DNA, the chemical that carries genes.

 1955 Doctors start using ultrasound scanners to see babies inside the womb.

 1967 Surgeon Christiaan Barnard carries out the first heart transplant.

 1971 Brain scanners come into use, allowing doctors to study living brains.

 1978 Louise Joy Brown, the first test-tube baby, is born in England.

Modern medicine

Doctors know more about how the body works than ever before, but there are still some mysteries, like why we hiccup or how the brain works.

Glossary

Artery A blood vessel that carries blood away from your heart to the rest of your body.

Bacteria Tiny one-cell creatures found all around us. Some are helpful, others cause diseases.

Blood vessel Any tube that carries blood through your body.

Capillary The smallest type of blood vessel. Your body contains thousands of miles of capillaries.

Cell The smallest living unit of your body.

Diaphragm A strong, flat sheet of muscle under your lungs. You use it when you breathe.

Digestion The process that breaks down food into tiny pieces that your body can absorb and use.

Enzyme A substance that speeds up a particular chemical reaction in the body. Digestive enzymes speed up the breakdown of food molecules.

Epiglottis A trapdoor-like tag of skin that stops food going into your breathing tubes when you swallow.

Oesophagus The tube from your mouth that takes food to your stomach when you swallow.

Genes Instructions that control the way your body develops and works. Genes pass from parents to their children.

Germs Tiny living things that can get into your body and cause illness. Bacteria and viruses are germs.

Gland A group of specialized cells that make and release a particular substance such as a hormone or enzyme.

Hormone A chemical produced by one part of the body in order to change the way a different part of the body works. Hormones are made in glands and carried by the blood.

Joint A connection between two bones.

Mucus Slippery liquid on the inside of your nose, throat, and intestines.

Nerves Threads of tissue that carry high-speed signals around the body.

Nutrients The basic chemicals that make up food. Your body uses nutrients for fuel, growth, and repair.

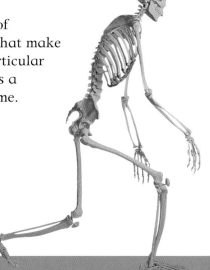

Organ A group of tissues that form a body part designed for a specific job. Your stomach is an organ.

Oxygen One of the gases in the air. You need to breathe in oxygen to live.

Proteins Vital nutrients that help your body build new cells. Food such as meat, eggs, fish, and cheese are rich in proteins.

Receptor A type of nerve cell that detects a change outside or inside the body, helping to create one of the senses. Touch receptors in the skin, for example, help create the sense of touch.

Reflex A reaction that is out of your control, like breathing or blinking when something gets near your eyes.

Saliva The liquid in your mouth. Saliva helps you taste, swallow, and digest food.

System A group of organs that work together. Your mouth, stomach, and intestines make up your digestive system.

Tissue A group of cells that look and act the same. Muscle is a type of tissue.

Umbilical cord The tube joining a baby to its mother's body while it is still inside her.

Urine Waste liquid that passes out of you when you go to the toilet. Urine is made of water and chemicals your body doesn't need.

Vaccination A substance that is swallowed or injected to protect your body from disease.

Vein A blood vessel that carries blood towards your heart.

Vertebra One of the bones that link together to form your backbone, or spine.

X-rays Invisible rays that pass through objects. X-ray photographs show the inside of your body.

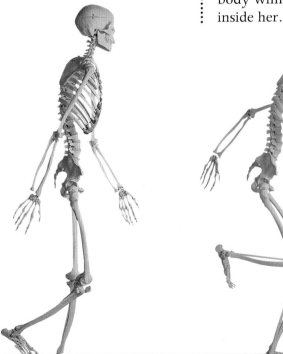

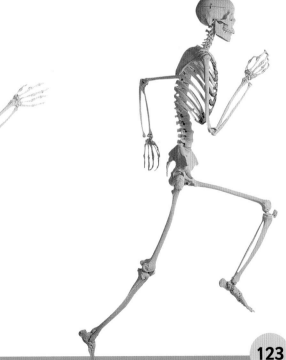

Index

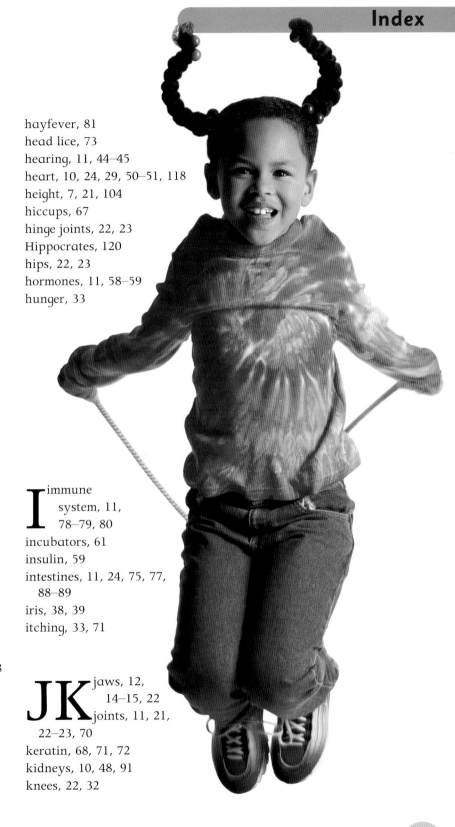

Reference section